PRINCE ARFA ʿ

Memories of a Bygone Age
Qajar Persia and Imperial Russia 1853–1902

Translated and edited by Michael Noël-Clarke

GINGKO
LIBRARY

First published in the United Kingdom in 2016 by

Gingko Library

70 Cadogan Place, London SW1X 9AH

Translation Copyright © Michael Noël-Clarke, 2016

A CIP catalogue record for the book is available from the British Library

ISBN 978-1-909942-86-8
eISBN 978-1-909942-87-5

Typeset in Times by MacGuru Ltd

Printed in the Czech Republic

www.gingkolibrary.com
@gingkolibrary

Contents

List of illustrations

Acknowledgements

I am grateful to many people for their assistance with this volume, but I owe a particular debt of gratitude to Dr John Gurney, Emeritus Fellow of Wadham College, Oxford, who originally advised me that this was a worthwhile project, and who has given me invaluable help, not least on the shape of the book, on Naser-od-Din Shah's 1889 visit to Britain and on Qajar personalities and titles; and to Narguess Farzad, Senior Fellow in Persian at the School of Oriental and African Studies, London, for her enthusiastic encouragement and for the time which, in a very busy schedule, she so kindly devoted to helping me with the finer points of the Persian language and poetry.

Monsieur Michel Bonneau, Prince Arfaʿ's grand-son, was kind enough to introduce me to Madame Françoise Aujogue of the Service des Archives at the Quai d'Orsay, to whom the ʾArfaʿ records have been entrusted and who made available to me the Prince's correspondence during his long years in Monaco. Farhad Diba, who is a descendant of the Prince's first protector, Mirza Mahmoud Khan ʿAlaʾ-ol-Molk, and who has a unique library of books on Iran, has been unfailingly helpful throughout, providing some excellent photographs to accompany the text. I would also like to express my gratitude to Catherine Taylor, Head Archivist of the Waddesdon Archive for help with research on the Shah's 1889 visit; to Tanya Lawrence for her comments on the historical background; to Antony Wynn, Marine Tigishvili of the Embassy of Georgia in London, Marina Alexidze and Anthony Stobart for their advice on the Prince's time in Tiflis; to Paul Wood of Morton and Eden Ltd for his advice on medals, Chiara de Nicolais and Lennox Money for helping to locate photographs, and to all those who have kindly authorised the use of their photographs, their contribution being acknowledged separately with each image. Among many others, I would also like to particularly thank Sir Patrick Fairweather and Dottoressa Caterina Cardona, former director of the Italian Cultural Institute in London; David Suratgar, Yanni Petsopoulos, Teresa Fitzherbert, Janet Rady and John Malcolm for their kind assistance; and of course my publishers, the Gingko Library, and my two editors, Rahim Gholami and Stephen Chumbley, who have believed in this project and worked so hard to prepare the book for publication.

TO VASHTI
WHO INSPIRED THIS PROJECT

Editor's Note

In 1936, Prince Arfaʿ returned to Tehran from Monaco, where he had mostly lived since his dismissal from Istanbul in 1910, and finished writing his memoirs shortly before his death in 1937 at the age of 84. It is not clear what sources Arfaʿ drew upon in writing his memoirs. There is no doubt that he had a prodigious memory, but in view of the length and detail of the book, the reader may wonder whether – as General Arfaʿ writes in his preface to the original Persian-language edition – the Prince wrote or dictated the whole story in the space of one month without referring to any notes or diary. The documents deposited by Monsieur Michel Bonneau, the Prince's grandson, at the Service des Archives at the Quai d'Orsay, however, contain no clues as to any original sources, and it may be that any surviving diaries or notes were confiscated at the time of the Islamic Revolution and are available to scholars in Tehran through the Institute for Iranian Contemporary Historical Studies (IICHS).[1]

The memoirs were published in Persian in early 1965 under the auspices of his son, Major-General Hassan Arfaʿ, a former Chief of Staff of the Iranian army who, like his father before him, had been Iranian ambassador in Turkey. In the early 1970s, he gave a copy to my wife, the Prince's great-granddaughter, and myself and she suggested that when I retired, I should translate them. That was the genesis of this project, which for someone who read Persian and Arabic at Oxford, married an Iranian and has been involved with Iran for most of his adult life has been a fascinating one. This is not, however, a well-researched evaluation of the Prince's importance as a historical figure. Nor have I looked closely into the achievements which he claims for himself. It is

---

1 http://iichs.org

rather an attempt to let him speak for himself in his own words, adding such historical notes as will, I hope, explain rather than irritate. I would ask for the reader's indulgence for any errors or omissions.

I have encountered the usual problems with transliterating foreign names into English, particularly Persian names, in respect of which I have adopted a phonetic method, based on the Persian pronunciation, even when the word is an Arabic one, except where the word is so well-known to the reader that it would be absurd to change the given version: Islam and the Qur'an, for example, and Isfahan rather than the Persian phonetic transliteration, which would be Esfahan. Persia or Iran? At the time, Europeans knew the country as Persia, which was indeed the official name of the country until 1935. The people, however, have always referred to their country as Iran. In the text, therefore, like the author I have used 'Iran' and 'Iranians' to describe the country and its people but 'Persian' to describe the language and culture. I have also retained 'Persia' where the country's official title appears in the context of international negotiations and treaties.

I originally translated the memoirs as literally as I could, but the occasional 'longueurs' of Persian narrative, have led me to adopt a slightly freer mode, which I hope reads better in English. The Prince does not mention his date of birth, about which he was notably coy: he once reproached his son, the General, for allowing a grey hair to appear on his head, and photographs of the Prince in his old age show hair of the deepest black. Nor was he good at dating events in his life, and when he gives a date it is almost always from the Islamic lunar calendar, in which the year is shorter than in the solar calendar. I have transposed these into solar years of the Christian era as best I can, but in some cases there could be a small error. Perhaps my biggest problem, however, has been with Qajar names and titles, which are indigestible to a Western reader and difficult to remember. I can see no alternative to reproducing them in their entirety as the Prince did, but hope that the addition of a Glossary of Qajar Titles and Names at the end of this volume, referenced to the first occasion a name in italics appears, will aid the reader to identify and add detail on the more important Iranian personalities in the memoirs.

In the 1920s and 1930s, the Prince was a distinguished relic of the Qajar *ancien régime* under the new, modernising but essentially insecure Pahlavi dynasty. Reza Shah had swept away and in some cases liquidated such people.

It may well be, therefore, that political caution was the reason why the memoirs were not published until General Arfaʿ deemed it prudent to do so. It is no surprise, therefore, that both the Prince in his introduction and the General in his preface, both of which I have omitted from the English-language translation, stress that the purpose of the memoirs was to contrast the benighted state of Iran under the later Qajars with the progress made under the enlightened rule of the Pahlavis.

As is often the case in countries where rote learning is the basis for education, the Prince's memory was indeed prodigious. Although there are occasional errors attributable to an old man's memory, he could even describe menus eaten decades earlier. The memoirs are very long and somewhat rambling: 559 pages of Persian text. Rigorous pruning has therefore been necessary. But what to cut? The Prince's prose is sometimes repetitive, so trimming the verbiage and the less interesting passages was relatively easy. To the Western reader, the Prince also appears intoxicated by the outward and visible signs of the respect paid to him by others. Much of that has also been omitted. He makes clear quite early in the memoirs that he preferred to live in Europe rather than Iran. Indeed, after his retirement, except for occasional visits to Tehran, he lived mostly in Monaco. The pages describing all this, together with accounts of his travels in Europe and to the United States, where he became something of a media celebrity, were designed for the Iranian reader but are of little interest now and have also been easy to omit.

Finally, it became clear that his life could be divided into two parts: the first from his birth in 1853 until 1902, the end of his time as Minister Plenipotentiary in St Petersburg, a period of continuous and meteoric rise, while the second was, one feels, increasingly marked by disappointment and disillusionment. Even his time as ambassador in Istanbul (1902–10), which should have been the peak of his diplomatic career, was professionally difficult. There are, however, interesting excerpts in the latter period: while he says little of his period as Minister of Justice from 1913–14, he describes his adventurous journey through bandit-infested Iran to Europe in 1920 with all his old verve, while his subsequent time as Iran's first representative at the League of Nations is perhaps worthy of separate research. However, it is the earlier period of his life which stands out, which forms a coherent whole and which is therefore the focus of this volume. His latter years from 1902–37 are summarised in a postscript.

C'est autant en Perse qu'en aucun autre pays du monde
que la condition des grands est la plus exposée
et celle dont le sort est le plus incertain
et souvent le plus funeste

Jean Chardin (1643–1713), *Voyages en Perse*
(Union Générale d'Editions Paris)

Introduction

Prince Arfa' was born, probably in 1853, the son of a Tabriz cloth merchant and money-changer whose stock was swept away in the great flood of 1872. Instead of becoming a Muslim cleric as his father had intended, he entered government service and rose to become successively Iran's Consul-General in Tiflis (1891–5), Minister Plenipotentiary in St Petersburg (1895–1901), Ambassador in Istanbul (1902–10), Minister of Justice (1913–14) and Iran's representative at the League of Nations (1920–8). He was honoured by Naser-od-Din Shah with the title of Arfa'-od-Dowleh and made a Prince by his successor, Mozaffar-od-Din Shah. A rising star and intimate of court politics and intrigue in the reign of Naser-od-Din Shah, under his successor he became one of the most influential Iranian diplomat-statesmen of his generation.

By 1853, when Prince Arfa' was born, the glories of Safavid Iran (1501–1736) were but a distant memory. The defeat and subsequent brutal occupation of Iran by the Afghans, then Nader Shah's (1736–47) brief and expensive military triumphs, followed by intermittent civil war for the rest of the century, left Iran a ruined, isolated and self-absorbed country. The new Qajar dynasty (1789–1925) re-united the country, bringing greater security and prosperity for its people. As the years went on, however, it became ever more evident that Iran was ill-fitted to face the challenge posed to its independence by the rise of two new empires on its frontiers, Russia to the north and British India in the east.

After disastrous military campaigns, under the terms of the Treaties of Golestan (1813) and Turkomanchai (1828) Iran had ceded its northern province of Georgia and eight Azeri khanates to Russia. Iran's forces were no match for the more technically advanced Russian army. In 1838, Iran had had to accept a British veto when Mohammad Shah attempted to reclaim the Afghan city of Herat for Iran; and, in 1857, conscious that a weak Iran might be persuaded by the Russians to allow them access to the city, Britain forced Naser-od-Din Shah to withdraw from a re-captured Herat by occupying the port of Bushehr in the Persian Gulf. Meanwhile, Russia continued its methodical conquests in Central Asia, until in 1881 its forces routed the Turkomans at Gok Teppe. From then on, Iran had a 1,000km frontier with the Russian Empire, which posed a direct military threat not only to Iranian Khorasan and Azerbaijan but, through Afghanistan, to British India. The 'Great Game' was being played out in Iran. As Arfaʿ illustrates in these memoirs, Naser-od-Din Shah's greatest fear was the loss of further territory to Russia. As Arfaʿ became a Russian specialist, the background to his career was the urgent need to safeguard, by non-military means, Iran's territorial integrity and independence against the Russian military threat.

Until the early nineteenth century, Iran, unlike the Ottoman Empire, had remained isolated from and largely immune to European influence. Few Iranians spoke European languages, let alone understood how the foreigners thought. Born in Azerbaijan, Arfaʿ spoke Persian and Azeri Turkish from birth. Although he received his primary education in a traditional religious school, it was his later foreign education which gave him his first opportunity. As a young adult student at the Greek school in Istanbul, he learnt French and some English, and then at the Russian school for Muslims in Tiflis,[1] he studied Russian. In 1878, still a student, he was called on to replace Naser-od-Din Shah's official interpreters, who had both fallen ill, when the Shah arrived on Russian territory on his second visit to Europe. Arfaʿs knowledge of foreign languages and foreign ways became the key to his future success.

The Prince's memoirs are not, however, primarily an account of his diplomatic career. He sometimes calls them a 'travel-diary', intended not only as a record of his own professional achievements but as a picture of a bygone age, written for the education of the younger generation of Iranians, for whom life in Qajar Iran and Tsarist Russia had faded into historical myth. We should not, however, be led astray by this description. Arfaʿ's memoirs not only chronicle what he considered to be his most important professional achievements but

---

1 Now Tbilisi, capital of Georgia.

include vivid descriptions of political, economic and social life in Iran, which will, I hope, become an important source for those seeking to understand the Qajar period.

The memoirs chronicle his own meteoric rise, packed with adventures, from modest beginnings to the highest pinnacles of the Qajar state: Arfaʿ describes the deadly intrigues of the Qajar court, the court cabals and the power of the eunuchs; and he gives a sympathetic picture of the weary, profligate Naser-od-Din Shah. On his travels, Arfaʿ sadly but implacably chronicles the inadequacy and insecurity of the roads, the deficiencies of the ill-equipped and underpaid army, the haphazard nature of state finances, the decay of Iran's archaeological heritage and latent social unrest, ever ready to break out into open revolt and, as always, channelled and exploited by the clergy. The background to his own life is the remorseless decline of Qajar Iran from a once-great empire to what had become by the end of the nineteenth century of the Christian era, an almost bankrupt and increasingly lawless state.

Against this backdrop, Arfaʿ chronicles the interaction between a weakened Iran and an all-powerful Russia and, to a lesser extent, Britain: Naser-od-Din Shah's third visit to Europe in 1889, enlivened by anecdotes from the Shah's visits to Britain and France; the splendours and eccentricities of the doomed Tsar Nicholas II's court; the Tsar's disastrous coronation; and Arfaʿ's own favour with the Tsarina and other court ladies, which he used to extract Russian concessions on matters of vital interest to his country: the delineation of the Akhal-Khorasan frontier by the Russian-Persian Boundary Commission (1883–6); the resolution of a damaging trade dispute with Italy and the other Western powers (1896); his role in defusing the Sistan crisis with Russia (1896), in which non-Muslim Russian troops were due to march through and thus defile the holy city of Mashhad; and the easing of the terms of a large Russian loan to a bankrupt Iran (1900).

Iranian history is full of stories of men who rose from humble beginnings to the pinnacle of wealth and favour, only to be cast low and executed. All favour emanated from the Shah, and one lie to the monarch could bring ruin at any time. Jealousy and deadly intrigue were rife. Nobody's position was secure. What was the secret of Arfaʿ's rise and rise and rise? In his later years he ascribed some part of his success to divine destiny. There is no doubt that luck played a role, particularly in his first employment by the Qajar state. It was, however, primarily Iran's desperate need for Arfaʿ's knowledge of foreign languages and foreign ways which led him on the path to fame and fortune. He soon became a favourite of Naser-od-Din Shah, who seems to have been intrigued by his foreign background and showed amused solicitude for his welfare in the snakepit of court politics. Having powerful enemies, including the court eunuchs, he was able to maintain his position by skilfully securing for himself a series of protectors, most notably the long-serving prime minister, the Amin-os-Soltan, who defended his interests at court. Throughout his career he was a skilled and persistent networker, surprisingly often, for a young traditionally-raised Muslim, with aristocratic foreign ladies. His knowledge of how foreigners operated and his many friendships in high places were important factors in his rise. He was quick-witted, energetic and tactful, and in foreign capitals, as an oriental who had absorbed Western ways, he seems to have been an exotic figure, almost a dinner-party trophy, an image which he himself sedulously cultivated. He was a superb diplomatic showman.

He was not, however, just a successful diplomat. He was also something of an intellectual. Traditionally educated in the works of the Persian poets Hafez, Saʿadi and Ferdowsi, as well as in the religious sciences, he had the characteristic Iranian poetic sensibility: he loved nature, gardens, trees and running water and he wrote poetry in both Persian and French, in which language his volume *Perles d'Orient* was published in 1904. His ability to compose an appropriate line of poetry also proved useful to him at key moments of his career. A constant theme in his memoirs was Iran's need for a modern Western-style educational system. As a young man, he wrote a treatise on a reformed Persian alphabet and in later years founded a craft school in Tehran. In building or re-decorating houses in the Persian style in Tehran, Tiflis, Borjom and Monaco, where from 1910 until his death in 1937 he made his main home, he took care to preserve the traditions of Iranian architecture and decoration. Furthermore, as Minister of Justice in 1913–14, in re-building the façade of the ministry on the model of Khosrow I's palace at Ctesiphon, he was an early proponent of the incorporation into the current vernacular of the lost pre-Islamic past, a policy later adopted by the Pahlavi dynasty.

As a product of both civilisations, Arfaʿ was both modern and traditional, Western and oriental. It has been suggested that he may have married a Tabriz girl during his early years in Tiflis. If so, he makes no mention of this apparently brief relationship. Moreover, the traditionalist scarcely mentions his two later wives, the first Anglo-Russian and a descendant of the Demidoff family, whom he married when he was consul-general in Tiflis, and the second the daughter of a violin teacher of Finnish origin, a member of the Stockholm Academy of Music, whom he met when he was concurrently minister in St Petersburg and to the Norwegian and Swedish courts. Both these ladies apparently lived the secluded lives of respectable Muslim women when the Prince was *en poste*. Nor, beyond mentioning the Shah's gift to him of all the revenue from the issue of Iranian passports at the consulate-general in Tiflis, does he mention the sources of his great wealth, much of which he deposited with the Imperial Russian State Bank and was later confiscated by the Bolsheviks. There is no doubt, however, that he took to heart Naser-od-Din Shah's words to him that in Iran only people with money are respected. Although not an unqualified admirer of Western culture or of Western policies towards Iran, he valued Western technical achievements and correctly discerned that the traditional Iranian religious education which he had enjoyed as a boy was a bar to Iran's progress in the modern world. He also liked the comforts and relative security of life outside Iran.

Like all good chroniclers, Arfaʿ was insatiably curious and he had a keen eye for the rogue and the charlatan, particularly among the self-consciously pious. His humanity, abhorrence of violence and understanding of human foibles shine through. Written with pace and verve and illuminated by witty anecdotes, not all of which end to his advantage, his dual identity is a theme which runs through the memoirs like a thread, to the extent that his wry descriptions of life at court and of traditional society in the provinces sometimes remind the reader of the satirical writings of the Englishman, James Morier.[2] On other occasions, however, with his abhorrence of conflict and his readiness to make pragmatic compromises, there is also an element of Haji Baba of Ispahan in Arfaʿ himself.

To what extent was Arfaʿ a figure of weight? A proper assessment is beyond the scope of this volume, in which the author speaks for himself. There is no

---

2 James Morier, Secretary to Sir Harford Jones, British Special Envoy to the Shah (1808), and Secretary at the British Legation in Tehran (1810–16). Author of *Haji Baba of Ispahan* (1824), a brilliant but sometimes controversial satire of Iranian *moeurs*.

doubt that he was vain. Throughout the memoirs there is rather too much emphasis on the respect paid to him wherever he goes. Nevertheless, his loyalty, skill and capacity for hard work clearly endeared him to successive chiefs. His ability to bounce back from setbacks which would have ruined a lesser man was remarkable. Nor did he lack courage: if he is to be believed, on more than one occasion he exceeded his official instructions to obtain important concessions for his country. Although he sometimes despaired at the state of contemporary Iran, he loved his country and was deeply proud of its artistic and cultural heritage. The one-time provincial religious student developed into a key intermediary in Iran's relations with Europe and one of the most important Iranian diplomats of his day. In unfavourable conditions his achievements for his monarch and, in the circumstances of the day, for his country were considerable. Fortunately for the sympathetic reader, he was also a born raconteur.

Life of Mirza Reza Khan Danesh, Arfaʿ-Od-Dowleh, Prince Arfaʿ

1853 Born in Tabriz, the son of Haj Sheikh Hassan, originally from Erivan in present-day Armenia.

1873 Left Tabriz for Istanbul, where he attended the Greek Galata School. Studied English and French.

1875 Ill, left for Tiflis. Attended Russian school for Muslims there.

1878 Naser-od-Din Shah's interpreter during his visit to Russia on his second journey to Europe.

1879 Appointed translator and Third Secretary in the Tiflis consulate. Awarded Order of the Lion and Sun (Third Class). Wrote his *Roshdiyyeh* treatise.

1880 Appointed interpreter at Russian-Turkish prisoner-of-war camps near Tiflis. *Akhtar* publishes article on his new alphabet. Appointed assistant Aide-de-camp to Mozaffar-od-Din Mirza, the Heir Apparent.

1882 Appointed First Secretary at Tiflis consulate. The ʿAlaʾ-os-Saltaneh replaces the ʿAlaʾ-ol-Molk as Consul-General in Tiflis.

1883 Interpreter for Iranian mission at coronation of Tsar Alexander III (27 May 1883).

1883 Summoned to Tehran. Appointed interpreter on the Russian-Persian Akhal-Khorasan Boundary Commission (1883-86).

1887 Official host to Count Donato, the newly-appointed Italian minister. Appointed counsellor at the embassy in St Petersburg under the ʿAlaʾ-ol-Molk.

1889 Interpreter on Naser-od-Din Shah's third visit to Europe.

1890 Recalled to Tehran. Appointed Consul-General in Tiflis.

1892 Visit of the Amin-e-Aqdas to Europe. Built Hôtel Firouzeh in Borjom.

1895 Appointed Minister-Plenipotentiary in St Petersburg and given title of Arfaʿ-od-Dowleh. Promoted Amir-Toman (Major-General).

1896 Death of Naser-od-Din Shah. Helps to resolve the Consonno Affair, a long-running trade dispute involving Mozaffar-od-Din Shah and the Italian government. Given title of Prince.

1896 Amin-os-Soltan dismissed as prime minister. Arfaʿ recalled to Tehran. Solves Cossack crisis in Khorasan/Sistan and is rewarded by being confirmed in his post at St Petersburg.

1899 Attended Russian-sponsored peace conference in The Hague.

1900 Russian loan agreement with Iran signed.

1901 Leaves St Petersburg. Founded the Danesh primary school in Tehran.

1902 Appointed Ambassador in Istanbul.

1903 Negotiated new customs convention with Ottoman Turkey.

1904 Attended coronation of King Alfonso XIII in Madrid. Promoted Amir Nouyan (General).

1910 Dismissed from ambassadorship in Istanbul. Retired to Monaco, where he built 'Daneshgah', now known as the Villa Ispahan.

1913 Offered Ministry of Education by Prime Minister ʿAlaʾ-os-Saltaneh. He becomes Minister of Justice in this government.

1914 Outbreak of the First World War. The Iranian government collapses and he returns to Monaco.

1918 Returns to Tehran.

1920 Appointed Iran's representative at the League of Nations.

1928 Dismissed from his post and returns to Tehran.

1931 Awarded Order of Homayoun (First Class) by Reza Shah. Leaves for Monaco.

1937 Dies in Tehran.

Chapter 1

My Childhood in Tabriz

The future Prince Arfaʿ, known in his youth simply as Aqa Reza, was born in Tabriz, probably in 1853, the son of a local cloth merchant who had emigrated from Erivan following the Russian conquest of the Caucasus. Tabriz, situated at the intersection of major trade routes and the capital of the early Safavid Shahs from 1502 until 1548, was and remains the main town in Azerbaijan, Iran's richest, Turkic-speaking province. The Afghan invasions of the 1720s, Nader Shah's brief, expensive period of military glory, followed by further internecine struggles for power and the severe earthquake of 1780 meant that by 1800 the town was largely in ruins, and its population is thought to have declined to some 30,000 people. By 1842, however, improving political security under the early Qajars and a construction programme under the prince-governorship of ʿAbbas Mirza (1801–33) led to increasing trade, greater prosperity and a doubling of the population. Nevertheless, recent humiliation at the hands of the rising imperial powers, Russia and Britain, and the proximity of the new frontier with the Russian Empire provided tangible evidence of Iran's diminished status. Furthermore, competition from cheaper Russian and English goods, and from the 1830s the arrival of foreign consuls and traders in Tabriz led to a feeling that not only Iran's territorial integrity but its traditional Muslim way of life was under threat, a recurring theme in these memoirs. Outbreaks of cholera, earthquakes, famine and floods were the backdrop to the author's childhood.

Nevertheless, the author's early memoirs give an intimate picture of a happy and protected childhood: the influence of a devout mother and father; a traditional Islamic education which was to have led to studies in Najaf and a career as a cleric; a narrow escape from accidental childhood death, which he ascribed to special protection from an all-seeing God who had from an early age destined him for great things; a beating from his teacher, which taught him a valuable lesson; and a great flood, probably in 1872, which ruined his father, led him to be detained by his father's creditors, and ultimately led to his dispatch to Istanbul as an apprentice to a merchant, his first step on the path to fame and fortune. All this is described with a sympathy and warmth for the closeness of the Tabriz merchant community and its support networks in times of difficulty.

I was born in Tabriz into a Tabriz merchant's family. Our father's name was Haji Sheikh Hassan, who had emigrated there from Erivan. Our house was in the Andarun-e-Shotorban, which was known as the Erivan district.[1] My mother was called Kolsom Khanom, the daughter of Aqa Safar of Tabriz.

My mother would relate to everybody until the end of her life that she had borne five sons and five daughters and she had breast-fed them all. She was a very religious woman and the only thing her father had taught her was to read the Qur'an from cover to cover. She had also learnt by heart most of the short suras of the Qur'an and used to copy out parts of it in *naskh*[2] script. She used to say that the nine out of the ten children whom she had breast-fed would cling very tightly with both hands to her bosom whenever one of her friends who also happened to have a baby would visit, for fear lest the other baby would grab away her breast. However, she swore on oath that when this happened to me, her son Reza, I would release her breast and would offer it to the other baby with both hands.

I remember, however, one winter, when I was about four or five, the weather was very cold and it was snowing. I was lying under the *korsi*[3] beautifully

---

1 After the Treaties of Golestan (1813) and Turkomanchai (1828), by which Iran formally ceded Georgia and the Azeri khanates as far south as the Aras River to Russia, many Turkish-speaking Muslims from Erivan (now Yerivan, capital of present-day Armenia) and other Caucasus towns emigrated to Tabriz and other towns in Iranian Azerbaijan.
2 Arabic calligraphic script used from the ninth century CE.
3 A small table covered with quilts and heated by a charcoal brazier, under which people sit or lie and warm their feet in winter.

warm, when someone knocked on the door. It was a beggar, who cried out: 'I have been hungry all night. Give me a piece of bread!' My mother took a piece of bread and gave it to me to give to him. I objected and replied that it was snowing and the weather was too cold for me to get out from under the *korsi* and cross the courtyard to give the beggar the bread. Why didn't she ask the maid to go? My mother angrily replied that she knew perfectly well that the maid could do this but she wanted me to give the bread, so that God would reward me. She forced me to get up and give the bread to the beggar.

In the afternoon it stopped snowing and the sun came out. Haji Samad Marandi, a respected local merchant, also had a house in our neighbourhood. His children sometimes came to our house to play in the snow and sometimes I would go to their house. On that day, however, it was my turn to go there. We threw snowballs at each other for a time. Then we rested our backs against a south-facing wall, trying to warm ourselves and unfreeze our hands. We were enjoying the sunlight and the whiteness of the snow, when through the open door of the courtyard we saw the neighbour's cock, a very strong and vicious bird, suddenly attack the owner's cock. As we all started to chase the cock out of the door, the wall on which we had been leaning caved in. All the children's mothers rushed out and began kissing their children and praising God for saving us from sudden catastrophe. When I went home I told my mother what had happened, and she said: 'Praise God that you got up this morning from under the warm *korsi* and went out into the cold to give the beggar bread with your own hands! Always remember this event!'

Now, I had a cousin called Ja'far, whose father was Haji Karim, a wealthier man than my father. Haji Karim was a man of property in Tabriz, for he owned a bakery, a shop selling cooked rice, and he was also sole proprietor of a public bathhouse and of two large gardens outside the town in the Sheshgilan region[4] . His son Ja'far would always boast about his father's wealth. One day when we were about five or six, Ja'far came to our house. As it was winter, we both sat under the *korsi* and were chatting about all sorts of things. Since I didn't take part in games played by my cousins, they called me 'Reza the Pretentious'. Ja'far said to me: 'Really, Reza, I always feel very sorry for you.'

---

4 The region of Sheshgilan is in eastern Azerbaijan.

I asked why. He said: 'If my uncle dies and the *mojtahed*[5] makes off with his money, you will die of hunger with this pretentious attitude. I am not proud, so if the same thing were to happen to me, I could earn my living by being a waiter in a tea-house, or an apprentice to a cloth-merchant. If those two fail, I shall take a begging bowl and a drum and become a *dervish*[6] and I will never starve.' I replied that I would neither become a waiter in a tea-house nor a cloth-merchant's apprentice nor a *dervish* but, I would become a great man like 'Abdollah, our chief district headman, and then I would have servants and give orders to people. He laughed and said: 'That is what I mean, you pay no attention to us, and you already give yourself airs and graces.'

Many years after this conversation, I was summoned to Jolfa[7] from my post as counsellor at the embassy in St Petersburg and joined the late Naser-od-Din Shah's entourage on his third journey to Europe. When we reached Iranian Jolfa on our way back, the Shah ordered me to accompany him to Tehran. On our arrival in Tabriz, however, I was given leave by the Shah to visit my family, so the next day, all my father's neighbours and friends came to call on me. The door was open, and through the window I suddenly saw a *dervish* carrying a begging bowl in one hand and in the other a drum, reciting poetry in praise of the Commander of the Faithful[8] (Peace be upon him!), in a very melodious voice. I was told that he was my cousin Ja'far. I was extremely surprised and asked the *dervish* to come up to where I was sitting. He came and sat down, and I asked him how he had fallen into this mode of life. He replied that after I had left, his father had died without leaving a will. Haji Mirza Baqer, the *mojtahed*, had appointed his son, a *molla*[9] who was himself on the brink of becoming a *mojtahed*, to administer the estate. The latter gathered

---

5 Leading religious scholars to whom people turned for advice on points of law and conduct and who were often entrusted with the administration of a dead man's estate.

6 A wandering beggar and storyteller, who claims religious status as a Sufi mystic.

7 At that time, the main route from Iran to Europe passed through Russia and the town of Jolfa, situated on both banks of the Aras River, was the main frontier post between the two countries.

8 'Ali, the Prophet's son-in-law, especially venerated by the Shi'a, who believe he was the legitimate successor to the Prophet and should have been chosen as the first Caliph of Islam instead of Abu Bakr.

9 Or mullah, A Muslim cleric, chiefly in Turkish-, Persian-, and Urdu-speaking areas.

in the whole estate but since Ja'far's father had had two wives and children from both, the administrator had caused everyone to quarrel over the division of the assets. Every asset that the administrator had, out of a sense of justice, wished to assign to his side of the family, had gone in lawyers' fees during the legal process. 'So now, as you see,' he said, 'I have no alternative. I have become a *dervish* and I spend my days singing praises to the Prophet outside tea-houses. I live off the odd coin that people give me.' I felt very sorry for him and I helped him as much as I could at that time, though I could not help remembering the conversation we had had as boys under the *korsi*. A Turkish proverb my mother was fond of quoting in came to mind: 'Everybody builds his house by his own efforts.'

There was a doctor in our district, called Mirza Ja'far, who had a daughter called Molla Sara. When I was six years old, my mother took me to Molla Sara's school, where she gave lessons to local children of both sexes until they reached the age of eight. The school consisted of a cellar, fortunately a dry one, eight steps below ground level, with a reed mat as its only furnishing. Parents had to send a small cushion for each of their children to sit on. Children were taught the Qur'an and some religious law. Sometimes Molla Sara would send me with messages to her father. Often he wouldn't ask me why I had come but would keep me waiting. As I waited, I watched the villagers who came to be cured of their various ailments and who were sitting in front of him. The doctor had various bottles of differing sizes, most of them full of herbal medicines, together with a small weighing machine in front of him. He would take the pulse of his patient and reflect for a while. Then he would take out a long rosary, shut his eyes, seek divine help by fingering his rosary and say in a loud voice: 'O God, do you think this person ought to be cured? Shall I give *folous*[10] to this servant of God?' If the rosary gave a positive answer, he would weigh out an amount of *folous*, administer it, and receive his fee. If the answer was negative on *folous*, he took an augury to see whether he should administer other herbal remedies and continued doing so until the verdict of his rosary was positive. After saying goodbye to his patient, he would deign to notice me and then I would be able to return to school.

---

10 A traditional cure-all Iranian herbal medicine, resembling liquorice.

The doctor, Mirza Ja'far, came from Zonuz.[11] In the autumn his garden-
ers would send him some grapes, pears, apples and quinces from his various
gardens for the winter. He had some rooms opposite his house in which he
hung his grapes and stored the rest of his fruit on sawdust in niches to prevent
it from going bad. One day he and his daughter were invited to lunch by
friends in another area of town, so they had asked a substitute teacher, who
was only two years older than us, to supervise us. We were about twenty-five
pupils, boys and girls. The sun was shining and we were all playing outside in
the courtyard. Suddenly a neighbour's daughter called Hajer had an idea. She
called out: 'Children, have you seen how much fruit they have stored there?
Come, let us find a way for one of us to get in and hand out fruit for all of us!
It's not fair that so much fruit should be stored there and that we should pine
for it from afar.'

Since as a child I was thinner and weighed less than anyone else, I was
chosen to climb through the window. The teaching assistant would put his
hands together, I would get on to his shoulders, wriggle into the room and
hand out as much fruit as they wanted. Suddenly, in the middle of this, there
was a knock on the door, and Mirza Ja'far and his daughter arrived back. All
the children ran away, but I was left behind, without even having had any fruit
to eat myself. The other children all rushed back to the cellar and sat down
in their places. Only I remained in the storeroom, with no one to rescue me.
Molla Sara opened the door and dragged me out. I hope that God will never
make anyone else suffer what I had to bear at that moment. I felt like a wolf
caught with blood on its mouth when it has not even touched its prey. The
molla then took me down and placed me in front of the other children in the
cellar and, before asking any questions, beat me with her punishment stick.
After beating me, she began to interrogate others. She identified two other
guilty children, the substitute teacher who had put me on his shoulders and
Hajer. The assistant received more blows of the cane than I did but since Hajer
was a girl like the teacher, her punishment was only two strokes. The others
were let off.

Talking of doctors, I should also record that at the end of the lane where we
lived there was a blind beggar who never asked any questions of anyone but

---

11 A town situated in the mountains of eastern Azerbaijan.

recited lines in praise of 'Ali, holding out his hand for the odd coin. He had
a son who used to lead his father to the same spot every morning and back
again in the evening. In time the boy grew up and became a house servant to
Mirza 'Ali, the doctor, on the sole condition that he could continue to take his
father to his begging spot in the morning and back again in the evening. After
spending some years there as a house servant to Mirza 'Ali, one day the blind
beggar's son started to wear a turban. He had suddenly become a doctor. Then,
one day he appeared riding a horse and wearing a shawl turban as he went
on his way to treat the sick. In due course, this unfortunate so-called 'doctor'
made a pill called the 'happy' pill, for which he charged a very high price, and
two people died after taking it. A relative of one of the deceased complained to
the chief judge at the Tabriz governor's court and took the doctor to court. The
governor asked the relative how many 'happy' pills the victim had swallowed
before he died. The answer was six. The 'doctor' was then asked what the pills
were made of. What had he made them from? It then became clear that one of
the components was a deadly poison, so the governor ordered some of these
pills to be brought and made the apprentice 'doctor' eat them on the spot. After
having eaten them he felt extremely unwell, so he was then sent home, where
a few hours later he died.

From Molla Sara's religious primary school my father sent me to Sheikh
'Ali, who had a secondary school[12] in the local mosque. Our lessons comprised
the study of Sa'adi's *Golestan*[13], the *Divan* of Hafez, Sheikh Baha'i's *Jame'-e
'Abbasi*[14] and the treatise of the late Sheikh Morteza Ansari.[15] This *molla* was
fond of poetry, which he made his pupils learn by heart. He decided that on
Thursday mornings there would be a poetry recitation competition. That is to
say, the pupils were put into two teams, a member of one team would start a
line and a member of the second would have to reply to his line, beginning

---

12 At this time education was in the hands of *molla*s, the *'maktab'* of Molla Sara being the
equivalent of primary school and the *'madraseh'* of Sheikh 'Ali of secondary school.

13 Sa'adi (1210–92) and Hafez (1325–89) were two of the outstanding poets of the classical
period of Persian literature.

14 First compendium of 'Twelver' Shi'ite canon law composed by Sheikh Baha'i for the
Safavid Shah 'Abbas (1588–1613).

15 A leading nineteenth-century theologian and 'source of imitation' for Shi'ite Muslims.

with the last letter the first child had used.[16] The winning team would be able to stay at home in the afternoon, but the others would have to come back in the afternoon and stay until sunset.

Whereas Molla Sara's monthly school fee had been ten *shahi*s,[17] Sheikh ʿAli's was one *kran*.[18] In addition to this, when their mothers had baked long-life bread, the children would sometimes bring him a present of a few pieces of bread and whenever there had been guests in the house they would bring him a plate of rice. As Sheikh ʿAli was doing rather well, he branched off and opened a big school, so that his primary school became a secondary school. He was an honest person with a good character, who hated lies and whenever any of us lied to him, he would beat the soles of his feet with a stick. His way of encouraging his students was to promote them according to how much effort and progress they made. The place of honour was on his right and the next was on his left. On first arrival, a student would be placed ten places from the *molla*. Gradually, as he progressed, he would move up to the place on the *molla*'s right or left. This was the highest point of achievement, for as had been the case in Molla Sara's school each student had his own cushion and his appointed place.

After the arrival of Molla Aqa Darbandi in Tabriz, *rowzeh-khwani*[19] became very popular in houses there. Those who recited these lamentations became very much in demand and our teacher, Sheikh ʿAli suddenly thought he would like to become one, so he borrowed notebooks containing poems of lamentation from some of those already reciting. An hour before the end of school on Thursdays, he would ask us to kneel and listen to him recite in tones used by the professionals. He ordered us to weep and he would beat anyone who didn't do so with a stick until he did. As a result, we were so frightened of the *molla* that as soon as he started to recite, we were already fainting with grief. He would say: 'Shout in a loud voice "Alas, My Lord"'! So, we would all start

16 This kind of poetic competition, known as '*moshaʿereh*', remains an integral part of Persian literary discourse.

17 There were 20 *shahi*s to the *kran*.

18 At that time worth approximately £3 or $4.50 in modern currency.

19 Ritual recitation of poetry and prayers lamenting the martyrdom of the Imam Hossein and his family at Karbala.

wailing. To do him justice, he began to do rather well for himself in this field, so that he would be invited to people's houses for this purpose and the *mojtahed* even gave him his turn to recite lamentations once a week in the mosque. However, he no longer had time or inclination to teach. Instead, he appointed one of his religious students to teach us in his place and would only come to the school when he had the time. Sometimes when one of the unfortunate children asked the meaning of a word, the student teacher would roundly curse the questioner and ask him why he wanted to know the meaning of this or that word and what use it would be to him if he did.

As by this time my studies with the *molla* had reached declensions and conjugations, the student could teach me nothing more. On one of his pilgrimages to the Holy Places,[20] however, my father had vowed at the immaculate tomb of ʿAli that if God granted him a male child, he would send him to most noble Najaf[21] to become a *mojtahed*. He therefore sent me to the Haji Safar ʿAli religious school, which was run by a *molla* called ʿAbdol-ʿAzim Ashlaghi, who was doing well from teaching there. This man didn't have many students but he charged five *kran*s for the fees and he was able to enjoy life on that sum. In those days life in Tabriz was very inexpensive and he and his fellow *molla*s could make a good living on this money. He never beat us, but when he wanted to punish one of us he would make the culprit sit in front of him in the presence of the other students, he would tell him what he had done wrong and rebuke him. As a result, we tried very hard never to upset him or to do anything which would merit a rebuke in front of our fellow students. He was also extremely polite but he never laughed, nor would he allow us to laugh. Nor would he allow us to sit cross legged in class: we had to kneel with our legs tucked under us.

My father heard that one Haji Molla Ahmad Tahbaz, who was from a line of highly-respected Tabriz merchants, had returned from Najaf and Karbala and gave group lessons by day in his house, where he taught Islamic Law and Jurisprudence, interpretation of the Qurʾan and the history of great men to religious students. As my father was a friend of the *molla*'s brother and Haji Molla

---

20 The Shiʿa holy places in Iraq, Najaf and Karbala, known as the Atabat.

21 Site of the tomb of ʿAli and leading Shiʿa seminary in Iraq, which together with Karbala, site of the shrine of the Imam Hossein, is a place of pilgrimage for Shiʿa Muslims.

Ahmad was a learned and pious man, my father asked him through his friend
to accept me in his group classes. The Tahbaz family all lived in the Nowbar
district, where they had built a small mosque, in which they performed the
dawn and evening prayers. All his relatives made sure that they stood behind
him five times a day and recited the prayers after him. As he was wealthy, he
never took any money for his teaching. Indeed he even gave a little financial
help to religious students who studied there.

From the day I started to have lessons with Haji Molla Ahmad, it was established that I would make the pilgrimage to Najaf and Karbala, for my father
had decided to send me there and thus fulfil his vow. At home my parents
would speak of it incessantly and my brother and sister began to call me Molla
Reza. My cousins would say that I was lucky because when I became a *molla*,
I would wear a turban and would always sit above everyone else and be invited
to weddings and funerals. I would always be given the breast of the chicken,
and by earning money from relatives of everyone who died, I would become
the dead man's heir and good fortune would accompany me. To tell you the
truth, I did not care for these jokes and had no wish to go and become a *molla*.

One night I dreamt that Naser-od-Din Shah came to Tabriz. Two court servants in uniform came to our house in a carriage and they said to me: 'The Shah
summons you.' They took me in the carriage to the North Garden,[22] where I
was summoned to the Shah's presence. He was sitting alone in the palace pool-
house in front of a large table full of succulent grapes. He gave me a bunch of
grapes and I bowed low and left the room. As I went out, a group of dignitaries
were standing in a corner with the Crown Prince. They all congratulated me.
At this point I woke up, extremely surprised, as the dream was so vivid that I
thought that I was awake. I didn't tell anyone about it as I was afraid they would
poke fun at me, as I knew from experience that whenever a neighbour or one
of the aunts had this kind of dream and repeated it, as soon as she left the room
people would laugh behind her back and say: 'A hungry hen dreams of grain.'

One day, however, my father's cousin came to visit my father and was
sitting in the reception area of our house. My father was out, so I brought him
tea. He very kindly told me to sit beside him, asked me how I was and said
that I was to go to Najaf and Karbala. He was so kind to me that I plucked up

22 Garden laid out by 'Abbas Mirza, when he was prince-governor of Tabriz (1801–33).

the courage to tell him about the dream I had had and said that I didn't know how to interpret it. He said he would tell me what it meant: I wouldn't become a *molla* nor go on a pilgrimage to the Holy Places; neither my father's wish nor his oath would be fulfilled. Instead, he thought, I would become a government servant and would rise to great heights in this profession. He adjured me not to tell anyone of this dream and especially not my father, but I must promise him that when I reached this position, I would not forget him or his children. If he needed my help, I was to assist him. Instead of being surprised by his words, it seemed to me that what he had foretold would actually happen and I very boldly gave him my word.

One summer's day, after lunch, I was sitting wearing a tunic of printed cotton with my mother, who was reading the Qur'an in her melodious voice, surrounded by her children listening to her. Our house with its small garden was situated five steps below the lane outside and our servant had gone on an errand to the neighbours. The door was open and we were only one house away from the river Chai. Suddenly we heard cries and wailing coming from the river. In an instant a huge wave two metres high flooded through the garden door into the courtyard and filled the area below street level. In her padded jacket and bare-feet, our mother grabbed us and took us up to the roof as fast as she could. The flood water filled the courtyard, gouged a hole in the cellar wall and rushed into our neighbour's house, but as the hole in the wall was not large enough for all the flood water to pass through it, the house shook like a willow tree at the force of it, but didn't collapse.

My father wasn't at home, as he was in his trading office in the bazaar. My mother placed the Qur'an on top of her head and then on ours in turn and, facing Mecca, recited: 'There is no God but God and Mohammad is the prophet of God,'[23] for she was convinced that the house would soon collapse and we would die. Meanwhile, we saw unfortunate people being tossed along and carried away by the raging river, which added to our terror. In total despair, we saw death in front of our eyes. All of a sudden, we saw that the district headman's men had brought a ladder, which they placed in the lane outside our house, and brought us down the ladder from the roof as fast as possible. In the lane the water was flowing so fast that the men had to make a

---

23 The Muslim profession of faith.

chain with their hands to stop us being carried away. They passed all three of us along the lane from hand to hand and then took us as far as the Shotorban cemetery, which was on higher ground and which the water hadn't reached. So many people, men, women and children were there that it was like the day of judgement. The cries of anguish among the tombstones were terrible, with people trying to establish where their mothers or sisters were. We were also weeping, as we thought that our father had been killed.

Grief-stricken, we stayed there until dark, when people in the Shotorban district whose houses had been spared took their friends in. Suddenly Haji Sadeq, a merchant from Salmas[24] whose office was next door to ours in the bazaar, came to look for us with his sons and took us off to his house. My mother and sisters were taken upstairs to the women's quarters, while room was found for me and my brothers in the men's area. We were all soaked to the skin, so our host very kindly provided us with dry clothes, and we were also given a good dinner and comfortable bedding. Eventually we went to bed but we couldn't sleep peacefully, as we were so worried about our father.

In the morning, our host and I went out to find our father and to see what had become of our house. I remember that the shoes, cloak and hat which I had been given were far too big: I was constantly tripping over my cloak, while one of my shoes would slip off after the other, as I walked along, and my hat practically hid my eyes. In this peculiar dress, I met one of the local children who had to wear his elder brother's hand-me-downs and he usually looked as I now did. We would all laugh at his appearance and make fun of him. However, as fate would have it, on this occasion his clothes, his shoes and his hat fitted perfectly. He stood in my path and bowed and said 'Greetings, Aqa Reza. How are you?' I realised I was being punished for having poked fun at him. It was a lesson for me and at that moment I vowed that I would never again poke fun at anyone who had suffered ill fortune.

When Haji Sadeq and I reached our house, all that remained of the two-storey house was a heap of mud. The rooms, the furniture, indeed all our possessions had vanished. On top of the mound the hunched-up figure of my father was standing, looking sadly in bewilderment at the surrounding desolation. When he saw me, however, his face lit up and when he heard that the whole

---

24 A town in north-west Iranian Azerbaijan.

family were safe, he prostrated himself, thanked God for our deliverance and vowed he would never complain to Him about the loss of his property.

The headman had placed guards on the ruins of some of the houses, so that thieves couldn't steal people's possessions from under the water, for no one knew what the flood had swept away and what was still there. His careful work was worthy of the highest praise, for he also saved many people's lives: if his men had arrived half-an-hour later, we should certainly all have been drowned. Haji Sadeq, my father and I then went to see what had become of the trading offices, as the caravanserai in which they were situated was in the arcade between the two bazaars. Everything belonging to my father and Haji Sadeq had been ruined by the water: damasks, Kashan velvet cloths of every kind, cushion covers, furnishing covers, velvet for clothes and curtains, quilts, printed cotton. Everything that we possessed had disappeared in just two hours. Haji Sadeq, however, had only lost his stock; his house, which was on higher ground than the Shotorban district, and his household possessions had fortunately survived. When my father saw the approaching flood, he had managed to escape to the upper bazaar. He had, however, been unable to cross the river from there to find us, so he had had to spend the night on a shop bench there without food or bedding. One can only imagine what his state of mind had been with worry, hunger and sleeplessness.

As bales of stock always had the owner's name written on the label, each merchant was able to identify his goods, which he then placed in front of his shop. As to the houses, our neighbours had paid workers to fish out trays, pots and copper plates, which they then sold in return for food, and we did the same thing. The first thing the workers who had gone into the water fished out was a silver halter which I had always put on our horse when we went out to welcome relatives returning from the pilgrimage to Mecca or Karbala. I remember that when I saw this kind of halter on Haji Naqi's son's horse, I had asked my father to have one made for my horse, but he replied that the Haji was very rich but we couldn't afford this kind of silver bridle for our horse. In the end I had succeeded in forcing my father to buy a silver bridle for my horse, so you can imagine how happy I was to see it now. It would fetch enough to pay for several days' subsistence for us. My father gave thanks to God that I had once browbeaten him into ordering it. He sold it the very same day to the goldsmith, received the money and recovered from his despair.

Life continued like this for two months, my father and I being busy from morning to night looking for our possessions in the ruins of our house. Apart from gold, silver and copper, nothing else we found fetched any money. At that time Haji Ahmad, the money-changer, died leaving small children. The dead man's uncle instructed me to go and sit in the money-changing office with Haji Akbar, the dead man's business partner, and with his clerk, make a list of claims on the estate and of the liabilities and, in effect, to supervise matters. It was agreed that until the dead man's estate had been administered, his business partner would give me a salary of twenty *tomans*[25] a month.

Anyway, it took nearly six months for us to settle the dead man's affairs. My father owed money to a number of people, and his creditors were very pressing. As he knew that I was with Haji Akbar in the money-changer's shop, he came and borrowed 400 *tomans*, which he paid to his creditors. When the administrator was about to close down the money-changer's shop, the 400 *tomans* had somehow to be paid back, but none of the ruined stock was available, for everything which had been rescued had already been sold at a very low price to a cloth-merchant, and my father had gone to Rasht with a relative to raise money. The six-month period of the loan came to an end, the two of them were unable to repay the loan note which they had given, and the credit granted by wholesalers was also coming to an end. Every day, creditors came and their assistants sat in the office asking me for their money. All I could do was to telegraph to Rasht. A reply came saying that I should assure the creditors that my father and his partner never made off with other people's money and that as long as they had breath in their bodies they would do their utmost to repay what was due.

These telegrams had little effect. Several creditors went to the Saheb-e-Divan Shirazi, who was the governor and judge of the province under the Heir Apparent[26] and also his financial comptroller, to file a complaint. I was summoned to the judge's house, where I was taken into the presence of his steward, a kind and just man who sat me down beside him and very gently asked me what had happened. When I did so, explaining that it was not my fault that a complaint had been filed and I had been brought to court, he was sympathetic. He reported the whole story to the judge, who summoned me and

---

25 A *toman* was equal to ten *krans*, approximately £30 or $45 in today's currencies.
26 The Heir Apparent was often appointed governor-general of Azerbaijan.

ruled that a claimant had no right to seek the repayment of a father's debt from his son, and in any case I owned no property myself. He then summoned his steward and told him to take me back to his house and look after me kindly until he had been able to summon the creditors and arrange matters.

About sunset, Haji Seyyed Morteza, a money-changer, arrive at the steward's house. He announced that he wished to see the judge himself immediately and when he came out again, he took me off to his house. It transpired that when my mother saw that I had been taken off to the judge's house, she had waited until noon but when I didn't return and had obviously been detained, she had gone to Haji Seyyed Morteza's house and told his wife that she would kill herself rather than allow anyone to detain her son for the night in the governor's house. The wife was a great friend of my mother's who had persuaded her husband to come and by hook or by crook to secure my return home. When my mother saw me in the Haji's house, however, she said that I shouldn't come home, as she feared that the creditors would come to our house and take me away again. I should stay where I was until an arrangement had been agreed with my father's creditors. She would come to see me every day. Since my reading and writing were good, my host gave instructions that until a satisfactory arrangement had been reached with my father's creditors, I was not to leave his house even for a moment and that I should occupy my time by giving calligraphy lessons to his two sons.

So it was that I stayed there for some months until Haji Reza Aqa from Salmas,[27] a relative of ours, came to see me at my kind host's house and said that there was no point in my staying there any longer. He would ask my host to arrange with my father's creditors that he, our relative, would pay my father's debts. He was leaving that very day for Istanbul, so he said that he would like me either to accompany him or follow him there and help him with his paper work. In return he would give me a proportion of his profits. He would make me his partner there, I would learn about business and become a man of property.

In view of this clear undertaking from Haji Reza, I happily agreed to this. My host, who had just received five bales of silk for sale from my father in

27 According to the author's son, General Arfaʿ, this man was the author's brother-in-law, married to one of his sisters.

Rasht, some of which he was to give to my father's creditors, was also persuaded to tell them to leave me alone. Haji Reza said that he was ready to give me enough money for me to travel to Istanbul. It took some time for the silk to be sold, however, so Haji Reza couldn't wait for me, but he insisted that I should follow him to Istanbul as soon as possible.

When my mother heard of this decision, she wept a great deal, as she loved me very much, but as she had seen me taken away once by the judge's man and didn't want this to happen again, she agreed that I should go. On the day of my departure from Tabriz, she came to Haji Seyyed Morteza's house and gave me a prayer which she had written out herself, saying that it was the Throne Surah of the Qur'an. She had wrapped this in oil cloth, which she enveloped in a shawl made from the finest wool for me to hang round my neck, together with three long shirts, three pairs of underpants, six handkerchiefs and two pairs of socks, all in a bundle, which she had placed in one side of a woven saddlebag. In the other she placed some dried fruit, a little cheese, some *lavash*[28] bread and boiled eggs for me to take on my journey. Haji Seyyed Morteza instructed one of his servants, Seyyed Mohammad, who was going to inspect their property, to take me along with him to spend a few nights at their house in Seyyed Larkandi, where all the inhabitants were *seyyed*s,[29] to treat me with respect and then after several days rest to send me on with a villager over the Khoda Afarin bridge to Ordubad. There he was to leave me and return to Tabriz.

---

28 Thin, crisp Iranian bread.
29 Descendants of the Prophet, highly respected because of their bloodline.

Chapter 2

My Journey to the Caucasus and Istanbul (1873–1875)

In 1873, at the age of nineteen or twenty, Aqa Reza set off from Tabriz for Istanbul. He had probably never even left Tabriz, let alone travelled outside Iran. Nor indeed had he been exposed to anything but the culture of his native city and the world to which a merchant's son could have access. He did not, however, travel by what would be to the modern traveller the direct land route across Anatolia; nor did he even take the long-established trade route from Tabriz to Trebizond on the Black Sea and thence proceed by sea to Istanbul. Insecurity on the roads of Eastern Anatolia made this impractical. At that time, there were no carriage roads in Iran, only rutted tracks, and he travelled the first sixty miles to the Aras River on horseback, escorted only by one man. Having crossed the Aras, he continued his adventure on horseback as far as Nakhchivan and then travelled by post-wagon to Erivan and on to Tiflis, staying in caravanserais, mosques and on one occasion, a post-house, a total distance of nearly 300 miles.

After leaving Iran, he travelled through territories which had once formed part of the Safavid Empire and which since the collapse of the Soviet Union now make up independent Azerbaijan, Armenia and Georgia. Although Russia had ruled all these territories since 1828 and Aqa Reza's father, like many other Muslim Azerbaijanis, had emigrated to Iran, most of the local inhabitants were still Muslims or Armenian Christians. Through a series of chance encounters, often with distant relatives or acquaintances of his father or grandfather, formerly chief minister to the Khan of Erivan, he was able to depend

on traditional Muslim hospitality most of the way. On his arrival in Tiflis,
however, where the Russians had started modern schools for local Muslims, he
was humiliatingly brought to realise the inadequacy of his traditional Muslim
education in this new order and the need for Western-style educational reform
in Iran. It was a seminal moment. He was also introduced to Muslim intellec-
tuals, who were by now taking Russian-style names and experimenting with
Western ideas: one of them advocated the replacement of the Arabic/Persian
alphabet by a new latinised alphabet as a basis for progress, an idea on which
the author wrote his own treatise, a reform which was eventually to be adopted
in Ataturk's Turkey, though not in Iran. He then travelled on the newly-opened
railway, another Western wonder, from Tiflis to Poti on the Black Sea, and
thence by sea to Istanbul, where he studied French, English, mathematics and
geography at the Greek school. He was thus launched on a voyage of discovery
which was to lead to him eventually becoming one of the Qajar court's leading
interpreters of, and intermediaries with, the West.

Agha Seyyed Mohammad and I set off, riding two of his horses, which had
been brought from his village. Agha Seyyed Mohammad was about thirty
years old and very kind, a saintly man who was punctilious in his religious
observances. At the half-way point for the day, we stopped at a caravanserai
and ate the lunch which he had brought in his saddlebag, together with some
grapes. After lunch we set off again and an hour after sunset we reached the
*seyyed*s' village, where we dismounted at Haji Sheikh Morteza's house, of
which he had built a few rooms. As yet, however, the courtyard had no walls
around it and there was only one floor. Two steps led up to the rooms but there
were still no doors or windows.

   That night around dawn there was a fierce rainstorm and it started to hail.
As I was very tired, I fell into a deep sleep. There were of course no beds:
cushions had been placed on the carpet for me to sleep on. I suddenly felt that
I was completely surrounded with water. I leapt up, terrified, and saw the flood
outside. The room itself was flooded to the depth of an inch. I just stood there
in shock and thought: 'Oh God, in Tabriz there was a flood and somehow I
escaped it. How is it that I have suffered the same fate here?' I was pondering
these thoughts when Seyyed Mohammad and two villagers came to look for
me and took me to high ground. As my bedclothes had been left behind in the

flood waters, they sent off to houses which had not been flooded, from where rugs and bedclothes were obtained and placed on the ground, so I was able to go back to sleep.

The next day dawned clear and sunny. The flood waters filling the courtyard had retreated but, as the floor of my room was very wet, Seyyed Mohammad bore me off to a relative's house, where I was given a room. After three days of generous hospitality, with the travel money which Haji Morteza Aqa had given me I hired a horse from a villager who agreed to escort me as far as Ordubad. Our journey that day took us through mountainous country and valleys. The mountains had once been covered with forests, but over time the villagers had burnt the wood to make charcoal, which they had sold in Tabriz and the surrounding areas. In the valleys on the riverbanks, however, there were still woodland trees and walnut trees, and there were plentiful wild raspberries in the valleys. Occasionally my guide and escort told me to dismount and we would eat raspberries and mulberries. The views were so spectacular that I felt no fatigue. We ate the packed lunch which Seyyed Mohammad had put in my saddlebag in a beautiful valley and rode on until an hour before nightfall, when we arrived at the village where we were to spend the night. As my escort had often travelled to this village, he knew the inhabitants and he said that he would spend the night in a friend's house. There was no caravanserai, however, but only a mosque where travellers spent the night under the arch in front of the mosque, so he took me there and left me. All I had was my saddlebag, which contained all my belongings and which became my pillow. Fortunately, as in the mosque itself, the floor under the arch was also covered with rush matting, so I didn't have to sleep on the ground.

My guide pointed out to me that a little further on from the mosque there was a valley into which water flowed from a waterfall at the top of the hill and which served as a bathing place for the villagers. Fridays was reserved for women, so they always placed a woman as a lookout at the entrance to the valley to stop men going there that day, while the rest of the week was for men, who washed their heads and bodies under the narrow natural gully from which the water flowed. As it wasn't a Friday, there wouldn't be many people there and the weather was warm, so I decided to go and take a look, my guide having said that I was welcome to bathe there. Nature had fashioned a real shower there for the local inhabitants. Granite lined the ground under one's feet and the water really flowed down like rose-water. Anyone standing under it was able to avoid oozing mud and sand by positioning himself on the natural stone carpet. I longed to go in, so I took off my clothes, had a delicious bath, dressed again and returned to the mosque.

I performed my ritual ablutions and then entered the mosque to say my prayers. The prayer-leader had not yet arrived, so I waited in line with some of the villagers. When the *molla* arrived, he saw that there was a stranger sitting among the villagers. He kept staring at me. Finally he came up to me and asked if I was Aqa Reza. When I replied that I was, he said: 'Don't you recognise me?' I looked at him closely and saw it was the Molla Moham-mad to whom my father used to give one *toman* a month.[1] When he asked me what I was doing there, I replied that it was a complicated story which I would tell him after evening prayers. We performed the sunset and evening prayers together and asked me where I was staying. On being told that I was sleeping under the arch in front of the mosque, he told one of the congrega-tion to bring my saddlebag and took me to his house. He owned a garden and on his first arrival in the village he had built an upstairs room as a reception area on top of the gardener's room, with a window overlooking the street, so that his guests couldn't see into his women's quarters. The room even had carpets and two bolsters and in the niche there were some flower-pots full of flowers.

There he welcomed me and I told the story of what had happened to me. He said that I should stay with him for as long as I remained in the *seyyed*s' village. I replied that I couldn't stay any longer, as we had hired a horse for two days and I had to go on to Ordubad. He said that he would pay the man off and so, as he insisted that he wouldn't allow me to leave, we agreed that I should stay one night and he would allow me to depart the next day. He provided clean bedclothes and a good dinner, and I spent a night upstairs untroubled by fear of floods. In the end, of course, he made me stay two nights.

He then told me his story: when he had studied enough in Tabriz for the requirements of this village, where he had been born and brought up, he had

---

1 The author had seen this young impecunious religious student working on a Tabriz building site and had asked his father to help him.

obtained permission from his teacher, Molla ʿAbdol-ʿAzim, to perform the ceremonies of marriage and divorce and to recite prayers for the dead and other religious functions. He had then returned home with the necessary approval from Tabriz, and he had trained for some years with the local *molla*, who appointed him as his successor on his death. He had married the *molla*'s daughter and since the old man had owned some agricultural land and a fruit-garden, together with some cattle and sheep, he now lived well on the small income he earned from performing marriages and divorces. He started to talk of the old days in Tabriz and said that on some days he had lived off 100 *dinar*s,[2] while sometimes only my father's offer of dinner had come to his rescue.

During my two-day stay, he paid for the cost of my horse and of my escort, whom he also treated as his guest. On the second morning, when it was time for me to leave, he filled every empty space in my saddlebags with bread and cheese, boiled eggs, chicken kebabs and fruit, and he escorted me on horse-back part of the way. We set off, ate lunch on the way and arrived at the Siyah Rud crossing-point in the afternoon. There we obtained a frontier pass and asked the way from the frontier official. Since we were to travel by boat, my horse was left behind on the Iranian side of the frontier but my guide accompanied me as far as Ordubad,[3] which was not very far away, and then returned home. He rented a mount for me for a few *kran* and gave instructions for me to be dropped at the first caravanserai. We reached Ordubad two hours before sunset and there I spent my first night in a foreign land.

Use of this caravanserai was restricted to postal service couriers and those travelling from Qaradagh[4] to Nakhchivan. It was not a hotel for merchants. We moved into one of the empty rooms, which didn't even have a mat on the floor. I asked the caretaker whether, if I paid him, he could bring me a mattress and some bedclothes for the night, so that I could leave for Nakhchivan the next day. The caretaker was a good man and said that I was not to worry: he would provide for my needs and would send me on my way the next day with the couriers. He went off immediately and brought me a mattress from

---

2   A *dinar* was worth approximately one *toman* or ten *kran*s.

3   First town in Russian territory on the other side of the Aras River.

4   Area of Iranian east Azerbaijan bordering the Aras River.

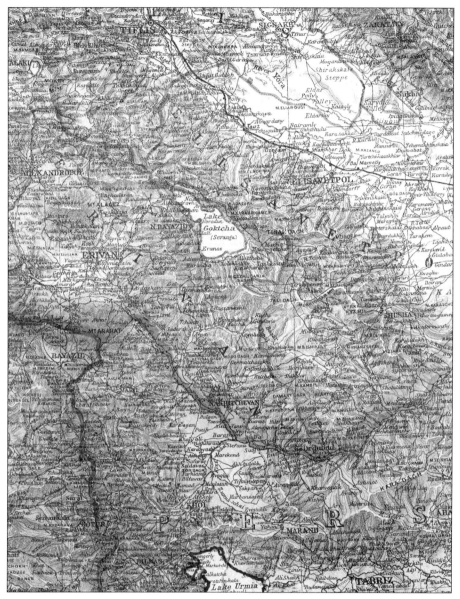

Map of Caucasia (Maps MOD) by the Intelligence Branch of the War Office in 1885 and revised in 1891. ©The British Library Board Maps MOD IB492.

his own room and spread it on the ground. There was a pool with running water in the middle of the caravanserai courtyard, where I went to make my ablutions before evening prayers. Suddenly I saw a distinguished-looking man who stopped me and said: 'Aqa Reza, what are you doing here?' It was Haji Mirza Ja'far, who was from Ordubad but who was also a close friend of Haji Molla Ahmad Tahbaz[5] and used to visit him in Tabriz and indeed sometimes attended his group lessons. Haji Mirza Ja'far's position in Ordubad was exactly like that of Haji Molla Tahbaz in Tabriz. He was a wealthy man and this caravanserai belonged to him. He was also the prayer-leader in the local mosque and he had a partner with whom he traded between Tabriz and Ordubad. He called the custodian, handed him my saddlebags and took me to his house, a building with both a reception area and women's quarters. The former was furnished with good Persian rugs, with crochet-work back-rests, velvet and fine curtains. In both the reception area garden and the women's quarters there was a pool with running water, fruit trees and roses. He was extraordinarily hospitable and we often went to the mosque together. Other local inhabitants also invited us to lunch and dinner. In addition to his little garden there, he had a large garden outside the town, from where load after load of grapes, quinces, pears and apples were brought every day to town. Next to my room in the reception area there were two storerooms, where all the grapes were hung for the winter.

There was such a profusion of fruit in Ordubad and so few buyers that fruit was very cheap and people sent presents of it to neighbours and friends. One day we were invited to one of the local merchants' house which lay at the end of a narrow cul-de-sac and, as we approached the house, I saw that a pile of at least one *kharvar*[6] of dark red peaches had been dumped in the street. I asked Haji Mirza Ja'far why this had been done. He replied that it was for the poor and those who didn't have a garden to come and take fruit away for free. Those who had gardens did this and even the poor became rather grand. They even took out the stones and gave the peaches to their donkeys. Such was my experience of the hospitality and kindness to strangers of the people

---

5 The author's teacher in Tabriz.

6 Literally, an ass-load. The measure varied in weight in different towns: in Tabriz, it was about 300kg.

of Ordubad that I wrote down in my notebook the following lines inscribed in fine *nasta'liq* script[7] on the wall of the mosque there:

> As the gazelle ran, she learnt from you
> To stop and shy and look behind;
> The moth learnt from me, the candle learnt from me, the rose learnt from
>   me
> To catch fire, to burn and tear its clothes.

Embarrassed by all the hospitality I had received, I wanted to set off for Nakhchivan, but every time I tried to do so, Haji Mirza Ja'far said that some distance from Ordubad local tribal bandits had made the road from Erivan to Nakhchivan unsafe. Anyone who tried to travel through this area at night was stripped of his clothes and his mount stolen. Anyone who resisted was killed. I must wait a few days and they would send me off when five or six travellers had assembled ready to travel together. Otherwise it would be dangerous, and he certainly couldn't allow me to travel alone. One day, however, he came and told me to get ready: some travellers were about to depart. He would place me in their charge and also send someone with me as far as the post-houses at Jolfa and Erivan, where the road was secure, and the man would then return home. The travellers were three tradesmen from the area and two young sons of local Muslim notables. The latter had good-quality rifles. They were also well-mounted and fully armed, while the merchants had revolvers and old pistols. I was the only person travelling unarmed.

Haji Mirza Ja'far accompanied us on horseback for a distance of about 600 yards,[8] recited the *azan*[9] in my ear and a prayer for good luck and entrusted me to them. Our first halt was to be at the post-house at Quri Cha'i, which lay on our way to Nakhchivan. Travellers on their way from Jolfa to Erivan also had to pass through Quri Cha'i, where we hoped to spend the night, and then all travellers would go on by the same road to Nakhchivan. When we dismounted for lunch, however, a foot-traveller coming from Nakhchivan told

---

7 The predominant Persian calligraphic script, developed in the eighth to ninth centuries CE.
8 A gesture of respect.
9 Or *adhan*, the Muslim call to prayer.

us that between Quri Cha'i and Nakhchivan mounted tribesmen had made the road unsafe. It was impossible to travel to Nakhchivan at night and Russian post-houses refused to provide lodging for those who were not travelling in post-wagons.

My companions thought about the problem for a while and then agreed unanimously that in order for us to be given a place to sleep in the post-house, I would have to be given the title of Khan. They asked me what my name was. When I replied that it was Reza, they said that they were going to call me 'Abdollah Khan or in Arabic 'Servant of God' Khan. After all, I thought, we were all servants of God. As we approached Quri Cha'i, one of the young gentlemen would gallop off to tell 'Ali Beg, the official in charge of the post-house, that 'Abdollah Khan, nephew of Asadollah Khan Nazem-od-Dowleh, Iran's consul-general in Tiflis, was travelling to Tiflis via Nakhchivan, accompanied by several consulate-general servants. As he was very tired from his journey, he wished to stay the night in the post-house before continuing his journey the next day. This solution was unanimously agreed. One half of me laughed and the other half trembled at the idea. I said to these gentlemen that I didn't know Mirza Asadollah Khan nor had I ever even clapped eyes on him. What would happen if 'Ali Beg asked his address, his age, whether he had a beard or what the name of the brother was whose son I was supposed to be? The young gentlemen said that if I would do exactly as they said that night, they would undertake to reply to any questions that 'Ali Beg might pose. They wouldn't let me open my mouth. Obviously on our arrival. I would be given a room to myself and the others would sleep elsewhere. They would say that the Khan was very tired and the post-house was to prepare a good comfortable room for him. For the benefit of 'Ali Beg and the post-house staff, the young men would pretend to be my servants and every time I emerged or when they entered my presence, they would bow, as is the Iranian custom. They would certainly not sit in my presence, at any rate until 'Ali Beg had been ushered into my presence and asked his questions. In the end I understood that I had to do as they ordered or else we would be in danger, so I told them to do as they wished.

As arranged, when we approached Quri Cha'i, one of the young men galloped off to see 'Ali Beg. I mounted the very beautiful horse with a fine saddle and bridle which he had lent me and he mounted my nag. We were still some way from the post-house when a courier and his son came up out to greet us and bowed low. He threw himself in front of my horse and introduced his son to me. The young gentleman with me replied to his polite enquiries on my behalf, saying that the Khan was grateful for his hospitality and for his welcome. Meanwhile, of course, I didn't dare say a word. We duly reached the post-house, where I was given a good room reserved for important Russians, while the others were lodged in other rooms, two young gentlemen in one room and the others elsewhere. 'Ali Beg wouldn't allow us to pay for anything: he gave us a good dinner and tea and breakfast the next morning. All this time, of course, he was kept well away from me. When we left, my travelling companions were happy to put together enough money to compensate 'Ali Beg for his expenses, which they gave to his son as a tip. Meanwhile, I mounted the young man's fine horse again, 'Ali Beg accompanied us on our way for about 300 yards, bowed politely and asked me to convey his greetings to my uncle the Khan, saying that although they were now Russian subjects and servants of Russia, they had not forgotten Iran and considered Iran's great men to be their own. When he spoke like this, I started to perspire with embarrassment and I was completely tongue-tied. The young gentleman, however, made the necessary replies on my behalf.

When we reached Nakhchivan, Haji Mirza Ja'far's man asked me where I wanted to stay. I replied that one of our fellow townspeople in Tabriz, Haji Mirza Aqa from Erivan, had a daughter who had married a man called Haji 'Abbas from Nakhchivan. I didn't know whether the latter was here now or in Tabriz, so he suggested that I should go to the caravanserai and wait there while he went to look for him. A short time later he came back with the Haji, who kindly bore me off to his house, a fine dwelling where he gave me a room in the men's quarters. Now the Haji was a wealthy man with good taste, so he had built a reception hall there in the Tabriz architectural style, that is to say with fine-tooled window panes of multi-coloured glass, plaster-moulded rooms and mirror work. Unusually for Nakhchivan, the Haji also invited us in the evening and he arranged for me to travel on with acquaintances who were going on to Erivan. In those days there was no railway from Nakhchivan to Erivan and Tiflis and travellers didn't travel on horseback, but in post-wagons, with horses being changed at every post-house. In some places the post-houses were run by Muslims from Nakhchivan and Erivan but in most they were headed by Russian villagers called *Malak*s.[10] The Muslims' houses were cleaner than those of the Malaks, but the latter's horses and carriages, which are called 'troikas', were in better condition than those of the Muslims.

On our arrival in Erivan, my companions said that those who could should stay with relatives or friends and those who couldn't should lodge at the new caravanserai belonging to the *Sheikh-ol-Islam*,[11] where it was suggested that I should go. When we reached the caravanserai and one of my travelling companions was about to rent a room for me, a local man stopped me and asked me whether I had any relatives in Erivan. I said that my father had a maternal uncle called Haji Rajab, an Erivan merchant. Haji Rajab was located, he reproached me for not having telegraphed him with news of my impending arrival and took me off to his house, where he gave me a room in the men's quarters.

The next morning I was taken to call on Haji Molla Baba, the First Deputy Qazi[12] of Erivan who was related to my grandfather, Mirza Ibrahim, formerly the chief minister to the Khan of Erivan. The Haji was a good-looking man of about fifty years old, with a substantial beard, dressed in sparklingly clean white clothes. His impeccably-fitted turban was made of fine muslin and added dignity to his face. Although he wasn't yet an old man, he improved his physical appearance by dying his hair with henna and coloured dye every week. As he had heard that I had studied Islamic Law and Jurisprudence in Tabriz with the late Haji Molla Ahmad Tahbaz, he said that unfortunately he had only studied in Erivan and that he feared that I was more advanced in the study of the Shari'a than he was. He would like me to remain in Erivan for a time, so that we could repeat the *Sharh-e Lam'eh*[13] together.

One day the Qazi said to me that there were some *Khans*[14] in Erivan who were very attached to Iran and who regretted having remained in what was now Russian territory. He wanted to take me to call on them. Except for one, who was the son of the former Sheikh-ol-Islam of Erivan, the others were

---

10 Greek Orthodox sect in Russia.

11 Leading government-recognised cleric in an area.

12 Government-appointed official and judge trying cases under Islamic law.

13 Learned work of biography and sayings of the Imams, much studied in Shi'a seminaries.

14 In this context probably tribal chieftains.

all of Mongol stock and from Mongol tribes. As they had heard from the Qazi that I was a descendant of Mirza Ibrahim, the minister of Erivan, one of them, Shokr Khan, invited the Qazi and myself to lunch one day. He had placed his two young sons, one of fourteen and the other of thirteen, in the government secondary school or 'gymnasium' in Tiflis, from where they had returned to visit their father for the summer holidays. After lunch the Khan summoned them and introduced them to me. He suggested that I should ask them a question so that he could know whether they had learnt anything or whether the money he was spending on their studies was being wasted. I asked them whether they knew any Persian (as they speak Turkish in Erivan). They said that they didn't. I asked them whether they knew any Persian poetry. They replied in the negative. In that case, I suggested, they certainly didn't know any Arabic. Again they said that they didn't. Shokr Khan was very embarrassed, since he imagined that as his sons were studying in the gymnasium, they knew everything. He said that as they didn't know any Persian, I should ask them a scientific question. I laughed and said that as they didn't know Persian or Arabic and that our sciences were written in these two languages, I really couldn't ask them any questions.

Then he turned to his two sons and ordered them to ask me a question. The elder son asked me how many countries our earth contained. In Tabriz I knew nothing of the divisions of the planet and had heard nothing on the subject, so relying on some of our poets, both Persian and Arab, who say that there are seven, I replied that the earth was divided into seven countries. They asked me what they were. I started to number them, saying: 'Iran, Turkistan, Afghanistan, India, Abyssinia, Europe and Arabia.' They said: 'What happened to America and Australia?' I had heard of America but this was the first time that I had heard of Australia, so I couldn't deny that it existed. As I knew that there was a country called America, I said that this was all I had learnt in Iran and that what they had said about Australia was not recorded in Iran. Then the elder boy asked: 'So they don't teach geography in Iranian schools?' As this was the first time that I had heard the word 'geography', this was yet another reason why I couldn't say a word. Nor could I possibly ask what 'geography' meant. Until that moment I had thought of myself as the most learned man in Iran and I cannot describe how ashamed I felt. Now that Shokr Khan had revealed the depth of Aqa Reza's ignorance, he didn't wish to embarrass me further. He told his sons to leave us. There and then I made a vow that as soon as I reached a place where this was possible, I would put aside all the subjects that I had studied up to now and start studying European subjects. The one thing which made me slightly less embarrassed was that when I left Shokr Khan's house, I went and asked the highly-respected Qazi about the different regions of the planet and I observed that like me he only knew those branches of religion-based knowledge which were known in Iran. He too knew nothing of the new sciences. After that I was no longer embarrassed in his presence.

Amidst all the entertainment provided for me by my father's friends, a telegram arrived from Tiflis from the Sheikh-ol-Islam of the Caucasus, announcing that the Russian government had accepted his proposal for the appointment of Haji Molla Baba as Qazi of Tiflis and that the latter should set off for Tiflis immediately. The Qazi thought this a god-send for me since he had been trying to find a travelling companion for me as far as Tiflis and his journey from Erivan to Tiflis would be entirely at government expense. In those days it was the custom for a post-wagon with room for four passengers to be provided for official travel and so if he was travelling on his own, he could take two or three people with him and there would still be room for his baggage. The Qazi had an assistant from one of the villages of Shureh-Gaz who worked for him on an unpaid basis and also studied religious texts with him as training to become a village *molla*. His name was Reza, a young man aged about twenty-two who was most punctilious in performing his prayers. The Qazi asked Reza to accompany him to Tiflis on the same terms as he had worked in Erivan. He would be given board and lodging there, he would have two hours a day to study and he would serve the Qazi the rest of the time.

We set off as a party of three, accompanied for about three kilometres on horseback by several of the Qazi's and my relatives and close friends. When we arrived in Tiflis, appropriate furnished lodgings had been rented for him in the house of the famous *Mirza Fath 'Ali Akhondov*.[15] The Qazi entertained me for ten days. Iranians living in Tiflis, both merchants and tradesmen, are very hospitable, especially so because they themselves are away from home. There were two caravanserais in Tiflis, one called the Khalatov and the other

---

15 Further detail on names printed in italics can be found in the Glossary of Iranian Names and Titles at the end of this volume.

the Mirzaiev, where Iranian merchants and tradesmen who had no family with them lodged. They rented two or three rooms there and these became both their trading offices and their lodgings. There were nearly 10,000 Iranians there, most of them workmen. All the kiln workers were from Salmas, Dilmaqan and the area round Urumiyeh, while the road workers of Tiflis were from Maragheh and the areas surrounding Tabriz, Marand and Khoi.[16]

The Qazi had supervised the preparations for my journey and found me a travelling companion in the shape of a Haji who was travelling to Istanbul. The Qazi sent me off via Poti,[17] which even in those days could be reached by railway, and accompanied me himself to the railway station with some of his friends. Obviously I travelled third class on the boat with the Haji. The Qazi had given me a Qarabagh prayer rug and a small travelling samovar as leaving presents. On the boat I put the rug under the samovar and the Haji made good use of the latter, which he lit and on which he made tea. My travelling companions had brought bread and cheese with them from Poti as they didn't wish to buy a thing on the boat. They were going on pilgrimage to Mecca and they would have been defiled if they had done so. In addition, they had a bag of dried fruit, walnut stones, raisins, herbs and dates, and I was their guest all the way from Poti to Istanbul. That was all the food we had and the pilgrims were grateful that I had provided the samovar, as it would have been unthinkable for them to have drunk tea from the ship's samovar.[18]

On our arrival in Istanbul I immediately went to Haji Reza Aqa's trading office in the Sonboli Han.[19] He showed me how to organise and make entries in his account-books and also instructed me on how to reply to the correspondence he received. I spent two days there paying and receiving calls. Most of the merchants there were from the same town as Haji Reza. Men from Salmas, Dilmaqan and Kho'i look after each other very well.

On the day after my arrival, Monsieur Kostaki, Haji Reza's Greek agent, came to see him and I was introduced to him. Monsieur Kostaki told Haji

---

16 All towns in Iranian Azerbaijan.

17 A port on the east coast of the Black Sea

18 Devout Muslims on a pilgrimage do not touch food prepared by infidels, which they consider unclean.

19 Part of the great Covered Bazaar.

Reza that his son had completed his studies at the Greek School in the last few days and had obtained his diploma. The boy now knew good French, English and Turkish. If the Haji agreed, he would bring his son to meet both the Haji and myself the next day, for as we were both young and of the same age, we would probably get on well. The next day he brought his son Nicholas to meet me. In addition to his good Turkish, Nicholas had also learnt a little Persian. I immediately asked him whether he had studied geography. He replied that the first subject which he had been taught at school had been geography. When I said that I really wanted to learn geography, he said that it was really very simple. He wanted to learn more Persian, as the family's work was essentially with Iranians. However, in order for me to study geography, he said, I first had to study French. He suggested that I should obtain Haji Reza's permission for him to come once a day for an hour to teach me French and in return I would teach him Persian.

Haji Reza gave his permission and so we went to the booksellers' bazaar where I bought a book on the French alphabet and he bought the *Golestan* of Sa'adi. We then spent several weeks teaching each other. One day, when Nicholas saw that I had made a great deal of progress and was gradually becoming able to read books, he said to me that he could see that I was very talented and that it would be a pity for me just to become a merchant. He suggested that I should obtain Haji Reza's permission for him to take me to the Greek School in Galatasaray, where he had studied, the headmaster there being a very kind man. As I already spoke good Persian and Turkish, I should learn French. I would then be given a good job in the Iranian consulate. Nicholas's words and his knowledge of geography made me start thinking but I doubted whether Haji Reza could be persuaded that I would be able to pay my own school fees. Nicholas replied that he would get his father to work on him, so that I could attend classes by day and spend the evenings after lessons dealing with correspondence and the Haji's office accounts. Kostaki duly persuaded the Haji and Nicholas took me with him to see the headmaster of the school. The fees weren't high, one Ottoman lira a month, so I was able to start my lessons. As I was much older than the pupils in the lowest two classes, Nicholas and the headmaster arranged that I should attend regularly when there were classes and that on other days I should do my homework in an unoccupied room there.

Obviously, in those days there was no tramway between the Sonboli Han and the Galata district. It was a long way to travel, too far to return to the trading office for lunch. Fortunately, next door to the school there was a tobacconist's shop kept by a man from Salmas, that is to say that from the same town as Haji Reza. I had to buy something small, a piece of bread and cheese, and eat it in the empty room. For three or four days at lunchtime I would leave the school, buy some bread from the baker next door to the tobacconist and return to school. One day the tobacconist greeted me and asked me why I bought bread and why I attended the school. I explained my circumstances and why I was happy to make do with this meagre lunch. He said that he was in the same position as I was in Istanbul: he too was a foreigner and as his house was also a very long way away near Eyyup, he always ate lunch in his shop, so he invited me to come and eat lunch with him every day.

The school programme was as follows: the Greek language, French, English and Turkish. Since I knew Turkish and didn't need Greek, we arranged with the headmaster that I should concentrate on studying French and some English.

One thing which is worth mentioning is the way in which the Iranians of Istanbul celebrated the ten days of 'Ashura.[20] Their *rowzeh-khwani*[21] was worthy of the highest praise. All along the passageways of the caravanserais which they occupied and in front of their trading offices they had hung black curtains, around which twelve verses of Mohtasham's poetry[22] had been written down and framed. Visitors, most of them Ottomans, were given tea and cigarettes or a water-pipe, while those serving the visitors, most of whom were the merchants themselves, rushed around receiving their guests like orphans at their father's funeral. However, the thing which I didn't like was the men cutting themselves with knives. They gathered in the Yildiz Han on the day before 'Ashura, clothed themselves in white shrouds and cut themselves so that their heads streamed with blood.[23] Crying 'Shah Hossein', they came

---

20 Annual ten days of Shi'a mourning, commemorating the martyrdom of Imam Hossein and his family.

21 Traditional Shi'a ritual lamentations to commemorate the martyrdom.

22 Mohtasham-e-Kashani wrote poetry commemorating this martyrdom.

23 A traditional Shi'a custom at 'Ashura.

out, passed through the Muslim districts and proceeded to the Valideh Han,[24] with many of them collapsing unconscious on the way. Some Iranians used to say that when those cutting themselves processed past Ottoman women in the street, they split open their heads with even greater enthusiasm in order to show the ladies how brave they were, but actually most of them lost consciousness before reaching the Valideh Han. I said at the time that if I ever became ambassador or consul there, I wouldn't allow this kind of thing to take place.

I continued to live like this until, as a result of the extreme humidity of the Istanbul climate, I became very ill just before I completed my studies and obtained my diploma. I began to suffer from such a bad stomach-ache that I was confined to bed and I really thought that I was going to die. In those days, Iranians thought that a sick man should not be sent to hospital in Istanbul where, it was claimed, foreigners were poisoned. Haji Reza couldn't be persuaded to send me to hospital, but the Iranian community had a Greek doctor in whom they had confidence and who told me that the climate of Istanbul didn't suit me. I should be sent back to Tabriz, where the climate would cure me of this illness, and I should stay there for at least two years. Haji Reza had to make hasty preparations for my departure, therefore, and he bought several cases of tea and cloth for me to take with me for him on my journey via Tiflis to Tabriz.

I set off in my sick condition and eventually arrived in Tiflis. I had warned the Qazi in advance of my arrival, so that he came out to welcome me and took me off to his house. He asked the head of the Russian government hospital, where the head doctor was German, to treat me and after a few days of the Tiflis climate I was completely cured. When I told the tale of my Istanbul life and of my French and English studies, the Qazi said that he couldn't allow me to return to Tabriz. He would do as Nicholas, the Greek agent's son, had recommended for me. The Russian government had recently opened two schools in Tiflis, one for Shi'a Muslims and one for Sunnis. The syllabus took in the Persian language and literature and enough basic Arabic to understand Persian literature. The major part of the syllabus, however, was the Russian language,

---

24 The Buyuk Valide Han, situated in the Sirkeci district of Istanbul, not far from the Grand Bazaar, had been commissioned by the Queen Mother Kosem Sultan in the seventeenth century and contained shops, publishing houses and coffee-houses, all owned by Iranians.

Russian grammar and syntax, together with geography, arithmetic, general
history and elementary physics. He said that as I didn't need to study Arabic
and Persian, I would be able to make rapid progress in Russian. My age made
it unsuitable for me to study these subjects in the same classroom with small
children, but the headmaster of the school was the Sheikh-ol-Islam and since
he, the Qazi, owed his appointment to the Sheikh's recommendation and the
latter had been kind to him, he was sure that I would be accepted in the school
on an exceptional basis. Consequently, I sent on through Rezaiev[25] all the commercial goods which I had brought with me to Haji Reza Aqa's son in Tabriz
and entered the Russian school.

We spent a number of evenings at home with Mirza Fath ʿAli Akhondov, where young men from leading Muslim families in Tiflis gathered of
an evening to chat. Akhondov was the Russian language interpreter to the
Viceroy and to the Caucasus General Staff and had chosen the family name
'Akhondov' for himself. His nephew, Mirza Mostafa Akhondov, also worked
in the General Staff and since many letters arriving there were in Turkish
or Persian, he was his uncle's assistant. Mirza Fath ʿAli Akhondov was very
well-educated in the Persian and Arabic languages and literature and he also
enjoyed complete mastery of the Russian language. However, he really didn't
like the Arabs at all. Indeed, he had an almost pathological hatred for them.
Whenever the history of the Arabs and Persians was discussed, he would
almost always cite the following verse of Ferdowsi:

> From drinking camels' milk and eating lizards,
> The Arabs have come to covet the Shah's Kayanian crown.
> Fie upon thee, O revolving world!

It was Mirza Fath ʿAli who first suggested to me the idea of changing the
Persian alphabet. Until then I had had no idea of our alphabet's defects. Whenever the subject of our alphabet came up, as soon as a few words were said,
he would suggest various ways of pronouncing them. He had a disputatious
way of looking at things. If the first word was Hassan, he would make his
audience look at the word and would ask someone to read it out. Someone

25 A large Tiflis trading company of Iranian origin.

read out 'Hassan'. He said that it wasn't 'Hassan' but 'Hosn'. Another would duly read out 'Hosn'. He asked why it should be 'Hosn'. It was 'Hisn'.[26] He considered contemporary *molla*s to be completely ignorant and ill-educated, and he would always say that eight year old primary school children knew more than *mojtahed*s[27] about world history and geography, I would remember my meeting with Shokr Khan's sons in Erivan and break out in a cold sweat with embarrassment.

He had one daughter, whom he had given in marriage to Khan Baba Khan, Bahman Mirza's son,[28] and whom he allowed to go out without a veil and who dressed like a Russian woman, whereas all the Muslim women there wore the veil. As a result of his free-thinking words and the fact that his daughter went out unveiled, the Muslims of Tiflis, who were very fanatical, thoroughly disliked Mirza Fath 'Ali and he himself used to say that when they saw him in the street, they lowered their eyes to avoid looking at him. He was, however, a very kind-hearted person. He had a steward whom he allowed to sit with him at meals when there were no guests. This steward used to recount that Mirza Fath 'Ali held a list of destitute Muslims in the town and on Thursdays and Muslim festival days he would always secretly send financial help to them through his steward, forbidding the latter to mention their names to anyone.

---

26 The Arabic-Persian script only contains consonants, vowel sounds being implied rather than written.

27 Pre-eminent Shiʿa religious scholars.

28 Perhaps Bahman Mirza, once prince-governor of Azerbaijan, a son of ʿAbbas Mirza and grandson of Fath ʿAli Shah.

Chapter 3

My Entry into Government Service
(1875–1883)

Until the early nineteenth century, Iran, unlike the Ottoman Empire, had remained isolated and largely immune to European influence. When it came up against the brutal reality of Russian and British power, few Iranians spoke foreign languages or understood how foreigners thought. In 1878 Naser-od-Din Shah paid his second visit to Europe. Due to an extraordinary combination of circumstances, Aqa Reza, who was studying at the Russian school for Muslims, was appointed Russian language interpreter to the Shah when the latter arrived on Russian territory on his way to St Petersburg. Thanks to this stroke of luck, a brilliant career opened up for him. No wonder that Aqa Reza later believed that he had been protected by a benevolent fate.

It is clear that he had exceptional charm and ability, for his two first chiefs at the Tiflis consulate-general valued his services and actively protected and encouraged him. Furthermore, his networking skills were already well-developed. His realisation that a modern education system was the key to Iran's progress and his ideas for the reform of the Arabic alphabet show a developing interest in educational reform which was to find more concrete shape later in his career. He sent a copy of his treatise on the subject to the Ottoman Minister of Education and dedicated the work to Iran's Heir Apparent, later Mozaffar-od-Din Shah. He was rewarded with decorations, appointment as an aide-de-camp to the latter and a magnificent uniform, which he wore with great pride tinged, to his credit, with a modicum of embarrassment at his complete lack of military experience. Throughout his career he had an inordinate love of decorations.

Aqa Reza, who had an almost mystical respect for the person of the Naser-od-Din Shah and whose career progression depended on the man who was the fount of all honours, was dazzled by the pomp and ceremony surrounding the royal personage. At the same time he noted the somewhat haphazard nature of public finances and was unimpressed by some of the lesser members of the royal family.

At the beginning of his government career, the author, now Mirza[1] Reza Khan, was acutely aware of the insecurity of his position and here the young upstart saw the first signs of his colleagues' deadly professional jealousy and intrigues, against which he would have to protect himself throughout his career. If the memories of an old man are to be trusted, however, he seems to have been very self-confident, sometimes almost fool-hardily so, in addressing his superiors, but his prospects do not seem to have suffered from this. Indeed the Shah seems to have shown him remarkable personal kindness.

In his later career, the author became part of both worlds, European and Iranian. Here we read of an essential stage in his social development: the first contacts between the young Muslim Iranian 'with a felt hat' and the Russian aristocracy in Tiflis and St Petersburg. He attends an archaeological congress, he learns to dance, he rides out with members of the aristocracy and above all he meets young, attractive Russian women. For the young Muslim from provincial Tabriz, there is an almost perceptible sensual frisson when he describes how Mademoiselle Taube, lady-in-waiting to the Tsarina, puts her arm on his. It is no wonder that many are jealous of him.

One day, two months before I completed my secondary school studies and obtained my school diploma, *Mirza Mahmoud Khan*, the consul-general, who later became the *'Ala'-ol-Molk*, sent 'Ali, the consulate messenger, to the Qazi's[2] house, saying that the consul-general wished to see me. The Qazi was somewhat put out that I had been summoned without him. The consul-general said that a strange thing had happened which he considered very auspicious

---

1 Mirza, when written before a name, means 'secretary' or 'learned man' and was a title given to bureaucrats. When it appears after a name, as in 'Bahman Mirza', it denotes 'Prince'.

2 The Qazi of Tiflis, Haji Molla Baba, was again giving him lodgings in his house, as he had done on the author's previous visit on his way to Istanbul.

for me. He said that His Majesty Naser-od-Din Shah, who was to make his second journey to Europe, planned to arrive in Tiflis in the next few days from Jolfa and Erivan. The Prime Minister, *Haji Mirza Hossein Khan Sepah-salar*, had telegraphed to his son-in-law, Ahmad Khan, the consul-general in Astrakhan, to come to Tiflis with his interpreter, Mirza Taqi Khan. He had also telegraphed Mirza Mahmoud Khan to bring his Tiflis interpreter, Mirza Maʿsoum Khan, to Jolfa to welcome the Shah.

Mirza Mahmoud Khan continued with the story: Mirza Maʿsoum Khan, who had been feeling unwell for several days, had had a fever the previous day. He had told his Armenian maid, Maryam, that he wanted quinine pills. Instead of giving him quinine pills, Maryam had given him mercury pills, the two bottles being very similar and the pills for both quinine and mercury being white. Furthermore, instead of taking two pills, Mirza Maʿsoum Khan swallowed four of them, thinking that he would shake off the fever more quickly. At the same time, Mirza Taqi Khan, who was staying with him and had just returned to the house, entered his room and, seeing the medicine bottle, asked him what it was. Mirza Maʿsoum Khan explained that since he had not been feeling well and had to set off the next morning, he had swallowed some pills. Mirza Taqi Khan said that he was also ill, so he too was given four mercury pills, which he duly swallowed. In the middle of the night, both men suffered from severe throat ache. He, the consul-general, had immediately sent for the head of the government hospital, who lived next door to the consulate-general and who examined the two men, inspected the pill bottle and said that they had eaten mercury pills. They were therefore both very ill, and he would have to transfer them to hospital immediately. Now both men were in hospital, the consul-general said, and his party absolutely had to set off that afternoon or at the latest the next morning. He had no interpreter, so I must go with them.

I replied that I was the Qazi's guest and he had been kind to me, so I couldn't promise to leave without first obtaining his permission. Furthermore, I still had two months to go before completing my studies and Mr Qarabashov had given me several subjects to prepare for my diploma examination. I was afraid that if I accompanied the consul-general on this journey, I would fall behind and would have to remain in school for a further year. I might not be able to come. The consul-general said: 'In so far as the Qazi is concerned, tell him from me that in my opinion the key to your future progress lies in not missing this opportunity! Tell Qarabashov that this journey will only last a few days and that he should continue to help you on your return and make up for the missed lessons! I promise that I will obtain the Shah's agreement to award him the Order of the Lion and Sun in the class appropriate to his rank.'

He gave me no further opportunity to delay, but simply said: 'Pack a small suitcase with what you need for the journey and come with us! From today onwards we will have to try to find a place to sleep in post-houses!' I returned to the house and told the Qazi what had happened. The Qazi was someone who very much believed in taking omens[3] from the Qur'an, so he said that he wouldn't give me his permission until he had taken an omen. He said that this kind of road was very dangerous. What if something awful were to happen to a carriage travelling through the Delijan Pass, which was a very difficult road, with its over-excited Malak horses? He wouldn't allow me to say another word but went to get his Qur'an. He took an omen and alighted on this verse from the Surah of Yusuf (12:19): 'Then came travellers, and they sent one of them, a water-drawer, who let down his bucket. "Good news!" he said, "Here is a young man"'! He congratulated me warmly and sent someone to fetch Qarabashov, so that he could tell him the story. The latter was thinking about the promise of a medal, for Russians are very keen on decorations, so he was delighted and readily gave his permission.

In the afternoon, 'Ali the messenger came back from the consulate and took my suitcase, while I went to the consulate. Mirza Mohammad 'Ali Khan Kashi, who had the contract for the paved road from Tiflis to Vladikafkaz, had prepared a fine new carriage, which he sent to Tiflis for the consul's journey. The three of us got into the carriage, as we weren't taking any servants with us. It was common knowledge that the Shah and his court had so many servants that there would be no room for ours. From his arrival in Jolfa until he left Russian soil, His Majesty was an official guest of the government and all his expenses would be paid by the Russians. Orders had been given that the post-houses on the road from Tiflis to Jolfa should be smartened up as much as possible, that carpets and rugs should be hung on the walls, that where

---

3 Iranians today still choose a passage at random from the Qur'an or, for example, from the poems of Hafez to decide on a course of action.

possible cut flowers or, where these were not available, wild flowers should be provided and that the door and window surrounds all should be decorated. Since the consul-general also had letters of recommendation from the governor of Tiflis, the horses were quickly changed on the way and we arrived at the Delijan post-house an hour after sunset.

Mirza Ahmad Khan said: 'We must divide our tasks between the three of us. As we have no servants, we will have to look after ourselves.' As I spoke Russian, I was told to be responsible for bringing water from the river and for purchasing bread and eggs, cheese and fruit. Mirza Ahmad Khan himself was to make the tea but I was to obtain a samovar and its various relevant parts from the *Malaks*. Mirza Mahmoud Khan was responsible for lighting the lamp, spreading the tablecloth and preparing the food. We agreed that we wouldn't prepare meat, kebabs or meat broth but that the 'Ala'-ol-Molk would cook fried eggs. I was delighted with this division of labour, for I saw that the consuls were treating me as an equal. Having spent the night in this way, we set off in the morning and reached Russian Jolfa[4] in the evening.

At that time, there was no bridge over the Aras River there. A thick rope had been tied to some kind of boat, and was also secured to both banks of the river. The oarsmen rowed the boat across, while the rope prevented the boat from being swept off course by the water. In this way we crossed the river. On the Iranian side, the passport department had built several rooms for the Shah, the Heir Apparent and the entourage. Tents had also been erected in front of the building on the barren land which stretched away into the distance. The late Mirza Afzal Khan Vakil-ol-Molk, the Heir Apparent's chief secretary who was also the consul-general Mirza Mahmoud Khan's brother, had heard of his brother's arrival by telegram. He had prepared three rooms and bedclothes in the same enclosed space which also housed the customs office and the passport office. On our arrival, we saw that the Amin-ol-Vezareh, the passport chief, and some of his friends had come out to welcome us on the banks of the Aras River. The next day, when the Shah was due to arrive in state from Marand, the Vakil-ol-Molk saddled three horses for us to ride out to welcome the Shah.

The Shah's personal cavalry escort, who were tribal khans from the Makou'i tribe, the Qarapapakh, the Kurds and the Shahsavan, had whipped up so much

---

4 On the north bank of the Aras River.

dust that really no one could distinguish one person from another. In accordance with the custom of the time, these tribal khans were putting on a show of horsemanship for the Shah. His Majesty entered the camp in great pomp. The next day, the Russian official hosts arrived with the two Beglarov brothers, who spoke good Persian. They crossed the Aras and, dressed in their official uniforms, were introduced to the Shah. They arranged that after lunch the royal party should set off and sleep the night in Russian Jolfa. His Majesty got into the boat with Haji Mirza Hossein Khan Sepahsalar and the rest of his entourage and crossed safely. Since there was no room for us in the boat, it was arranged that the boat would return and take us across.

Unfortunately, however, as we were waiting to cross, the rope snapped and the current swept the boat away. The oarsmen could only manoeuvre the boat to shore much further downstream than at the planned crossing point. The consuls were all weeping and saying: 'What will happen to us? The Shah will arrive in the Caucasus and we won't be there. What will happen to His Majesty and his entourage? It isn't our fault, but we will be punished for this.' Mirza Mahmoud Khan, who was a brave man and had no fear of death, said to his brother: 'Can you find a boat to take us to the other side? Even if we perish, we will at least die in the service of the Shah.' The Vakil-ol-Molk said that a boat could certainly be found but the crossing was dangerous. 'I cannot allow you to do this. The Aras is in spate and as it can sweep even a large boat away, how do you think that you can cross it in a small one?' The 'Ala'-ol-Molk insisted that by hook or by crook he had to get to the other side that night, so the Vakil-ol-Molk asked the Amin-ol-Vezareh, who was also the local governor, to take care of the matter and a boat with six oarsmen was obtained from the local khans. Even the boatman said that he didn't think such a crossing a good idea, claiming that the Khan had forced him to cross the Aras, which was thoroughly dangerous when it was flowing as fast as this. Mirza Ahmad Khan agreed with them. However, as the 'Ala'-ol-Molk was the consul-general for the Caucasus and was in charge, Mirza Ahmad Khan had to take his orders from him. There were only three of us in the boat. No one else dared to come with us, although there was plenty of room in the boat. As soon as we had gone a short distance from the shore, the power of the river overwhelmed the oarsmen and swept the boat away. The boatman said: 'You would not listen to anything I said. Now you had better recite the Muslim testimony of faith. I can do no more. Only hope in God's bounty remains for us.' Then all six men on board kept on crying out in unison: 'O 'Ali!' but only occasionally asked for the help of God himself. For a time the river swept us away, heaven knows how far, with the oarsmen trying their utmost to avoid being pulled away from the Russian bank of the river. They kept on saying that if only we could reach Foyuj between Ordubad and Jolfa, the local people would come out and we could ask them for help. As they cried out 'O 'Ali!', they suddenly saw a light from the camp at Foyuj and the boatmen recovered their spirits.

Everyone cried out 'Help! Help! Help!' over and over again as loudly as they could. The Foyuj people heard their cries and they all rushed down to the riverbank. Those who knew how to swim threw themselves into the water, while the boatmen cast their ropes into the torrent. The people of Foyuj on one end and the oarsmen on the other hauled the boat to the shore and we landed in the middle of the Foyuj tents. Tea was immediately brought and a fire lit for, although it was summer, the nights were very cold there. Having drunk the tea by the fire, we began to warm up a little. Then the 'Ala'-ol-Molk told their chief to provide horses and send someone to escort us to Jolfa. We asked how far it was to Jolfa. One replied that the distance was two *farsakh*s,[5] while another said that it was three *farsakh*s. A horse for the guide and three others were brought up. It was a dark night, but anyway off we set. Luckily, as the road ran along the river, it was straight and as the horses knew the way, they made good progress. However, about half a *farsakh* from Jolfa, the 'Ala'-ol-Molk's horse started to play up and kicked out at my horse. Its hoof struck my leg, however, injuring me quite seriously, and it started to hurt very badly. The 'Ala'-ol-Molk was very upset that he had insisted on taking me with him, for he thought that his horse had perhaps permanently damaged my leg. He kept on comforting me, saying that I shouldn't be afraid, as on the Russian side of the river there was a Russian military hospital and I would be taken there.

Thus, in great pain I reached Jolfa. The two consuls took me off to the Russian hospital and called for the attendants, who got me off my horse with some difficulty and put me on a stretcher and then on to a bed. A surgeon arrived immediately. He said that the bone was broken, but it was reparable

5 An informal and somewhat variable measure of distance, usually thought to be about 6km.

and I shouldn't worry. He immediately broke it and bound it up again, but I couldn't sleep from the pain. When we arrived, it was long past midnight and everyone was asleep, but as Naser-od-Din Shah was an early riser, he was told the whole story: what happened to the boat, the help given by the people of Foyuj and my leg being kicked by the consul-general's horse. This was the first time that His Majesty had heard my name and he asked the consul-general through the prime minister who Reza was. The ʿAlaʾ-ol-Molk said that I was the Russian language interpreter. The Shah felt sorry for me in that this injury had happened to me while in his service, so he sent Dr Tholozan,[6] his chief personal doctor, to the hospital to see me so that he could re-set my leg if this had not been properly done. Luckily, because the mooring rope had broken, the whole party was forced to stay two days there until, after the rope had been repaired, they were able to load the royal baggage and supplies onto the boat and bring them across. My leg improved a great deal during our two day stay there and the pain had eased. I was now able to walk a few steps with difficulty. When all the luggage had arrived with the servants, His Majesty left for Erivan but at every stopping-point on the road, the Shah sent either Dr Tholozan or one of his attendants to ask how I was, and the Sepahsalar did the same.

When we reached the Quri Chaʾi post-house, I told the story of what had happened between ʿAli Agha and myself[7] some years previously. The ʿAlaʾ-ol-Molk summoned ʿAli Agha and thanked him for his kindness to his 'son', as he called me, on the occasion previously described and presented him with a gold medal, which he had obtained through the Sepahsalar from the Shah. ʿAli Agha was so delighted that tears of joy flowed from his eyes and he didn't know how to thank him adequately. This story also even reached the Shah's ears. On his arrival in Erivan, where he rested for three days, the garrison welcomed the Shah with an official parade outside the town. When he arrived in Tiflis, His Majesty, the prime minister and his principal courtiers were lodged in the palace of the Viceroy of the Caucasus,[8] while the rest of the party stayed at the Caucasus Hotel.

---

6 The Shah's French doctor.

7 See Chapter 2, in which, on his youthful journey from Tabriz to Tiflis, Reza had pretended to ʿAli Beg that he was a Khan in order to obtain a bed at a post-house.

8 The Grand Duke Mikhail Nikolaievich, the Tsar's uncle, Viceroy of the Caucasus from 1862 to 1881.

One evening, the consul-general gave an official dinner, to which the prime minister, the royal entourage and His Majesty's official hosts from St Petersburg, together with the governor of Tiflis, were invited. Even I was invited to the dinner. At this point, two things happened to me which I will recount here. First, the Sepahsalar told the 'Ala'-ol-Molk to go and make arrangements for him to visit the best mineral baths and as he would spend some time there dying his hair with natural dye and henna, the baths had to be entirely cleared for three hours. So the 'Ala'-ol-Molk sent me to the Erakle Baths[9] to make the necessary arrangements. I duly returned to the viceroy's palace at the appointed hour, where the governor's carriages with their Orlov horses,[10] were waiting at the door. The Sepahsalar came out with Agha Ibrahim Amin-os-Soltan, the father of *Mirza 'Ali Asghar Khan*, and got into the carriage. The Sepahsalar told me to sit beside the coachman. I replied that it was not right for me to sit there: my school friends might see me and be surprised at my sitting in such a menial position. He was extremely displeased by my words, but very angrily told 'Ali Khan, his steward, who was carrying the fine lawn bath bundle containing the Sepahsalar's under-shirt and gold-embroidered clothing under his arm and who was supposed to sit in another carriage, to sit next to the coachman. The steward got into the carriage and sat down, his dignity offended.

The 'Ala'-ol-Molk was standing next to the coachman and angrily demanded why I had spoken like this to the prime minister of the kingdom. He then asked me whether I had given them the address of the baths. I said that I hadn't. He hit his head with both hands, saying that now I had ruined him too. There were several bathhouses in Vorontsov Street and they would probably go to one of them, find that there was no room there and return. That would really be a disaster for us. When I saw how upset he was, without a moment's hesitation I got into one of the waiting carriages and set off, but how could it catch up with the Orlov horses? I was getting desperate. Unlike the Grand Duke's horses, ours just limped along, until we reached the top of the Ard Square, where I saw the prime minister's carriage standing motionless, while some twenty

---

9 Named after Erakle II, penultimate king of Kartli and Kakhetia, who gained independence from Persia and in 1783 placed Georgia under Russian protection.
10 The specially-bred Orlov horses were the fastest trotters in Russia and by 1867 the fastest in Europe.

cattle wagons loaded with flour were blocking the street in front of it. When I saw those cows, I became a cow-worshipper like the ancient Egyptians: I wanted to bow down before them in adoration, for they had saved both the consul-general and me. We remained there for an hour until the police came and removed the cattle-wagons, so that I was able to go up to the Grand Duke's coachman and tell him to go straight to the Erakle Baths. The 'Ala'-ol-Molk laughed uproariously when I told him what had happened and said that I had been born under a lucky star: I should go and pray to the cows.

The second important event happened when on the morning of their departure from Tiflis, the Sepahsalar's steward, 'Ali Khan, told me to go and buy two umbrellas of the best quality silk with fine handles from the shops. I was to go and tell the shopkeeper to bring a selection, so that he could choose the ones he wanted. I went to a recently-opened shop which had very good-quality stock and took the shop-assistant with his umbrellas to the viceroy's palace. Only a few minutes remained before the party were due to depart, so 'Ali Khan took the umbrellas to the Sepahsalar, who chose two of them, while the others were brought back to be returned to the shop. 'Ali Khan told me to recover the money for the two umbrellas from the consul-general. It took me time to go and find him, but his head was in such a spin because of the imminent departure of the Shah that I had to ask the shop-assistant to wait a moment until I could find an opportunity to obtain the money from him. The two of us waited and waited. Suddenly the consul-general got into a carriage and left for St Petersburg, leaving me behind wondering what to do. The shop-assistant and I went back to the shop keeper and explained what had happened. He became quite angry, so I asked him to wait for the consul to return to Tiflis, when I would be able to pay him his money. He had no alternative but to accept my proposal.

Two weeks later the consul returned, so I told him the story and that the value of the two umbrellas was 50 *manat*,[11] as they were made of silk. The 'Ala'-ol-Molk said that his travelling companions had carried no money on them and so the umbrella-seller would have to wait for him to write to Paris on the subject, as the money for the umbrellas would have to come from there.

11 *Manat* is derived from the Russian word '*moneta*', meaning a coin. The author seems to have used the *manat* synonymously with the rouble. The *manat* has survived as the currency of the modern countries of Azerbaijan and Turkmenistan

Once again I explained matters to the umbrella-seller, who said that he knew neither the prime minister nor the consul, so that he would have to recover the money for the two umbrellas from me. As I didn't have that much money on me then, he wrote out an undertaking for me to sign that I would repay this money to him by instalments.

When the consul-general returned, he showed me great kindness, saying that I should go and persuade the Qazi that until I finished school, I should come and live at the consulate. He would tell his staff to give me a room, I would eat lunch and dinner with him and since his son, Javad Aqa, was studying Russian in the middle school of the Russian Gymnasium and he had brought a governess from Paris to teach him French and look after him, I could speak Russian with Javad Aqa and perfect my spoken French with her. Obviously I was delighted with this proposal, so I went and obtained the Qazi's permission and took some of my personal effects with me to the consulate. Since there wasn't a great deal of room there after the arrival of the governess, I was given a room which doubled up as the office of Mirza Mohammad Khan, the first secretary, who had rented a separate house for himself and his family, so he only came to the consulate for a few hours in the daytime, being responsible for passport work. The consul-general also had a private secretary who was responsible for his correspondence and when Mohammad Khan was working, I was either at school or with Javad Aqa, so that we didn't get on each other's nerves.

On my arrival, the consul-general made no mention of a salary for me. Two days later, he instructed his steward Mirza Faraj that until Mirza Reza's duties had been defined, he was to give me 25 *manat* as pocket money and a weekly allowance of one pound of sugar and sufficient money to cover what I would have needed to spend on tea. When Mirza Faraj gave me this good news, I was of course delighted. As there had been no reply from Paris to the consul-general's letter, however, I was embarrassed to bring up the subject of the umbrellas again, so I said to Mirza Faraj that as I didn't drink tea in the morning, he should give me the sugar and tea money in cash. I then went to the shop-owner and arranged that he would receive 5 *manat* from me every month until the debt had all been repaid, an offer that he accepted. The 'Ala'-ol-Molk really treated me as his son and made no distinction between me and Javad Aqa. Whenever he went to the circus or to the theatre or even went out for a spin in his carriage, all four of us would go. Mademoiselle the governess sat next to him, while Javad Aqa and I would sit on the seats opposite him in the carriage and we would all occupy a box at the theatre or the circus.

The 'Ala'-ol-Molk adored his son, who was then his only child. He had sent for a Persian teacher from Tehran, so that the latter should learn to speak Persian as sweetly as the people of Shiraz. The teacher, who was given the title 'Excellency', would give him calligraphy to copy. As 'Excellency's' hand was not as good as mine, the consul-general arranged that nominally his son would get his calligraphy homework from the teacher, but whenever the latter was not actually in the room, Javad Aqa would get his copying exercise from me. In this way we would avoid humiliating the teacher.

Obviously, I had never seen such a thing as a play before. As soon as autumn arrived and the government theatre in Tiflis opened, the 'Ala'-ol-Molk reserved a box and we all four went to see *Mary Stuart*, in which a tall, very beautiful Russian actress played the title role. When, on the orders of Queen Elizabeth of England, the Protestant judges condemned Mary Stuart to lose her head, the executioners went to escort her from her cell to the scaffold. Before leaving her cell, she started to say her prayers. At this point I was so moved that I started to weep uncontrollably, which was heard by everyone in the neighbouring boxes, and the 'Ala'-ol-Molk and Mademoiselle started to reproach me, pointing out that it wasn't the actress whom they wished to kill. I said that I knew that it wasn't the actress whom they wished to kill: it was the fate of the unfortunate queen which had so affected me.

The 'Ala'-ol-Molk really loved his son more than words can describe. In those days it was the fashion for wealthy Tiflis people to order very beautiful one-horse wicker carriages from Europe, in which two people could sit and drive around in the evenings. Mademoiselle Louise, Javad Aqa's governess, who was socially very ambitious, forced Javad Aqa to ask his father for one of these. The 'Ala'-ol-Molk ordered one from Europe, which duly arrived, and he also bought a fine Qarabagh Arabian horse, which was harnessed to the carriage the very same day. Mademoiselle Louise said that she was perfectly capable of driving it and didn't need a coachman. She invited me to sit in the carriage with Javad Aqa while she drove, an invitation which I accepted. Before Mademoiselle was ready and we could set off, however, an Iranian came to lodge a formal complaint with the consul-general that an Armenian had beaten his son without due cause. As neither father nor son knew Russian, the father had gone to the police department, while the son had been taken off to prison. As the petitioner had made a huge fuss, the 'Ala'-ol-Molk told me to go to the police department with the governess and the Armenian to get the son released. As the police department was not very far away, he told me to come back quickly and then go for the drive with Javad Aqa.

As luck would have it, the chief of police was away from his office, and by the time he had returned, the Iranian's problem had been resolved and I had returned to the consulate. The servants told me that Mademoiselle had waited for me for a short time but when I didn't come back, she had flown in a rage and she and Javad Aqa had left together. I rushed after them on foot, as I was sure that they would stop outside the coffee-house, but when I reached Mikhailski Avenue, I saw a policeman leading the horse, which was gushing blood from an open wound to its chest, and the carriage, which had a broken wheel, back to the consulate. I was told that neither the consul's son nor his governess had been able to control the horse, which had bolted with the carriage. When people went to their assistance and tried to restrain the horse, it had crashed into a gas lamp post in front of the government hospital and then reared up. The consul's son's brains had spilt out and Mademoiselle had suffered a broken leg. You can imagine in what a state I was. I rushed to the hospital, on the stairs of which there were fresh drops of the poor young man's blood.

They had placed Javad Aqa's body in a room, guarded by a soldier, and no one was allowed to enter the room. Mademoiselle had been put to bed in another room. I went to see her and could see that the poor unfortunate woman was weeping, more for what had happened to Javad Aqa than for her own broken leg, and crying: 'O God, please let me die, so that I do not have to look on his unfortunate father's face!' At that moment, poor Mirza Mahmoud Khan, who had been told the news, arrived and went to Javad Aqa's room with the director of the hospital. As soon as he clapped eyes on his son's shattered skull, he let out a wail and struck his head against the wall with such force that it split open, blood gushed out like a fountain and he fell on the ground in a swoon. The doctors rushed up, bound up his head and brought him back to his senses, but he looked paler than a corpse. A doctor then took him to the consulate, where they put him into bed. May God never visit the fate of this unfortunate on any other father!

When he had been brought to his senses with eau de cologne, he leapt out of bed and ran out of the room, intending to rush back to the hospital in the state he was in. The doctor in charge and members of the consulate staff stopped him and brought him back to bed. He tore his clothes and if people hadn't known of the calamity which had befallen him, they would have thought him completely mad. He was just able to say that his son's body should be embalmed and taken to Tabriz for burial in the family's private tomb. The body was embalmed and as soon as the 'Ala'-ol-Molk had partially recovered his senses and his head wound had healed, he took his son's body to Tabriz.

Mirza Mohammad Khan, the first secretary, now became the acting consul. Thinking that perhaps I might one day take his place, he started to mistreat me and this is how he did it. As I shared my room with his office, the consul-general had instructed him that in my absence, when he went home he should leave the key with the head consulate servant. He never ever did so but took advantage of the fact that I wasn't there to take the key home with him. As his house was a long way from the consulate, I had to remain outside on the balcony for the lengthy time it took to find a consulate servant and send him to get hold of the key. Whenever one of my fellow students or friends came to see me, I was very embarrassed but couldn't tell them why I couldn't receive them in my room but was standing outside. One day I asked Mirza Faraj Khan to go and tell Mirza Mohammad Khan that I knew why he was doing this. He was afraid that I would gradually progress until I replaced him as first secretary. However, my ambition was greater than this: I wouldn't be content with becoming first secretary. He should fear the day when I was promoted straight to the post of consul-general and that when he stood before me, I would remember his actions and take my revenge. Mirza Faraj Khan looked at me, thinking that I was delirious. He said that as he wasn't even the third secretary in the consulate, he couldn't go and say this to the first secretary. I could see that in a way he was right. After all it was astonishing that I, who couldn't even afford to drink tea in the morning and who received his tea money from Mirza Faraj Khan, should have such pretentions. Nevertheless, it was as though I was divinely inspired to say this, for instead of becoming more careful and being embarrassed by what I had said, I told him that I insisted that he go and repeat my words to Mirza Mohammad Khan exactly as I had said them. The latter roared with laughter when he heard what I had said and suggested that I should go and pray to have my intelligence restored to me.

When Mirza Mahmoud Khan returned from Tabriz, I had finished at school and obtained my diploma. On his return, the poor man really treated me like his son Javad Aqa and said that I reminded him of him. When he took me to Jolfa to welcome the Shah, he had even included my name in the list of members of the royal entourage without telling me. One day he summoned me and presented me with the Russian Order of St Stanislas (Third Class) and congratulated me. As it was the first decoration which I had received (and although it was of course the least important Russian order) medals were very rarely given to Muslims in the Caucasus, so I was delighted. Indeed I was so pleased that I sewed it to my pillow and whenever I woke up in the night I would look at it before going back to sleep. A few months later, the consul-general sent for me again and decorated me with the Order of the Lion and Sun (Fifth Class). Furthermore, I saw that in the royal *farman*[12] I was called 'Mirza' and named as interpreter at the consulate-general. The consul-general said that I must be the first consulate interpreter to have been appointed by royal *farman* under the signature of the Prime Minister. Mirza Mahmoud Khan explained that as only the foreign ministry had the right to grant this title, he had done this on purpose so that when he was posted somewhere else, his successor couldn't dismiss me on a whim.

When at school, I used to visit Mirza Fath 'Ali Akhondov with the Qazi and every evening I would hear about the defects of our alphabet, so I fell to think-ing about changing and reforming the Persian alphabet, and wrote a treatise in Persian called the '*Roshdiyyeh*' Treatise, using mostly Latin letters but with some Cyrillic ones. I showed it to Mirza Mahmoud Khan and asked his per-mission to send it to Istanbul so that it could be printed in the journal *Akhtar*.[13] He gave his permission, saying that he could see that I had a fire in me which drove me to do this kind of thing and he wanted to do his best to help.

In those days, the Russian police didn't accept passports issued to Iranians in Tehran, Tabriz or at the frontier, on the grounds of incompatibility with local law: any Armenian, Georgian or Tartar who wanted to evade Russian military

---

12 Written decree or order signed by the Shah.
13 Persian-language journal published in Istanbul from 1876 to 1896.

service or other obligations went off to obtain a passport from Iran. Until then, no authority had taken responsibility for the validity of these passports: there was no statement in them as to the city in which they had been issued or indeed any indication of who had signed them. Consequently, whenever we found one of these irregular passports in the hands of a Russian subject, we sent it to the Russian Embassy in Tehran. The Caucasus police agreed, however, that when a passport had been validated by the Iranian consulate and counter-signed by the police, the consulate would give an attestation certificate to the holder of the passport and the Caucasus police would then issue a one year residence permit to him. The Iranian Ministry of Foreign Affairs was of course aware of these arrangements.

A price of 1 *manat* for each certificate had been fixed. The 'Ala'-ol-Molk had given instructions that each certificate, which had to be handwritten and not printed, was to be in my own handwriting. One tenth of the fees received were to be mine, so my financial situation certainly improved as a result of this. As there were many Iranians in Tiflis and the Caucasus, some nights I sat writing out certificates until two o'clock in the morning, and on occasion certificates flowed from my pen until dawn. The more I wrote, the happier the 'Ala'-ol-Molk became at my increasing income. This matter increased jealousy among the consulate staff, but as this act of kindness came from their chief, they could do nothing about it.

At this time, the Russo-Turkish war, known as the Kars War, broke out. After the defeat of the Ottomans at the Battle of Kars,[14] nearly 10,000 prisoners of war were lodged in tents outside Tiflis. Since the Russian general staff officers didn't know Turkish, Caucasian Armenians who knew the language were appointed to supervise their custody. The chief of staff had written to the 'Ala'-ol-Molk asking him to introduce a trustworthy person speaking Ottoman Turkish who could accompany the Russian officers on a tour of inspection and ask the prisoners how they were being treated by the Armenians. The 'Ala'-ol-Molk put my name forward, so I accompanied a staff colonel and two first lieutenants to the camps. It became clear that these unfortunate Turks had been very badly treated. They were not given enough food, and most were hungry. The Armenians hit them for no reason and either kept the whole twenty kopeks

14 The Battle of Kars, a decisive Russian victory in the Russo-Turkish War (1877–8).

provided as pocket money by the Russian government for the prisoners to buy cigarettes, or they kept half that sum. When this report reached the Viceroy of the Caucasus, he ordered the Armenians to be removed, and Russians to replace them. The Russians asked the 'Ala'-ol-Molk to allow me to go one day a week to inspect the camps and submit a report. After a few months, however, a peace agreement was reached and the prisoners left.

The Ottomans then opened a consulate-general in Tiflis. On his first call on the 'Ala'-ol-Molk, the Ottoman consul-general asked to see me and bestowed on me the Majidiyyeh Order (Fourth Class) for service to the prisoners. He also very kindly advised me to send a copy of my treatise on the alphabet, which I had had printed in French in Tiflis, through him to Kamel Pasha, Ottoman Minister of Education and later Prime Minister. As the third secretary of the consulate-general, I didn't dare to write directly to such a distinguished figure, but encouraged by our consul-general, I gave my letter to the Ottoman consul-general, who sent it off. I didn't expect a reply but Kamel Pasha wrote back, praising my idea for such an alphabet. Greatly encouraged by Kamel Pasha's reply, I sent a copy of my *Roshdiyyeh* treatise with a copy of Kamel Pasha's letter to the *Sani'-od-Dowleh, Mohammad Hassan Khan, later the E'temad-os-Saltaneh*. At that time, the official newspaper in Tehran was called *Iran*, and its editor was *Mohammad Hossein Khan Foroughi*, the father of the Zoka'-ol-Molk. To my great surprise, this newspaper certainly didn't reject my idea out of hand but warmly praised the treatise in its columns.

At this time, *Prince Malkom Khan*, the Iranian minister in London, passed through Tiflis on his way back to his post after his leave of absence, having been summoned back to Tehran. On the way, his brother Alexander Malkom had fallen ill and so he stayed a few days in Tiflis to receive treatment. Since Malkom Khan had written a book on the reform of the alphabet and had actually proposed a new alphabet, I presented him with a copy of my treatise in Persian, explaining that the French translation was in the hands of the printers. He wrote a foreword in his own words, and suggested that I should now adopt a family name, which should be 'Danesh'.[15]

When the treatise was published in Persian and French, the 'Ala'-ol-Molk saw fit to dedicate it to the Heir Apparent, Mozaffar-od-Din Mirza, and to

---

15 A play on words, as 'Danesh' means knowledge.

present him with a copy of it. As a reward, I was then appointed an assistant aide-de-camp to the Heir Apparent. The uniform for this position was very beautiful, so I had one made which I wore to an evening reception at a local prince's house. Some young local noblemen who were present saw that the hostess paid more attention to me than to them. Their jealousy came to the boil and they wanted to humiliate me in her eyes, so one of them asked in a loud voice: 'So, which military academy did you attend?' Of course, they knew that there were no military colleges in Iran at the time and military ranks were honorary. I replied stiffly: 'I regret when I have had the privilege of talking to this kind lady for a few minutes, you wish to waste my time in this inappropriate way. I am living in the Iranian consulate-general. If the impression I have made on this lady is a concern for you, come to the consulate-general at 10 o'clock tomorrow, so that I can give you my reply!' Instead of humiliating me, he was himself humiliated. The lady clapped her hands to show her appreciation of my reply. I really had no alternative to replying in this way, but my conscience tormented me all that night. On the one hand, I was pleased by the uniform and rank of aide-de-camp to the Heir Apparent, but on the other hand my conscience gnawed at me: why was I wearing a uniform to which I had no right? I decided, therefore, that I should try to acquire as much military expertise as possible.

As one of the 'Ala'-ol-Molk's friends who visited the consulate was a staff colonel who had been very kind to me, I went to his house that very day and told him the whole story from beginning to end. He burst out laughing at my exchange with the Russian officer and promised to teach me all that I needed to know about the rudiments of military science. He taught me the syllabus of the Tiflis Cadet School.[16] First he took me to his armoury. There he showed me in turn every kind of rifle from its first invention and explained how each one worked, how to manufacture gunpowder and how to fire a flintlock rifle. He explained the workings of all the rifles, even the Berdanka.[17] He then taught me drill, both with and without a rifle, as if I was a soldier, and how to salute.

16 The Tiflis military secondary school for the sons of the nobility and officers, examples of which existed in all the main cities of the Russian empire.
17 The Berdan rifle, a single-shot breech-loading rifle of American design, adopted by the Russian army from 1870. Later manufactured domestically.

When I had acquired sufficient skill, he gave me two large army manuals, the one on military tactics and the other on military logistics. I kept up my lessons with the Colonel until I was recalled to Tehran. Most of the time, the colonel would accompany me to St David's mountain, where a soldier would bring a revolver and the colonel would instruct me how to shoot at a target.

When the 'Ala'-ol-Molk was later recalled to Tehran, the *'Ala'-os-Saltaneh* took his place as consul-general. He too was very kind to me. By that stage, I had become first secretary at the consulate. Before Tiflis, he had been consul-general in Baghdad, where, being a great horse-lover, he had bought three Arab horses, which he brought with him to Tiflis, together with a stable-manager and a good groom. One of these horses was very beautiful. As I had bought a horse from Salmas in Azerbaijan, I sometimes went out riding with officers and young ladies. The 'Ala'-os-Saltaneh suggested that as my horse was not a good one, I should sell it. Whenever I wanted to ride, I could take one of his horses. Strange to say, and I have no idea why, the 'Ala'-os-Saltaneh never once rode a horse during the whole of his stay in Tiflis. It was his stable-manager and groom who exercised the horses, to prevent them being ruined by staying too long in their stables.

One day at a reception in the viceroy's palace, the viceroy's wife introduced me to a certain Mademoiselle Taube and her brother, saying that she was a lady-in-waiting to the Tsarina and her brother was an outstanding student at law school. She said that they were on a tour of the Caucasus and would stay in Tiflis for two weeks. She added that Mademoiselle always rode in St Petersburg and as she was very keen to ride here, she suggested that I should accompany her on rides around the town and to scenic places. Since I was very grateful for the 'Ala'-os-Saltaneh's kindness to me in lending me his horses, I suggested that the two of us might go riding together. Mademoiselle said that she had brought her lady's saddle with her from St Petersburg, she would send it over to me so that we could ride out together the next day. We went out riding together four or five times and she was very grateful, particularly for being given very beautiful Arab horses to ride. As I will describe at the appropriate moment, at the coronation of Alexander III, when I was an attaché to the Embassy Extraordinary, and later when I was ambassador in St Petersburg, this same young lady was very kind to me and often when I had political matters to discuss, she would accompany me to my audiences with the Tsarina and the Tsar.

At this time a telegram arrived from the 'Ala'-ol-Molk saying that Prince 'Ezz-od-Dowleh, Naser-od-Din Shah's brother, was travelling to Moscow with an important delegation to offer congratulations to Tsar Alexander III on his coronation.[18] He wrote that since the delegation had no Russian translator, he had asked the Nazem-od-Dowleh, our minister plenipotentiary in St Petersburg, to propose me to Tehran and the Russian government as its interpreter. I showed the telegram to the 'Ala'-os-Saltaneh, who took it and telegraphed the Ministry of Foreign Affairs to say that as he had only just taken up his post, if his deputy was to attend the coronation and he was to remain in Tiflis, this would damage his reputation in the eyes of the people of the Caucasus. He asked the Ministry to include him in the delegation. His request was granted. The Ministry telegraphed that as Mostafa Qoli Khan Mirpanj, the governor of Ardebil, also a senior Iranian officer, would be the military attaché, and *Mirza Javad Khan Sa'ad-od-Dowleh* would be the counsellor. The 'Ala'-os-Saltaneh would be put forward as the first secretary of the delegation. We made hasty preparations and set out.

On our arrival in Moscow, we repaired to a hotel as guests of the Russian government. The Nazem-od-Dowleh, our minister, the 'Ala'-ol-Molk, counsellor, and the Mostashar-os-Soltan, first secretary, were already in Moscow where they had rented a fine house and taken up residence. The 'Ala'-os-Saltaneh was related to the Nazem-od-Dowleh and to the 'Ala'-ol-Molk on his mother's side.

When we went to the Kremlin, the Tsar received Prince 'Ezz-od-Dowleh and his suite and spoke very graciously, but unfortunately the latter, who had his speech in his hand, suddenly became tongue-tied and was unable to say a word. For a time we remained in silence, and then the Tsar, unwilling to add to his visitor's embarrassment, made the appropriate reply and withdrew. Since the 'Ezz-od-Dowleh was also incapable of introducing us, Monsieur Zinoviev,[19] Russia's well-known former minister plenipotentiary in Tehran, who had now become an under-secretary in Russia's foreign ministry, introduced us on his behalf.

---

18 Tsar Alexander III succeeded his father in 1881 and his coronation took place in 1883.

19 Ivan Alekseevich Zinoviev, Russian minister plenipotentiary in Tehran from 1856 to 1883, was then Director of the Asian Department at the Iranian Foreign Ministry (1883–91).

The same evening there was a great ball and all the reception rooms of the Kremlin Palace were opened up. It was quite an occasion. As the Tsar and Tsarina hadn't yet emerged from their private quarters, all the ministers pleni-potentiary had been placed in a separate room. Suddenly, it was announced that everyone should go to the Great Hall and all the ministers plenipotentiary should stand in a circle. As I was passing through the crowd in the Great Hall and I was looking down, someone put a hand on my shoulder. I looked up and saw that it was the same Mademoiselle Taube with whom I used to go riding in Tiflis. She said that as soon as I could leave the circle of diplomats, I was to come and find her at the same spot and she would show me all the rooms of the Kremlin with their antique treasures and introduce me to her friends.

When the 'circle' broke up, those ambassadors extraordinary and the ambassadors who were resident in Russia and knew those present went to another room to talk to each other, but the members of our embassy, who knew no one, stood around in a corner looking at each other. Mademoiselle Taube placed her hand on my arm and showed these rooms to me. As we reached the ambassadors' room, where the 'Ezz-od-Dowleh and his suite, together with our minister plenipotentiary and his staff were standing, they saw me with the Tsarina's lady-in-waiting, dressed in her white court dress with the diamond-encrusted Order of St Catherine. They were astonished and wondered how I had come to know members of the Tsarina's court so intimately. Mirza 'Ali Taqi Khan was sent over. He whispered in my ear that the 'Ezz-od-Dowleh wished to speak to me. I replied that as soon as Mademoiselle released me, I would be at his service.

At this moment, Monsieur Zinoviev saw us and greeted Mademoiselle in a very respectful way. He was astonished that an Iranian in a felt hat had been able to attract the favour of the Tsarina's lady-in-waiting to such an extent that we were walking around together. Anyway, as a result of the kind attentions of the young lady that evening, I became an object of curiosity among the Tsar's 6,000 guests, who began to talk about me and ask questions. When the 'Ezz-od-Dowleh saw what was going on, from then on, except at official functions where he had to take the most important members of his suite with him, he would take me with him in his carriage and he would often even talk to me at meals. Those members of the imperial family who saw us together also asked why Mademoiselle Taube was showing me so much favour.

The coronation of this Tsar was truly magnificent. From every corner of the world heirs to thrones and their wives, together with dignitaries from many countries had come to Moscow to offer their congratulations. Princess Marie, wife of the Romanian heir apparent and the granddaughter of Queen Victoria of England, who was not more than twenty and so beautiful that she was constantly surrounded by both men and women, attended the celebrations. The person who attracted most attention as a spectacle was the Chinese representative, Li Hong Chank, who unlike most Chinese and Japanese was exceptionally tall and was renowned among the Chinese for his intelligence, shrewdness and understanding, so the Chinese government used to choose him for important missions. The Russians also paid him extraordinary respect. In second place was the Amir of Bokhara, whose robes really attracted attention, for they were entirely made of Bokhara gold thread: dressed in a long tunic, a turban, a fine shawl and with his chest covered with his country's medals, all of which were diamond-encrusted, he was the cynosure of all eyes.

During our few days as tourists in St Petersburg, however, our money ran out and we were consequently extremely embarrassed. I suggested to the 'Ala'-os-Saltaneh that we should write to the consulate-general in Tiflis to ask for money but he didn't like this suggestion. He said: 'Let us wait and perhaps God will send us money from somewhere!' As I understood matters, he had withdrawn a sum of money in cash on departure from Tiflis and he didn't want his staff to spend too much. As we were talking, I saw Mirza Mohammad 'Ali Khan Kashi, the maternal uncle of the *Mo'aven-od-Dowleh,* enter the room. He said that he had been summoned to St Petersburg by a telegram from the Compagnie des Chaussées, so he had asked for news of us at the best hotels and he had come to see us, as he was returning to Vladikafkaz the next day. He sat down and the 'Ala'-os-Saltaneh invited him to lunch with us, an invitation which he accepted. After lunch the 'Ala'-os-Saltaneh wrote something on a piece of paper and gave it to me. I saw that he had written: 'Don't say anything on my behalf but on your own behalf tell him that your money has run out! Get 300 *manat* from Mirza Mohammad 'Ali! We will return it to him from Tiflis when we get back there.' As the latter was leaving, I accompanied him as far as the corridor, where I asked him for 300 *manat.* He took out his purse and opened it. I saw that it contained more than 2,000–3,000 *manat.* He said: 'Take as much as you want!' He insisted that I would need more money for my journey, but I only took the sum which the 'Ala'-os-Saltaneh had authorised, 300 *manat*.

In due course we bought our train tickets and set off on our return journey. In Rostov, however, we realised that we had completely run out of money and we didn't even have enough to pay for lunch or dinner, so we had to leave the train and book into a hotel. There was an honorary Iranian consul there who was Jewish. The 'Ala'-os-Saltaneh, however, didn't want to go and ask him for money. It was summer, and the national park there was very beautiful and peaceful. An orchestra was playing music and there was a small theatre in the middle of the garden, so the 'Ala'-os-Saltaneh suggested that we should go to the garden, as we couldn't spend the evening in the hotel in that heat. He pawned his gold watch to the hotelier for 30 *manat* and we stayed in the garden until midnight, when we returned to the hotel. The next day I said to the hotel owner that I would send him 30 *manat* from Vladikafkaz and asked him to return the watch to the person who brought the money. The hotelier seemed to understand our situation and think that we were trustworthy, or perhaps he recognised us, because he brought back the watch, saying that we could take it and he would give us as much money as we needed, for he trusted us. In recognition of his chivalrous behaviour, we sent him 40 *manat* from Vladikafkaz.

When the consul-general left for Tabriz, he had handed over responsibility for the consulate's affairs to Mohammad 'Ali Beg, the Secretary, and put me in charge of his personal affairs and accounting matters. Two months after reaching Tabriz, he telegraphed me that *Sultan Morad Mirza Hesam-os-Saltaneh*, the conqueror of Herat,[20] would be arriving in Tiflis on a certain day on his way back from Mecca. I was to go to the railway station with all the consulate staff to welcome him formally, prepare the consul-general's rooms on the upper floor for the Prince, his suite and his wife, as they were to be his guests during their stay in Tiflis. I was to pay for their meals and all their other expenses and ensure that he was happy with the way he had been treated. On the appointed day, we went to welcome the Prince. He was a very dignified, taciturn person, with grandeur imprinted on his physiognomy, and his son,

20 In October 1856 Iran, with Russian encouragement, occupied Herat. War between Iran and Britain immediately followed. Britain would eventually force the Iranians to withdraw from Herat by occupying the Gulf port of Bushehr .

Malek Mansour Mirza, was a very polished youth aged about eighteen. He had with him a teacher, who was both a doctor and a French language teacher, called Mehdi Khan Nabavi, who later became the Mofakhkhar-od-Dowleh. Respect for the family was shown in the following way: the young man could not enter a room without the Prince's permission, and when he had been summoned and had entered the room, he would make a low bow on the threshold and stand there without daring to greet his father. A few minutes would pass, the father looked at the son, and when he looked, the son bowed again until his father asked him some questions. The son would reply and then the father would give him permission to withdraw with a nod of the head. The son would then bow again and leave the room. It was clear that as the son behaved like this, Mehdi Khan and I had to act in the same respectful way. Only the son, Dr Mehdi Khan and I were invited to sit at meals with the Prince but he didn't invite any other members of the consulate, the only reason for my presence being that I was his interpreter, for he knew no foreign language.

Although the Prince was not paying an official visit, the Russian government treated him with great respect. A guard of honour of two soldiers stood at the entry to the viceroy's palace; two soldiers were similarly stationed for the Prince. Every morning, the Tiflis assistant chief of police came and asked through me what the Prince's wishes were for the day, when the government carriages should come to pick him up and whom he would be receiving that day. During his week's stay there, apart from the deputy chief of police and the governor of Tiflis, the prince received no Iranians or indeed anyone else. He accepted no invitation from the viceroy, he only received one official call from the deputy viceroy and attended only one tea party with the latter's wife. He even refused to pay an official call on the governor of Tiflis, but instead sent me with his visiting card. At that time, there was no railway line to Ganjeh, Baku and Erivan, so a few days were needed for the government to make arrangements for his onward journey, and he stayed in Tiflis for a full week. The Prince, who remained alone in his room all this time, spent his time reading history books in Arabic and Persian. He also had two or three volumes of poetry, although he was not particularly fond of poetry. During that week, in which I spent the whole time with the Prince and Dr Mehdi Khan, we got to know each other very well and became friends. On the day of his departure, the Prince summoned me. I saw that Mehdi Khan had in his hand a sword. The

Prince said that it was one of the swords which had been given to him by the Khans of Mashhad on his journey to Herat. It was this sword, a present from the people of Khorasan, which had made him victorious. 'I know that it will bring you good fortune,' he said, 'so I am giving it to you to wear at your side at official ceremonies.' The Khorasan sword was a real rarity: its handle and scabbard were the work of fine craftsmen and goldsmiths. The blade of the sword was engraved with the verse: 'There is no hero but 'Ali and no sword but *Zu-l-Faqar*!'[21] and the name of the Hesam-os-Saltaneh was engraved on it. The scabbard was coloured a kind of dark purple.

On the day of the Prince's departure, the Viceroy's deputy came to the consulate-general to bid him an official farewell. The Governor of Tiflis and the chief of police were nominated to accompany the prince out of the city, together with an escort of twenty-five Cossacks and their officers accompanying the Prince's carriage. I also accompanied him as far as the first post-house, where the horses were changed. There I took my leave and returned to Tiflis, where my colleagues were very jealous of my sword.

---

21 'Ali's legendary sword.

Chapter 4

My Journey from Tiflis to Khorasan to join the Russian-Persian Akhal-Khorasan Boundary Commission until my Appointment as Counsellor at the Embassy in St Petersburg (1883–1887)

In 1881, following the overwhelming Russian victory over the Turkomans at the village of Gok Teppe earlier that year, the Russian minister in Tehran, Ivan Alekseevich Zinoviev, and Mirza Sa'id Khan, the Iranian minister of foreign affairs, signed a treaty delineating the Akhal-Khorasan border between the two countries from the Caspian Sea eastwards to the village of Baba Dormez. Further east, some 100 miles of the new frontier as far as Sarakhs remained undelineated. Mirza Reza Khan again owed this promotion to his linguistic abilities: chosen as the Russian language interpreter for the Iranian delegation on the new boundary commission, he had to spend nearly four years in Khorasan in conditions of great discomfort, but he won the personal favour of his sovereign and an introduction to his most constant and powerful protector, 'Ali Asghar Khan Amin-os-Soltan, the future prime minister.

This chapter is full of amusing stories, but underneath this there is serious observation of Iran's plight: the incompetence, unscrupulousness and martial prudence of Iran's ill-paid tribal levies; the decline of law and order caused by the weakness of central government and the depredations of greedy provincial governors, resulting in outbreaks of violence by over-taxed and oppressed citizens; the disorder of public finances; the power of the Shi'a clergy to incite or calm the exasperated populace; and at the highest political level, the desperate attempts of the author's chief to defend Iran's interests against inflexible Russian demands, contrasted with Naser-od-Din Shah's weary acceptance of the reality of Russian power. Iran ultimately gained from the removal of the Turkoman slavers' threat to the security of the road from Tehran to Mashhad but the Shah feared the looming threat of a Russian invasion of Iranian Khorasan and the holy city of Mashhad.

Through all this, the author wends his resourceful, quick-witted way. Flexible but supremely self-confident, with a keen eye for religious charlatanry, he stood up for himself when attacked. Beset by jealous intrigues within the delegation, often considered by the local populace, stirred up by clerics, as a westerner and an infidel, sometimes at risk of his life, he was nevertheless able to rely on the idiom of his past as a religious student to defuse the wrath of local clerics and, while his apparent boldness in speaking the truth to his superiors could owe something to rose-tinted hindsight, he seems to have got away with his bravura. In a wonderfully Iranian touch, the author's extempore composition of appropriate lines of poetry so affected the local governor that he ordered the immediate resumption of long-overdue salary payments for the delegation. Finally, from early on he was a skilful cultivator of potentially useful contacts, and a constant in this story is his relationship with a succession of European women, who seem to have been intrigued by him as an exotic novelty: it was to his carefully-cultivated friendship with the family of General Komarov, the Russian commander-in-chief in Ashkabad, that he owed his success in re-drawing the map of the frontier to Iran's advantage.

In 1883, by divine destiny, I was First Secretary at the consulate-general in Tiflis and, together with the late ʿAlaʾ-os-Saltaneh, who at that time held the title of Moʿin-ol-Vezareh and was appointed first secretary for the occasion, I was given the rank of attaché and we attended the coronation of Tsar Alexander III in Moscow in the entourage of Prince ʿEzz-od-Dowleh.

On our return to Tiflis from this journey, a telegram arrived from the late *Mirza Saʿid Khan*, the Minister of Foreign Affairs, saying that an interpreter was needed who knew Russian, who was capable of translating from Persian to Russian and vice versa and who could act as the interpreter for the commission charged with delineating the new Akhal-Khorasan frontier. Without showing me the telegram, the consul-general replied saying that he only had one man on his staff, Mirza Reza Khan, but that although the latter was needed at the consulate, in view of the importance of the matter, he was prepared to put his name forward. The minister telegraphed back to instruct him to send off Mirza Reza Khan, adding that my travel expenses would be paid. The ʿAlaʾ-os-Saltaneh sent for me, showed me the two telegrams, confirmed that he had made his arrangements and ordered me to leave at once. I said that following the Russian conquest of the Akhal, Ashkabad and Merv the new map showed that Iran's new frontier started in the east at Sarakhs and Kalaat-e Naderi and from there it ran westwards from the Quchan mountains and through Bojnourd to the valley forming part of the barren Gorgan plain. I had heard from travellers that nothing except scorpions and tarantulas existed there, I had no experience of living under canvas in these areas of the country and did not have the constitution for it, so I asked to be excused this mission. I do not know what telegram was actually sent but several days later the following telegram arrived from the minister addressed directly to me: 'Mirza Reza Khan, when do you arrive in Tehran? Minister of Foreign Affairs.' I was so puffed up with pride by this telegram that I said to myself: 'What an important fellow you have become for the minister to write personally to you!' I replied that I would be honoured to attend on him very shortly.

As I knew that the road was infested by Turkoman and highway robbers from other tribes, I made an official request to the consul-general, who wrote to the military authorities asking them to provide me with a pair of American revolvers, like those used in the Russian army, for the pommel of my horse, together with 200 rounds of ammunition. I made my preparations in the space of two days, took my servant ʿAsgar Beg with me and set off.

When I reached Baku, the consul, Baba Khan Ansari, came to welcome me and invited me to stay, so that when a ship became available I could set off for Enzeli. A young merchant called Haji Mohammad Hossein, a native of Tabriz, approached the consul and suggested that as I did not know the road, he could accompany me and act as my guide, so that no misadventure should befall me. Obviously both he and I were delighted by this arrangement. When I was about to embark on the ship, however, I saw that Mohammad Hossein had several boxes with him and that he was telling the customs officials that they belonged to Mirza Reza Khan, who was exempt from customs examination.

Because of the letters of recommendation which I was carrying, the Russian officials didn't examine the boxes. Furthermore, when we reached Enzeli, the Haji gave the same explanation of the boxes to the Enzeli customs as he had done in Baku and succeeded in passing the boxes through customs.

In Enzeli, we stayed at the governor's residence and the deputy governor welcomed us in a fitting manner. The rest-house, situated in the marshes on the edge of the sea, had a fine view of the sea. Situated in the middle of a grove of orange and sour orange trees, it was also aesthetically a fine building. The beauty of the view, the kindness of our host and the pleasant weather had so distracted me from the prospect of my journey to Iran that I thanked my lucky stars for my good luck.

Shortly afterwards, Haji Mohammad Hossein came up to say that the boat was ready and asked me to embark. At that time there was no road from Enzeli to Rasht and one had to travel by boat from Enzeli to Pirehbazaar. Large boats, lined with comfortable rugs and with flags flying from the mast, crewed by eight oarsmen, arrived and took the three of us and our baggage out on to the lagoon. When we reached the other side of the lagoon, the sea-bed became shallow and it was impossible to row, so the oarsmen got into the sea and the eight of them dragged the boat along with ropes and cables, chanting harmoniously 'O Mohammad, O 'Ali!' to a particular tune. The woodland trees lining the lagoon were reflected in the clear water of the lagoon and the beauty of the wild flowers made the journey so enjoyable that only those who had actually experienced it could have the faintest idea how beautiful it was. And so we reached Pirehbazaar, where Haji Mir Qasem, a native of Rasht, had built a caravanserai and a tea-house on the shore of the lagoon. Above the gate of the caravanserai there was one room, built in the Iranian style, with windows looking out over the lagoon. The door was open and I saw that in the usual Iranian way there were two felt rugs at the side of the room, together with a rug at the furthest end from door, and in the middle a large carpet. They had thrown a linen cover with a blue and white pattern over the felt, and anyway I didn't think it right to walk on that fine carpet in my rather muddy half-boots, so I took them off and put them behind the door. As the room had no table or chairs, I sat down on my knees very politely[1] in front of the window with my eyes humbly cast down.

---

1 The polite way to sit in traditional Iranian society.

Suddenly the tea-boy ran up and told me that Mohammad Khan, an artillery colonel, had arrived from Tehran on his way to Enzeli with his staff. Since I had never seen an artillery colonel, I thought that this personage must be very important, indeed one of the great men of the kingdom. Suddenly the colonel entered the room carrying a bamboo cane in his hand. I immediately got up and made a low bow. To my astonishment not only did the colonel not reply to my bow but he didn't even look at me but, playing with his cane, he walked up and down the room several times. He then went and sat down to wait for one of his servants whom he had sent off on an errand.

In due course I became tired of sitting alone and got up to call my servant saying that if the horses were ready, we should leave. I was about to put on my boots when I saw that they were missing. I called the tea-boy and asked him where my shoes were. He searched inside and outside the door but found that they were missing. When I asked how this could have happened, he said that the colonel had taken them, adding that this was not the first occasion on which the colonel had stolen something that had caught his eye. I asked where my servants were. He said that they had gone to hire baggage animals and went to call them. Haji Mohammad Hossein said that as he knew the area, he would go and recover my boots from the colonel. As I stood in front of the window watching, I saw the merchant get into the boat with Asgar Beg and start to make a huge fuss. Then the colonel's man came up and ordered the boat to cast off. When I saw the boat pulling away from the shore, I shouted out: 'Colonel, I don't want my boots, just don't take my servants away!' I asked myself what in heaven I would do if the colonel kidnapped my servants. A short time later, I observed ʿAsgar Beg and Haji Mohammad Hossein making their way back. They said that the colonel had given them a good beating and dropped them on the beach, which was so full of camel thorn and raspberry bushes that there was no path through them. All their clothes had been torn to shreds and they had had a great deal of difficulty in finding their way back again. I told ʿAsgar Beg to open my suitcase to get out my other pair of boots, which I put on and we set off for Rasht. In those days there was no carriage road and the track was only suitable for post horses. Indeed the road through Caspian tribal territory was so arduous that sometimes we had to dismount and travel some way on foot. After the post-houses, which didn't even have windows or doors, the recently built guest house at Qazvin was a delight and from there to Tehran one travelled by coach.

In the rest-house at Shahabad I observed a very dignified personage, dressed in a tunic with a fine shawl round his waist, a tall Bokhara fur hat on his head and a beard freshly dyed black, coloured with henna and looking like shiny jet, who came up to me and said that his name was Mashhadi[2] Kazem Amin-os-Sofara' and that he was the 'Ala'-os-Saltaneh's agent at the ministry of foreign affairs. The minister's respected wife had sent him with this carriage to greet me and welcome me, saying that they were expecting me in Tehran. The Amin-os-Sofara' was really an excellent conversationalist. He was also very knowledgeable on the country's leading families and wealthy classes and their life histories. When we arrived in Tehran, we alighted at a fine house, where the Amin-os-Sofara' took me into a large room on the second floor, in the middle of which there was a table laden with Persian sweets and fine fruit. There I was welcomed for the second time on behalf of the 'Ala'-os-Saltaneh's wife. A short time later, another gentleman entered. Mashhadi Kazem introduced him as the Sabah-ol-Molk, one of the senior under-secretaries and deputy to the future foreign minister and prime minister, *Mirza Nasrollah Khan Moshir-od-Dowleh*. After a lengthy exchange of courtesies, the Sabah-ol-Molk said that the minister had instructed him to make travel arrangements for me as soon as possible, for the Commission was late in starting its work. He had been ordered to take me to the minister's house the next morning and the minister would then take me in his carriage to Doshan-Tappeh,[3] where I would be received in audience by His Majesty Naser-od-Din Shah.

At sunrise the next day, the Sabah-ol-Molk came to take me to the minister's house. Although it was very early in the day, he took me in to a large hall where the minister and several important personalities were already seated. I bowed. Since there were no tables or chairs, the minister indicated a place and told me to sit down. As I hadn't sat on my knees on the ground for a long time, I found it very difficult to sit properly for any length of time. Mirza Sa'id Khan was a very dignified person with a fine beard. He had dyed this black and applied henna to it, but the henna was the dominant colour. He was wearing a long tunic with a shawl round his waist and a long shirt over his

---

2 Prefix given to a person who had performed a pilgrimage to the shrine of the Eighth Imam at Mashhad.

3 Royal hunting lodge north-east of Tehran, where the royal menagerie was also kept.

vest like a traditional cape. His conversation with his guests was entirely about Arabic literature and he used to recite the poetry of Imra'-ol-Qays.[4] He had a real taste for poetry and had composed an epic poem which he had written on the walls in Arabic, of which the opening verse was this: 'In the time of the reign of Naser-od-Din, the Sun of Kings and the Most Fortunate of Sultans.'

After we had drunk our tea, the servant came and announced that the carriage was ready. When we reached the palace of Doshan-Tappeh, one of the Shah's servants asked us to wait in the ante-chamber, as His Majesty hadn't yet arrived. The minister went into the ante-chamber, instructing me to accompany him. He sat down at the top of the room and indicated to me that I should sit below him. At this juncture, a very good-looking, fresh-cheeked young man aged about twenty-two or twenty-three years entered the room. The minister and the rest of us got up. He came up and then sat down at a respectable distance from the minister and said: 'I have been in His Majesty's presence. He has instructed me to look after Your Excellency until he comes out.' The minister thanked him warmly. The young man then called for tea to be brought. After the tea, they brought a pipe for the minister and a very magnificent water-pipe with a gold top for the young man. The minister smoked a pipe of the old-fashioned kind rather than a water-pipe.

This distinguished personage, whose identity I still didn't know, looked at me kindly and made a sign with his eyes to ask whether I would like to smoke a water-pipe. With my head I nodded to say 'yes' but with my eyes I said 'no, because I do not dare to smoke in the presence of the minister.' Smiling, he asked the minister whether he would allow the person accompanying him to smoke a water-pipe. The minister said that he had no objection but he said it in such a way that it would have been better if he had emphatically said that he wouldn't allow this, so although they pressed me to smoke, I dared not take the water-pipe and smoke it. At this moment a servant entered and told the minister that His Majesty had ordered him to bring Mirza Reza Khan into his presence. The minister asked me whether I had ever been received by the Shah before. I said that on His Majesty's second journey to Europe, I had gone to Jolfa with the 'Ala'-ol-Molk and had been part of the entourage accompanying His

---

4 Celebrated Arabian pre-Islamic poet, whose poetry was reputedly praised by the Prophet Mohammad.

Majesty to Tiflis. He said that an audience when His Majesty was travelling was quite different from one in Tehran. 'As we go in, as soon as His Majesty appears on the balcony, watch me and follow every movement I make!' From then on, I paid no attention to anything else but concentrated on the minister's movements.

When the Shah appeared on the balcony, the minister stood and made a bow as low as or even lower than his knees, and I did the same. When we had completed our bow, we straightened up and the Shah ordered us to come upstairs, so we went upstairs and there bowed again. The Shah then approached us and after a few kind words, said to the minister: 'These young men who come from Europe to Iran are not used to the difficult journeys one has to make in Iran. You must do your best to make arrangements for Mirza Reza Khan's comfort on his journey and he must have no problem with his expenses.' Then he turned to me and said to me that he had heard that some of the Qarabagh tribes had revolted against the government in the Caucasus and had made the roads unsafe. He asked me what information I had on this. I humbly offered the opinion that if this kind of thing happened in Russia, the government wouldn't allow news of it to appear in the newspapers. If trouble did break out, however, in view of the considerable forces which the Russian government had at its disposal in the Caucasus and had particularly concentrated in and around Tiflis, any revolt could only be an insignificant event and would be rapidly suppressed. I, however, had heard nothing of such a revolt. His Majesty said nothing further to me but began to talk to the minister. Then the Shah looked at us in a particular way, so we bowed and he left. The minister said that I shouldn't have talked like this. I replied that I didn't know about these things, but the Shah had asked me a question and I had told the truth. If His Majesty asked me another question like this, however, I would of course give the reply which His Majesty wanted.

From there we travelled back to town. On the way, I asked the minister who the young man in the ante-chamber had been. He said that he was *Mirza 'Ali Asghar Khan*, the son of Aqa Ibrahim, butler-in-chief to the Shah. In other words he was the *Amin-os-Soltan*. His father had died a week ago, leaving several of his sons at court. As the father lay dying, he had made the following dying request to the Shah in his will: 'If after my death you hand on my responsibilities to my sons, my second son is the best of them.' Three days before the father's death, His Majesty had summoned Mirza 'Ali Asghar Khan and conferred on him his father's old position, giving him the title of the Amin-os-Soltan. (His elder brother was the private secretary to the Shah or, as he was known, the Amin-e-Hazrat.) The minister praised the young man's intelligence and pleasant demeanour, saying that his father had spared no pains in his education and training, the young man being thoroughly competent and able.

When we arrived at the minister's house, I was told that arrangements had been made for me to set off the next day. He had obtained the necessary letters of recommendation from the *Amin-od-Dowleh*, under whose department all the post-houses came, so that I should have someone with me on the journey. As my journey was to take place only a few months after His Majesty's visit to Khorasan and the road had seen a great deal of traffic, all the post-house horses were limping or injured and the only horses capable of being ridden were the ones which were provided for us in Tehran. At one post-house near Khorasan, they gave us donkeys to ride and at another a camel carried our baggage.

As the Ministry of Foreign Affairs in Tehran had extracted a promise from me that I wouldn't take more than ten days to reach Mashhad, we travelled night and day. We reached Mashhad on the tenth day, having only slept four hours in every twenty-four. Some *seyyed*s in Mashhad used to furnish their houses to provide lodgings for travellers, and then came to blows in their efforts to grab each new arrival. After fisticuffs and a struggle, one of the *seyyed*s bore us off to his house. As it was late at night and I was tired, it was too late to call on *Soleiman Khan Saheb-e-Ekhtiyar*,[5] who was staying at the house of the Rokn-od-Dowleh, the governor-general of Khorasan.

The next day I went to the baths to purify myself for the pilgrimage[6] as I wanted to visit the Holy Shrine before going to call on the Saheb-e-Ekhtiyar. As soon as I entered the baths, a foul, really nauseous smell from somewhere in the vicinity reached my nostrils. I went down the steps leading to the room where people placed their valuables before bathing. Without exaggeration, I cannot describe how filthy and full of hair the water was. After my experience

5 Head of Iran's delegation to the Boundary Commission and the author's chief.
6 To the shrine of Imam Reza, the eighth Shi'a Imam, in Mashhad, together with Qom one of the two holy places of pilgrimage for Shi'a Muslims in Iran.

of the spring-water baths in Tiflis, where there is running water, readers can imagine what effect the smell of the pool had on me. I turned round in front of the valuables room, went down the stairs and was about to leave the building when the barber stopped me and asked why I was leaving. I told him what I had seen. He said that the remedy was simple. 'All you have to do is to pay two *kran*s, and then you can go to a private bath where there aren't many people. Wait where you are, then send your servant to hire a large cauldron for one *kran* and spend another *kran* on buying wood which he can use to heat the water! He can then bring the hot water for you to wash yourself,' I agreed. Before the cauldron could be brought in, however, a huge furore broke out in the middle of the baths. Everybody wanted to come to the private area of the baths but the barber wouldn't allow them to do so. I got up and went to see what was going on. The barber said that two religious students were saying that I was Armenian[7] and had polluted the baths. I asked why they thought that I was Armenian. He said that as this was a holy place, Armenians weren't allowed to enter it. Since everybody shaved the back of their necks and I hadn't done so, they thought that I was Armenian.

I told the barber to bring in these men so that we could look into the matter and I could prove that I wasn't Armenian. The two students approached and we all stood together with the barber. I said: 'Gentlemen, you are mistake in thinking that I am Armenian (may God give me a peaceful death!). First let me prove to you that I am a Muslim. I say: I bear witness that there is no other God but Allah, Mohammad is the prophet of God and 'Ali is the Commander of the Faithful and the Vice-Regent of God'.[8] However, in order to give them absolute proof, I also wanted to gently discuss a point of theology with them. From all the body of religious law that governed predestination and free will, they should tell me whether performance of such and such a religious injunction was compulsory or whether one had the right to use one's own free will in deciding whether to obey it or not. At which point they bowed their heads in submission and withdrew.

Clean water was then brought in, so I washed myself, gave a tip to the barber and went to perform my pilgrimage at the Holy Shrine. By the blessed

---

7 Christians and therefore unclean.
8 The Muslim declaration of faith, with a specifically Shi'a addition.

tomb I started to perform the two obeisances of the pilgrimage with a pure mind, when a woman, probably from Shiraz, came up to me and, just as I was praying, whispered in my ear: 'Mr Mashhadi, I am honoured to see you, I can come to visit you at an appropriate place and time.' She completely destroyed my peace of mind, so I finished my prayers as best I could and returned to my lodging place. From there I went to the citadel to call on the Saheb-e-Ekhtiyar, to whom I handed over the documents from the Ministry of Foreign Affairs.

As I had promised the Ministry, I reached Mashhad on the tenth day of my journey, When I arrived there, however a telegram arrived ordering me to leave immediately as, although at the time I was unaware of this, all the members of the Frontier Commission had reached Mashhad earlier than me and indeed had already reached their destination in the wilds of Khorasan. I was given a list of the supplies I would need and was told to obtain all these things in less than two days. In addition to 'Asgar Beg, I was provided with a groom and an attendant to erect and pull down the tents. I was given a colonel's tent, there was a small tent for the servants and one as a kitchen. Five riding horses were provided, with two old nags to carry the bedding, travel equipment, the kitchen, two chairs and a travelling table. I was given 300 *tomans*[9] extra to purchase all these things, and we somehow managed to acquire the lot within two days. It was agreed that I, like the other members of the Commission, would receive a monthly salary of 60 *tomans*. I need to say this because in those days when an egg cost one *shahi* and other things were just as cheap, this would be the equivalent of 300 *tomans* today.

The Saheb-e-Ekhtiyar sent orders for us to set off that night. Everybody was told that we would take the road to Lotfabad and Quchan and that we should wait at the crossroads, so that we could all leave from there together. Luckily, I was introduced to a Shahsavan tribesman called 'Ein-e 'Ali, who had escorted Naser-od-Din Shah to Mashhad and who hadn't yet returned to Tehran with the rest of the mounted escort and was looking for work. 'Ein-e 'Ali was a rough fellow but an excellent horseman and a good shot, as well as being brave and physically strong. Through 'Asgar Beg, he intimated that even if I didn't wish to hunt myself, I should nevertheless buy a rifle and 200 bullets, so I bought the rifle of his choice with 200 rounds and gave them to him.

9 Ten *krans* made one *toman*.

Anyway, when we reached the designated meeting point, where everybody was assembled, the Saheb-e-Ekhtiyar ordered us to take the Kalaat-e-Naderi road. As this was the very beginning of our journey, everybody was surprised by this and nobody could understand why the route had been changed, since the road to Lotfabad goes left and the Kalaat-e-Naderi road goes to the right. We rode till morning and reached Kalaat-e-Naderi around midday. There we saw the Shoja'-od-Dowleh, governor of Quchan and chief of the local Za'faranlou Kurds who had his own cavalry, the Sahham-od-Dowleh, governor of Bojnourd and chief of the Shadlou Kurds of Khorasan with his Bojnourd cavalry, and Mohammad 'Ali Khan from Darrehgaz[10] with his horsemen.[11] In addition, an infantry brigade raised by the Saif-os-Saltaneh from Khalaj and commanded by a brigadier, one of his relatives, was also camped there.

On the journey I had worn my uniform as an aide-de-camp to the Heir Apparent. One evening, one of the Saheb-e-Ekhtiyar's servants gave me a message from his master that I should attend a military council. When I arrived, all the army officers were gathered there, together with the brigade commander and the Saheb-e-Ekhtiyar, but 'Alam Shah Mirza was the only courtier. When I entered, the Saheb-e-Ekhtiyar said: 'First I want to explain why I have come to this spot. A courier has arrived in Mashhad from Sarakhs, with a message saying that a black-robed *seyyed* wearing a black veil has appeared in Merv. He has assembled 30,000 Turkoman horsemen around him and intends to conquer Khorasan. He says that he is the Hidden Imam[12] who has returned and that he will send half these tribesmen to Mashhad and the other 15,000 against Kalaat and Quchan and Darrehgaz in order to capture Khorasan in one fell swoop. The *Rokn-od-Dowleh* has enough soldiers and equipment in Mashhad. The Shoja'-od-Dowleh can maintain control of Quchan, but you must take 200 cavalry from Quchan, Bojnourd and Darrehgaz to repair the ruined fortress

10 All three were local governors.
11 The Shah's cavalry regiments were largely raised by tribal chieftains and were, as we shall see later, a source of pride to Naser-od-Din Shah.
12 The occultation refers to a belief that the Messianic figure of the Twelfth Imam, the Mahdi, who is the infallible descendant of the Prophet Mohammad, was born and then disappeared. The Twelver Shi'a believe that he will return at the end of time and fill the world with peace and justice.

at Hesar, even the gates of which are in total disrepair. Mohammad 'Ali Khan has given orders to the governor of Lotfabad that the village headmen of Hesar and Shalangan must immediately provide you with all the carpenters and workmen you need. Your orders are to leave this evening with the cavalry and proceed to Hesar, where you are to await orders.' This had been decided by the military and I hadn't been consulted, but I had no alternative but to obey. Actually, I was secretly very happy to have swapped the role of secretary in the consulate-general for that of commander of two hundred cavalry. Having received my orders, I returned to my lodging, left my baggage in Kalaat and took 'Ein-e 'Ali and 'Asgar Beg with me. The cavalry were waiting for me. These undisciplined troops operated as follows: every twenty-five soldiers had a 'chavush', whom we would call a junior officer, while every hundred men had a 'moshref' or more senior officer. Their marching order was in fact completely undisciplined. Each individual travelled separately, and if there was a problem on the road and there was a need to assemble his troops, an officer would simply gallop up and say to the cavalry: 'Come on, you sons of no-good fathers, get moving!'

Anyway, we set off and rode until morning. Just before noon the next day, when we reached the foot of a hill, a junior officer galloped up and said that the seyyed's troops could be seen in the distance. We went up to the top of the hill and indeed I could see a cloud of dust on the horizon. Then the officers gathered around me and said that as they were only 200 men, they couldn't possibly fight a thousand enemy troops. They asked for my permission to flee. I replied that in the first place, I did not give them permission to flee and that in any case even if I were to give permission, their horses were completely exhausted from the journey, so we weren't in a position to flee. They said that there was no alternative. I said that there was an alternative, which was to remain here and fortify our position. We could then see who the troops were. In any case, an honourable death was better than shameful survival. They could not make up their minds what to do, so they stayed where they were, paralysed with fear. I told my men that I wouldn't leave and ordered them to gather rocks and place them all around us, so in the end, realising how parlous our situation was, they all decided to build fortifications. When I gave the order, the officers went off to assemble the cavalry, who were spread out all around, and bring them up. As they were in fear for their lives, in a short space

Map of Khorasan and Neighbouring Countries illustrating the paper by Lt-Colonel C E Stewart, 5th
Punjab Infantry, from Proceedings of the Royal Geographical Society July-December 1881. Most
maps of the period are in Russian, and this map pre-dates the Boundary Commission delineation of the

Akhal-Khorasan frontier in 1886. Reproduced by kind permission of the Royal Geographical Society (with IBG).

of time they had collected enough stones to provide some form of defence. I of course had a revolver, as did 'Asgar Beg, while 'Ein-e 'Ali had the rifle. The cavalry, who had flintlock rifles stacked in conical piles, copied us and prepared themselves for battle. Most of the rifles, however, had no bullets but only guncotton and gunpowder.

After a long wait, we saw a column of 300 camels loaded with flour and wheat bought in Merv being transported to Ashkabad by a Russian Cossack escort. When they saw us behind our fortifications, they came up and enquired why we were sitting there. Our cavalry replied that we were waiting for the black-robed *seyyed* who, we had heard, had gathered 30,000 troops and was coming this way to attack. They roared with laughter and asked whether we were unaware of the fact that General Skobelev[13] had made Merv and all this Turkoman area Russian territory. It was unthinkable that he would allow some black-robed *seyyed* to raise an army there. They said that they had heard that a certain veiled *seyyed* claiming to be the Imam of the End of Time had appeared and that some Turkoman ruffians had gathered around him, but there was no question of horsemen or of an army.

When the camel caravan had gone on its way, I ordered my men to bring up the horses so that we could leave for Hesar. However, all the officers replied with one voice that after such a signal victory, they would not leave until an official report of their victory had been sent to Kalaat. I laughed and said: 'My good fellows, what is this talk of victory or of a victory report?' They replied that it was clear that I didn't know how governors of these frontier provinces behaved. When they wanted to obtain some privilege, title or medal from Tehran, they would mount their horses, ride off into the Turkoman wastes, and when they spotted a poor shepherd or a traveller, they would cut off his head, which they would then send to Tehran with a letter announcing a victory. In this way the governors would obtain what they wanted from the government. 'Why', they said, 'do you ignore justice, when, having given up our livelihood, money and family, we are even prepared also to give up our lives? It is not our fault if the black-robed *seyyed* doesn't have an army or if he does have one, it hasn't appeared. He should have come, and then he would have been beaten

---

13 The Russian victor of the Battle of Gok Teppe (1881), in which he had comprehensively defeated the Turkomans.

to a pulp. He would have seen what lions we are in Iran.' At this juncture, one of the more senior officers wrote out a victory letter, which he sealed, and brought to me, asking me to sign and seal it. I read it and saw that they had written: 'Today, about midday, in the distance we saw the black-robed *seyyed*'s cavalry approaching Hesar, so we dismounted, tied our horses to bushes, and very bravely fortified our position with stones until their cavalry, approximately 4,000 or 5,000 in number, approached. We didn't allow them to get close, but killed many of them with a single volley. When they experienced our knock-out blow, they fled taking their dead with them. Praise be to Almighty God, that in the shadow of the immortal government we have won this victory! As for other matters, we rely on the liberality of the authorities.'

They all signed this victory letter and brought it for me to sign as well. I refused to do so, whereupon they roared with laughter. I said that it was a joke to talk of the approach of the black-robed *seyyed* or of any volley of shots. In utter disdain, they said that I had obviously come from Europe and knew nothing about how things were done in these parts. Clearly, one Turkoman's head was very like another, so they got what they wanted from Tehran. They then said that if I didn't sign the letter, they would leave me there to make my own way to Hesar on my own. I saw that they weren't joking, so I asked all the officers to witness the fact that I was signing this report under duress. To keep them quiet, I also sealed the report, for I was certain that when the senior officers and brigade commanders investigated this matter, they would ask me some questions and I would tell them the truth. Nevertheless they gave the victory letter to a horseman and sent it off to the military council in Kalaat.

In due course we mounted our horses and went on to Hesar, where we saw that one of the gates to the fort had collapsed, as indeed had most of the walls and towers, while almost all the inhabitants had abandoned the place as a result of Turkoman attacks. We sent the remaining inhabitants to Lotfabad to look for carpenters, workmen and masons to repair Hesar. At this point, the courier we had sent off returned with three other horsemen, who brought a letter in which the military council lauded our bravery and our victory to the skies. They wrote that they had sent a reward of 300 *toman*s to be fairly divided among everyone. They gave 200 *toman*s to the 200 horsemen and said that one-tenth of this sum, that is 30 *toman*s, was for me. The remaining

*toman*s were divided between one senior and seven junior officers. I really
have no idea what happened, whether the officers thought that the military
council really believed a word of this victory story or even accepted that the
black-robed *seyyed* had appeared at all. I heard conclusively, however, that the
military council had sent the victory letter on to Tehran and had received two
bejewelled swords, a senior position and 5,000 *toman*s as their reward. The
governors of Quchan, Bojnourd and Darrehgaz were then ordered to return
to their seats of authority, while a letter arrived for me from Soleiman Khan
Saheb-e-Ekhtiyar ordering me to stay where I was because, as a result of the
complaints of the people of Lotfabad to Mashhad, orders had been received
from Tehran that the bilateral Border Commission should first resolve the
problem of the people of Lotfabad and then go to install the frontier demarcation posts. I was ordered to go to Lotfabad and wait there.

Two days later, our delegation reached Lotfabad and the Russian delegation, who had been waiting nearby, came and pitched camp near Lotfabad
on Russian soil. They had an escort of 300 Cossacks and their officers. The
delegation itself consisted of ten men led by Staff Colonel Guzmin Kara-
vayev, the interpreter being a Monsieur Pakhtianov. They also had several
engineer surveyors. One was Kapilov from the Qarabagh, who was also an
engineer-surveyor to the General Staff. On their arrival, Monsieur Pakhtianov
came to congratulate the Saheb-e-Ekhtiyar on his safe arrival on behalf of the
colonel. Then the Saheb-e-Ekhtiyar sent me to the Russian camp on a reciprocal courtesy call. It was agreed that the two sides should meet without delay
and consider the requests of the people of Lotfabad, agree the frontiers and
then erect the frontier posts. As Soleiman Khan Saheb-e-Ekhtiyar was an old
man, a much respected titular chief of the Afshar tribe, with the title of Amir-
Tomani,[14] it was decided that as a mark of respect the first meeting should be
held on Iranian territory. From Mashhad we had been sent all the equipment
we needed to entertain our guests such as tent covers, camp chairs and every
kind of utensil for a party of twenty-four.

A magnificent tent was pitched and all the other furnishings installed. At
the appointed hour, the Russian colonel arrived, preceded by an escort of ten
Cossacks in front of his carriage and followed by ten others. After official

---

14 A senior Iranian military rank roughly equivalent to major-general.

Members of the Russian-Persian Akhal-Khorasan Boundary Commission 1883–1886.

introductions and refreshments, it was agreed that negotiations should start the next day but that our delegation should now pay a reciprocal call. Since we had twenty-five Iranian Cossacks[15] under the command of 'Ali Khan Yavar, we paid our call in the same manner with ten Cossacks in front and ten behind. The first meeting had gone as well as we could possibly have hoped.

It had been agreed that the negotiations would take place in our tent. First, the agenda and the maps, copies of which had been given to both sides, were placed on the table. The agenda, which had been prepared by the Russians,

15 The Russian-officered Iranian Cossack Brigade was formed in 1879 at the request of the Shah after his second visit to Europe. It was an elite cavalry unit modelled on the Cossack Brigade of the Imperial Russian army and was widely recognised as the only effective military unit of the Qajar state.

was in both Persian and Russian, their Persian text being identical to our own. When we looked at the maps, however, which were to be signed by the Russian foreign minister and Zinoviev, the Russian minister in Tehran on the one hand and by our foreign minister on the other, we noticed that the course of the new frontier had been traced with a green line under the very walls of the citadel of Lotfabad. They had placed all the farms and pasture lands belonging to 500 Iranian families outside this line and in Russian territory. We were all left aghast by this. We were astonished that, without sending a single engineer surveyor to the spot, those in Tehran had signed these maps and given them to the commission. The Saheb-e-Ekhtiyar said to the colonel: 'Do you see how Tehran has signed these maps on the basis of a total lack of information? How could the sense of justice of the Russian authorities and indeed your own sense of justice allow all these people to go hungry? Is it possible for a village or tribe anywhere in the world to live without farming land?' The colonel very gently replied: 'Your Excellency Saheb-e-Ekhtiyar, we have been instructed by our government to determine the frontier on the basis of these maps and this green line. We have no instructions to show pity or consideration. Our instructions are simply to put this map into effect in due course.' The Saheb-e-Ekhtiyar said: 'Now that you can see that your minister in Tehran and our Minister of Foreign Affairs have been misled into signing this map, now that you are actually on the spot, your duty as a human being is to report this matter to your government, explain matters and act justly.' The colonel replied that his response was the same: he had not come here to do justice.

Thereupon, the old man flew in a rage and lost control of himself. He got up and said: 'You insignificant little man, I have now spent an hour pleading with you, but now I insist that you act justly. You say that the green line must be adopted. I will give you your green line.' With that he slammed the map down on the table and said: 'I won't work under these conditions. I resign, and you and your government can deal with the matter.' God was merciful because Pakhtianov did not translate the Saheb-e-Ekhtiyar's speech word by word but translated 'insignificant little man' as 'Monsieur', but when they saw his anger and how he slammed down the map, they got up and said that if this was going to happen, their mission was over. They then left the tent without shaking hands.

Soleiman Khan Afshar-Ghassemlou
Saheb-e-Ekhtiyar, chief of the
Afshar tribe and head of the
Persian delegation to the Russian-
Persian Akhal-Khorasan Boundary
Commission.

Obviously, both sides reported what had happened to the appropriate ministry by telegram. Three days later two telegrams arrived for the Saheb-e-Ekhtiyar, one in code from the Shah and the other, a short one, from the Minister of
Foreign Affairs. The latter said that the Saheb-e-Ekhtiyar's instructions from
His Majesty were clear: his resignation would not be accepted and he was
to fulfil the mission with which he had been entrusted. The Shah's telegram
was very long and detailed: After the customary amendments by the court it
read: 'Do you really think that I am happy with this division of our territory
and demarcation of our frontiers? When General Skobelev dug under Gok
Teppe and blew up all the Turkoman fighters there with dynamite, he captured
Ashkabad, Merv and the Akhal. When he saw that the land he had conquered
was just a barren waste without water or vegetation, he thought of conquering

all Khorasan. Once he had established himself with his staff in Quchan, he brought up his whole army there. I had neither troops nor money with which to repel him, so with a thousand entreaties, I entered personal negotiations with the Tsar and with great difficulty I was able to make Skobelev withdraw from Khorasan. If a portion of land around Lotfabad is lost, this is unimportant in relation to the great danger we have avoided. There is no place for argument. You must carry out the instructions which you have been given.'

Fortunately Monsieur Zinoviev was not given a copy of this telegram in Tehran, but he was given a copy of the Iranian Foreign Minister's uncoded telegram. Obviously, the text of the latter telegram, which Zinoviev had sent to the Russian Foreign Minister, was passed on word by word to the colonel, who wasted no time in carrying out his instructions. A note from Pakhtianov reached me in which he said that I should gather together workers and the Russians would assemble their share of the work force, so that we could start installing the frontier posts. I knew three members of the Russian delega-tion from previous acquaintanceship. One was Pakhtianov, whom I had got to know well when he had been the official host's interpreter for the 'Ezz-od-Dowleh's embassy to the coronation of Alexander III, at which I had been an attaché, when I had got to know him well over the two-week period we spent together. The second was the Colonel's deputy, Lt-Colonel Sripitski, who was a departmental chief on the Caucasus General Staff. The third was Kapilov from the Qarabagh, the engineer surveyor, who was a Muslim. Following the insult which he had received from the Saheb-e-Ekhtiyar, the colonel refused to write to him and wrote to me privately instead.

When the Saheb-e-Ekhtiyar was alone, I showed him the letter, and he asked me whether I had seen the Shah's telegram. He said that if he agreed to the Russians' green frontier line, he and his family would be disgraced for all time. He said that he simply could not explain to the people of Lotfabad, all of whom were illiterate, what the green line was nor could he show them a copy of the telegram. People would say that the Saheb-e-Ekhtiyar had taken 100,000 imperials[16] from the Russians and in return handed over to them the pasture land belonging to the people of Lotfabad. The inhabitants of Lotfabad

16 A Russian imperial gold coin issued in various denominations from 1835 until the Bolshevik Revolution. Also issued in silver.

had sent a message to him saying that if their pasture land was given up, they would all become Russian citizens. If this happened, nothing could be done about it. He added that he had heard that my father had been a devout man in Tabriz, and he had no doubt that I too was a loyal, patriotic citizen and would serve the government in a straightforward manner. Since he had seen how warmly the Russians had shaken my hand on the day of the opening meeting and how relaxed they had been in talking to me, it was clear that they respected me. The fact that their interpreter wrote to me and not to him was a clear indication of this respect. He continued: 'There is no one at this meeting except you and I. God is my witness of the mission with which I am about to entrust you. If you succeed, you can be certain that the happiness of the world and a brilliant future for you will result from it. We will both come out of this in a good light and be happy. First of all, you must go and somehow persuade the Russians to come and drink tea with me. I know that they will say that I should go there and apologise. You must explain to them, however, that from the day I arrived here, the inhabitants of Lotfabad, accompanied by their wives and children, have come to me in tears saying that for some time now the Russians have stopped them enjoying the use of their own pasture land. They demand justice and I have given them a promise to set the matter to rights. In the face of the Colonel's definitively negative reply, I didn't know what to do and lost my temper. I am very sorry and am ready to send my Arab horse to bring him here and I will even make a present of this horse to him. Second, you know the Russian language well and you must somehow secure Russian agreement to give up sufficient cultivable land for 500 peasant households. As God is my witness, I will obtain rewards for you beyond your dreams from the Shah.'

I replied: 'Your Excellency Saheb-e-Ekhtiyar, if on this journey I am able to serve and achieve complete or even partial success, I will do so out of loyalty to the government and without expectation of reward. However, it seems very unlikely that the Russians will accept these two points. These instructions seem to me impossible to fulfil, not least because the Russians have a copy of the Ministry of Foreign Affairs' telegram.' He said that he would ask me a question: could I reply that I believed in God, his prophets, the Qur'an and the power of personal prayer? I replied that of course I did. He said that he knew a prayer which he recited before sending an official to make an important call on someone. I was to get ready to leave and come to see him, when he would recite the prayer and send me off. I therefore sent a Cossack to Pakhtianov with a message that I was coming to call on him, and the Saheb-e-Ekhtiyar duly sent me off after reciting the prayer. At the end of my meeting with Pakhtianov, he himself suggested that I might wish to meet the colonel, who received me well. First, I expressed great regret for the events of that day in a personal capacity. When I saw that he was not displeased by this, I quickly apologised on behalf of the Saheb-e-Ekhtiyar, who, I said, had sent me for this purpose. As the Saheb-e-Ekhtiyar was a highly respected old man, a tribal chief who held the rank of Amir-Tomani, which was senior to a brigade commander, would he not see fit to come to pay a friendly call the next day, so that this unfortunate incident could be put on one side and we could start work? He looked at his interpreter, as though he wanted his opinion. Happily Pakhtianov agreed and it was arranged that the next day they would come to meet the Saheb-e-Ekhtiyar, and there would be no talk of the exchange of words which had taken place that day. Nor would they say that the colonel had come to apologise. The colonel asked me to have a word with the Saheb-e-Ekhtiyar, in case the latter brought up the same subject again and continued in the same vein about pity and human kindness. If so, my chief would be troubling himself to no purpose, he said, as his own instructions were simply to give effect to the provisions of the map. If the Saheb-e-Ekhtiyar wouldn't accept this, we could hold a farewell meeting without any reproach on either side and simply go our separate ways. If the Iranian delegation had been in his position, would they have acted any differently? If the Iranian side wanted agricultural land or pasturage, however, they should address an official request to St Petersburg, for the Russian were not so brutal as to starve people to death. The subject was then closed. I got up, said goodbye and returned to our camp.

I saw that the Colonel and Pakhtianov weren't being difficult or obstinate: they themselves had suggested to me that if St Petersburg gave instructions, they would carry these out. It occurred to me, therefore, that we must find a way to achieve this. When I gave the Saheb-e-Ekhtiyar the news that I had persuaded the Russians to pay a call the next day, he got up and kissed me several times. I suggested that he should send a telegram to the Ministry of Foreign Affairs reporting on the progress we had made here and suggesting that they should start negotiations with the Russian court and that orders should be given to this effect. He thought for a moment and then pointed out that I had absolutely no knowledge or experience of how things worked in Tehran. Our Minister of Foreign Affairs would have to make this request to the Russian Foreign Ministry through Zinoviev, the Russian minister plenipotentiary in Tehran. If without informing Zinoviev, we negotiated through our minister plenipotentiary in St Petersburg so that he approached the Russian foreign ministry, the latter would seek the views of their minister in Tehran and since the latter had been responsible for drawing up this map which had brought this misfortune on the people of the frontier, he would reply in a way which would only make the situation worse. He added that I had lived for some years in Tiflis and he knew that I had made some good friends there. He invited me to think whether it might be possible to bring this manifest injustice to the attention of the Russian authorities and even find a medicine for this incurable pain.

I thought about what the Saheb-e-Ekhtiyar had said and resolved to leave Lotfabad for Ashkabad to meet the commander-in-chief of the army in the newly conquered territories, General Komarov, whom I had known in Tiflis with his family and who had invited me to parties and balls there, to ask him to find a solution for this problem. I told the Saheb-e-Ekhtiyar of my idea. He immediately ordered five Cossacks to accompany me. He then gave me enough money to cover my expenses, those of my servant and of the Cossacks, and sent me off to Ashkabad, accompanied by the same prayers for my well-being.

Ashkabad had previously had a Turkoman citadel, a kind of stockade made of thick, rough cloth. In the two years since the Russian victory, however, the Russians had started to build a large town. They had laid out a town plan in chalk and had marked out the plans for the town on a grid. They announced that anyone, Russian or foreign, who wanted to build a caravanserai, a shop or a house would be given the land free of charge and would be helped with all kinds of building materials. A wealthy Iranian merchant resident in Mashhad, Haji Mehdi Kuzeh Kanani, took over several blocks of land with the intention of building a caravanserai, shops, a bathhouse and other facilities. He had already built the caravanserai, in which I lodged. The rooms were habitable, as the Russians had designed them. They had built comfortable quarters for men and animals, and every two rooms had a shared kitchen. The chief merchant in the bazaar there was one Hossein Qarabaghi. I asked to see him and questioned him as to whether General Komarov was on his own or whether he had brought his family with him from Tiflis. Fortunately, the chief merchant said that the general's family had arrived from Tiflis about a month previously and that they were now all together, so I wrote a letter to Madame Komarov to tell her that I had arrived in Ashkabad.

Divine destiny works in a wondrous way for the human race. Following my return to Tiflis with the 'Ala'-os-Saltaneh from the coronation of Alexander III, on the very day that I was appointed to join the Boundary Commission, I had gone to the Komarov house to say my farewells to the family. Both Madame Komarov and her daughters had made me promise that when I reached the Akhal, I would go to see them in Ashkabad, which was of course close to the Akhal. The eldest daughter had in her hand a hand-towel, which she was embroidering. She said that she would embroider my name and hers together with the date 1883 of the Christian era and send me the towel so that I shouldn't forget my promise. This same towel is now in my museum in Monaco.

Anyhow they were very pleased to see me and asked me how many days I intended to stay in Ashkabad. I replied that the length of my stay depended on the general and I hoped that he could be persuaded that I should not bother them for too long. At that moment, the general entered the room, his wife introduced me and described how kind they had been to me in Tiflis. The general asked about my journey to Tehran, Tiflis and Ashkabad and why I had come to Ashkabad. I politely asked him when he would have time to receive me in his private office so that I could explain my purpose in coming to Ashkabad. He got up and said: 'Let's go to my office!' When I got up, his wife said to me that when I had finished my work I was to come back, as it would be lunch time and she invited me to lunch with them.

I explained the problem truthfully to the general: I told him that unfortunately the Russian Embassy in Tehran had informed our Foreign Ministry that the green line was to be the frontier and had thus left the people of Lotfabad completely destitute. I said that if the Boundary Commission acted in this manner, the whole of the Akhal, Khorasan and Astarabad would rise up against the tyranny and injustice of the Russian government, saying that they had deprived the poor, orphans and the defenceless of their livelihood. I added that as the Russian Embassy in Tehran was responsible for this matter, we couldn't do anything about it through diplomatic channels. I had left the Boundary Commission and come to see him, therefore, placing my hope in the sense of justice of the Russian court and having confidence in his own friendly and humane feelings. I humbly requested him to give orders for a solution to be found through the Russian General Staff, of which he was the representative with full powers. I showed him a copy of our own detailed map, which I had brought with me. He was very well informed about the situation in Lotfabad but was very surprised that we had been given a copy of this map. He promised to report what I had said the same day by telegram to the appropriate quarters. I was somewhat re-assured by his words and by his tone that the problem would be solved. I then got up and returned to the ladies, spending three days in Ashkabad, lunching or dining at his house as his guest.

On the third day, the general gave me the good news that the Russian delegation had received orders to deal with us fairly. I returned in triumph and brought the good news to the Saheb-e-Ekhtiyar. Before I arrived back, however, the Russian delegation had already sent a message that they were prepared to negotiate on this matter. Several days later, therefore, acting on the basis of the letter of authority which the Saheb-e-Ekhtiyar had earlier given me, I went to the Russian camp and we looked into all the points at issue. It was agreed that an area one and a half *farsakh*s long and half a *farsakh* wide of pasturage, agricultural land and woodland should be given to the people of Lotfabad and that the patrols which had been placed round the walls to prevent the local inhabitants from going to their fields should be removed. The Saheb-e-Ekhtiyar gave me a letter, and told me to read it. In it he had written: 'In view of the great service which you have rendered to Iran, I give you my sincere promise that when I reach Tehran, I shall obtain the title of Adjutant General[17] and the appropriate salary for you from His Majesty.' I was very surprised by this, as were the members of our delegation, because at that time only one person in the whole of Iran held this title and he was one of the first-grade princes. I thanked the Saheb-e-Ekhtiyar warmly and took the letter, which I have kept in my possession.

The Saheb-e-Ekhtiyar then said that now that I had relieved the people of Lotfabad of the problem of their pasturage and fields, the remaining problem

17 It seems that this was a semi-honorary title as a very senior aide-de-camp to the Shah.

was their water supply. He gave me another letter of authority and he told me to go and solve that problem too. When I showed the letter of authority to the Russian delegation, they nominated Kapilov to accompany me to the valley through which the river flowed so that we could see what should be done. When we got there, we saw that all the river water originating from the Quchan mountains flowed through the Quzkhan valley into the barren Akhal territory. All the mountains from which water flowed were situated in Iranian territory. Nevertheless, the lie of the land made it suitable for making an appropriate division of water between the two parties: this could be achieved by allotting the waters naturally belonging to the Turkoman settlements to the Turkomans and those inside Iran, which properly belonged to us, to Iran. Turkomans had settled near the source of the river, while the lower stretches belonged to the people of Lotfabad. The objective was that after our departure, the Turkomans shouldn't interfere any further with the water rights of the people of Lot-fabad. After we had taken this decision, the next problem was on what basis to divide the water. Kapilov said that he had been instructed by his chief to divide the water on the basis of the number of households, that is to say that he was to calculate on the basis of thirteen Turkoman fort settlements and the three fortified villages of Lotfabad, Shalangan and Hesar. If we had put into effect this kind of agreement, it would have meant that we would have had to divide the water into sixteen parts, of which thirteen would have gone to the Turkomans and three to Iran. I wasn't happy with this and said that this was unjust because after the Russian victory the inhabitants of these three fortified villages had abandoned them, whereas in contrast the number of inhabitants of the Turkoman fortresses had greatly increased. If we counted households in this way, the people of Lotfabad would not even obtain three shares out of twenty. It was agreed that we would both go and consult our respective chiefs on this point and then return to the river at Hesar, pitch our tents and start work.

The next day I was summoned to the Russian camp, where it was clear that by this time that their attitude had softened and there was no trace of their original inflexibility. It also became obvious that at the time of their conquest of the Akhal they had conducted a census of the population of the Akhal and Lotfabad and so there was no need to argue over population numbers. As at that time Lotfabad was a village, we called it 'the village' and assigned one-third of the water to us and two-thirds to the thirteen forts. As the old channel of the river was to remain in the hands of the Turkomans, they were to provide two-thirds of the workforce and equipment for digging a new channel, while the people of the three fortified villages would provide the other third.

The weather was cold and it was a Tuesday evening just before Nowruz.[18] The headman of Hesar was an old man called 'Ali Khan Beg, who was a great storyteller. He said that the Turkomans had looted Hesar eight times and taken him off into captivity. On some occasions he had managed to escape and sometimes his people had ransomed him with horses and sheep. They had even taken him as far as Merv, Khiva and Bokhara. He recounted his experiences as a captive, and I could not make out whether he was lying or telling the truth, but he invited me to go and have supper at his house and said that as it was the last Tuesday of the year, we should light a fire and eat *polow*[19] and fruit. He lit the stove but it smoked so badly that while my host was preparing the dinner, my eyes were watering from the smoke. Instead of candles, a bowl full of fat with two wicks in the old-fashioned way, all badly put together, was burning. The two wicks added to the smoke from the stove.

Suddenly, a horseman from Darrehgaz, wearing a typical Turkoman hat, with a sword in his belt and dressed in a long tunic and villager's boots, entered the room. He gave a cursory greeting, but it was clear from his manner that his purpose was not a happy one. He gave me a letter, which I opened by the light of the wick, and saw that it was in the handwriting of the Saheb-e-Ekhtiyar. The beginning of the letter was proof enough of his displeasure with me. Whereas in other letters he had addressed me as 'beloved light of my eyes', here he had written: 'Sir, I regret that I considered you a Muslim and a patriot. I now see that I made a mistake. As I have been informed that you have betrayed Iran, as soon as you receive this letter you are not to remain there a moment longer but you are to strike your tents and, escorted by the Cossacks, return to Lotfabad with this horseman.' I asked the rider what his orders were. He said that they were to take me and my servants back to Lotfabad immediately and that he was not to delay for one instant.

I went out and gave orders for the tents to be struck and the horses saddled. We mounted and rode until morning. At about dawn we arrived at Lotfabad.

---

18 The Iranian New Year, celebrated across the Persianate world on 21 March.
19 Dish of rice with chopped vegetables and meat.

Shaking the dust of the journey off my feet, I went to pay my respects to the Saheb-e-Ekhtiyar, who was at the local governor's house. I saw that the kind and polite way in which his servants used to look at me had changed and that they were looking at me in an entirely different way. I asked where the Saheb-e-Ekhtiyar was. They replied that having said his prayers, he was now busy reciting verses of the Qur'an and telling his beads. I entered the room and sat down before him. I saw that as he was telling his beads and reciting verses from the Qur'an, he was looking at me angrily from under his eyelids. I said nothing but bowed my head. I saw that the verses he was reciting were to calm his anger. The late Saheb-e-Ekhtiyar did not know Arabic, but he had a book in Persian which indicated which verses he should use to calm anger and which to recite when he was summoned to the Shah's presence. I had seen that book and I recognised the prayer he was reciting as one that he had recited to me when I went to call on the Russian delegation.

When he had finished reciting prayers, he made a formal obeisance in the direction of Mecca and one in the direction of the holy city of Mashhad in the East. The servants came in and gathered up his prayer mat and the book of prayers. He then sat down near the window and indicated where I was to sit. He turned towards me and repeated more or less the contents of the letter which he had written. Very calmly, I asked him: 'Your Excellency Saheb-e-Ekhtiyar, I do not know how I have betrayed Iran. Please tell me.' He replied that the headmen of Lotfabad had got together and written two petitions, one to him and the other through the governor-general of Khorasan to the Shah. They had stated that the water channel which I was creating for the villagers on the basis of his letter of authority and into which I was channelling the water was next door to the old one and that as the level of the new one was about a metre higher than that of the old one and the soil there was like sand, all its water would flow into the channel of the river belonging to the Turkomans. Not even a spoonful would reach the complainants. Not only would the eighty families of Lotfabad be deprived of their hope of water but the inhabitants of Shalangan and Hesar would all abandon the area. Not a single person would remain there. Worse than this treachery to my country, how could I wish to disgrace him, an old man, in the eyes of the world, which would say that he had taken money from the Russians and sold all the water in the area to them?

I said to him: 'Excellency Saheb–e-Ekhtiyar, the Arab has a proverb of which the translation is: "every piece of news which reaches you is probably both true and false." Thanks be to God that you have a healthy constitution and that you are a better horseman than a young man! In your delegation you have appointed two learned engineer surveyors. When this petition arrived, you, 'Ali Ashraf Khan and Mirza Mohammad 'Ali Khan should have mounted your horses. You should have ridden up to the river and seen the nature of the terrain with your own eyes. If the complaints of the people of Lotfabad had been true, you could have questioned me. If I had made this agreement through ignorance, you could have repudiated it and cancelled my authority. If you had seen that I had intentionally acted in this way, rather than insulting me as much as you have now done, you could have dismissed me and sent me off to Tehran, where I would have been tried by a court and punished.' I realised that I was really getting very angry and feared that I would say something which would offend the old man, so I got up, saying that I would go straight to Tehran, where I would insist on being tried in court.

I left the room, went to my lodgings and told my servants to pack everything we had, load them up, mount our horses and leave for Mashhad. We had not travelled for more than half a *farsakh* before Heydar Khan, 'Ali Naqi Khan, Eskandar Khan and several other government officials came up behind us on horseback and stopped us. 'Ali Naqi Khan said that his grandfather had sent them after me to apologise. The headmen had forced him to write that letter to me in a moment of anger. 'Come back', they said, 'and he promises that as you say, he will investigate the matter and from now on he will report what you have done directly to the Shah.' I insisted that I would not return, but in the end I had to comply. They ordered their men to escort my servants back there, and so I had to go. We arrived at the Saheb-e-Ekhtiyar's house at lunch time. My determination to leave for Tehran had had an even greater effect on him than his prayers, for his reception of me was extremely gracious. His servants brought him pigeon kababs, but he told them to serve them to Mirza Reza Khan, as although he had shot them himself, I deserved to eat them. It was arranged that the next day, we should ride to the Quzkhan valley with the whole delegation. There he would hunt and we would also inspect the lie of the land in the valley. There they were able to confirm with their own eyes that the level of the new channel we were to make was a little lower than the old one. If water leaked, it would be from the old river to our new channel rather than vice versa and as the river-bed had not one ounce of sand, the whole complaint was complete nonsense.

The Saheb-e-Ekhtiyar had given me complete authority to punish the headmen who had made the complaint against me as I saw fit. One day, therefore, I sent for eight of them, who were brought before me in front of the same fort where the tents had been pitched. I told them what they had done wrong and read out their punishment, which was, in accordance with the local custom, eighty strokes of the lash. However, since I was not accustomed to the business of striking people, I abandoned the idea of having them whipped but said that they would have to explain why they had sent this petition to the Saheb-e-Ekhtiyar and to Mashhad. They replied that they were not at liberty to name their informant but this much they could swear on the Qur'an: some members of the Iranian delegation to the Boundary Commission had spread the rumour among the people that Mirza Reza Khan was not a Muslim but a Russian and he was betraying them. The villagers said that the reason why they considered me a traitor was that on several occasions I had summoned them to attend on-site investigations, I had translated what they had said for the Russians into a foreign language which they did not understand and had distorted their words. That is what they had written in their petition. Despite their efforts to explain the incident, I roared with laughter but unfortunately, however much I tried, I couldn't make them understand that if the Russians had understood our language, there would have been no need for an interpreter. I saw that it was no use: they didn't understand what an interpreter was.

After that I did not pursue the question of their misdeeds, but I asked the Saheb-e-Ekhtiyar to instruct his private secretary to show me the petition, which was in his keeping. He told me to request it from Mirza ʿAli Khan, his secretary. I duly made the request but I observed that he prevaricated for several days and didn't want to show it to me, so I dropped the matter.

After we had finished work on Lotfabad, we returned to Kalaat. Kalaat-e-Naderi is famous as a natural fortress, surrounded by hills. It is as though millions of years of rain have washed around the mountain creating a kind of wall. Millions of years of combined rainfall and water from far-off springs have divided the mountain into two parts, creating two gateways, both of which Nader Shah greatly strengthened. Above the gates he made a bridge and on top of the bridge a guard-house. In the old days there were no rapid-firing guns, battering rams or heavy-calibre artillery, and the citadel could be defended for a long time against 50,000–60,000 soldiers. These gates are known as the Nafteh Gate and the Khorasan Gate, in the case of the former because there are so many oil wells there that oil can clearly be seen lying on the ground. Of the buildings built by Nader Shah, only one dome remains, the bottom of which lies four or five metres below the level of the ground. They used to say that after his return from India, Nader Shah left all the treasure which he had brought from India there but if so, the treasure has disappeared.

All the food available was grown locally, both cereals and summer crops. The water, however, was so contaminated with oil that although the local inhabitants drank it, we couldn't. Consequently, water was brought from mountain springs for us to drink. The principal crop there is rice, but since the water used to remain standing in their fields for a long time, it created germs, which were unfortunately malaria ones. Since most of the population thus suffer from malaria, there are not many inhabitants and there is a high mortality rate. All over Khorasan, there is a saying that if you want to die, go to Kalaat! The local brigade commander used to say that of every brigade sent there as a garrison, if there were 500 soldiers on arrival, on their return to base 200 of them would be sick and dying. Indeed when the Russian delegation to the commission sent a doctor there to report on the state of health there, after examining the situation he told the Saheb-e-Ekhtiyar that the latter's first humanitarian duty there should be to forbid the cultivation of rice and to replace it with wheat, barley and other cereals.

When we were at Kalaat, the local governor died. He had a son called Yanktush Khan, who was seventeen or eighteen years old. This young gentleman had travelled with his father to Mashhad, where he had picked up some expressions from 'modernisers' such as 'civilisation', 'civilised', 'education' and 'progress of the country'. From them he had heard that people in Mashhad regretted that Iran was not making 'progress' and they were asking why. Because of our proximity in age, I being the youngest member of the delegation, he used to spend a lot of time with me. He used to make great play with the above words. I saw that as the poets say, he had 'sniffed the smell of the tavern without tasting the wine' and his ears had picked up words like 'civilisation' without understanding them. I told him in forceful terms everything that the Russian doctor had said. I then told the Saheb-e-Ekhtiyar that according to our government's instructions issued to this young man,[20] all the local governors had to do what he told them. So the Saheb-e-Ekhtiyar made him write out that at the next sowing season, in order to eradicate malaria, the local farmers should sow half the rice-growing fields with another crop, either wheat or only as much rice as they needed for their own consumption, but not for sale.

Unfortunately during the few days we were carrying out our investigations in and around Kalaat, our chief doctor contracted a severe case of malaria and died. Then it was the turn of our Cossacks and our Quchan cavalry escort to contract the disease. We had no doctor and no medicines. God was merciful in that the Russian doctor was still there and he helped as much as he could. His posting had come to an end, however, and he had to return home, so he summoned me to the bedside of a patient who had collapsed and gave me all his supplies of sulphate of magnesium and quinine, saying that he would send more medicine as soon as he reached the Russian camp. He said that there were weighing scales in a suitcase and other medical supplies in a suitcase belonging to the deceased chief doctor. He told me to get this equipment out and demonstrated it to me. Then he said that if a patient was young and strong, as soon as he fell ill I was to give him five *mesqal*s[21] of sulphate of magnesium. As soon as his stomach was clear, I was to give three quinine pills every four hours. However I was not to count the time the patient was sleeping, which meant that I was to give him three quinine pills a day. As to those who were weak, thin or not very strong, I was to give them four *mesqal*s of sulphate of magnesium and two pills. I should also telegraph to Tehran to send a doctor. After his departure, I did as he had instructed and became known as the 'Hakimbashi' or 'Chief Doctor' and was nicknamed Mirza Reza Khan 'Hakimbashi'.

Since our mission lasted more than four years, we used Quchan as winter quarters twice. On each occasion things happened to me which I must mention. The first was as follows: in all Khorasan and the surrounding area a certain

---

20 Acting as his father's successor.

21 A *mesqal* (*mithqal*), a measure generally used to weigh valuable materials such as saffron, jewellery and gold, was the approximate equivalent of 4.7 grams.

faqir[22] by the name of Faqir Mohammad ʻAli had been well-known for some years among the Turkomans as having gone into seclusion in the area. He had made two underground rooms on one side of a garden, neither of which had even a vent through which he could breathe. Only the first one had steps down to it, from which light penetrated the underground room. The second only had an air vent for the stove but this gave no light. Very little fresh air reached the room. Faqir Mohammad ʻAli had lived for some years in the second underground chamber, in which absolute darkness reigned. His servant lived in the first chamber, looking after him and taking him food. They had stopped light entering the second chamber by placing a rough curtain over the door. The people of the area believed in this *faqir*, especially the women, who if they were ill or did not have children, sought a remedy from him and took him offerings. They would say that from the time that this man had withdrawn from the world and given up the pleasures of the world, and shut his eyes to waterfalls, flowers and beauty, he saw the whole world from there and, if he wanted to, wherever you asked him about, he could describe what was going on there.

I asked Amir Hossein Khan Shojaʻ-od-Dowleh, where this man was from and what he thought of him. He said that the man was originally from Quchan, and his father was a hat-maker. 'When I first became governor, having succeeded my father in the post, a religious scholar stirred up the people against me. This *faqir* had a rifle, and he was an unusually good shot with it. Before he went to his shop, he would go out hunting and he never returned with empty hands. Because of his courage the rebels chose him as their leader. They clashed with my men over a period of several weeks, but in the end the rebels were either killed or they surrendered. But since the *faqir*, Mohammad ʻAli, had caused me a great deal of trouble, he dared not surrender but fled, living for some time from what he shot in the mountains. In the end he came down from the mountains while I was away on one of my journeys to Tehran, which lasted a year, and he built the two underground rooms in this same garden, which belonged to his father. He abandoned the world and became an ascetic. When I returned, I saw that he wouldn't cause me any further trouble and changed my mind about him. I have not been to see him myself, but I have

22 An ascetic or holy man.

sent some of my servants, who tell strange and wonderful things about him. Now his garden has become a place of pilgrimage for the villagers.' I asked the Shoja'-od-Dowleh whether I might go and see this person. He said that he himself had no objection but people said that in order to gain access to the second underground chamber, one had to obtain permission to enter from the man himself. I said that it would be easy to obtain this permission from him and I would do so.

The next day, accompanied by 'Asgar Beg and three Iranian Cossacks, I mounted my horse and rode over there. The garden gate was open and from a distance one could see a kind of curtain on the stairs leading down into the cellar, obviously to prevent rain and snow going down the stairs. There had been a lot of snow in the night and the weather was so cold that my hands were frozen and my tongue was so frozen that I couldn't speak. At the sound of the horses' hooves, the *faqir*'s servant appeared from underground. As I was dying of cold, I dismounted so as to go underground. The servant stopped me, saying that I had to get the permission of the *faqir*. He would not allow me to go down the stairs. Then I began to assert myself. I told the Cossacks to grab hold of this rude fellow, which they did, and I then went downstairs.

As there was no door from the stairs to the chambers and I thought that perhaps the second underground chamber would be warm, I pulled back the rough curtain and entered. What did I see? Pitch darkness darker than any night. I called out a greeting but heard no reply. I was able to feel that there was no carpet on the floor but that boards had been laid on the ground. As I couldn't see in front of me, I sat down cross-legged. The *faqir* remained completely silent, so I said to him: 'O Faqir, I have come on a pilgrimage to you in this cold weather. Why do you receive me in this way?' In a weak voice, the *faqir* asked me what my nationality and religion was. I said that I was from the same nationality as himself and was a Muslim. He said that he wanted to ask me a question: in what religion was it permissible to enter a house without the permission of the owner? I had said that I was a Muslim and had certainly read the Qur'an. God particularly commanded that one should not enter a house without the owner's permission. To whom did this garden belong? Who had made the underground chambers? He said that he was the owner, for a long time ago he had chosen this dark corner as his abode, so as not to have to look on the faces of despots and oppressors like me.

When he said this, my sense of justice made me realise that he was right and I could make no reply to this. Instead, I said: 'O honoured Faqir, I see that you are an educated man and so you have certainly heard the proverb: "Necessity forgives what is forbidden." I was dying of cold. If it had been summer or spring, I would have been very happy to sit in this garden and wait for your permission. I was thinking that if I asked for permission and you didn't grant it, I would freeze to death from cold up there. This was why I said that it was better to enter without permission, for it was necessity which made me enter by force.' He remained silent for a moment and then gently asked me why I had come to Quchan. I replied that I had come to delineate the borders between Khorasan and the Akhal. He said that for *faqir*s like him my kind of work was of no importance. They did not believe in borders or frontiers but believed that the whole world belonged to the whole human race.

I saw that he was beginning to get into politics. I didn't want to have this kind of conversation or indeed to have any kind of disagreement with him. Since the underground chamber was very dark and the air foul and heavy, I wanted to ask him one question and then leave. So I said to him: 'O Faqir, now that you have kindly agreed to talk to me, I want to ask you a question: all Quchan says that as a result of your strict asceticism you have discovered the power to see the whole world and that when you concentrate, everything takes concrete form in your eyes.' With a great deal of humility he said: 'I too have heard that they say this but one shouldn't believe everything one hears.' I saw that he was not seriously denying that he had these powers, so I said: 'Faqir, only God knows whether I will come back here or not. Please now turn your gaze to St Petersburg.' He asked what I wanted there. I asked him to look and see in what street the Iranian Embassy was situated. He said that in the middle of a very wide street there was slightly narrower street, roughly in the middle of which the Iranian Embassy was situated and it had three floors. I asked him to look carefully and tell me what was opposite the Embassy. He said that there was a house, also with three floors, of which the windows were smaller than those of the Embassy. I said: 'No, Faqir, listen carefully! Opposite the Embassy there is a Turkish bath.' He said, however, that the Embassy was situated four or five houses away from the bath.

I saw that he was making things up and that he hadn't actually seen the place, because that same year, after the coronation of Tsar Alexander III, we had gone on a tour of St Petersburg with the ʿAlaʾ-os-Saltaneh. Afterwards, the Nazem-od-Dowleh, our minister there, invited us to lunch. A building constructed in what I thought resembled the Arab architectural style and the Alhambra, with a tower, an awning and Turkish bath stood in front of the Embassy. Consequently, I thought that the *faqir* was talking nonsense and that I was wasting my time, so I got up and returned to the Shojaʿ-od-Dowleh's residence. They were waiting for lunch and both the Saheb-e-Ekhtiyar, the Shojaʿ-od-Dowleh and the members of the delegation all asked me what I had seen. I said that he was not uneducated and had a semblance of education but what he had said about St Petersburg was completely untrue.

Now, some years after my posting to the Boundary Commission, I was appointed counsellor at the Iranian Embassy in St Petersburg and left Tehran. The late ʿAlaʾ-ol-Molk had sent Mirza Ishaq Khan, the First Secretary, to the station with his own carriage to meet me and we returned to the Embassy in it together. As soon as we reached the Turkish bath, I saw that the carriage didn't stop but continued on its way. I asked Mirza Ishaq Khan where we were going, as the Embassy was here. He replied that I had forgotten: we still had four houses to go before the Embassy. Then I remembered my meeting with the *faqir*, Mohammad ʿAli. I was so ashamed of having called him uneducated and ignorant that if it had been possible I would have leapt up from there and gone straight to Quchan to apologise to him. In this world there are secrets which only scholars of mysticism have even guessed at. To some observers, there exists in man a power which can be strengthened 'mystically' by ascetic practices and which gives man the power to do remarkable things.

The other noteworthy event to happen to me at this time was the following: since each member of the boundary commission was given lodging in the house of a local merchant, I lodged in the house of a *seyyed* who was highly respected as one of the town's great men, a man of letters and a poet, whose brother was a Bojnord merchant of good standing. My stay, which lasted three weeks due to the severe weather, in the house of this hospitable man, Mirza ʿAskari, was very enjoyable. However, one day I was given news of an extraordinary event: the leading religious scholar and Friday Imam[23] of the town

---

23 Government appointment as the senior cleric in a town who spoke from the pulpit on Fridays.

had cursed me, calling me an infidel, and declared that it was a religious duty to kill me. One of those who attended the meetings of the Friday Imam had immediately reported this to my host, so that the latter should expel me from his house. Before giving me this news, my host started speaking as follows: 'I have unpleasant news for you, but before giving you details, I want to reassure you that there is no need to worry, because I have found a timely solution to the problem. Someone has shown your *Roshdiyyeh* treatise on changing the alphabet to the Friday Imam and asked for the issue of a *fatwa* condemning a person who wishes to change the Qur'an into European letters, as some of Arabic letters, such as strong *h, 'ein, t, z* and *s* can't be properly enunciated using the European alphabet. In fact he wants to oblige all the Muslims in the world, both Sunnis and Shi'a, to change the Word of God.' It was clear what the contents of the *fatwa* would be: it would be as I had been warned. Luckily the *Roshdiyyeh* treatise was in my suitcase, so I took it out and read the following passage to him: 'I submit that my purpose is not forcibly to transform the Islamic alphabet into another script: my fundamental objective is that all letters of the alphabet should be written separately and that vowels should be inserted between consonants, the lack of which has caused many disadvantages for us and has held us back. That is all I have to say.'

When Mirza 'Askari had read the treatise, he said that I had greatly clarified matters. He hadn't known the details but he had now worked out my reasons and he was sure that the book would be valuable. He said that I should send out and purchase four sugar-loaves, two pounds of tea, one bag of henna, one bag of dye and five *sirs*[24] of Kerman cumin. He then placed all these on a tray, which he covered with a cloth, and he wrote the following letter, which he gave to me and of which I copied out in my own hand: 'Muslims, since I have long heard of that world-famous *Hojjat-ol-Islam*'s[25] reputation for piety, I had long hoped to be honoured by being admitted to his lofty presence and being able to kiss his feet. By good fortune I am in Quchan for a few days. I humbly request that tomorrow, before the devotees of the blessed threshold are present, you give this humble servant permission to be admitted to your holy presence. I would like to submit a few words to your eminence without

---

24 A traditional measure of weight approximately equal to 75 grams.
25 Mid-ranking Shi'a religious scholar.

anyone else being present. Thus I hope that your holiness will not stint in your kindness. I will also offer a small present to your devotees, so you may divide it among them. Your hopeful and devoted servant, Reza.' I gave the letter and the tray to my host's servant who, accompanied by my servant, took it to the great man. They brought the following reply: 'With God Almighty's permission, your letter has arrived. As you have requested, come tomorrow after the dawn prayer and I will see you!'

The next day at the appointed hour, after the great man had finished his prayers and was sitting on his prayer rug saying his supplementary prayers, I went to call on him. I greeted him respectfully and he gave me permission to sit in front of him, so I sat down very politely and kissed his knee. He was aged between sixty and seventy, thin, with a full hennaed beard, and his clothes were immaculately clean. He had a large white turban on his head and as he had spent some time in Najaf, he had an Arab accent, albeit an attractive one. After repeating what I had written in my petition, I said that since I was afraid that the many pilgrims would enter his presence and interrupt us, I requested permission to bring the subject of my request to his attention. I said that I knew a learned man called Mirza Reza Khan who had spent some time in Istanbul and Cairo. He had recently written and had published a treatise on simplifying the alphabet. As most of the people of Europe wanted to learn Persian and to become acquainted with the Word of God, indeed even to learn about the truths of Islam and to accept Islam, Mirza Reza Khan had invented an alphabet in European script, for he wanted to write some introductory books in Persian in the European alphabet, thus providing an easy means for Europeans to learn the language. Since I had heard that people had misrepresented this matter in his blessed presence, I had brought with me the treatise which he had written in order to show the truthfulness of what I was saying. I humbly requested him to look at the passage at the end of the treatise written by Mirza Reza Khan. When he had read this part of the treatise, he cried out: 'Praise be to God, I take refuge in God, they never described the matter to me in this way.' When I saw that he agreed with me, I showed him the whole alphabet, which he read carefully. I then asked what conceivable objection there could be to our writing the Divan of Hafez or the *Golestan* of Sa'adi in this script and teaching them to Europeans. He said that he could see no objection to it nor was it in any way contrary to religion or custom.

I was then emboldened to say that I was Mirza Reza Khan, the writer of the treatise and the unfortunate individual whom he had condemned to death the previous day. I then recited to him the following verse from Hafez:

We did not come to this door seeking dignity and status;
Rather we have come to take refuge from ill-fortune.

I then said that obviously if I left his presence with the threat of the previous day's *fatwa* hanging over me, I wouldn't get out alive unless he gave me a written safeguard in his own divinely-blessed handwriting. He then called for a servant, paper and a pen-case and wrote: 'As I have now read in the *Roshdiyyeh* treatise, this alphabet which Mirza Reza Khan has written and in which he has suggested that the rudiments of the Persian language should be written, is in no way contrary to the light-giving Shari'a. Mirza Reza Khan is a religious and god-fearing man and I wish him all success.' He signed and stamped this letter, which I put in my clothing. I then kissed his knee again and left. Haji Mirza 'Askari was waiting for me at home to hear the result of my meeting. When he had read the great man's handwriting, instead of throwing me out of his house, he wrote a *qasidah*[26] about me which was printed fifty years ago in *Danesh's Selection*.[27]

At lunchtime the Shoja'-od-Dowleh's servant came to invite all the members of the delegation as his guests for lunch and I was included. The Saheb-e-Ekhtiyar was sitting in the most important place with the Shoja'-od-Dowleh. In addition to the members of the commission, several local khans and members of our host's family were present. Since I knew that those friends who had stirred up the people of Lotfabad against me were present, when the Saheb-e-Ekhtiyar asked where I had been and what I had been doing, I took out the Friday Imam's letter and showed it to him, saying that I had been defending myself against the evil actions of false friends. I then read the letter out from beginning to end, but stopped at that: I did not wish to search any further for

26 Originally an Arabic elegiac poem which typically ran for more than fifty verses, later adapted by Persian poets to articulate philosophical, theological and religious themes.
27 A compendium of poems selected by Mirza Reza Khan and published in French in Istanbul in 1891 and in Russian in Tiflis in 1893.

the culprits. Slander is of course not a good thing, but I said to myself that they had already been punished enough. As I have written, Mirza ʿAli Ashraf Khan of the Qaradagh,[28] who was a straight and sincere man, came to my house after we had left the Shojaʿ-od-Dowleh and said: 'Reza, I am completely amazed by what you have done. You are not like us. Where did you learn your cleverness?' I replied: 'Colonel, if you had been the object of envy and the victim of a sentence of death, as I have been, you would have acted more cleverly than me. The best form of self-education is dire necessity.'

One day, while we were talking, the Shojaʿ-od-Dowleh told us the following story: in Quchan there was a small village called Khakestar, whose inhabitants lived to more than a hundred years old. Their teeth remained in good condition and their beards didn't turn white until they were eighty years old. In Tehran, the Mesbah-ol-Molk had told me that if I saw extraordinary things on my travels, I was to note them down and on my return report them to him. He would pass them on to the Minister of Foreign Affairs, who would relay them to the Shah, for the Shah liked to hear this kind of thing. So I asked the Shojaʿ-od-Dowleh how far Khakestar was from Quchan. He said that if someone started early in the morning, he could eat lunch there and return to Quchan by evening. I asked him to provide a good horseman to escort me there, so that I could enquire on behalf of Tehran how the local population lived.

The village of Khakestar has a spring in the middle of it, and it is surrounded by hills, while there is a real mountain about a thousand metres high in the form of a sugar loaf on one side of it. A Quchan horseman took us to the house of the village headman. The walls of all the houses there were made of mud, while the roofs were sometimes made of wood and sometimes of reeds. The headman was very hospitable. He ordered fresh bread to be made for us, a lamb was killed and they started to prepare our lunch. The villagers had gathered round us to see the spectacle. I noticed that the headman and most of the villagers were old. I asked their age in order to note it in my journal, but they didn't know their age. The headman said that he was ninety-five and described the others as between eighty and a hundred. He said that as I could see, eighty families lived there. Their farms produced just enough food for them but not enough for even one more family to live there, so as soon as the young grew up

---

28 The military member of the Iranian delegation to the Boundary Commission.

and married they had to emigrate from the village. Consequently, most of the inhabitants of Shirvan, Quchan and the neighbouring areas were the children of people who had left Khakestar.

I asked them about their food. They replied that in times of prosperity, when the harvest was good, they ate wheat bread, with milk and cheese and yoghourt. As I would see, they didn't have any fruit gardens there, so when they took a sheep to Shirvan or Quchan to sell, they would buy clothes and fruit, which they would bring back with them. When they ate meat, it was when a sheep or goat from the flock had fallen on the mountain and broken its leg. In years when the wheat harvest was poor, they would eat barley bread. Their whole subsistence depended on their livestock, cattle, sheep and goats. They sold the wool and when they needed clothes or dishes, they sold from their flocks in proportion to their needs.

I asked them whether when they fell sick they had a doctor. They replied that they never became seriously ill, and anyway they were their own doctors. Every time one of them had a cold or a stomach ache, they treated him with watered yoghourt. In cases of stomach pain, they placed the sick person in a piece of woollen cloth and bound the four corners to poplar trees, which grew in great numbers on the banks of the river, with rope in a kind of cradle. They then gave as much watered yoghourt as possible to the patient and shook the cradle hard, so that the patient vomited so much that he regurgitated whatever he had in his stomach. As for the patient with a cold, either a stomach cold or a head cold, they put him in bed and two strong young men would massage him in turn so that he sweated. They would then cover him with several quilts. When he had slept for a time and woken up again, he would be entirely cured. I asked them how many people died a year. They said that two people had died that year and this was because they had fallen on the mountain. After having gathered this information, I said goodbye to my hospitable host and returned to Quchan, where I reported to my friends.

In the summer of that year, because of the exceptional heat, we went to a place called Firouzeh, the Quchan hill-station, which had good spring water flowing from the Killab mountains. Firouzeh had many gardens with excellent fruit, but not many inhabitants, who just planted their crops there. A strange thing happened here which I must mention. As I wrote at the beginning of this journal, at the time when our delegation reached Mashhad, the Prince

Rokn-od-Dowleh, who was Naser-od-Din Shah's brother and the Saheb-e Ekhtiyar's son-in-law, was the governor of Khorasan. Our salaries were transferred to him and because of his relationship with the Saheb-e-Ekhtiyar, he ensured that our salaries were paid on the first of every month, wherever we were. A year later he was recalled to Tehran and he was replaced by the late Nasir-od-Dowleh, who was given the title of the Asaf-od-Dowleh.

Malicious people pretending to be his friends had written to the Asaf-od-Dowleh that the Saheb-e-Ekhtiyar was intriguing against him with the governors of Quchan, Bojnourd, Darrehgaz and Kalaat. He had, they alleged, persuaded the governors to criticise the Asaf-od-Dowleh to Tehran so that the latter would be recalled and the Rokn-od-Dowleh should once again be sent to take his place as governor. Unfortunately, when this letter reached the Asaf-od-Dowleh, he believed it and gave orders that the delegation's salaries should no longer be sent on to us. He said: 'Let them go and get their salaries from Tehran! This is not the right place for them.' Our salaries didn't arrive for several months, and so everything we had was either sold or pawned. We were in a desperate situation.

On a Wednesday morning at the end of the month of Safar, Mirza 'Ali Ashraf Khan's servant came and invited me and the other members of the delegation to lunch on behalf of his master. Since I knew how bad his financial situation was, I wondered how he had the means to host such a meal. The other members of the commission were equally surprised by this invitation. When we arrived, we saw the colonel, who was an amusing character and loved a joke, sitting on a chair smoking a water-pipe. He said: 'Friends, I know that you are all surprised that in our poverty-stricken state I have been able to invite you to lunch. Before you ask, I will give you a reply. Before I was appointed to the delegation, I was sent on a mission to Sanandaj. The governor of Kurdistan, who was a generous man, gave me a very fine Kurdish horse-rug as a present. Since I had nothing else to sell or pawn, yesterday I sent my groom to Ashkabad to sell it. He did so and bought today's lunch with the proceeds. In addition to something to eat before lunch, I was only able to buy meat soup with yoghourt, bread, cheese, and I have picked some pennyroyal mint from this riverbank, the like of which cannot even be found in paradise. That is all we have, so we must make do with little, as the *dervish* does.' The guests sat down and everyone started to talk. One said: 'Today we will enjoy our lunch with the colonel, but what will happen to us tomorrow? An intelligent man must always think of his future,' a sentiment with which we all agreed.

Consequently, we agreed that after lunch the assembled company would write a petition clearly setting out our catastrophic situation. Each person would then describe his own indigent state in his own handwriting in the margin and sign it. The same evening the petition would be sent by hand of one of the servants directly to the Asaf-od-Dowleh in Mashhad. After lunch, Mirza 'Ali Khan, who was of course the nephew of Mirza Sa'id Khan, the Minister of Foreign Affairs, who had a fine, cursive hand, wrote the petition out beautifully and in well-chosen phrases. Everyone else wrote in the margin as agreed. Since I was the junior member of the delegation, they gave me the petition last to finish. I who had never composed a word of poetry in my life was so overcome with distress that the following lines came to my mind and I wrote them down:

I am penniless. What a surprise in this world!
Although it is now the month of Safar,[29] my profession is fasting;
In the hope that at least one day's expenses may be covered,
Today I have sold the boots on my feet.

Mirza Mohammad 'Ali Khan's groom then took the petition to the holy city of Mashhad. A few days later, he returned accompanied by other riders, who had brought our unpaid salaries, including our salaries for the current month of Safar. The groom reported that when he arrived in Mashhad he had been summoned to the governor-general's presence. The Asaf-od-Dowleh was sitting with the chief financial officer of the shrine, the head of the telegraph office and a number of other important officials of the holy city of Mashhad. The Asaf-od-Dowleh asked the groom who this Reza Khan who had signed the petition was. The latter replied that he didn't know him but he was said to have come from Europe and to be an interpreter. Then the Asaf-od-Dowleh read out my poem in a loud voice to the assembled gathering. He then said: 'This person has described financial misery in an incomparable way. A man has to be really miserably poor to have to sell the boots from his feet in order

---

29 Arabic month which follows that of Ramadan, the month of fasting.

to provide his evening meal. It would be unjust to make such people wait.' That very hour he gave orders that our salaries should be sent off and that in future they should be paid on time, as had previously been the case. When my travelling companions heard this description from the groom, with one voice they proclaimed: 'You are really the greatest of Iranian poets: with one verse you have rescued us.' One even said that nobody should be surprised if the title 'King of Poets' was actually given to me.

The following winter, as we had reached a point near the frontier at Bojnourd, we were ordered to go and spend a month in that town. The Sahham-od-Dowleh was from Bojnourd, where all the inhabitants are, like the people of Quchan, of Kurdish background. Although they have no experience of anywhere else, either in Iran or in Europe, nature has, in my view, endowed them with good taste. They borrow ideas from foreign photograph albums and illustrated newspapers and their fine houses are very clean, both inside and out. Their gardens are all planted with flowers. Outside Bojnourd, they had made a very wide street, with water channels on each side and trees such as planes and poplars had been planted on each side of the channels. At the end of the street, they had made a spacious park with a lake and a fountain; when it was working, jets of water could be seen from the street. It was really very magnificent.

The Sahham-od-Dowleh himself, who was also the chief of the Kurdish Shadlou tribe, was always talking of progress and renewal. I encouraged him to visit Europe, as this would greatly help the country to make progress. He had provided lodging for me in the house of his steward, so that I should be completely comfortable. I gave him a copy of my alphabet and explained it to him, for his knowledge of Persian was good.[30] He had three sons, the oldest from his first wife and the other two from other wives. Since he had learnt from history that in the age of Cyrus and Darius, the Iranians had taught three things to their sons, to ride, to shoot straight and to tell the truth, now that the gun had replaced the bow, the Sahham-od-Dowleh sent his sons hunting every fine day and the head groom was instructed to teach them riding skills and to ride up and down hill at a gallop. Although their young age did not require this, they were also taught how to shoot. According to the customs of Iran's

---

30 Despite his first language being Kurdish.

great men, a boy who has not reached the age of twenty years doesn't have the right to sit down in front of his father and only has the right to ask questions or reply when strictly necessary, so I asked the Sahham-od-Dowleh whether he had instructed his sons in the third of these Iranian customs, telling the truth. He laughed and said that he entrusted the duty to teach them never to tell a lie to their mothers.

There I witnessed the following astonishing scene: the Sahham-od-Dowleh's teeth were giving him pain, so at great expense he had sent to Ashkabad for an Armenian dentist, who was staying at his residence when I was there. One day I came out of the house and saw the steward sitting outside in front of the flower beds. The dentist had pulled fifteen sound teeth from his mouth and was continuing to pull them out. The steward was one of those burly, strong Kurds who only once cried out while this was going on. I just couldn't watch this and so I said to the dentist: 'Stop! Tell me what is going on!' He said that the Sahham-od-Dowleh's teeth were so rotten that they couldn't be treated. The dentist had suggested to the latter that he should pull out all his teeth and replace them with a set of false ones, which would make him comfortable. The Sahham-od-Dowleh, however, wouldn't believe that he could eat with artificial teeth. So he called his steward, and told the dentist to pull his teeth, all of which were sound, and make artificial teeth for him. If the steward could eat, then the dentist was to pull all the Sahham-od-Dowleh's teeth and make him false teeth. I was sorry that I hadn't heard this in time. Otherwise I would have informed the Sahham-od-Dowleh that it was indeed possible to eat with false teeth. However, it was now too late, as more than half the steward's teeth were lying on the ground.

Another surprising thing which I observed took place on the day when we left Bojnourd for Gorgan. Our first stopping place was in the beautiful valley of Simlaqan, which had wonderful views and which Ferdowsi[31] called Semmanqan. I had been given lodging in the house of one of the most important local landed gentry. As a result of my acquaintanceship with the Sahham-od-Dowleh, who owned the village, a dish of rice and chicken had been prepared for my dinner. When they brought me my dinner, 'Asgar Beg came in and said that a village woman had come and entreated him to bite off a chicken

---

31 Tenth-century Persian epic poet and author of the *Shahnameh* or *Book of Kings*.

leg, eat some of the flesh, put the rest in bread and give it to her. I told him to go and ask why the woman wanted this chicken leg. The woman said that it was the custom in this valley to give the left-overs from the meal of an important person who had just arrived to any incurably ill person, who was then promptly cured. 'Asgar Beg said that since she had tearfully entreated him to give her the chicken leg, he had done so. The next day when the head of the delegation and the members were ready to leave, the local people brought in a seven year old child, together with presents of two new baskets, filled with several pieces of bread, four roast chickens, twenty boiled eggs and some pieces of cheese. They pointed me out to the child and told him to kiss my hand and to throw himself at my feet. They explained that the child had been mute from the time he was a baby and, although they had taken him everywhere and done all they could, he had remained mute. However, last night they had made him eat the chicken leg and this morning he could talk. They added that that since this child was like a slave whom I had set free, I could take him with me as my servant, or if I would leave him in their care, they would pray for me all my life.

From Simlaqan we went on to Jajrum. Since Karim-Dad Khan was the father of one of Sahham-od-Dowleh's wives and supervised all the latter's affairs, he acted as host to the Saheb-e-Ekhtiyar and the rest of us until we left Bojnourd. Karim-Dad Khan had observed the Sahham-od-Dowleh's kindness to me. In Jajrum, where the latter was also governor, he owned several houses there, so he lodged the Saheb-e-Ekhtiyar in one and allotted another to me. There he brought a boy, about five or six years old, to me and said: 'We Kurds are expert in physiognomy. I am certain that you will go exceptionally far in life. Please agree to take this son of mine, who is very intelligent, with you and treat him as your own son. His name is 'Abdol-Hussein.' I replied that I very much hoped that his knowledge of physiognomy would prove to be correct, and I happily accepted the boy as my son.

Some eight years later, I became minister plenipotentiary in St Petersburg. One day, a servant came in and said that a tribesman, accompanied by a child, wished to see me. When they came in, I saw that it was Karim-Dad Khan and his son, 'Abdol-Hossein Khan. I asked them to sit down. The father did so, but he had told his son not to sit in my presence. I saw that the boy was frightened by the embassy and the servant, so I asked the latter to bring a chair. I told him to sit down, which he did after politely declining to do so many times. Karim-Dad Khan said that of course I hadn't forgotten his prophecy and my promise. He had brought my son to hand over to me and I could do what I wanted with him. I thanked him and asked him what he wanted for the boy. In what field should I educate him? He replied that as I had no doubt observed, the Sahham-od-Dowleh's sons were learning to ride and his son had ridden with them. His son had now learnt to ride and he wanted him to follow in his father's footsteps. Through the minister of foreign affairs I asked His Majesty the Tsar to place him in the principal cavalry school known as the Nikolai Cavalry School. My request was granted, he duly entered the above-mentioned school and in the end he became Iran's Court Minister.[32]

At this point I should mention the following story: In the hijra year 1307, 1928 according to the solar calendar, I was recalled to Tehran from the League of Nations. By this time, the minister of court had chosen the family name Teimurtash and royal favour had brought him to the peak of his career. Indeed it can be said that this man was the most important man at court. The whole of my time in Tehran, he showed me filial respect. He never failed to show me the appropriate regard and he never took precedence over me in any official or unofficial party in an Embassy or a minister's house, although he insisted on his own seniority over all ministers. He made me very pleased with his behaviour in every way. Indeed, without my prior knowledge he had even proposed to his Imperial Majesty that rather than becoming a senator, I should become prime minister. One day, he invited me to call on him officially at court and communicated to me His Imperial Majesty's command in this respect. I respectfully declined but asked him to convey my humble thanks to His Imperial Majesty, saying that after seven years at the League of Nations I was tired and asking his permission to return to Monaco to take some rest. Although the minister of court continued to press me, I continued to make the same reply. Since he saw that I had taken a firm decision, he informed His Majesty of this and the latter conferred on me the Order of Homayoun (First Class) with the sash in reward for my faithful service at the League of Nations.

---

32 As 'Abdol-Hossein Teimurtash served under Reza Shah Pahlavi, who later imprisoned him and had him murdered.

Three months before the end of our mission, the Saheb-e-Ekhtiyar, who was tired by the continual travelling involved, fell ill and was unable to continue on the road. He obtained permission to go to Mashhad and after treatment to leave for Tehran. With Tehran's permission, he appointed me as his representative. As we had finished placing the frontier flags, the Russian and Iranian surveyors only had to make new maps of the frontier and have them signed by officials of both delegations. It was agreed that this should be a joint effort, but since the necessary equipment wasn't available on the spot, we went to Ashkabad and prepared the maps there. On behalf of the Saheb-e-Ekhtiyar, together with Brigadier Mirza Mohammad 'Ali Khan, Colonel Mirza 'Ali Ashraf Khan on the one hand and Guzmin Karayev and his surveyors on the other we first signed all the new maps, consisting of about twelve large pages. Then, to celebrate this occasion, General Komarov gave a magnificent dinner in honour of the two delegations. After dinner, speeches were of course made in honour of the illustrious monarchs of Iran and Russia by the Saheb-e-Ekhtiyar, Komarov and Guzmin Karayev.

I set out for Tehran by way of Semnan and Damghan with an escort of twenty-five Iranian Cossacks under the command of Yavar 'Ali Khan, the delegation's Cossack commander. On the day before Nowruz, half way between Semnan and Bojnourd, we were approaching a large village at about sunset when we were stopped by a villager who told us not to enter it because the villagers had risen up against the local governor: they had shut themselves up in the citadel, had gone up on to the fortifications and had sworn not to allow anyone coming from Bojnourd to enter. If we approached the citadel, they would shoot. I asked why they were doing this. He replied that in the past year they had paid all they possessed in taxes to the government. Now that it was the New Year, a new tax collector had arrived who wouldn't accept that they had paid their due to the previous one. The villagers had nothing left. They had therefore sworn an oath either to die or to make the government treat them justly in the future. We took the local man with us and approached the village. About 300 yards short of it, there was a garden with an open gate and a hut with a room for the gardener in it. Since it was very cold, I went in, wood was brought and a fire lit in the middle of the room. I sent the villager ahead to the village to tell the headman and the *molla*s that I hadn't come on behalf of the Sahham-od-Dowleh. He was to tell them who I was and that I had nothing to do with taxes. On the contrary, if I could help them, I would, as I had heard that they had been badly treated. It was the eve of Nowruz and neither I, my servants nor my escort had dinner to eat or a place to sleep and our horses had neither straw nor barley. If they gave us space somewhere in a corner of the village, I would pay them in advance for everything I bought and we would leave the next day. The man then went off with my message.

The villagers then appeared on the walls and on the towers, making threatening gestures at us from afar. They sent the messenger back to say that they didn't believe us and that if we approached, they would open fire. I told the messenger that this was my last word to the villagers, for we had nothing but a gardener's room in the garden where we were and we and our servants were not prepared to die of cold and hunger. He should go and tell the village elders and the *molla*s that I did not wish to use force against them. However, as they were threatening us with guns, I wished to point out that our guns had a far greater range than theirs. In order to test this, I intended to order the Cossacks to form a line. The villagers should then fire a volley at them to test their rifles. When they saw that their bullets fell short of the Cossacks, I would order the Cossacks immediately to fire a volley, aiming about a yard above the villagers' heads as they stood at the top of the towers in such a way that they should not be hit. If this lesson was not enough for them, since it was a question of life or death, I would then order the Cossacks to aim to hit them, and it would all be the fault of the village elders and the *molla*s. The messenger went off but brought no reply but the villagers didn't shoot, so I ordered the twenty-five Cossacks to line up a yard from each other and fire a volley over their heads. At the first volley the gate of the citadel opened and about a dozen elderly villagers, accompanied by their *molla*s and headman, came towards us, carrying copies of the Qur'an in their hands. They escorted me, my servants and the Cossacks into the citadel and although darkness had fallen two hours previously, they brought out a sheep which they were about to sacrifice when I told them not to. They were really very hospitable to us and our servants. In the morning we paid our bill in full in the presence of the *molla*s and headmen and promised to lodge their complaints in the appropriate place in Tehran. They all came out to see us off and we arrived in Damghan in the evening.

At about six kilometres from the town, news was brought to us that the locals had rebelled and surrounded the governor's residence and would not allow the besieged governor, his servants and a number of other people out of the building. Two days before, the governor's small son had fallen into the pool there and drowned, and they would not even allow his body to be taken to the graveyard and buried. I exclaimed: 'O God Almighty, what a time to leave Ashkabad, for wherever we go we get caught up in rebellions and trouble!' However, as the town wasn't fortified, we would probably have been able to enter the town, but we nevertheless dismounted in a garden some distance from the town and had our tents pitched there. We were able to buy whatever we needed in town. I then sent for a local man and asked him what was going on and why they had rebelled. Why had they surrounded the governor's residence? Who was the governor? He said that the governor was Anushirvan Mirza, the son of Bahman Mirza.[33] The governor had left for Tehran a month ago, leaving his deputy, his son, in charge.

Some months ago, a young Armenian merchant had come from Tehran and opened a shop, where he was selling Russian goods such as printed cotton, felt and shirt cotton. Since he sold his goods a little cheaper than the local merchants, he had taken the bread from local merchants' mouths, as both men and women went to his shop and bought from him. Recently a young Damghan woman had gone to his shop. Some of the locals had followed her and from a distance had seen the Armenian take her to a room at the back of the shop. They rushed into the shop and grabbed the woman, while the Armenian jumped off the roof into the lane and took refuge in the local governor's residence. The people took the woman away and stoned her. Now they had gathered to ask the acting governor to hand over the Armenian so that they could take him away and kill him. The government had told them to wait until two officials arrived from Tehran, one from the Russian Embassy and the other from the Ministry of Foreign Affairs, as the Armenian was a Russian citizen. If the Armenian was found guilty, then the Russian Embassy would punish him according to Russian law, as Iran did not have the right to punish foreign citizens. The locals were not satisfied by this reply and wanted a formal guilty verdict for the Armenian.

As it was night and time was short, there was nothing I could do. The following morning the prince, who had learnt of our arrival, managed to send a

---

33 A son of ʿAbbas Mirza and grandson of Fath ʿAli Shah.

servant out of the building to me with a written message in which he repeated the same version of events. He wrote that in a coded telegram his father had forbidden him to give up a Russian citizen to the mob to take away and stone. The governor had then instructed him to call on the senior *mojtahed* who had stirred up the people against the government. First, however, he was to obtain the cleric's permission for the infant's body, which remained in the governor's residence unshrouded and unburied, to be taken away and buried. If, simply because of the hostility of cloth-dealers who wished to remove a competitor to local merchants and without any kind of investigation, Iran was to impose the same fate on a Russian Armenian as had befallen the unfortunate Damghan woman, the Russian government would hold the Iranian government responsible and the whole responsibility for this would lie on the shoulders of the same *mojtahed*. His father, the governor, would arrive within the next two days and the officials responsible for investigating the matter were also on their way. When everyone had arrived, the necessary investigation would start in the presence of the *mojtahed*. If the Armenian was found guilty, officials of the two governments would be informed and he would be punished.

I wrote back to him saying that he needn't worry, as I would do what was necessary. I sent a message to the *mojtahed* by hand of the Cossacks asking when I could call on him. He immediately gave me an appointment, so I set off with an escort of three Cossacks and came on a chaotic scene: the courtyard, the street and the cleric's room were full of people, all hanging on his words. As the poet says: 'We are heart and soul slaves of the sole of your foot, and our ears are slaves of your command!'

As soon as they saw me, they left the *mojtahed* and started to make a huge uproar, as they demanded that I allow them to kill the Armenian, shouting that if an Armenian was allowed to dishonour a Muslim woman in a Muslim town, they could not bear to live any more. Two Cossacks walked in front of me and cleared a path for me to the *mojtahed*'s room, where I greeted him formally. His Holiness did not move but returned my salutation and showed me a space just large enough for one person to sit. I sat down but the level of the room was not much higher than the courtyard, which was full of people, with many directly outside the windows, and the room had only limited space, it was very crowded with people all respectfully sitting on their knees. His Holiness had a very long unlit pipe in his hand. With exaggerated courtesy he asked what commands I wished to give him. I said that I entreated him to listen to my humble requests for just two minutes. I said that of course his honoured person would well remember the last war between Iran and Russia many years ago, when despite the calls for jihad by the most eminent religious leaders, Iran had been unable to resist Russia. I did not need to describe this. The result had been that a treaty had been concluded between the two governments at Turkomanchai. One of the clauses of this treaty was that if a Russian citizen was accused of a crime in Iran, Russian and Iranian officials should jointly carry out an investigation on the spot and if he was proven guilty, responsibility for punishing the criminal would lie with the Russian government, who would punish him according to Russian law. Iran had no alternative but to comply with the terms of the treaty, because in every Russian town there were many Iranian tradesmen, merchants and labourers and if we acted in a manner contrary to the treaty, then Russia would deal with our subjects in an illegal manner.

Until this point, His Holiness listened calmly but those sitting in the room and outside were shouting: 'Why has this person come here to talk such non-sense? What is a treaty? Who has even heard of Turkomanchai? Give orders for this unclean Armenian to be handed over to us for punishment! Today is the day for Your Excellency to give the order. We are your devotees, ready to sacrifice our lives for you.' In the face of these declarations of willingness to die for him, the mood of the great man suddenly changed completely. He looked at me angrily and said: 'For three days now, government representatives have been assuring me that the Tsar's representative is coming to investigate and solve this problem. They keep assailing my ears with the name of the Tsar.' At this point he banged the mouthpiece of his pipe down on the ashtray so hard that it broke and ash scattered over the rug. He had been put in a terrible position, he said. When the people heard the great man's bold words, however, they all cried out, praised God and his prophet and implored His Holiness to do as they asked. I was lost for words and did not know what to do. I waited silently to see what would emerge from him. We sat for a time looking at each other. Then I said that if he had no more commands for me, I would humbly withdraw. He suddenly said: 'Will you smoke a water-pipe?' I saw that he had become silent and from his appearance that he slightly regretted what he had said. I replied that although I didn't smoke, with God's blessing I would gladly smoke Aqa's pipe in his honour.

After we had taken a few puffs, I from the water-pipe and he from the pipe, I suggested that now that he had smashed the head of the Tsar, he might give orders for me to be allowed to take that unfortunate child away and bury him, that the people should stop besieging the governor's house and that the governor's staff who had left the building should be able to buy what they needed from the bazaar. Either that evening or the next day, the governor and the committee of investigation would probably arrive. Then the investigation could take place in complete tranquillity in His Excellency's presence and the whole fuss would end to the greater glory of his blessed reputation. He asked what my name was and I told him that it was Mirza Reza Khan. He asked what my occupation was. I told him that I had been a religious student in Tabriz for a time and that I had studied Islamic Law and Jurisprudence under Haji Molla Ahmad Tahbaz and had been about to go to Najaf when a flood had destroyed our house and I had been obliged to become a servant. I was now the servant of the government. As soon as he heard the name of Haji Molla Ahmad and the words 'Islamic Law' and 'Jurisprudence', his expression completely changed from its previous severity. He said that he was very grateful for my visit and politely suggested that I could now go. He would try to calm the people by the evening. As I could see, it was impossible to do this now. We should then await the arrival of the government party. I expressed my fulsome gratitude but asked that two of his men should accompany me when we went to bury the body of that unfortunate child. If God Almighty permitted this, we would wait until the evening, however, by which time His Excellency would have calmed the populace.

The great man agreed. He called out and two *seyyed*s acted as my escort. Then His Holiness half got up to show his respect for me, so that the people should see that his attitude towards me had changed from the way he had looked at me when I entered. Escorted by the two *seyyed*s, I went to the governor's offices, where I saw the deputy governor and offered my condolences on the death of his son. With some members of the deputy governor's household we then took the corpse of his son to the graveyard and the boy was buried in the plot indicated to us. We then returned to town, where as the *mojtahed* had promised, he had duly calmed the populace. We were greatly relieved and set off for Tehran.

Chapter 5

Tehran in the Time of Naser-od-Din Shah, 1887

During his stay in Tehran, Mirza Reza Khan was rewarded by the Shah for his services on the Boundary Commission: he received the title of Adjutant General to the Shah, a fine military uniform and a salary of 200 tomans a year, a considerable sum. As is often the case in Iran, however, all was not as it seemed: in the dilapidated financial situation of Qajar Iran, he had to call on his protector, the Amin-os-Soltan, for help in order to receive the money to which he, more used to the European ways of Russian Tiflis, naively thought he was entitled. Furthermore, the acquisition of power and influence brings concomitant financial obligations: the need to make gifts to those further up the tree who can help a career if obliged but can ruin a man who does not understand his obligations, and to a host of hangers-on who hope to benefit from the rising star's good fortune. Having been thus stripped of every asset he had gained in Khorasan, he was reduced to pawning his last possession to pay for one night's food for himself and his horse so that he could present his petition to the Shah. The unofficial pawnbrokers were ironically the guards to the chief government accountant for Azerbaijan. The author reluctantly accepted the system, pointing out, perhaps tongue-in-cheek, that the chief extortioner in his case, Yahya Khan Moshir-od-Dowleh, then Minister of Foreign Affairs, was not independently wealthy and had many expenses. He clearly thought, however, that the latter went beyond the bounds of propriety in developing and refining a highly efficient system of extortion, dignified by the name of 'gifts'. While one may doubt whether Mirza Reza Khan spoke as frankly to his nominal chief as he claims, his revenge was sweet: many years later, his former minister's son, reduced to destitution on the death of his father, asked for his help. He says that he helped him to the best of his ability.

Although in Tehran the author was required to report to the Foreign Ministry three days a week and to the court for three days, he didn't actually have a great deal to do except make friends and contacts. He was finally appointed official host to the first Italian minister to Iran, who was due to travel to Tehran with his wife, her companion and staff, from Russia via Enzeli. The roads were almost non-existent, the conditions appalling but he admired his guests' stoicism and endurance and did his best to make their journey as comfortable as possible. Delighted when his guests liked what they saw or ate (his memory for menus eaten even fifty years before being remarkable), he was nevertheless constantly humiliated by flagrant evidence of Iran's backwardness. Having spent most of his adult life in the Russian Caucasus, it was no wonder that, although a devoted servant of the Shah, he formed a lifelong aversion to actually living in Iran, with its petty jealousies and lack of personal security, which he compared to living in 'a dark well'. He was delighted to be appointed Counsellor at the Iranian Legation in St Petersburg, where he would be further from the hothouse politics of the Iranian court.

In Tehran I rented a modest newly-built house opposite the house of *Mirza Ibrahim Mostowfi*,[1] the *Vossouq-od-Dowleh*'s father.[2] On the day of my arrival I took the maps of the new frontiers to the Saheb-e-Ekhtiyar's house. He came out, took me in his arms and repeatedly kissed me. He then took the maps and said that, having been summoned to court that day, he would personally announce my arrival to His Majesty. He invited me to lunch the next day at his house in the Sangalaj area of the city, which had both women's quarters and a reception area, both of which were large and spacious, and in the middle of which there was an ornamental pool with many flowers and plants around it.

---

1 The title 'Mostowfi' denoted that Mirza Ibrahim was a government accountant.

2 Vossouq-od-Dowleh, later a leading proponent of the Constitutional Revolution and three times prime minister, on the last occasion at the time of the abortive Anglo-Persian agreement of 1919.

His wife was a daughter of Fath 'Ali Shah. The Princess was the mother of the Saheb-e-Ekhtiyar's eldest son, Khan Baba Khan, who was the father of 'Ali Naqi Khan. The mother of Hassan Khan, however, was a temporary wife.[3] Despite the fact that they had different mothers, the brothers, the third of whom was 'Ali Khan, also the Princess's son, got on very well together. The same was true for their children and nephews. Since the Saheb-e-Ekhtiyar was by descent the chief of the Afshar tribe, he was one of Iran's most important personalities and was the object of particular attention from the Shah. When he sat in his receiving room in the afternoon, ministers, senior clerics, generals and the most important merchants all came to call on him. He was an extremely well-intentioned, patriotic, pious man and was much respected by the people. His favourite occupation, on which he spent most of his time, was falconry. He had several personal falconers, whose task was to look after the hunting falcons. The greatest mark of respect he could pay to a friend was to send him a pheasant or partridge he had hunted himself. In Iran, this kind of thing is so important that if the Saheb-e-Ekhtiyar or someone like him were to send a 100-*toman* horse as a present to a friend, it wouldn't be as highly valued as the gift of a pheasant or partridge.

Anyway, on the fifth day after my arrival, the Saheb-e-Ekhtiyar instructed me to come to his house, as we had been summoned to Sahebgharaniyeh,[4] where we were to take the maps. There we were first received by Mirza 'Ali Asghar Khan Amin-os-Soltan. After waiting there for a short time, we were invited into the Shah's presence. It was summer time and Naser-od-Din Shah was sitting on a chair at a writing table in the garden. A number of ministers, princes and court officials were standing in front of him. The Saheb-e-Ekhtiyar bowed from a distance and the Shah ordered him to approach, so he went and stood with the princes. The Shah spoke kindly to him for a few minutes. The master copies of the maps were under my arm. When the Saheb-e-Ekhtiyar was dismissed, the Shah looked at me, as I was standing about twenty paces further away than the princes, and shouted in a loud voice: 'Mirza Reza Khan, come here!' From a distance of twenty paces, after bowing three times in the manner prescribed by Mirza Sa'id Khan when I first arrived, I advanced

3 A contractual temporary marriage for a defined period, permissible for Shi'a Muslims.
4 Royal palace, then outside the city limits but now an affluent part of north Tehran.

and stood below the princes. The Shah commanded: 'Bring the maps!' I took the maps, the Shah made a sign to me and I placed them on the table. He then ordered me to take out the map of Lotfabad. I extracted the relevant map from the ten frontier maps, took it out of the fine gold compass-case in which it had been put and laid it on the table.

The Shah then called out for the *Mohandes-ol-Mamalek*, who was then a mathematics teacher at the Dar-ol-Fonoun school.[5] The latter came forward and gave the compasses to the Shah, who ordered the old map given to the Saheb-e-Ekhtiyar by the Ministry of Foreign Affairs to be brought. The Shah studied it very closely, while I showed him the relevant points. He told me to show him the old and the new frontiers. I pointed out to him the old, green line, which ran directly under the walls of the citadel of Lotfabad, and the red line which on the new map had been drawn further from the Lotfabad citadel. The Shah ordered the Mohandes-ol-Mamalek to measure the area with the compasses. He measured this with great precision and suggested to the Shah that there was a considerable difference between the green line and the red one. One *farsakh* and a half in length and half a *farsakh* in width had been added to Iranian territory beyond the green line. The Shah ordered me to take away the maps and told the Moshir-od-Dowleh to register and file them in the Ministry of Foreign Affairs. He then spoke very graciously and kindly to the Saheb-e-Ekhtiyar.

The latter then said: 'Your Majesty, may I be your sacrifice! I am now nearly eighty years old and not much time is left to me to devote to your blessed presence before leaving this world. Whatever I have received in terms of good luck, pleasure, honour and happiness has come to me from the generosity of your blessed person and the blessings of the noble saints of God. Now is not the time for me to be reticent in describing the services rendered by the servants of your government. Nor should I take credit for the services rendered by others. I swear by the earth under your foot that on this journey every achievement that has been accomplished in relation to the extension of the agricultural land belonging to the people of Lotfabad has been as a result of the honesty, expertise and loyalty to the Shah of this young man who is standing before you. I promised him that as a reward for his service you would grant

---

5 Established in 1851 by Naser-od-Din Shah's reforming minister, the Amir Kabir, the Dar-ol-Fonoun was the first polytechnic or institution of Western-style higher education in Iran.

him the position of Adjutant General to Your Majesty.' The Shah turned to *Yahya Khan Moshir-od-Dowleh*, the minister of foreign affairs, since I was on the staff of the ministry. He gave orders that the next day the order should be drafted giving me this position together with a salary of 500 *toman*s and sent to him for sealing. Then the Shah got up, dismissed us and we all withdrew.

The next day the members of the delegation went to the Saheb-e-Ekhtiyar's house to see Hassan Khan, his son, and moaned and complained, saying: 'Tell the Saheb-e-Ekhtiyar that he is eighty years old and has experienced everything that is to be experienced in the world. We also want to be eighty years old and we hope to enjoy the same experience. Why did he not say a word about the services we have rendered? Why did he talk of Mirza Reza Khan the whole time and attribute every achievement to him?'

Furthermore, for a time they also looked at me in a hostile manner. I later heard from Hassan Khan that in his reply to the gentlemen of the delegation, the Saheb-e-Ekhtiyar had reminded them that they shouldn't forget their own role in the division of the Lotfabad water, as a result of which he had almost dismissed Mirza Reza Khan. If he had done so, all the latter's services would have gone to waste and he himself would have been branded as useless in front of the Shah. After that, relations between the Saheb-e-Ekhtiyar and the members of our delegation were severed.

One day the Amin-os-Soltan invited me to his town residence and said that His Majesty had given instructions that since I had started my government service as an employee of the Ministry of Foreign Affairs and I had gained experience in Tiflis and on the Boundary Commission, it would be better for me to attend the ministry one day a week and court one day a week until a suitable post could be found for me abroad. Naturally I obeyed and, on account of my new position, I was able to form friendships with senior court officials. My expenses, however, also increased as a result.

During my travels in Khorasan, whenever we went to Quchan or Bojnourd or Darrehgaz for recreation or work, all the expenses of feeding us, our retinue and our pack animals had, in accordance with the well-known old Iranian custom of hospitality, been borne by the local governors, Amir Hossein Khan Shoja'-od-Dowleh, the Sahham-od-Dowleh and Mohammad 'Ali Khan.[6]

---

6 Governors of Quchan, Bojnourd and Darrehgaz.

Furthermore, every time we left a place, we were given a horse or a camel to carry the baggage or the kitchen tent. Consequently, after the Firouzeh disaster,[7] which I have mentioned, as a result of the generosity and hospitality of the above-mentioned governors, together with the horses which I had bought in Mashhad, I had seven horses and six camels and I also had a sum of cash in Tehran. I had found space for these with 'Ein-e 'Ali in a caravanserai but I had been thinking of selling them. However, fortunately or unfortunately, you will be able to judge which, Yahya Khan Moshir-od-Dowleh helped to relieve me of the expense of keeping these animals.

Now I think that I should say a word about the minister of foreign affairs. He was very good-looking, spoke very well and had a beautiful voice. Whenever he opened his mouth, it was as though a nightingale was singing. Anyone sitting opposite him was enchanted by his words and the manner in which they were spoken. He was about sixty years old and despite this, whenever he went on a journey to Europe, particularly on a recent journey to convey condolences to Tsar Alexander III on the murder of his father, he attracted the attentions of the ladies in every town he visited. However, he had one fault. He was very hospitable and every day his large tablecloth was spread out on the carpet in one of the ministry's rooms and lunch was prepared for forty people. Every day two or three kinds of *polow*, with a stew and five or six other dishes such as soup, mincemeat and stuffed vine leaves, rissoles full of finely-ground meat and split peas, rice pudding, halva and other things were served. Not only did everyone in the ministry from the most senior official and his deputy down to the registry clerks attend these lunches but the Moshir-od-Dowleh would also keep those who had come to call on him for lunch and would not allow them to leave. In addition to these dishes, when everyone was seated on the floor around the cloth, his head chef would come in dressed in a clean white uniform and bringing various kinds of European food such as cutlets, roast leg of lamb and other dishes which he had cooked. These he would place in front of the Moshir-od-Dowleh, who was the only person allowed to use a knife and fork. Before sitting down, everyone else had to wash their hands

---

7 A reference to the period when the new governor of Khorasan, the Asaf-od-Dowleh, stopped paying the salaries of the Iranian delegation to the Boundary Commission, reducing them to indigence (see Chapter 4).

with soap in jugs brought by the numerous servants, dry their hands on a towel and then eat with their hands. The Moshir-od-Dowleh would offer a morsel of that European food to his most favoured guests and this was the highest proof of attention he could bestow on anyone. In addition to his official wife, who was a sister of Naser-od-Din Shah, he had a young temporary wife, but out of fear of the Princess he had found her a place to live far from his residence and he spent a great deal of money on her. His fault was this: although he had to pay all these very onerous expenses, he was not wealthy and his income was insufficient to cover them, so inevitably anyone in the ministry who was sent on a mission or was promised one was obliged to pay him money through his private secretary and he extorted as much as he could from him.

I do not write these words out of a desire to find fault with this highly-respected man. My purpose in writing the story of my journey is only and I repeat only to explain the state of affairs existing at that time and to describe the morals and the attitudes prevalent in those days. This is the only reason why I am revealing so much and why I have written an eyewitness account of how Yahya Khan Moshir-od-Dowleh treated me. Since he knew that the Shah wanted to give me a post in the Ministry of Foreign Affairs and that I had no ambition for a post elsewhere, as the minister responsible he acted with me in the same manner as with others who were seeking positions. One day his principal private secretary, Mirza Asadollah Khan, wrote me a note saying that His Excellency the ʿEzzat-od-Dowleh was going to Shemiran and needed camels to carry his luggage. I was to bring my camels so that they could be loaded up there. I immediately told ʿEin ʿAli to hand over my camels to the Moshir-od-Dowleh's camel driver. That was the last I heard of my camels. One day I asked Mirza Asadollah Khan what had happened to them. He replied that it had never been agreed that the camels should be returned to me. Another day, the chief secretary wrote that the Moʿtamed-ol-Molk, the minister's son, had been summoned to the royal camp and needed a horse for his servant: I was to send one of mine, so again I immediately obeyed.

One day at lunch, he gave me a place above the other guests at the table and kindly gave me one of his cutlets on a fork. After lunch he invited me to his private office and invited me to sit in front of him, so I sat down next to his private secretary. I had a good turquoise ring on my finger. He said: 'Mirza Reza Khan, today is the birthday of a minister plenipotentiary's daughter.

Give your ring to the chief secretary so that he can send it as a birthday present from me!' Obviously, I gave it to him immediately and since I felt that my horses would shortly follow my camels, I kept two, one to ride myself and the other for my groom, and sent one as a present to the Mesbah-ol-Molk, who had taken a great deal of trouble for me on my arrival in Tehran and continued to help me. As to the other one, the chief secretary had once again demanded it on some excuse or another and had taken it away.

On the matter of the royal *farman* granting me the title of Adjutant General with a salary of 500 *toman*s, I waited and waited but there was no sign of any salary. Whenever I brought the matter up with the official accountant responsible for this kind of thing, he said: 'Wait until there is a vacancy!' I was too embarrassed to ask once again, only to be told to wait. All the money I had brought back with me was exhausted. Engineer Mirza ʿAli Ashraf Khan who had become like a brother to me, came to see me and said: 'As you know, on this journey the governors wanted to give me horses and camels, but I declined to accept them. I said that instead they should give me mules, so that I could send them to Mazanderan with the groom to buy coal, which I could then sell to help with my living expenses. On their way back from Mazanderan this time, one mule went lame and another went sick. I have to tell you that tonight the mules have neither straw nor barley.' I had a turquoise water-pipe top, which I gave to ʿAsgar Beg, who pawned it for five *toman*s, which I gave to the colonel. He asked why I was pawning a water-pipe top when I had a salary of 500 *toman*s. He thought that I was doing this on purpose so that he would never ask me for a loan. I told him that so far not one *dinar* of the 500-*toman*s had reached me and that I was pretty well in the same state as he was. I brought out the royal *farman* and showed it to him. He said: 'You poor fellow, you are naïve. You won't get any money out of this *farman*.' I asked him how that could be. He replied that it stated that I should be given 500 *toman*s from the 'vacancy'. This salary was a mirage. I asked him what 'vacancy' meant. He replied that this meant a vacancy caused by someone going missing or dying. I would not be paid until a government servant who enjoyed this 500 *toman* salary fled the country or died. He said: 'I am telling you clearly that there are so many *farman*s of this kind in the hands of people that the wretched owners give monthly sums to doctors so that when someone with a real salary is dying, the doctor informs them and the *farman* can be issued in their own

name before the other actually dies. This kind of *farman* also has its own
expenses attached to it, as the beneficiary has to give commission money to
the government accountants.'

That very same day I took the *farman* to the Saheb-e-Ekhtiyar's house. I
told him that he knew that I wasn't wealthy and had no financial resources, for
my father had lost everything he had in the flood of 1280 of the Muslim era. [8]
In Tiflis I had had a salary from the issue of passports on which I had managed
to live. Although I had given satisfaction on our journey in Khorasan and had
been given presents, the money had all been spent. I had even had to pawn
my water-pipe top for 'Ali Ashraf Khan. What would happen to me? Tehran
was a foreign town to me and no one would give me a loan. He replied: 'You
know and I don't have to repeat how much affection I have for you. I think that
tomorrow you should go to Niavaran to the house of the Amin-os-Soltan, who
is at present highly esteemed by the Shah and knows you. I have praised you
highly to him. You should submit a petition to the Shah through him, saying
that you have no financial resources and cannot wait for a place to be vacated
by a dead man or a fugitive. Neither bakers nor grocers nor fodder merchants
listen to this kind of thing. They want cash for their goods. You must act from
one direction and I will do so from another. Tomorrow or the day after tomorrow I will go and explain everything to the Shah. Don't worry! After the great
services you have rendered, you will not be allowed to fall into financial difficulties in this way.'

The next day I drafted a petition, telling 'Asgar Beg to saddle the horses for
us to go to Niavaran. He told me that the horses had had nothing to eat since
the previous day and we had absolutely no money. If we were to go to Niavaran, the horse would need barley and we couldn't stay the night in the desert:
we would need to stay in a caravanserai. I asked him how much we would
need for our journey. He said that we would need at least one *toman*. Since
there was not even a *dinar* in our purse, 'Asgar Beg said that the soldiers who
were guarding the house of Mirza Ibrahim Mostowfi took sureties and loaned
money at interest. With my permission, he should pawn something with them
in return for one *toman*. I agreed, but I had nothing else to pawn, having

---

8 There could be a mis-print here, as 1290 or 1872–3 is believed to have been the date of the
flood.

already pawned the water-pipe top. On my first Khorasan journey, however, I had bought a Turkoman rug for twenty-five *toman*s, so we pawned the rug and negotiated a ten *shahi*s a day interest rate for the *toman* we received, so one month's interest on one *toman* was fifteen *kran*. Finally we were able to go to Niavaran, where we lodged in the straw-dealers' caravanserai. We gave straw and barley to the horses, we ate bread and cheese for lunch and in the late afternoon I went to the Amin-os-Soltan's house.

When I entered the house, there were a number of men sitting around, but the Amin-os-Soltan had left for an audience with the Shah, so I waited there until he returned. I gave him the petition to the Shah in an unsealed envelope. He read this from beginning to end and said that he greatly sympathised with me. I had written a few words especially for him in the petition explaining how I had travelled from Tehran and how the guards had lent me money. He was not particularly surprised by this, but said that as I had rendered a service to the government, he would arrange my affairs. I was not to worry. Then he gathered up a few petitions from others and went to the Shah. When he returned, he had a very happy expression on his face. He gave me a *farman* from the Shah which he had written out and the Shah had signed. It read as follows: 'From the Amin-os-Soltan to *Haji Mohammad Hassan Amin-oz-Zarb*,[9] pay to Mirza Reza Khan for now the sum of 200 *toman*s in cash as a gratuity and take urgent care to pay him 200 *toman*s from the first available monies, so that he has no worries.' When the Amin-os-Soltan gave me this document, he said that a vacancy for the same sum had been found the previous evening and that the next day he would order the minister of finance to publish the *farman* concerning me.

I was so grateful to the Amin-os-Sultan that on the spot I swore that I would be his devoted and loyal servant until the end of my days. I showed the order for 200 *toman*s to 'Asgar Beg, who was overjoyed. We returned to Tehran and the next day I sent 'Asgar Beg with the draft money transfer to the Amin-oz-Zarb. After a short time 'Asgar Beg returned, accompanied by two porters.

---

9 Haji Mohammad Hassan was often called the first Iranian entrepreneur. A self-made man, he was the wealthiest and most influential merchant in the late Qajar period with interests throughout the country and abroad. The title 'Amin-oz-Zarb' means that he was also in charge of the royal mint and thus responsible for minting the coinage of the realm.

I asked what the porters were for and what they were carrying. He replied that each one was carrying 100 *toman*s of 'black money'. I asked him why he had brought black money. He replied that he had been reluctant to accept this kind of coinage but the Haji Amin-oz-Zarb's steward had said that for the past year his master had obtained a concession from the Shah that he could strike 100,000 *toman*s of 'black' coinage, so he had gone to Europe himself to purchase copper, which he had then brought back to Iran. He gave a share of the profit to the Shah and a share to ministers.[10] He himself was reaping an enormous profit from the operation. All the coins now struck were in denominations of 100 *dinar*s, 50 *dinar*s and 25 *dinar*s. The porters were paid off and the coins were brought and placed under my bed. 'Asgar Beg said that when they had reached the corner of the street, the porters had said that they hoped that there were no thieves or tricksters in the neighbourhood who might attack me in the night. It would be better to bring something with which to bundle it up or a covering, so that the coins could be concealed, and that is what 'Asgar Beg had done. The first thing we did was to give one *toman* plus two days interest to the accountant, Mirza Ibrahim Mo'tamad-os-Saltaneh's guards and recover the rug from pawn. (His title was later conferred on his son.) Some time later, the Amin-os-Sultan was as good as his word and found a 'vacancy' for my salary of 200 *toman*s. This sum in those days was the equivalent of a thousand *toman*s in today's money. I no longer had to worry about having enough money to live on and little by little I was able to socialise with and lay the foundations of friendship with members of the court and of the Ministry of Foreign Affairs.

One day, Mirza Zein-ol-'Abedin Khan, Deputy Prime Minister, who later acquired the title of the Sharif-od-Dowleh, invited me to lunch. It was a very hard winter, and that day it had also snowed heavily. In the middle of the room, a *korsi* had been placed, very clean, with a quilt and bolsters and cushions, all of them freshly cleaned. On top of the *korsi* a silk cover from Kashan had been placed. Obviously, I took off my half-boots in the corridor and sat down under one side of the *korsi*. Truly, sitting under the warm *korsi* being agreeably supported by cushions behind one was a pleasurable experience. In fact it was the first time that I had sat under a *korsi* since my days in Tabriz. In

---

10 Normal practice with concessions granted in late Qajar Iran.

addition to myself, an old mystic was sitting in the place of honour under the *korsi*. Mirza Zein-ol-'Abedin Khan introduced me to him. Then he told me the name of this highly-respected personage, who was Abu Nasr Fathollah Khan Sheibani. He introduced me as the man who with one poem had relieved the worries of an entire people. Fathollah Khan asked what country this people belonged to. I told him the story of Firouzeh and Asaf-od-Dowleh, whom he knew. Indeed, it became clear that the latter was a close friend of his. He spent some time praising his qualities and a very friendly discussion ensued. Mirza Zein-ol-'Abedin Khan said: 'with this bad weather and heavy snow, please do not go but stay the night here as my guests, so we can carry on talking!' As this was clearly a genuine invitation, we both accepted.

Sheibani was a considerable literary figure and very eloquent. He recounted the story of his life, saying that he and Soltan Morad Mirza Hesam-os-Sal-taneh had been very good friends, having often invited him to eat with him. When the latter left for the Herat war,[11] he had insisted that Sheibani should go with him as a special adviser and most of the correspondence which the Prince held with the Khans of Herat and the besieged population had been through him. Furthermore, he said, the Prince had been very kind to him and chosen him as an intimate companion. After the victory at Herat, mischief-makers wrote to Tehran saying that he wanted the Hesam-os-Saltaneh to proclaim himself Shah in Herat and appoint him prime minister. This story was completely false, for neither did the Hesam-os-Saltaneh have any such intention nor did the local population particularly want this. Furthermore, he was well aware that to become Shah was no joke and couldn't be achieved so easily. As the saying goes, there are a thousand things finer than a hair's breadth. Nevertheless these false reports were believed in Tehran. His friends and relatives in Tehran wrote to him that no one would dare to take action against the Hesam-os-Saltaneh in Tehran. The worst that could happen to his chief would be to be told to spend time under house arrest. However, they wrote, he would probably be treated differently and they would take their revenge on him, Sheibani, as they would have liked to do on the Hesam-os-Saltaneh. His friends had therefore advised him not to return to Tehran until the Hesam-os-Saltaneh had

---

11 In 1856, the Prince had captured the town for Iran before British occupation of Bushehr led to the withdrawal of Iranian forces.

done so and had managed to allay the suspicions of which he was the object. He should remain for a time in Turkestan and Afghanistan. Since he couldn't remain in Afghanistan, however, he went to Bokhara, where the language is also Persian, having heard that the Amir loved Persian literature and poetry. On the day on which the Hesam-os-Saltaneh left Herat for Tehran he left for Bokhara, where he remained until the Prince reached Tehran. The governor of Kashan plundered his Kashan property, which consisted of a few villages, and incorporated them in crown lands. The Amir of Bokhara however, had been really very kind to him: he appointed an official host for him and gave him lodgings in the precincts of the royal palace. He stayed there until the Hesam-os-Saltaneh interceded with the Shah and recalled him to Tehran. He continued: 'If you come to my house, you will see in what language my petitions to the Shah were couched, one of which was as follows:

The divine judge gave the power of judgment to the Shah,
So that he would save mortals from injustice.
If you do not dispense justice to oppressors, O earthly judge,
The heavenly judge will protect us from them.

I stayed the night there and in the morning, when I was about to say my farewells to my host and leave, Fathollah Khan Sheibani said to me: 'Of course you know that poetic talent is a gift from heaven and that it *emanates* from divine generosity. Once this light has appeared in you, it would be a pity to allow it to die. Since, to use the Persian expression, we have shared bread and cheese in one place, we must continue this hospitality. I suggest to you that for as long as you are in Tehran, whenever you have an opportunity, you must come and see me. I have a garden outside the town. It is a sad and withered garden because of the wrongs that I have suffered, but there is a stream flowing through the middle of it. On one side of it, I have pitched a modest tent. There is no one on the gate, but some days scholars and literary figures come to join me there. If it is lunch-time, according to established custom, we eat a peasant stew informally together and in the afternoons we have a glass of weak tea. Since I can see how talented you are, I would like to teach you about prosody, rhyme and poetic metre. I am certain that you won't allow my teaching to go to waste.'

I accepted his invitation and, whenever I had an opportunity, I used to visit him, sometimes for lunch and sometimes simply to drink tea. As he had promised, he taught me this strange and wonderful art. One day I saw seven books written in his own handwriting. They were very well-written and they had very poetic titles. He showed me these one by one and expressed his regret that as all his possessions had been stolen, he couldn't afford to have them printed, so they would all be lost on his death. I could feel the old mystic's heartache. There and then I swore to my God that in so far as he gave me the power, I would not allow him to take this sorrow to the grave with him. I would have his works published. During the first year of my time as consul-general in the Caucasus, therefore, I wrote to Tehran and he sent me a selection of all his writings, which I had printed and bound in his name in Istanbul, and sent back a thousand copies to him.

Let us return to my days in Tehran! One day, Mirza Asadollah Khan, the private secretary to Yahya Khan Moshir-od-Dowleh, invited me to the latter's house. He said: 'His Excellency wishes to be kind to you because of your presents to him. An Italian minister plenipotentiary is coming to Tehran. Since this is the first time that an emissary has come from that country, in accordance with usual custom it has been decided that he, his staff and servants will be official guests of the government until they reach Tehran. In view of the inadequacy of the roads and the poor facilities for hosting these people on the way, it will be a very demanding job. However, Mirza Reza Khan Mo'ayyed-os-Saltaneh, the official host to the first German embassy, acquitted himself well of his responsibilities and so was made minister plenipotentiary in Berlin. If you perform your duties well and the Italian minister is pleased with you, it may be that you could become minister plenipotentiary at the Italian court.' I said that of course I would do my best. He continued that the court would provide all the travel equipment such as tents, camp beds, cutlery and china, chairs and tables, together with servants and cooks. An annex to the royal *farman* would be sent to the governors of Qazvin, Rasht and Enzeli ordering them to provide me with whatever was needed to entertain this guest. As they had promised, everything was provided from the royal stores.

The private secretary said that 200 *toman*s had been allotted for my personal expenses, but that I would have to give half of this as a gift to his master. I accepted but the money was paid to me by money transfer which only arrived as I was leaving, so that I didn't have an opportunity to make the required gift. One of the secretary's men brought me a note stating that at Rasht I should obtain for His Excellency an embroidered carpet cover consisting of a side piece and a head piece and specifying the precise dimensions and colour required.

It was winter time and in those days there were no paved roads between Qazvin and Rasht. We had to travel down from the summit of the Elborz mountains and the roads were very bad. Sometimes we even had to dismount and travel on foot. After many tribulations we reached Gavdam, where we spent the night. There were also a few other travellers from Europe and Qazvin there. We were about ten people to spend the night at that altitude. Never mind about beds! There was not even enough bedding to cover us. The travellers had placed their suitcases under their heads and lain down. A little after midnight we heard a great commotion in the courtyard of the post-house and the sound of several shots being fired. Then the assistant courier opened the door with a lamp in his hand. He said that thanks to him we had just escaped great danger and promptly asked for a reward. I asked him what had happened. He said that a huge leopard had come down from the mountains. As the door had been left open, the servants realised that it was about to come upstairs. He saw the leopard first, so he shouted out and roused the other couriers from their beds. The leopard had then taken fright and fled. We saw that he was standing there, clearly wanting a tip as a reward for his service to us, and wouldn't leave until he received something, so we all gave him as much as we could, he said a prayer and left. When we got back to Tehran, however, we heard a completely different story: a European who had been present had spread it about in Tehran that at Gavdam he had been attacked by a huge leopard, at which he had fired a few shots, wounding the leopard, so that its wounds had started to bleed and it had taken refuge in the mountains.

When we reached Rasht, I met the local governor, the son of the Rokn-od-Dowleh, Naser-od-Din Shah's brother, to whom I showed the annex to the royal *farman* and the minister's order. He summoned a local notable and gave orders for the minister plenipotentiary and his travelling companions to stay at his residence for two days before resuming their journey. He ordered his coach to Pirehbazaar to transport the minister and his wife and he also gave written orders for the deputy governor at Enzeli to carry out Tehran's programme for an appropriate official reception and to furnish the rooms of the governor's official residence for the guests.

The deputy governor had really done his best to furnish the rooms and provide bedclothes. The menu for the guests' meals had also been given in advance to the government cook. I slept in a room allotted to me in the governor's residence. Since it was winter-time, the ship was a day late in arriving, as it had had to remain at sea off Astara.[12] My orders were that when the minister plenipotentiary stepped ashore from the royal launch which had carried him from the Russian ship to Enzeli, a guard of honour of twenty-five soldiers under the command of a senior officer should salute him on shore and a salvo of eleven artillery rounds was to be fired from the arsenal in his honour. Consequently, I asked the deputy governor whether everything was ready. He replied that everything would be ready and that I should relax. I insisted that everything must be ready. Once again he told me to relax, as everything would be ready: the appropriate orders had been given. The next day I stood waiting on the shore, but there was no sign of either soldiers or of any senior officer. The deputy governor was with me, and the more I urgently reminded him of this, the more he repeated that the soldiers would come. The minister plenipotentiary arrived and still there was no sign of the guard of honour. Instead of eleven guns only three fired their salvo and then fell silent. Very embarrassed, I greeted the minister and took him to the governor's residence, where chairs and tables to receive guests had been set out in exemplary fashion in the upstairs reception room and cakes and sweet things were offered to the guests.

First, I asked the deputy governor why there had been no guard of honour and only three rounds fired by the artillery. He replied that the truth of the matter was that the soldiers had indeed turned up as ordered but that neither their uniforms nor their rifles were up to standard for them to parade. It had therefore been decided that it would be better for the guard of honour to be absent rather than to show the minister the men's torn uniforms, old caps and shoes, with each one of them dressed in a different colour. It would have been the ultimate disgrace for the government. As for the artillery, as I was aware, there was no ammunition and no gunpowder in the arsenal at Enzeli nor was

---

12 An Iranian town on the Caspian Sea border then with the Russian Empire, now with independent Azerbaijan.

there any gunpowder manufacturer there. Gunpowder had been ordered from Rasht a week ago. That morning just enough gunpowder had arrived for three rounds.

The Italian minister made no comment on the hospitality he had received at the governor's residence but his deputy did ask me why there had been no guard of honour when the minister had stepped onto Iranian soil and why a salvo from three guns had been fired. I replied that as he was aware, we didn't have railways or steamships yet and, as he would see the next day, he would travel to Pirehbazaar and Enzeli in a wooden boat or as he would call it a 'lighter'. Unfortunately on the day when the boats should have brought the guard of honour to Enzeli, the rough sea which had delayed the guests by a day had been the reason for the absence of the guard of honour. As to the salvo, unfortunately the gunner had not understood his commander's orders and had thought that he was to simply fire a salvo of three rounds. No doubt from politeness, he said nothing but from his expression it was clear that he didn't believe my excuses. He had no doubt often read about the state of Iran's infantry and artillery in the newspapers and so he understood that my conduct didn't stem from carelessness or lack of respect. He said nothing and the minister also remained silent.

The next day we boarded the royal lighter and progressed as far as the depth of the lagoon allowed. When the water became too shallow, however, for us to go any further, anchor was cast. Numerous rowing boats lined with fine rugs were waiting there to transport us to Pirehbazaar, but since they couldn't row all the way to Pirehbazaar from there, ten boatmen dragged each boat along with a rope, singing out 'O Mohammad! O ʿAli!' as they pulled, to the great pleasure of our guests, for whom this was a completely novel experience. As, the boats pulled them along in the fresh, pleasant air, it must have been an entirely different experience for them to being shut up in a train.

The names of the guests were as follows: Count Donato, Minister Plenipotentiary and Countess Donato; Mademoiselle Bari, the Countess' companion; a first secretary, a second secretary and the military attaché, together with an Italian servant. As I had understood from foreign embassies in Tehran, this minister was close to the court: the father of the present King of Italy, Victor Emmanuel, had had a liaison with one of the Queen's ladies-in-waiting, who was herself from an Italian noble family, and when she gave birth to the fruit of their love, the Count, the king gave her in marriage to one of his courtiers. The young man was given the title of Count Donato, which means 'Given by God'. Both he and his wife were congenial companions and very kind-hearted. Anyone who travelled in those days between Pirehbazaar and Qazvin in winter with snow, ice and ankle-deep mud, knows how difficult the journey is, particularly for Europeans and their wives. Indeed it is truly unbearable for European women. As I shall mention, despite the hardships of the road, I heard not one word of complaint from these people. They never ever moaned about their lot, which was indeed an arduous one. On the contrary, wherever they went and whatever they saw, they would say how happy they were to see new things in their lives.

Anyway, in Pirehbazaar, the Prince Governor had sent officials to greet them, together with his personal carriage for the minister and his wife, as well as carriages loaned by the wealthier local inhabitants for other members of the embassy and myself. After a reception lasting an hour drinking tea and eating cakes in Haji Mir Qasem's upstairs rooms, we got into the carriages and set off. There was so much mud, however, that the horses had great difficulty in moving. Because of the delay, we arrived a little late in Rasht, it was night time and as the welcoming party had been waiting for a long time, they had all gone home, leaving an orderly to tell us that we should alight at the house of one of the local Rasht notables, a fine newly-built house in the middle of a garden full of different kinds of citrus trees. The entrance was made of brick covered with new and very fine turquoise-coloured tiles. When one entered the house, instead of a corridor in front of one, there was a fine gallery, the south side of which was completely covered in glass, which they called a greenhouse. All along the gallery, flower pots full of winter flowers had been placed between the windows and the walls and there were some orange, tangerine and lemon trees laden with fruit, all worthy of paradise. Three steps led from the gallery up to the main room, with a very long corridor on each side, onto which other rooms opened rather like in a European hotel. All these rooms were placed at our disposal and we all moved into our rooms in considerable comfort.

A hearty supper was then served in the dining-room, which was even furnished with tables and chairs. On the table, in addition to meat soup and stuffed vine-leaves, a vegetable omelette, meat-balls and rice, there was pheasant and several large dishes of *polow* and seven kinds of Gilani stew. To drink, we had watered butter curds and several kinds of orange and pomegranate juice sherbet. Our dear guests, who had never seen this kind of spread before, took one or two mouthfuls of each dish to try them and were so pleased that they kept on praising the food and expressing their gratitude for the opportunity to travel to Iran, all of which was a cause of great satisfaction and honour to me. However, one thing which greatly worried me was what they would say about the journey which was about to take place. It was planned that we should stay two nights in Rasht, so the guests spent the next day bathing in a leisurely fashion, as the owner of the house had had a very clean bathhouse installed with two marble baths, one for hot and the other for cold water, the latter having continuously running water.

As far as Qazvin, the governor had provided us with an official escort, who was to arrange our staging posts, provide horses and mules to carry us and our luggage, and buy the food needed for the kitchen. The upstairs rooms of the Gavdam post-house had been made ready for us to spend the night and staff from Tehran prepared our supper. We stayed the night there and on the next day, we sent the carriages back, for they had saddled up horses for us. When we mounted our horses, the minister's wife, who had ridden in Rome and had brought a lady's saddle with her, was very grateful for an opportunity to ride. Her companion, however, who was a pretty young girl of twenty-two, had never ridden in her life. When, faced with a horse, she saw that she had to ride like a man on an Iranian saddle, she burst into tears and protested loudly to the Countess, asking to be sent home. Very gently the minister and his wife entreated her to mount her horse. The Countess even got off her horse to help her. With one of the grooms, they got her onto the horse and put the bridle in his hands. The Countess told her always to ride immediately behind her horse: there was no need to be afraid. In this way, they managed to convince her and off we set.

Our first night's stop was at Rudbar, where we stayed at the post-house and where the governor's chief *farrash*[13] had furnished rooms for us with beds but no bedclothes. Our second night's staging post was at Manjil and the third at Pachenar, from where we had to climb up to the pass at the summit of the mountain. There it really was hell for the Countess's poor companion.

---

13 A senior attendant generally in charge of household furnishings

At every step the poor girl would fall off her horse. We had to get two villagers, one to hold one knee and the other one the other. Since she was a modest
young lady, she was in tears, saying that it was not necessary for them to hold
her knees: they should just hold her feet.

Finally, after many trials and tribulations we reached the head of the pass.
After the problems we had experienced in climbing as far as this, we had lunch
there and a short rest, after which we once again mounted our horses, but we
couldn't reach Qazvin that day. About a *farsakh* from the town, there was a
fine caravanserai with good upstairs rooms, where we stayed the night. In the
evening, we sent one of the villagers to announce our arrival to the Saʿad-os-
Saltaneh, maternal uncle of the Great Atabak,[14] who was the governor of the
town. The next morning at about ten o'clock we reached Qazvin. On behalf of
the governor, the deputy governor, the governor's chief *farrash* and the local
mayor came out to welcome us and escorted us with great marks of respect to
the post-house, which the Saʿad-os-Saltaneh had just had built. The rooms had
been furnished with fine carpets and the walls draped with Kashmir shawls
and fine printed cloth. It was really very splendid and we spent the night there.

Our host invited us to stay two nights there as his guests. The next day
the Italian minister said that he would like to go and see the Friday Mosque,
but the local religious leaders had indicated to me that Europeans were not
allowed to enter it. However, as the Saʿad-os-Saltaneh had paid an official call
on the minister, the minister wished to pay his return call on the governor, and
as the Saʿad-os-Saltaneh's residence was in a Safavid building, the minister
very much wanted to see this.

At the appointed time, the servants arrived and led the way, as the minister
wanted to walk there. We set off with his staff and when we reached the door
of the residence, we could see that there was a tower next to the wall around
this building. The minister wanted to climb up the tower to look at the view
from the top, but suddenly the governor's chief *farrash* gesticulated that he
must not be allowed to do so. Before I had time to ask him why, the minister
had started to climb to the top of the tower with his staff following behind
him. He came down again very quickly crying out: 'Don't come up! Go back!'
The minister said to me that it would not be a good idea for anyone to go up

---

14 Another title of the Amin-os-Soltan was the Great Atabak.

the tower. I did go up, however, and there I saw that the guards had defecated and the foul smell was unbearable. Embarrassment was piled on my previous embarrassment at Enzeli and I didn't know how to look the minister in the face. As it was summer, when we reached the courtyard, the Saʿad-os-Saltaneh had arranged the reception there and it was really the most superb reception. After having seen so much filth, however, the minister wouldn't touch a thing. Whenever food was brought to him, he said: 'No, thank you!' The Saʿad-os-Saltaneh asked me in Persian whether the minister was fasting or whether he was angry, since he wasn't drinking anything and had eaten no fruit. I replied that it would be better to leave him to recover and that I would tell him the reason later.

A few minutes later, the Saʿad-os-Saltaneh came to my room and asked what had been the cause of this unpleasant incident. When I explained the cause to him, he was very embarrassed. He said that as I knew, he had only been governor for a few months and he had been so busy building the splendid post-house that he hadn't had the time to look into other matters. He would give orders that very day for the tower to be cleaned and for the necessary facilities to be provided for the guards, whom he would forbid to climb the tower. The Saʿad-os-Saltaneh spoke very sincerely, but unfortunately his words were not enough to take away the foul smell from the minister's nose. Nevertheless from Qazvin to Tehran the roads were straight, the post-houses newly-built and good rooms had been prepared in the places where our guests had to spend the night. The Saʿad-os-Saltaneh had also provided good car-riages for them, but as we reached the Tehran gate, a crowd of some 200 people, mostly *seyyed*s and beggars, threw themselves in front of the carriages carrying the minister and his staff and demanded money. The chief *farrash* and his men then behaved disgracefully by beating these men around the head and face with staves. We got away from them in some ignominy. We didn't know, however, that worse ignominy was yet to come.

We had sent on the kitchen tent ahead with the steward to Yeng-e-Imam with instructions to prepare dinner and rooms for the minister and his trav-elling companions. We reached our destination at about sunset. Chairs and tables, cutlery and china had been set out, and as soon as we sat down to dinner, the soup was brought. However, when he had taken just one mouth-ful, the minister let out a cry: 'Don't touch it! I have been poisoned.' I took a spoonful to see what was wrong and immediately had a burning pain in the stomach. I ordered the head cook to be summoned, but was told that he was too drunk to be brought in. His assistant was summoned. The latter explained that they had been given supplies of alcoholic drinks in Tehran, not all of which had been drunk: one bottle of brandy remained. The cook had said that as we were due to reach Tehran on the morrow, he had no intention of handing this over to the royal pantry. He would drink it. The head cook had a full mustard tin in his hand, which he had then poured into the soup. When the guests heard this story and realised that they hadn't been poisoned, we asked for the other dishes to be brought in. Everything they brought in, however, was burnt to a cinder and inedible. The food had been completely ruined, so we had to resort to the post-house food. We waited and waited until they had cooked some eggs and grilled some chicken kebabs, which they brought in and served to the guests, who had to be content with what was provided.

Next morning, when the carriages were ready and we were about to set off, the cook, who was by now sober and who knew what punishment awaited him in Tehran, suddenly appeared with a rope round his neck. Quick as lightening, he threw himself at the feet of the minister's wife and tied one end of the rope to the lady's foot. He cried out: 'Noble lady, either pardon me or hand me over to have my head cut off here and now! Let the lady deign to notice what misfortunes have befallen me and what indignities I have had to endure!' The lady asked me what he was saying and what had happened. I said: 'As the cook's behaviour last night was unpardonable, he knows that he will be seriously punished in Tehran. He has therefore bound his future to your foot and he is asking you either to promise that you will intercede for him in Tehran or, if you wish to mount and ride away, he will refuse to untie the rope from his neck and he will suffocate.' The Countess, who had never seen anything like this in her life and hadn't read in any book that someone could come and tie himself to her foot, started to laugh from pure astonishment and said that she promised that she would entreat the authorities not to harm him. Immediately, he untied the rope from his own neck and the Countess' foot, threw himself on the ground before her and embraced the ground under her feet. We then set off.

We had lunch in Shahabad and arrived in Tehran in the evening. The governor of Tehran had sent a delegation to greet us accompanied by representatives from the German Embassy, which had been responsible for Italian interests until then. They had rented a house for the Italian minister near the German embassy, where they went and made themselves at home. It wasn't a bad house either, with good rooms and a pool. Before I went to my own house to relax, the minister said to me: 'On this journey, I have seen how much trouble you have taken for us and I will never forget it. I will inform His Majesty the Shah and my own government. I have, however, heard that according to Iranian court custom, when a foreign government appoints a minister for the first time, on the same day but just before such a minister or ambassador is received in audience by the Shah, he is sent a horse with a golden halter from the government stables. I have also heard that for some time the Shah's master of the horse has been in the habit of changing this for a silver gilt one. Please ensure that he does not do this in my case.' I promised to put in a word in the appropriate quarter.

I went home and saw that one of the minister, the Moshir-od-Dowleh's secretaries was waiting for me. He said that the chief secretary had sent him to recover the 100 *toman*s I owed. In place of the 100 *toman*s, I handed over the receipt for the eighty *toman*s I had spent on the embroidery he had asked me to buy for him, I gave him twenty *toman*s in cash and I also gave him the rug-covers, which he took away with him. The same evening when I went to the minister's house to make my report on recent events, I saw that the Moshir-od-Dowleh was somewhat preoccupied. When he said goodbye to me, he behaved in a rather discourteous manner, so I went to see the chief secretary. He asked what I had done to offend the minister, who had been so kind to me. I asked him what I had done. He asked me why I had sent the receipt for the present I had given him and why I had accounted for it as part of a debt. I replied: 'Sir, you gave me 200 *toman*s, telling me that half of this was the minister's and half for me. You told me what the minister wanted, and of my 100 *toman*s only seven or eight remains, as I spent it all on the journey. In Rasht I even bought an embroidered table cloth and gave it as a present to the Italian minister's wife and I also bought a few small flower embroideries to present to my friends.' He replied that he didn't want the money for himself but that he thought it would be in my interest to send the remaining eighty *toman*s the next day. I said that if I had been able to, I would certainly have done so. I asked him, however, to tell his master the whole story, for I simply didn't have eighty *toman*s to hand over. He said that he would tell him, as I wished. There was no pecuniary advantage in it for him.

Very angry, I returned to the house. Indeed, I was so upset that I couldn't sleep all night. The next day the chief secretary's man again came and asked to see me. He said that he had told the story to the minister, who was angry and said that he now regretted being so kind to such a low-class individual, the son of a cloth merchant. He had asked the minister how the matter could be resolved and the latter had replied that I must provide the money from whatever source I could lay my hands on and send it to him. Since I could see that the chief secretary was secretly unhappy with this behaviour but had been forced to speak in these terms, I asked him to promise that he would convey my words to the minister. I then spoke as follows: 'When he says that I am a low-class individual and that my father was a cloth merchant, I will refrain from saying who his grandfather was, for he knows better than me. He should be ashamed. My grandfather, however, was Mirza Ibrahim, minister to the Khan of Erivan,[15] and the whole world knows that. His Excellency should be afraid lest I remember this day when his son the Mo'tamed-ol-Molk stands humbly before me and I make the son pay for his father's unpleasant behaviour. However, he shouldn't worry: I am not a low-class person like him. I will help his son as much as I can.' On that note, I left.

After this incident, I didn't go to the Ministry of Foreign Affairs again but I continued to go to court on the three days a week ordered by the Shah until the day when the minister had to send his chief secretary himself to my house and ask me politely to go to the ministry. The 'Ala'-ol-Molk[16] had sent a telegram to the ministry saying: 'When I was consul-general in Tiflis, my secretary and translator was Mirza Reza Khan, who was an industrious and competent young man. Please send him as Counsellor to St Petersburg.' Before the telegram reached the minister himself, the telegram had had its effect, for the Shah issued an order that I should be sent to St Petersburg and this was communicated to Yahya Khan. Consequently, he was very gracious and kind when I went to see him and paid me many compliments. He said that my letters of appointment were ready and I was to leave as soon as possible.

---

15 Before the Russian takeover of the Caucasus in 1828, after the Treaty of Turkomanchai.

16 The 'Ala'-ol-Molk was now minister plenipotentiary in St Petersburg.

He needed a few things in Astrakhan such as some silver writing instruments, which I was to buy and send to him. I thanked him very much. Of course I bought everything he wanted in Astrakhan and sent them back to him.

Many years later, I was recalled from the embassy in St Petersburg to Tehran and was given lodgings in the little palace with a bathhouse in the late Amin-os-Soltan's park.[17] The latter lived in a town house but sometimes in the evening he would come to the park and sit in the large hall there. Ministers, leading religious scholars, nobles and wealthy men would come to call on him and he would receive them. One day a servant came and said that the Atabak wanted to see me. I went to the big house, where I saw a young man who kept bowing to me from a distance. Surprised, I stopped and asked the servant who he was and why he was doing this. He replied that the young man was the Mo'tamed-ol-Molk, Yahya Khan Moshir-od-Dowleh's son. His father had died heavily in debt some time ago, all his possessions had been sold and the son was destitute. He had submitted a petition to the Atabak asking for some kind of arrangement to pay him a living allowance. The boy was now waiting for me so that I should intercede for him with the Atabak. When I heard these words, I felt genuinely sorry for him, for I had seen the splendid style in which he had lived in the days of his father. I called him over, he came up to me and I took him up to the great hall to see the Atabak and I showed him a place to sit. Some time later the Atabak had said goodbye to his guests one by one and it had been arranged that he would have dinner in my house. He made a sign to me asking why the Mo'tamed-ol-Molk didn't leave. Then he realised that it was I who had brought the young man and had shown him where he should sit. I said that of course he knew this young man, the Mo'tamed-ol-Molk. After the death of his father, his fate was a pitiful one. He had submitted a petition to His Excellency and asked me to intercede on his behalf. My humble request was that the Atabak might bestow on him the same kindness he had shown me. The Atabak agreed and in our presence he summoned one of his secretaries whom he instructed to draw up a list of the Mo'tamed-ol-Molk's requests and

---

17 After the Amin-os-Soltan's assassination in 1907, the Atabak's Park, as it was known, was bought by Arbab Jamshid, the leader of the Zoroastrian community, and was later used to house Morgan Shuster, the American financial adviser, who was brought in to reform Iran's finances in 1911.

give it to him for use when he was next received by the Shah. He then said some kind words to the young man and dismissed him.

Since on the whole I hadn't really enjoyed my stay in Tehran, on the day when I went to say goodbye to Sheibani, he asked me, on the occasion of my departure from Tehran, to write a few words of poetry describing my experiences in that tumultuous town as a souvenir for him. On the spot I recited the following:

On the day when I leave to see the object of my desires,
I will load my horse for the journey from Tehran;
I shall be as relieved of all worry and pain,
As Bizhan escaping from the king of Turan's dark well![18]

---

18 In Ferdowsi's *Shahnameh* or *Book of Kings*, the Iranian national epic poem, composed in the late tenth and early eleventh century, Bijhan, is an Iranian hero who falls in love with Manizheh, the daughter of Afrasiab, the King of Turan's daughter, Iran's hereditary enemy. He is imprisoned in a dark cave and is eventually released by Rostam.

Chapter 6

My Time as Counsellor in St Petersburg and my Journey to Europe as a Member of Naser-od-Din Shah's Entourage on his Third Journey to Europe (1887–1889)

Mirza Reza Khan arrived as counsellor at the Embassy in St Petersburg in 1887 to serve under the Iranian minister, the 'Ala'-ol-Molk, his former chief in Tiflis. His real opportunity for advancement occurs, however, when in 1889 he is chosen as interpreter to the Shah on the latter's third journey to Europe. This lasted four months and included a month-long visit to Britain planned, so the courtiers said, to secure commercial concessions for British interests. Interestingly, Tsar Alexander III, influenced by the reports of his aggressive minister in Tehran, Prince Dolgorukov, was reluctant to receive the Shah on his passage through Russia and the atmosphere of the visit there was cold. For the Russians the Shah and his prime minister, the Amin-os-Soltan, were too close to Sir Henry Drummond-Wolff, the British minister: in January 1889 they had signed an agreement with Britain for the long-desired opening of the Karoun River to foreign traffic, designed to increase British trade penetration of the country, and a concession to open the Imperial Bank of Persia, with a monopoly to print Iranian bank-notes. More concessions were to follow the visit to Britain.

The author's delight at his good fortune is unabashed: all favour flows from the monarch, and he will have continuous, direct access to him throughout the tour. The great opportunities thus presented for advancement were counterbalanced, once again, by the jealousy of courtiers and particularly of the household eunuchs, who on two occasions almost succeeded in having him cast into outer darkness. He describes in detail the occasionally absurd but always menacing jockeying for position around the Shah and the perennial uncertainty surrounding the position of a rising star at court. In addition to his interpreting duties, he was entrusted with the social education of the Shah's favourite, Malijak,[1] a teenage boy of humble Kurdish origin whom the Shah treated almost as his own son; he demonstrated his financial trustworthiness to his sovereign, gained a reputation as a poet and advised the Shah on how to behave with European ladies. The Shah even appears to have believed that Mirza Reza Khan had hypnotic powers over the Princess of Wales. He describes in lyrical terms the splendour of parties given in the Shah's honour, his enchantment with the Scottish landscape and, a recurring theme, the visible charms of Western ladies. However, it is his description of Naser-od-Din Shah's personal interests and foibles which particularly stands out: the Shah's fascination with Western technical devices, such as the camera, the gramophone and the machine gun; his weariness with the burdens of kingship, which made him long to roam the streets of Warsaw incognito to see how ordinary people lived; his dislike of the Scottish kilt; his fury at being ridiculed in the French press; his pride in Iran's tribal cavalry and his consequent interest in the manoeuvres of the Austrian Hussar regiments; his fascination with the love-life of Louis XIV, as recounted to him by the author; and his purchase from Istanbul of a Circassian girl to minister to the royal desires while on tour.

When at the end of his European tour, the Shah crossed the Iranian frontier, the fragility of the author's position was brought home to him: after the glory of being intimately associated with the monarch for months, for just a moment a chasm opened up before his feet: it seemed that he had been forgotten and that without money, without position and without horse or escort, he would have to fend for himself on the long journey to Tehran. Happily, aided by his customary presence of mind, he was summoned to the presence and royal favour once again shone on him.

---

1 Known as 'Malijak-e-Dovvom' or 'Malijak the Second', whose father 'Malijak' or 'Little Sparrow' had been the royal favourite in the 1860s. They were respectively the brother and nephew of the Amin-e-Aqdas, the Shah's influential wife, who used the relationship to strengthen her hold over the Shah.

When I arrived in St Petersburg, in addition to the reception rooms at the embassy and the 'Ala'-ol-Molk's private apartments, there were two rooms for members of staff: Mirza Ishaq Khan, the first secretary, had one and I was given the other. The door to Ishaq Khan's room led off mine. He had been living there for a number of years. He was a very polite and well-mannered person, who had got to know all the great families, and he played *Vingt-et-Un*, the card game, very well indeed. Every evening he was invited out to dinner and soirées which lasted until two or three o'clock in the morning, and when he passed through my room on his way to bed, he woke me up. When I left Tehran, the Russian minister plenipotentiary there was Prince Dolgorukov, who wrote a letter of introduction for me to his mother the Princess, who had once been the head of the Tsarina's household and who was herself a leading member of the Russian aristocracy. She therefore introduced me to many prominent Russians. Out of courtesy, therefore, I had to call on them and they returned my calls. However, I didn't have a room in which to receive them. Although the 'Ala'-ol-Molk was kind enough to let me use the embassy drawing rooms to receive this kind of guest, this was not altogether appropriate, as either my guests arrived while the 'Ala'-ol-Molk was receiving or vice versa, and the same thing sometimes happened with Mirza Ishaq Khan. Since the embassy rooms were very large, I suggested to Mirza Ishaq Khan that we should order a folding screen made of reeds, thus dividing his room so that half of it should become his sleeping quarters and the other mine. We would make my previous bedroom, which gave on to the long embassy corridor, into our reception room and that is what we did.

Mirza Ishaq Khan introduced me to the families he knew. Since Russians in general and the people of St Petersburg in particular are very hospitable, they used to invite us to dinner and to their soirées. Since it was then the custom to pass the time playing Vingt-et-Un, and I didn't know how to play this game, I became somewhat of a burden to whoever was my host, who didn't know what to do with me, so I had to learn the game and only Mirza Ishaq Khan could teach me. In the daytime, however, he worked and in the evening he was invited out. At nine o'clock in the evening, I would come out of the minister's office and go to my room. Since the minister also played cards and went to parties, I didn't know what to do in the long St Petersburg winter nights or how and when to get up, so I slept from nine o'clock until two or three in the morning when I had just about had enough sleep, by which time Mirza Ishaq Khan would return and wake me up, but then I didn't know what to do with myself until morning. So when I saw that he had well and truly gone off to sleep, I had to wake him up, so that he should sit with me and teach me how to play the game. From then on, we used to come and go together and the problem was solved.

One day that winter, the 'Ala'-ol-Molk said: 'Let's go for a walk! We really shouldn't always stay inside. We should take some exercise.' The promenade area in St Petersburg was the 'Gostiny Dvor'. In the middle of this area lay a great caravanserai built by Peter the Great many years previously. On all four sides of it there were rooms which gave on to very long, wide corridors, so long that anyone who walked round the building once would feel quite worn-out. On both sides of the corridor there were also substantial merchants' shops where the best merchandise was on show: there were jewellery shops, silverware shops, shops selling samovars and samovar accoutrements and very fine brass dishes, shops selling felt, gold, 3,000–4,000 *manat* fur coats made of seal skin or Siberian furs, all made by first-class tailors. Then there were shops full of men's hats and women's hats and things of this kind; all lit by electric lights even brighter than daylight. In the evenings in particular, the leading families, together with their grown-up daughters, used to come to shop or just to look. These passageways had eight large doors and on each of the four sides of the old caravanserai facing the internal courtyard there was a gallery. In those days, when there were no cars, carriages and high-class cabs with fine horses would wait there for their masters or mistresses.

The late 'Ala'-ol-Molk was particularly partial to a pretty face. In one of the corridors, his eye fell on a remarkably lovely girl, to whose beauty, figure, eyes, eyebrows and curled locks no written description can do justice. She was about eighteen years old and she was walking with her mother. The 'Ala'-ol-Molk followed this moon-faced wonder for a while until they reached their carriages. Then from the bottom of his heart he let out a great sigh and exclaimed: 'If only you were here, Sa'adi, you could recite a *ghazal*[2] in

---

2 Persian ode or love poem consisting of rhyming couplets and a refrain, with each line sharing the same metre.

praise of this *houri*[3] from paradise. Now that she has gone, there is no point in remaining here. Let's go home!' This sigh from the very soul of my highly respected chief had a strange effect on me. I returned to the embassy, went to my room and composed the following *ghazal*:

In Petersburg I saw a beautiful young girl;
No finer lass have the eyes of the world beheld.

I wrote down the *ghazal*, took it to 'Ala'-ol-Molk and said: 'If you have no electric light to read this by, make do with a lamp with a wick!' I gave him the *ghazal*, which he read and liked very much. From then on, whenever he introduced me to a family, he would say that the embassy counsellor was a good poet. Indeed, he made me famous as a poet in the city, as it was the custom in Russia and indeed in Europe at that time for every young lady to have an album which she would bring out when a literary figure, poet or scholar entered their house and ask the learned guest to write some lines of poetry or prose or a thought in it. The 'Ala'-ol-Molk's introduction to these ladies therefore caused me considerable exertion. Some of my poems were later published in my book, *Perles d'Orient*.[4]

One morning, Mirza Ishaq Khan came up to me and said that he had happy news to give me. However, he would not give it to me until I gave him the sword which the Hesam-os-Saltaneh had given me in Tiflis. I asked him how he could possibly imagine that I would give him a sword which had been a gift from a very distinguished Iranian hero. He replied that I had become a military man but this sword was for a civilian and I didn't need it. It had brought me good luck and he couldn't understand why I wouldn't give it to him so that it would bring him luck too. 'Give it to me as a souvenir of our having shared lodgings!' I replied that I had no intention of leaving our lodgings so there was no need for me to make a gift as a souvenir. He said that if he had not known that I was about to leave our lodgings, he would not have made this suggestion. I lost patience and said that if I really was going to a better place,

3 The Qur'an states that a believer who goes to heaven shall be rewarded with more than one houri or beautiful girl.
4 Published in Istanbul in 1904.

then I would give him the sword. On that very day Mirza ʿAli Asghar Khan Amin-os-Soltan, the prime minister, had sent a coded telegram from Tehran to the ʿAlaʾ-ol-Molk which he showed to me. It announced that the next day His Majesty would leave Tehran on a journey to Europe with his entourage. He was instructed to send Mirza Reza Khan to Jolfa with the official Russian host as fast as possible. I was so pleased by this news that I immediately presented Mirza Ishaq Khan with the sword.

The next day, Colonel Count Keller, the Tsar's adjutant, came to the Embassy to say that the Russian minister in Tehran had telegraphed proposing that at the request of the Iranian prime minister I should be invited to go to welcome the Shah to Russian soil. Admiral Popov, the inventor of the icebreaker, who had the title of General Adjutant and was close to the imperial court, had been appointed official host. He, Count Keller, would be Popov's deputy and six senior cavalry and infantry staff officers had also been appointed as part of the welcoming party. I therefore travelled to Tiflis, from where I set off for Russian Jolfa, which we reached a day before the arrival of the Shah's cavalcade. I duly crossed over to Iranian Jolfa, where most of the princes and Tabriz notables were staying in the passport building or the customs-house.

The Shah arrived the next day in great pomp. After a night's rest, the official hosts announced that the Tsar had ordered them to convey his invitation to His Imperial Majesty and to accompany him to St Petersburg. Horses with gold and silver bridles and saddles, ridden by grooms from the imperial stables, arrived to carry the admiral and his companions from the river-bank to the Shah's tent, which was sewn with pearls, on the Iranian side of the river. An Arab horse with a gold saddle and harness, not quite as elaborate as the admiral's, had been provided for me, so I mounted in great state and rode with the others. The official hosts entered the tent to make their welcoming speeches, His Imperial Majesty said some kind words to them and then the cavalcade set off towards the river. Happily, the Russians had learnt from the experience of the Shah's second journey to Europe, when the boat had been swept away by the current, and this time they took every precaution. His Majesty and his entourage crossed the river comfortably and safely and from Jolfa to Tiflis nothing out of the ordinary happened. The Shah was received everywhere with great respect and suitable welcoming ceremonies took place all the way to Tiflis.

As consul-general, the 'Ala'-os-Saltaneh went out to welcome His Majesty a day's journey from Tiflis with the members of his staff. Dondukov-Korsakov,[5] who at that time had gone on a tour of inspection of the provinces of the Caucasus, went to be received in audience by His Majesty to Akhstafa, at that time the first staging-post from Tiflis. In Tiflis, elaborate preparations had been made for receiving the guests. At Akhstafa, a cavalry division had been drawn up to pay their respects to the Shah, who rested for two days in Tiflis and then travelled by train to Moscow. The 'Ala'-ol-Molk, who had come all the way from St Petersburg to Jolfa, was received in audience by His Majesty and accompanied the Shah everywhere he went.

At St Petersburg, Tsar Alexander III, together with the grand dukes, his brothers and uncles, came to the railway station to greet the Shah. A guard of honour, cavalry and Cossacks from the Imperial Guards were present. Iranian and Russian flags, rugs and golden hangings decorated the streets through which the Shah passed. On that journey, *Gholam-'Ali Khan 'Aziz-os-Soltan,*[6] who was twelve years old, was also part of the entourage. On his arrival in St Petersburg, the Shah summoned me alone for the first time and instructed me as follows: 'The 'Aziz-os-Soltan is the *Amin-e-Aqdas*'s nephew and I wish to educate him. This is why I am taking him with me while he is still young so that he can see courts and kings and learn about the world. I am entrusting him to you. Whenever we go to a reception, you must take him with you and find a place for him. Explain to him how to go into society and greet people appropriately. If he is happy, I shall be happy.' From that moment on, the 'Aziz-os-Soltan's head tutor, who accompanied him everywhere, became my deadly enemy.

As the Shah had become rather tired on the journey, he asked to stay ten days in Warsaw, where the weather was better than in St Petersburg. At the official dinner in St Petersburg, the Tsarina Maria Feodorovna sat at the centre of the table. On her right was the Shah and on her left sat the Grand Duke Vladimir. The Tsar sat at the top of the table. He would walk behind the Tsarina, the Shah and the Grand Duke and would occasionally approach the

5 Prince Alexander Mikhailovich Dondukov-Korsakov, a distinguished cavalry general and hero of the Russo-Turkish War who became governor-general of the Caucasus (1882–90).
6 Otherwise known as Malijak the Second, as described in the introduction to this chapter.

Shah and speak to him. I stood behind the Shah and translated for him. Sometimes the Tsar would ask about the weather in Tehran and about the beauty of the royal palace there. He said that people had particularly praised the Hall of Mirrors there, which was like nowhere else in the world. On the day after the dinner, the Shah left for Warsaw and the Tsar and the Grand Duke said their official farewells at the railway station.

General Gorkov, who had won victories in the recent Russo-Turkish War, was the governor-general of Warsaw, that is to say he was both the military and civil governor. He welcomed the Shah in a fitting manner as instructed by St Petersburg. The Shah and his entourage were lodged at the Lazienki Palace, the palace of the old Polish kings, which was situated in a large garden.[7] Enormous numbers of Poles of both sexes, gathered in front of their former kings' palace and greeted the Shah and his entourage with happy faces. As the Russians in general and Gorkov in particular had been merciless in crushing the last Polish revolt, when the Tsar and Tsarina visited Warsaw, not a single person had appeared in front of the palace to salute them. On this occasion, however, the reception accorded to the Shah on his arrival was in fact an expression of hatred for the Russians and although this was ill received by them, they could say nothing.

Up to that point of the journey, I had worn military uniform. On the second day after our arrival in Warsaw, however, His Majesty summoned me to his rooms and said to me that as his programme had been entirely official on his first two journeys and indeed until now on this his third visit, he had learnt nothing of the situation in the towns, about the people, trade or shops. He said that on this visit he would like to come with me incognito on evening excursions to see the town. He took ten imperials which were lying on the table and gave them to me, telling me to go and buy a good civilian suit for myself. He told me to wait for him at the courtyard gate after dinner that evening. He twice asked me if I had understood. I replied that I had. He called out again: 'Don't wear an Iranian hat! I will wear a Qarabagh hat.' I went and bought the clothes, including a hat which was half European and half oriental, that is to say that it didn't have a brim. At the appointed time I went and stood by the

---

7 The Lazienki Palace, built in the eighteenth century in a 76-hectare park and known in Polish as 'the Palace on the Water'.

gate. I had to tell the guard on the gate who the person going out and in was, so that they didn't stop him, but I told them on no account to salute him. At that moment, his Majesty appeared alone and came up to me. As it was summer, he was wearing a summer coat buttoned up to the collar. It showed no gold and he was wearing an unremarkable black hat like those worn in the Caucasus. He said that he wanted to see the National Park, where he understood that all Warsaw families went to walk, so I asked the passers-by where the National Park was. It seemed to me that they had recognised the Shah, for a young man stood in front of us and very politely said that he would be honoured to show us the National Park. The Shah was displeased by this. He felt that he had been recognised and insisted that I should thank the young man but say to him that he didn't want him to accompany us. A few steps later, the Shah stopped, looked round and said: 'Look! Those terrible fellows haven't given me a moment's peace for the last hour. Despite my emphatic command that no one was to follow me, once again some of them are following me.' I saw that he was very angry and dared not say a thing. When the courtiers came up to him, the Shah cursed them roundly. I don't want to mention the names he called them, but he firmly ordered them to go away. They said that they couldn't possibly leave the Shah alone, as a thousand misadventures could befall him and they would then be left without a master.

Finally, they withdrew and we entered the National Park. The Shah started walking down the central avenue looking around him. The park was full of people, including a group of very good-looking young ladies from the dance academy, accompanied by students from the military academy. Naser-od-Din Shah, who was a talented painter and was also something of a poet, was partial to a pretty face. Looking at the eighteen-year-old girls' faces, which fasci- nated him, shining like tulips under the bright lights, he asked me: 'Would they be offended if I looked at them for a long time?' I ventured that one couldn't simply stand and stare at these ladies, for they would be offended but that if one was strolling around and kept glancing at them, there was nothing wrong with that. At this moment the Shah again seemed to catch sight of his entourage and servants, as he said abruptly that we should return to the gate. He said: 'It seems that these wretches have come back to the gate and will not even allow me to go for a walk by myself for an hour.' As the Shah had guessed, two attendants were at the gate but the moment they spotted him from afar, they vanished into thin air, so we returned to the centre of the park, in the middle of which there was a square, in which people were standing around a little pool taking turns to drink water from it. The Shah instructed me to stand in the queue and give him some water, as he was thirsty. This I did, and he took the water and drank it, commenting that it was good, clean water. We were about to leave, when the Shah said: 'No, now I want to give you some water, for I am not the Shah and we are on an equal footing until we reach the Lazienki Palace.'

The Shah then said that we should go and sit on the benches near the drinking fountain and watch the passers-by, but there were no empty seats. All the park benches were very long, with room for five people to sit. People understood from the way the Shah was standing looking around him that he was an important personage. Suddenly they all got up and indicated to him a place to sit. There could no longer be any doubt that they had all recognised the Shah: everyone who passed us was looking only at him. The Shah said: 'Let's go! Clearly fate has ordained that I, unlike Shah 'Abbas or Haroun Al-Rashid,[8] can't walk around at night unrecognised or go to *dervish* gatherings and talk to them. Here come my staff, who despite my formal orders forbidding it, have followed me! Despite my having no royal insignia and wearing other clothes, the local people have all recognised me too.' Just as he had said at the drinking fountain, we were on an absolutely equal footing until we reached the gates of the palace. Instead of observing protocol, which dictated that I should walk two or three paces behind him, he ordered me to walk with him.

In the corridor I met the Sadiq-os-Saltaneh, the Master of the Royal Saddlery, who asked me to go to his room, as he wanted to talk to me. He said to me: 'Reza, you have ruined yourself.' I asked why. He said: 'From the day on which the Saheb-e-Ekhtiyar had you appointed general adjutant to His Majesty, one of the requirements for this post being that you should become part of his intimate circle, that is to say that you should have uninterrupted access to the Shah whenever you want, it was inevitable that you would excite jealousy in the royal circle. The Shah was well aware of this and when he said to the Amin-os-Sultan in their presence that you should sometimes attend

8 Celebrated early ninth-century 'Abbasid Caliph who would roam Baghdad incognito at night to find out what was happening in his capital.

the Ministry of Foreign Affairs and sometimes the court, he was trying to slightly limit the scope of these men's jealousy. You were then lucky in that you were appointed to a post in St Petersburg, so that you left court. Now from the moment we arrived in Jolfa, all the members of the inner circle, private attendants, stewards and court officials, indeed all those who have unlimited access, are following the Shah's dealings with you with a beady eye. Although I am Master of the Royal Saddlery and part of the royal circle, I know that you will never interfere with my work, so I have no reason to be jealous of you. As the Shah took you with him tonight and sent them away several times with curses, they are very jealous of you and this will certainly end badly for you. I am a humane man and I feel for you. Be very careful and don't give them a pretext to go to the Shah, speak ill of you and ruin you!' I thanked him very much and returned to my rooms.

Two days later, Gorkov invited the Shah and his entourage to visit a water purification plant, where water was purified and bacteria killed, and from which water was piped to private houses. In the afternoon, Gorkov came to the royal palace in a four-man carriage, which had been assigned to the Shah. On the right of our carriage was the 'Aziz-os-Soltan, while I sat on the left. Two young attendants sat on the box at the front of the carriage. A few moments before we were due to set off, Mirza Mohammad Khan, the 'Aziz-os-Soltan's father, came and stood in front of our carriage and harshly ordered one of the two attendants to get out. He obeyed. Mirza Mohammad Khan then got up into the carriage, grabbed my hand and said: 'Get up and sit in the servant's place! I have to sit next to my son.' At that moment the carriage started to move and I sat down. He was still standing but he held on to my hand hard to stop himself falling over. Suddenly he swore at me and said: 'I order you to get up and sit here!' I returned his curse and said to him: 'I am wearing military uniform and so you can see that I cannot sit in front. Why have you got into this carriage? You had a carriage and a place allotted to you.' He said: 'As you refuse to get up, I will go and tell the Shah, who will put you in your place.' He then jumped out of the carriage like a madman but fell over. I was afraid that he might be crushed under the hooves of the horses of the mounted Cossack escort, so I shouted out to their officer to dismount and take this madman to the Lazienki palace. He was then carried off and we went on to the water purification plant. Those travelling behind our carriage had seen what had happened and some of them didn't dare to talk to me afterwards, saying that I was a ruined man. Since I saw nothing wrong in my actions, however, I was not unduly disturbed.

As soon as we reached our apartments and the Shah and General Gorkov alighted from the carriage, Mirza Mohammad Khan threw himself on the ground in front of the Shah. He had rehearsed this little drama and he had undone the buttons of his waistcoat, torn the collar of his shirt open down to his chest, and was shrieking and crying out and tearing his hair, saying: 'Let them kill me! I should live no longer. This nobody Reza has foully insulted my sister, the Amin-e-Aqdas, on the streets of Warsaw.'

Obviously this incident was humiliating for the Shah in front of General Gorkov. He didn't know what had happened so, having ordered Mirza Moham-mad Khan to be taken to his room, he said that he would personally investigate the matter. The Shah then retired to his apartments and said goodbye to the General. I, however, had no experience of the antics practised by these people. I was absolutely flabbergasted and went to my room, for of course I had never even mentioned the Amin-e-Aqdas's name. The ʿAlaʾ-ol-Molk, the minister plenipotentiary, who was supposed to be in attendance until the Shah left Russian soil, had been present. He came to my room and, very distressed and sympathetic, asked me whether I realised what I had done. I asked him why people were condemning me without knowing what had actually happened. The Shah's intimate circle was doing this out of jealousy: they were afraid that I would take their places. Half an hour later, an attendant came and said that the Shah had ordered me to go to the Amin-os-Soltan, the prime minister's apartment. I asked what was going on. He replied that he had been ordered to take me there for the trial of myself and Mirza Mohammad Khan.

I saw that some of the most important members of the Shah's entourage including the *Mokhber-od-Dowleh* and *Mirza Mohammad Hassan Khan E'temad-os-Saltaneh* were present. As the Shah was aware that the Amin-os-Soltan was my protector, the latter would obviously have to be severe with me in order to show his neutrality in the matter. The Amin-os-Soltan asked me in a particularly harsh manner: 'Why did you, whom I considered intel-ligent and competent, cause a scandal in front of the people of Warsaw and in particular its governor-general?' I replied respectfully that I was not the complainant in the matter. Another had complained about me and he was not present. Whenever this person was present in person to submit his complaints for judgment by His Majesty, then I could reply to the complaints. If not, I suggested, whatever I might say would be like going before a judge with no witnesses. As the assembled gentlemen saw that there was no alternative, the Amin-os-Soltan sent a servant to bring Mohammad Khan. He was brought in with his torn collar and shirt and with his hair in disarray. He sat down above me, but the Amin-os-Soltan addressed him very fiercely and said that His Majesty had given orders for a proper investigation to be carried out to establish the truth behind this scandal. He asked what Mirza Reza Khan had done to him which caused him to throw himself at the feet of the Shah in this way. Mirza Mohammad Khan replied in a trembling voice that as the servant of His Majesty's person, he had submitted a petition to the ground before His Majesty's feet asking for this person (and here he pointed to me with a scornful gesture) to be punished, and he would see me punished. There was no need for the Amin-os-Soltan to conduct a trial.

In the face of this harsh, rude reply, the Amin-os-Soltan turned to me and said: 'We are gathered here at the Shah's command. You have heard Mirza Mohammad Khan's statement. I wish to know the cause of this row. What was it about?' I replied that I had one request to make from the assembled company, which was that they should ask Mirza Mohammad Khan what he was doing in my carriage and why he had leapt into it. Fortunately, I added, all those present were aware that on our arrival in Warsaw the governor-general's office had written down the names of the Shah's entourage in Russian script and had given them to the coachmen. Each carriage except His Majesty's had been numbered and the numbers given to the entourage. The authorities had even decided who would sit on cushions and who on hard seats. The reply to whatever questions they wished to ask lay in this one point and it would be clear who was at fault. When Mirza Mohammad Khan heard what I had said, he could find nothing to say. He suddenly got up and said: 'I knew that you were all protecting this individual, and that is why I didn't respond to your invitation to attend. On the second occasion, I came at the Shah's command and not yours.' The meeting then broke up and I returned to my room.

Since I had been due to attend the theatre that evening, dinner was served early. The carriages were ready, and the whole party set off. In accordance with the Shah's orders, I had been supposed to accompany the 'Aziz-os-Soltan from

St Petersburg onwards, but when we were about to get into the carriages, the Shah ordered the 'Ala'-ol-Molk to accompany the 'Aziz-os-Soltan and sit in the carriage with him. One other person besides myself remained behind in the palace: Mirza Mohammad Khan, who was lying sick in bed. In my room my eye fell on an envelope lying on the table, so I opened it: a general's daughter had written to me that as there was to be a parade on the Warsaw parade ground in honour of the Shah and her father was to command the parade, she and her mother had come from St Petersburg. As she had access to the royal garden, she asked me to come and walk with her for a time at seven o'clock at a place which she indicated. I looked at my watch and saw that it was a little past the hour she had set. I went out to greet the Sadiq-os-Saltaneh and wish him a good evening before leaving. He asked me where I was going, so I showed him the letter and asked him to read it. When he saw the contents, he was really astonished and said: 'All your friends are weeping at the ill fortune which has befallen you and you go off for a walk with a young lady!' I replied: 'My dear Sir, haven't you heard the saying that what will go goes, what will come comes and what will be will be? Yet we still worry. Or as the *dervishes* say, as long as you have breath in your body, enjoy the moment, O Lord! I am convinced that the fact that I am going for this walk will have absolutely no effect on my future fortunes.'

It was a moonlit night and the garden was looking very beautiful. As we were walking along the paths in the garden talking, someone came down the steps of the royal palace and came straight towards us. As he came up to us, I saw that it was the Amin-os-Soltan's uncle, who was the Shah's butler-in-chief and treasurer. He said: 'Come immediately! The Shah wants you at the theatre.' I accompanied the young lady to the garden gate, said goodbye to her and went with him to the theatre.

The opera was *La Belle Hélène*[9] in Russian and since no one in the entourage spoke Russian, I had been summoned to translate the story of the play from beginning to end for the Shah. In the interval, cakes, sherbet and ice-creams were served in a tent pitched in the garden for the Shah. There he was able to talk to any of the aristocratic ladies he wanted through me, and I was able to make acquaintances through introductions performed by Count Keller. Meanwhile, the guests, who felt very honoured to be in the Shah's

---

9 The opera bouffe by Offenbach.

presence, stood around eating cakes and ice-creams. Then the bell rang for the
last act and everyone returned to their places, so I too returned to the Shah's
box, where only the Shah and the Amin-os-Soltan were present. The servants
stood behind the Shah, as indeed did I. However, when the play was over, the
Shah told me not to sit beside the 'Aziz-os-Soltan on the return journey to the
palace: the 'Ala'-ol-Molk should sit beside him and I was to return alone in the
spare carriage, which I did.

As soon as the Sadiq-os-Saltaneh heard my footfall, he summoned me to
his room and asked me to tell him what had happened, so I did so. He said that
when the Shah left the palace saying that I was not to sit next to the 'Aziz-os-
Soltan, he had been worried for me. Someone who has fallen out of favour is
redundant. However, the fact that the Shah had summoned me to the theatre
and had been able to converse with the ladies through me gave him a little
hope for me. With my usual trust in God, I should go off to bed and sleep
peacefully and we would see what God would cause to happen.

What actually ensued was entirely to my advantage. The Shah's attendants
all gave Mirza Mohammad Khan the same report on the events at the theatre,
which made him end the evening in a rage. The next morning, as soon as
the Shah woke up and before his butler could take away his chamber pot
for him to perform his ritual ablutions and say his morning prayers, Mirza
Mohammad Khan entered the Shah's bedroom without permission, fell on
his knees and banged his head hard on the floor. Since the Amin-os-Sultan
and the trial judges had already reported the events of the previous day in
detail to His Majesty, the Shah ordered him to be picked up from the floor and
rained curses of every kind on him: 'You so and so, reply to this one simple
question! Stop playing these tricks! You knew the number of your carriage,
for you got into it every day. What were you doing in the 'Aziz-os-Soltan
and Reza's carriage? Get lost! I never want to see your wretched face again.'
He then threw him out ignominiously. Mirza Mohammad Khan didn't dare
show his face for several days until the Mokhber-od-Dowleh interceded for
him to be allowed to return to the Shah's service. From that day onwards,
the Shah ordered me to sit in the carriage with the 'Aziz-os-Soltan and the
raging torrent subsided.

One day the Shah sent me to the market to buy certain articles. On my
return, when I entered the corridor, I saw a tall, thin old man with a white

beard coming out from the Shah's palace talking very angrily to himself at the top of his voice, '*Ils sont fous. Ils sont fous*', or 'They are mad.' I stopped him and very gently asked him who he was saying was mad. He opened his eyes wide and in an angry voice said: 'Your ministers, your ministers.' I asked him to come to my room, which was nearby, for a few minutes to explain the cause of his anger and inappropriate words. He said: 'Of course, and I hope that you will agree with me.' We went to my room and sat down. I offered him a cigarette and suggested that he should smoke, calm down and explain. He explained why he was angry. 'My family name is Posselt. I am of German race and German nationality. I have a thread-spinning factory in Warsaw and a cloth factory near Berlin. I buy nearly three million sheep and camel skins a year in Khorasan and Astarabad, from which I make thread in Warsaw, which I send to Berlin to be woven into cloth. Three thousand workers work in this factory, of which 800 are Iranians, whom I have brought from the Caucasus. I have built houses for 3,000 workers near the factory and have created a large garden for their families to walk in, with a pavilion, to which I bring a military band to amuse them every year at the time of the ʿEid. I have also built two primary schools for them, one for boys and one for girls, and two bathhouses with showers.'

Since the Shah of Iran was visiting Warsaw, he had wanted to invite him and his entourage to the park. He had approached the governor-general and enquired about this. The latter had approved the idea and said that if the Shah accepted his invitation, he would send a military band there to play while the Shah was present. 'So I came to this palace, where I met a young courtier, who spoke a little French. I told him my idea and asked to whom I should refer it. He wrote down the name of the Eʿtemad-os-Saltaneh on a piece of paper and gave it to me. Having obtained permission from the court servants, I went to the latter's rooms. He approved my idea and kindly said that he would put the matter to His Majesty that evening and would give me the reply at 11 o'clock the next morning.' However, this was the fourth day on which Monsieur Posselt had come to the palace twice a day but in all this time he had failed to obtain a reply. Either the Shah would come or he would not come. He had heard that the Shah would only stay two days in Warsaw. Receiving the Shah as one's guest wasn't easy and required several days preparation and organisation. He feared that either he would make the necessary arrangements and the Shah wouldn't come or that he would make no preparation and one day before the Shah's departure he would be told that the Shah was coming. He was concerned that he would be gravely embarrassed. Whatever was the problem in saying either yes or no? He had sworn an oath to the E'temad-os-Saltaneh that he had no ulterior motive, neither financial reward nor a decoration. For the honour of his factory, he simply wished to print on his business notepaper that His Majesty the Shah of Iran had honoured the factory with his illustrious presence. If this was not considered appropriate, he was even prepared not to write this. His Majesty's presence alone would be sufficient to raise his prestige among his Iranian workers. It was teatime, so I rang the bell and suggested that he should drink tea while I went to submit the matter to the appropriate quarter and bring back a reply. I told the Amin-os-Soltan, who said that this was the first time that he had heard of the matter and that since the Shah was anyway waiting for me to return from a shopping expedition, I should immediately go and explain the matter exactly as it was to him.

The Shah said that the E'temad-os-Saltaneh had indeed informed him of this invitation but he hadn't yet made up his mind as to whether to go or not. However, now that this man had come and given so much detail, he would go. Truly, I don't know how to adequately describe with my pen Monsieur Posselt's gratitude. He took my hand and squeezed it several times, saying that he didn't know how to express his gratitude. As I left, he said that he had one further request to make: as he wished to show the schools and infirmaries to the Shah, I should entreat the Shah to come at three o'clock. The E'temad-os-Saltaneh had told him that if the Shah accepted his invitation, no one should be invited except the Shah's suite so that the Shah could relax and spend an hour or so listening to the music. Monsieur Posselt had obviously complied fully with his request and had decided not to invite his wife and children to the factory garden, not wishing to cause trouble.

On the appointed day, the Shah entered Monsieur Posselt's factory, his carriage escorted by a squadron of Cossacks. His suite consisted of courtiers and servants, the chief doctor, the tutor to the 'Aziz-os-Soltan, together with two of his more intimate servants, the royal barber and the gentleman of the bed-chamber, for Naser-od-Din Shah didn't sleep in a bed but had his bedding spread on the carpets. Together with the attendants of his private quarters, his butler and his assistant butler, his suite consisted of forty-two people in all. Of

these forty-two men, however, the *Amin-od-Dowleh* and *Naser-ol-Molk* had
gone on ahead to Paris to await the Shah's arrival. Of the others not more than
four people had remained behind to attend to the luggage and other effects,
while thirty-five actually accompanied His Majesty to Monsieur Posselt's
reception.

First of all, the Shah briefly inspected the schools and infirmaries and
enquired after the health of two patients. He then visited the factory, where
he was shown the whole process from the point at which the dirty wool was
rinsed in running water and then put into vats until it was finally made into
spools of thread. From there the Shah went on to visit the garden. The pavilion
had been superbly decorated with Iranian carpets, Italian brocaded silk and
other decorative objects. For the person of His Majesty a velvet chair braded
with very beautiful gold lace had been prepared and in front of him there was
a table large enough to seat twenty-five people, completely covered by many
kinds of sugared nuts, sweets, cakes, and several kinds of biscuits with various
fruit jams. This wonderfully-laden table was solely for the Shah. Marquees
had been pitched in the park, however, one for the Amin-os-Soltan, ministers
and nobles, with a second tent for other court officials such as the chief butler
and the servants, while third-class courtiers were placed in a third marquee.
His Majesty invited the Amin-os-Soltan and the ministers to the pavilion and
gave them permission to help themselves to tea and cakes. All the while Monsieur Posselt and I had been standing in the pavilion: he explained things and
I translated. At 5.30 His Majesty indicated that he wished to leave. Then a
strange scene unfolded. Monsieur Posselt's staff popped up from under the
ground like *jinns*[10] and handed out valuable gifts such as silver tea sets, silver
writing sets, gold watches and other precious things. He presented these to
those attending according to their rank. Thus he gave presents, each valued at
3,000–4,000 *manat*, to the Amin-os-Soltan and the ministers. To the servants
he gave gold watches, while the fifth-level servants received a silver watch and
a silver pen. Monsieur Posselt then accompanied the Shah back to the palace.

In Warsaw I saw a ballet, the like of which I haven't seen anywhere else
in the world. It is well-known that the best ballerinas are Polish and as this

---

10 *Jinn* are supernatural creatures, probably of pre-Islamic origin, who have a chapter or
Sura devoted to them in the Qur'an and can be either good or evil.

part of Poland, Warsaw, has been part of Russian territory for many years, the Warsaw Ballet is called the Russian Ballet. In fact it is not the Russian Ballet but the Polish Ballet. Most Polish girls are well-proportioned and beautiful, with small hands and feet, nicely-rounded knees, fine eyes and eyebrows, oval faces, small mouths and auburn hair. These girls are the best ballerinas in the world. The former Polish kings imitated the architecture and gardens of Louis XIV in France and one of them built a very beautiful summer theatre in the middle of the Lazienki Park. The theatre itself is quite small: only half the size of a reception-room. Think of a large reception-room covered with a dome and then cut it in half! A thing which really adds to the beauty of this theatre is the crescent-shaped lake which lies just below the theatre. The water is so close to the theatre that the dancers seem to be up to their knees in water and when they are dancing it is as though there are two dancers, one dancing in the water like a fairy and one on the stage, while the stage itself is framed with arrangements of many different flowers.

Anyway, after ten days stay in Warsaw, Mirza Reza Khan Mo'ayyed-os-Saltaneh, minister plenipotentiary in Berlin, came and joined the retinue, which then left for Berlin. A Russian train took us to the German frontier, where the Kaiser's private train, together with the official hosts and guard of honour, was waiting. On our arrival in Berlin, the Kaiser and his brother were present at the station to greet the Shah. The guard of honour had been chosen from the tallest soldiers, the likes of which cannot be found anywhere else in Europe. Their weapons and uniforms sparkled.

As there was a great deal of jealousy among the Shah's personal servants and courtiers at that time, each faction had got together and sworn that when in the presence of the Shah, one member of their 'committee' would speak ill of and indulge in backbiting against the other and defend his own group. As I had seen instances of this backbiting in Warsaw, I also formed a four-man committee consisting of Mehdi Khan, son of the Amin-od-Dowleh, the court minister; the Fakhr-ol-Molk, the son of the governor of Kurdistan; Ahmad Khan, grandson of Khan Baba Khan Sardar of Erivan, all three of whom were highly-respected servants of the Shah; and myself. The names of Mirza Mohammad Khan and our four names were on the list of Iranian courtiers provided by the Amin-os-Soltan to the German court. On our arrival in Berlin, because of my knowledge of the language, the minister had introduced only me to our German official host. On the day of our arrival at the palace, I was sitting drinking tea with four people in the dining room when Mirza Moham-mad Khan, who knew all three members of our committee, came and sat down with them and asked for tea but he wouldn't look at me. At this moment the German general and his deputy, a colonel, came up to me and asked me to make the introductions. I introduced my three fellow oath-swearers but didn't mention Mirza Mohammad Khan's name. Our hosts then shook hands with the three men, made some polite remarks and left. They paid no atten-tion to Mirza Mohammad Khan, however, and didn't shake hands with him. Of course the latter was very upset and angry. When we left the dining-room, he took the Fakhr-ol-Molk, who was a friend of his, off to his rooms. They remained there for some time, and then the Fakhr-ol-Molk came to see me to tell me that Mirza Mohammad Khan regretted his behaviour in Warsaw and he wanted to be reconciled with me. I should wait half an hour and then come to his room so that he could put my hand in Mirza Mohammad Khan's, and we should then embrace and make up. I said that I was by nature a man of peace but that I would not make peace with him now. The suspicion which he had cast on me was of the kind which would linger in people's minds and almost certainly some of the mud thrown by his accusation would linger in His Majesty's mind. I wouldn't make up with him until I had succeeded in removing this suspicion from the Shah's mind. He asked what my conditions for reconciliation were.

I said that my condition was that we should all four go and wait at the Shah's door and that Mirza Mohammad Khan should tell His Majesty that when he had made the accusation against Reza in connection with the Amin-e-Aqdas, he had done so at a time when, because of his fall from the carriage, he was completely out of his mind and didn't know what he was saying. He should say that Reza had in no way shown a lack of respect to the Amin-e-Aqdas. Furthermore, so that His Majesty should be certain that I had not been rude to the Amin-e-Aqdas, he should ask His Majesty to give me a present. The Fakhr-ol-Molk said that he didn't think that Mirza Mohammad Khan would accept these conditions. I replied that it was not I who had sought reconcilia-tion. He had done so, and these were my final conditions. The Fakhr-ol-Molk said that he was not the supplicant either but, as commanded by the Prophet on the delivery of messages, he would go and give him my message. Mirza

Mohammad Khan could make of it what he wanted. After his meeting with Mirza Mohammad Khan, the Fakhr-ol-Molk returned laughing and said: 'This man is such a low-born wretch that he has accepted both conditions. He even told me why: first, as you know the language and are the Shah's aide-de-camp and the official hosts only deal with you and members of the Ministry of Foreign Affairs, he fears that you won't introduce him to the official hosts nor will you give his name to the Ministry of Foreign Affairs staff when decorations are being handed out.' I said that I hadn't even given a thought to preventing him getting a decoration, but since he thought me such a difficult character but he had nevertheless accepted my conditions, I had nothing further to say on the matter.

Since Mirza Mohammad Khan had permanent right of access to His Majesty, it was arranged that the next day he would let us know when the moment was right, so at the appointed time the four of us went and stood at the door of the Shah's apartments. Mirza Mohammad Khan said: 'Your Majesty, I threw myself at your feet in Warsaw when I was in such a state that I didn't know what I was saying. I said that Mirza Reza Khan had insulted my sister, the Amin-e-Aqdas. As I know that he is a very calm person, I do not wish this accusation to remain in your august mind. My sense of justice does not allow this. I submit that he is completely innocent of this accusation. So that I can look him in the eye, I entreat you to give him a present which I can take to him, so that he knows that I have retracted this accusation.' The Shah started to laugh and said: 'Mohammad Khan, you are a remarkable ass and Mirza Reza Khan is a clever fellow. Go and get £50 from my treasurer and give it to him, saying that it is a present from the Shah!' Mirza Mohammad Khan went and got the money, which he brought to me and the Fakhr-ol-Molk made us shake hands in reconciliation.

From Berlin we went on to Kassel, Munich, Wurttemberg and finally Baden-Baden. Haji Baqer Khorasani, who lived in Vienna and had been a trader and agent there for many years, had come to Baden-Baden from Vienna, thinking that he could make purchases for the Shah and his entourage. One day he said to me that the local custom was that if someone introduced a customer to a shop, when the buyer had left after making his purchase, the introducer had the right to return and receive a 5 per cent commission. It did not matter that he was not a professional agent. On our second day there, the Shah summoned me and said: 'I see that you are good at buying at a good price. Come with me, help me and let us buy some crystal worked in gold for Tehran!' We went to look at the goods in the crystal shops, which he inspected one by one until he chose one particular shop. There I asked the price of each object and I wanted to bargain with the shopkeeper, but the latter showed me a board on the wall on which he had written: 'Fixed Price'. The Shah was pleased that he would not be cheated and he started to select what he wanted. He told them to bring out any chests for sale, from which he chose four small enough to be carried on mules from Enzeli to Tehran. His Majesty had brought a great deal of money with him, so he paid for the goods in cash and we gave them the invoice to receipt. The cost of the four chests was about 6,500 marks.

When we left, the Shah wanted to return to the hotel. I humbly suggested, however, that he might care to rest a few minutes on the benches which had been placed there for that purpose, so that I could return to the shop. I remembered what Haji Mohammad Baqer had said and wanted to render a service to the Shah. The Shah asked why I wanted to go back to the shop. He had bought and paid for everything he wanted. I respectfully submitted that I would tell him the reason later. He didn't insist but sat down. I went back to the shop owner and asked for my commission. Without any argument he took out 325 marks and gave it to me. Without even putting it in my pocket or my purse, I took it in my hand and gave it all to the Shah, who asked what this money was. I explained what Haji Baqer had told me. He said that this money was rightfully mine and I should keep it. I quoted the Arab proverb to him: '"Anything in the servant's hand belongs to the master". This is Your Majesty's property.' He gave me 100 marks and kept the rest. From that moment on the Shah realised that I was honest and my position with him was assured.

From Germany we went on to Belgium. After the official receptions at the royal palace in Brussels, as the weather was very hot, the Shah was invited to Spa where people go in summer from other Belgian towns and indeed from other countries. There is a park and a club where they play cards and roulette. Some evenings the Shah would visit the club incognito and stake one imperial at a time, sometimes winning several imperials but sometimes losing. One evening he took me with him and told me to play. I suggested that I had heard that this game was risky and that, once addicted to it, one could very well lose one's shirt. He said: 'Bravo! Well done! I wanted to test you.' He took a napoleon from his pocket and said: 'I am wagering one napoleon on your good fortune.' He won two napoleons, which he gave to me saying: 'I am giving them to you but do not play yourself!' One day he sent me, together with the Fakhr-ol-Molk and Ahmad Khan from Spa to Brussels to buy a few things. On our return journey, a young girl of about seventeen entered the carriage with another girl of perhaps eight or nine. We were alone with them. The elder girl was exceptionally beautiful with an elegant figure, and the Fakhr-ol-Molk asked whether it would be all right to ask for their address so that he could give it to the Shah. I replied: 'My dear fellow, we are in Europe now. It is very rude to ask a lady where she lives until one is introduced to her and she shows that she wishes to talk to you.' He replied: 'I had no ulterior motive in asking this question. It was simply that on our return the Shah will ask what we have seen and we could say that we had seen an extraordinary beauty. However, now that I understand that it would be discourteous, there is no need for you to ask.' As the weather was hot, the younger girl wanted to put her hat on the rack above her head, but she couldn't reach it and the hat fell on the floor, so I quickly picked it up and placed it on the rack. The girl went as red as a tulip and said: 'Thank you!' Her sister told her in French to thank me properly. The little girl was tongue-tied. I replied, saying: 'Mademoiselle, I have done nothing to deserve thanks from this young lady.' Thereupon we started to chat and I introduced my travelling companions. It transpired that when the Shah arrived at Spa, they had come to the railway station to watch the spectacle and had seen us among the entourage. She asked in which country we had been before coming to Spa. She had read in the newspaper that the Shah was visiting as an ordinary visitor. I said that we had come from Baden-Baden in Germany. When we arrived at Spa, I asked where she was staying. She said that she had come with her parents to spend the summer and that they would take part in the Red Rose Day there. I joked with her that I was not surprised: of course a heavenly fairy should live in a rose-garden. Anyway, we said goodbye and went our different ways. When we reached the hotel, my friend went and recounted the whole story to the Shah, who summoned me and said that the reply I had given that lady was very poetic. How had it come into my head? For the Shah was himself a poet and liked ready replies. The lines of Hafez came to mind and I recited:

In its longing for the rose the nightingale learnt words;
Otherwise all these odes would have been but noises in its beak.

The Shah was very pleased and was loud in his praises.

Two nights later, the municipality of Spa gave a ball in honour of the Shah
to which the distinguished people spending the summer there were invited.
The Shah was sitting in the place of honour, he had accepted an ice-cream
which had been offered to him and we were all standing in a line some way off
awaiting his command. Suddenly I saw that young lady and her mother enter.
Everyone present were stunned by the radiance of her beauty. When they were
about to pass in front of the Shah, he could bear it no longer. He summoned
me and said: 'Reza, the courtiers were telling me that you compose poetry. I
want to know how far your talent for poetry goes. Improvise something about
this young lady and bring it for me to see!' I said to myself: 'O Lord God, I
have escaped from the clutches of the ladies of St Petersburg, who forced me
to compose poetry for them. Now I have fallen into the hands of a mighty
king who has power over my life and limb. Have mercy on me!' I took a piece
of paper from the chest of drawers and went outside. With heaven's help, the
following lines came to my mind:

My beloved is the calamity of the age;
The least of her skills is the pursuit of royal hearts!
Her locks are sometimes a noose and sometimes a chain,
Her eyebrows the bow and her eye-lashes the arrow!

The Shah was absolutely delighted by this and told me to go and take twenty
napoleons from his treasurer as a reward for this piece. He then wrote down
the poem in his travel diary. Before leaving for Ostend, where we were to take
the Queen's private yacht to London, we went to Liège to buy rifles as home-
coming presents for tribal chiefs. The Shah had been informed that the whole
population of a particular district in Liège made guns, together with all the
parts such as stocks and firing pins, which they made by hand. I was to take
one of the policemen who had been designated to look after us and go and buy
two hunting rifles. The very helpful policeman and I went off, and I bought
two good hunting rifles. I took out ten napoleons to give him but the gunsmith

would only take four napoleons, saying that each rifle cost two napoleons. Truly two napoleons was very little for so much work.

The Shah gave the order that the other rifles which the eunuchs had gone to buy for him should be brought in and placed beside these rifles. When he saw that both sets of rifles were of the same quality, he gave orders for the eunuchs to be fined three napoleons for each rifle they had bought and then punished in Tehran for theft. I didn't know anything about this, however, but when my group of close friends heard about this, they told me that I was already the object of envy to the Shah's intimate servants, but now the eunuchs would also be jealous of me. Did I not know how influential the eunuchs were? Clearly I didn't know what the enmity of these people would mean. They had right of access to the Shah at all times, before he went to bed and early in the morning and they were skilled talkers. If they struck to wound, the wound was mortal. I said: 'Gentlemen, what can I do? I either have to steal or make enemies. I prefer to speak the truth and make enemies rather than to steal.'

From Liège we travelled to London by way of Ostend, where the royal yacht *Victoria and Albert* was waiting. The editor of the *Graphic* newspaper had been invited to sit on deck. He came up to me and asked if the Shah would sit for a few minutes for him, as he wished to publish a photograph of His Majesty in his newspaper, the leading illustrated journal in England. His Majesty accepted on condition that he was shown the photograph before it was given to the newspaper. When I brought the photograph to the Shah, he said that it was not a very good likeness but as it was for a newspaper, it didn't matter. He told me to go and tell the editor that he should come and sit so that he, the Shah, could take a photograph of him. When the Shah had taken the photograph, it was such a good likeness of the editor that the latter asked His Majesty to sign his name beneath it, so that he could frame it and his family could be eternally proud of it. When both photographs were printed in the *Graphic*, readers were very surprised and said that it would have been impossible to produce such likenesses of a face with a pencil and paper.

As Her Majesty Queen Victoria had abandoned London some time before and now resided in one of her palaces outside London, never taking part in official receptions, His Royal Highness Prince Edward,[11] the heir apparent, had

---

11 Later King Edward VII, who reigned from 1901 until 1910.

come to the railway station as her representative, together with members of the court, the minister of foreign affairs and the prime minister, who was then Lord Salisbury, to greet the Shah. The guard of honour and the Household Cavalry took their appointed places, His Majesty entered London in great pomp and circumstance and resided at Buckingham Palace. Apart from the servants, the intimate companions and some ministers who stayed in the Buckingham Hotel at their own request, the rest of the party stayed at the royal palace. The lawns and flowerbeds of this palace are really wonderful and as it mostly rains in London, they are emerald green and the eye never tires of looking at them.

The Shah was scheduled to spend ten days at Buckingham Palace. When we arrived there from the railway station, Her Royal Highness Princess Alexandra, the wife of the heir apparent and the daughter of the King of Denmark, was awaiting His Majesty's arrival in one of the palace reception rooms with senior members of her court and her principal ladies in waiting. The Prince of Wales introduced the Shah to her and she held out her hand to him and inclined her head but said nothing. The Shah introduced the principal members of his entourage to her, but she didn't hold out her hand to any of them, which displeased the Shah. When we came out of the Shah's apartment, the Amin-os-Soltan asked our official host the reason for this cold reception. The latter explained that the princess was unfortunately a little hard of hearing and therefore when she was with people whom she didn't know well she didn't speak, fearing that if she was asked a question, which she misheard, this would be humiliating. The princess was then a woman of about forty years old and in a country which is a mine of the most beautiful women in Europe, by common consent she had no equal in beauty among English women and no one would have given her more than twenty years of age.

It had been arranged that during the Shah's ten-day stay in London, a ball should be given in his honour at Buckingham Palace to which the diplomatic corps and the aristocracy had been invited. The ball was a splendid occasion, with all the ladies in ball gowns and dripping with jewels, diamonds, rubies and emeralds and the men in uniform with decorations. It was a brilliant scene. The colonel who was one of our official hosts was so kind as to introduce me to several young and beautiful women, but as the Shah had charged me with looking after the ʿAziz-os-Soltan, I was unable to take advantage of the opportunity to talk to them.

In accordance with protocol, one day the members of the diplomatic corps in uniform were received in audience by the Shah. Then Lord Salisbury, the prime minister, called on the Shah to say that as it was summer, the best season in Scotland, the peers felt an obligation to invite him to spend forty days there as their guest. He could thus spend a day as the guest of each peer at his stately home, both on the way up to Scotland and on the way back. In this way he would see more than half Britain and would learn how the British nobility lived. His Majesty accepted this proposal on condition that as most country houses had a limited number of rooms, which would not be enough to house his whole suite, he would only take with him ten members of the entourage. It was therefore arranged that in the absence of the Shah, the rest of the suite would stay at the Buckingham Hotel as guests of the British government. On one of these days, *Abol-Qasem Khan Naser-ol-Molk*, who had successfully completed his studies at Oxford University and had taken his degree, was presented to the Shah by the Amin-od-Dowleh and was appointed by him as his official interpreter.

At the Lord Mayor's reception for the Shah at the Crystal Palace, which was the most splendid reception given by any mayor during the visit, there was an incomparable display of fireworks and illuminations. Life-size images of the Shah and the Prince of Wales made of fireworks were part of the show. At the dinner, the Lord Mayor made a speech lasting half an hour, in which he gave a short history of relations between Iran and Britain, and the Shah made a short speech in Persian in reply, asking the Naser-ol-Molk to reply in English on his behalf. The latter stood up and gave an approximate translation of the Shah's words but, by adding descriptions and some detail, he really acquitted himself very well. The English clapped him for a very long time and were surprised that such a young Iranian could speak English so well. From that day onwards, he was favoured by the Shah but since he was part of the Amin-od-Dowleh's and Malkom Khan's group, he only had official dealings with the Amin-os-Soltan. Therefore, on the day when the Amin-os-Soltan was deputed by the Shah to go and present two pictures to the Prince of Wales's sons, the latter took me with him as interpreter for these two elder princes, who must have been Prince Edward, who died in his father's lifetime, and the prince who later became King George V, who lived until the age of seventy-four.

One day, the inventor of the gramophone had an audience of His Majesty at Buckingham Palace. The Shah asked him to say something into the gramophone so that it would be recorded on a record. Mehdi Khan, who was licensed to say very daring things in the Shah's presence, used to say things in the form of a joke which no one else would have dared to say. The Shah had forbidden the young to go to certain tea-houses and places of pleasure at night. As the Shah didn't want to say anything himself into the gramophone, he ordered Mehdi Khan to say something, so the latter recited these lines of Hafez:

Although wine gives pleasure and the breeze wafts the scent of the rose,
Do not drink wine to the sound of the harp, for the *mohtaseb*[12] is fierce!

The Shah understood to what he was alluding and tweaked his ear very hard.

On another occasion, the inventor of the machine gun which could fire sixty bullets a minute,[13] brought it to the pool in the palace grounds, and demonstrated it to the Shah. Ten receptions were given in honour of the Shah at Buckingham Palace, some inside the palace and some garden-parties in the grounds which were attended by all the leading citizens and their wives. Of all the exhibitions which had been organised for him perhaps the most remarkable was one given by a couple who were brilliant shots.[14] First, the woman would throw hollow eggs into the air with all her strength and the man would shoot them down. He didn't miss a single time. Then the man would throw the eggs into the air and the woman would shoot them down. People were so impressed that they kept on clapping. Then the Shah said to me: 'Tell the man to throw an egg up into the air, and let the Majd-od-Dowleh shoot at it!' So the Majd-od-Dowleh hit an egg, which fell to the ground. There were cheers and loud shouts of 'Bravo!' from the audience. When the Shah heard the plaudits, he had an idea: he pulled out a sovereign and gave it to me, telling me to give it to the man, who should load the gun and throw the coin up into the air. The

12 Religious police.
13 *Sic.*
14 The *Illustrated London News* of 18 July 1889 mentioned a shooting display given before the Shah by Captain G. H. Fowler and Miss Louie at Hatfield House rather than Buckingham Palace.

Shah came out in front of the crowd, the man threw up the coin with all his strength and the Shah's shot turned the coin into a half-moon, with half of it carried away and the other half hitting the ground. People cheered so enthusiastically that the sound rose to the heavens. The Shah gave orders that the coin should be given to Princess Victoria, the Prince of Wales' daughter, as a souvenir. But the shooting was not over yet. The woman then placed herself at a distance from the man. She then placed an egg on the top of her hat, which she only wore to cover her hair so that the egg should not fall off. The man fired and the egg split in the middle. Obviously, everybody cheered wildly and shouted 'Bravo!' Then the man went and placed an egg on his head and the woman did exactly the same thing. The Shah was so delighted by this that he ordered the Amin-os-Soltan to give a medal to each of them on his behalf.

Another day, a mounted demonstration by specially-chosen horsemen from the Household Cavalry, was staged for the Shah in the Park near the palace. An iron ring, just large enough for a human hand to pass through it, was brought and hung on one of the branches of a tree growing in an avenue in the Park. The riders then broke into a gallop and as they approached the ring, they hurled their lances through it. Everyone who succeeded in doing so had his name written down and was given a prize. Akbar Khan, the Deputy Steward, asked the Shah if he could be given a horse and a lance, as he had occasionally practised this sport in his own garden. He added that as he hadn't tried this for a long time, the umpire should allow him three throws of the lance. At the Shah's command, I obtained permission from the umpire, who was a colonel. Akbar Khan succeeded in throwing the lance through the ring at the third attempt.

On the day of our departure from Buckingham Palace, the British government awarded decorations to all the royal party. The Shah was given the Victorian Order encrusted with diamonds and everyone else received one according to his status. The Mohandes-ol-Mamalek, the Fakhr-ol-Molk and Mehdi Khan, aide-de-camp extraordinary, Ahmad Khan and I myself received a decoration, which was also a medal. It was the most beautiful thing that I had ever seen. It was in the form of the sun, with all its rays. In the centre of the sun was the head and face of Queen Victoria portrayed in a very prominent way. Around that were the rays of the sun, slightly separated from the centre.

During our ten-day stay at Buckingham Palace, the British gave the most superb receptions for the Shah. The entourage, who spend their time searching for motives behind such things, said that the reason for this was that through Malkom Khan the British were discussing the possibility of obtaining very important commercial concessions[15] from the Shah. One day, Malkom Khan invited the Shah and the entourage to the embassy. He presented his wife and his daughters to the Shah and the courtiers. His embassy[16] had a garden and was in every way a prestigious building. He had also invited several British ministers, as well as members of the aristocracy and leading personalities. As minister plenipotentiary in London, Malkom Khan spoke good English but as he was a member of the Amin-od-Dowleh's group,[17] the latter's supporters gained in influence during our stay in London, while the supporters of the Amin-os-Soltan were starting to tremble. At the very end of our time in London, the Shah and his party were invited to the British Museum. There the rivalry between the two groups was revealed for all to see. As the Shah had to take Malkom Khan with him to make the introductions, the Amin-os-Soltan didn't want to enter the museum behind the Amin-od-Dowleh and Malkom Khan. So the Shah, the Amin-od-Dowleh and Malkom Khan walked on the right-hand side of the museum, while the Amin-os-Soltan and his people walked on the left-hand side. At the beginning, the fact that there were more people on the right than the left wasn't apparent. However, when we reached the middle of the museum, there was no one on the Amin-os-Soltan's side except the Saheb-e-Ekhtiyar and myself. Everyone else had moved to the other side of the museum. The Amin-os-Soltan was very upset. In angry tones, he repeatedly asked us why we had become separated from the others and told us to join them on the other side, saying that otherwise the damage to his position would also adversely affect us. As we saw that he was very distressed and angry, we said nothing. He didn't wish to prolong his visit to the museum and after visiting half of it, he returned to the palace with us.

---

15 In late 1889, after the Shah's return to Iran, a lottery concession was granted to a London-based consortium and in 1890 a tobacco concession was awarded to the British-owned Régie. These concessions caused such discontent throughout the country that by 1891 Qajar Iran was in ferment. The ensuing protests are often considered to have been the dress rehearsal for the Constitutional Revolution.

16 In 1889, the Iranian Embassy in London was at 80 Holland Park.

17 The Amin-os-Soltan and the Amin-od-Dowleh were long-time rivals for the post of prime minister.

When the British government wants to receive a guest and treat him royally, they are infinitely better at this than other courts. We saw the proof of this with our own eyes one evening at an official theatre evening arranged for the Shah. It would be simply impossible to put on a play in a more splendid environment. The Shah had been invited to the Empire Theatre, where all the boxes were decorated with every kind of flowers. Obviously all the aristocratic families, as well as those of the most important men of the day, ministers, senior officers and government officials had been invited. The Shah had been given the central box. On his right sat Princess Alexandra, wife of the Prince of Wales, while on his left was Princess Victoria, the Prince of Wales' daughter. Next to her was the Prince himself and next to Princess Alexandra sat the Duke of Kent, the Prince's brother. In the second row, only members of the royal family were seated. Ministers and peers sat in other boxes. As we left for the theatre, the Shah summoned Ahmad Khan and myself, saying that tonight he wanted the two of us to act as cup-bearers in the theatre that evening. When the Shah was invited to the theatre in an official capacity, the chief butler always had to bring a gold cup with him and remain standing in the royal box. Meanwhile the assistant butler would hold a jug of water, so that when the Shah asked for water, the Amin-os-Soltan's uncle[18] could fill the cup and take it to him. He would do this three or four times in the course of a theatre evening.

In order to describe the theatre evening properly, I should describe the layout of the Shah's box, which was directly opposite the stage, with no wall behind it on the corridor side, so those strolling in the corridors could see those sitting in it. The boxes were of course semi-circular in shape. When the British royal family wished to move at the first curtain, I went to stand on the right of the Shah with the gold cup in my hand, awaiting his order, so that whenever he wanted it, I could give the cup to him without delay. In that position, I couldn't turn my head to look at the stage. It would have been discourteous. I had to keep looking at the Shah. Naturally, as I looked at the Shah, I was also looking at Princess Alexandra, who was sitting on the Shah's right. I didn't know whether the Shah had noticed my gaze.

When the curtain came down for the first time, the Shah and the royal family repaired to a large room with a long table covered with flowers, on

---

18 The Shah's chief butler.

which were laid out all kinds of drinks and sweet things. The Shah summoned me there and said: 'Reza, on the day of our arrival, you saw how coldly Princess Alexandra greeted the ministers and the entourage and how she wouldn't shake hands with anybody. I have told you on many occasions that your eyes have extraordinary mesmeric powers. When you were looking at the Princess during the play, she was also looking at you. This evening I want you to hypnotise the Princess so that she comes and talks to you, and in talking to you the cold demeanour which she showed on that evening melts away.' I explained that in order to hypnotise someone, one had to look at the person directly and fixedly for some time and this was impossible in the circumstances.

The Shah replied that he had heard that it was possible for those with the greatest hypnotic power to look at the back of a person's head and hypnotise that person from behind. I humbly suggested that I knew this but I did not feel that I had this power myself. Nevertheless, he asked me to hand over the cup to Ahmad Khan, who should be in attendance for the whole evening. When the second curtain went up, I invited the Fakhr-ol-Molk and Mehdi Khan to come with me into the corridor so that we could see the stage. I gazed intently at the back of the Princess's head, but this had no effect. I then took the pulse of the Fakhr-ol-Molk, taking strength from it, and looked at the Princess's neck. This still had no effect. Then I took Mehdi Khan's pulse and pressed it so hard that he cried out. I said that this was the Shah's command and had to be obeyed. Then I saw the Princess move, throw off the swan-feather collar which women put round their necks at balls and parties and put it behind her. As she took it off, she turned round and her eyes met mine. I let go of my friends' hands and said that the operation was complete.

At that moment, the curtain fell and His Majesty and the ladies of the royal family all went to the furthest end of the room set aside for the interval. I stood by the door, waiting to be of service. A few moments later Princess Alexandra left her husband, her daughter and His Majesty and came up to me and said: 'Why are you standing there? Why don't you come and have some of these sweet things and soft drinks?' I replied that Iranian court custom did not allow me to eat or drink in the Shah's presence. I was standing there to carry out the Shah's commands, as I was his aide-de-camp. She replied: 'Come with me! I will stand between the Shah and you, so that he does not see you eating.' Since the Shah himself had ordered me to persuade her to talk, I obeyed her command. We went to the bottom of the table and with her own hand the Princess gave me a chocolate and poured me a glass of orange juice, which she placed on the table in front of me. Of course I didn't eat the chocolate nor did I even see the orange juice. At this point His Majesty came up behind me and said: 'Reza, that is enough. Go home!' When the Princess saw the Shah, she turned to him and I left the theatre and went back to the palace. After that act of hypnosis, I was in a state of complete nervous exhaustion and fell asleep.

In the morning before sunrise, I heard someone pounding on my door. I got up and saw the Shah's butler standing there. He said: 'The Shah wants to see you. Come!' I asked him to wait for me to dress as it was not right to appear in the Shah's presence in my night-wear. He said that the Shah had ordered me to be brought in whatever state I might be in: I wasn't allowed to dress. I was taken off to the Shah's room in my pyjamas. I saw that the Shah was sitting on a cushion with a felt hat on his head, while the royal barber was preparing his shaving kit with two eunuchs in attendance. The Shah told his barber to leave the room and instructed the eunuchs to search me.

I had been told that when the Amin-od-Dowleh became very close to the Shah, the courtiers had become very jealous of him. They wanted to destroy him, so one day when the Shah was about to carry out his ablutions, they placed the Shah's diamond ring in the Amin-od-Dowleh's pocket, in such a way that he was out of sight for a time and then the 'theft' was revealed. I was terrified and said to myself: 'O God! What is going on?' The eunuch searched me and brought out the prayer which my mother had hung round my neck when I left Tabriz. The Shah ordered them to break open the Kashmir shawl wrapping round the prayer. When they did so, they saw that a piece of oil cloth was inside it. They opened this up and saw that it contained the Throne Verse from the Qur'an and two other verses to ward off others' jealousy. There was nothing else in the paper, so they returned these things to me and the Shah told me to go back to bed. As a result, for some time I thought that the eunuchs had stolen something from the Shah and were seeking to blame me for the loss, so that was why I had been brought into the Shah's presence. However, sometime later a courtier who was very close to the Shah told me that when he left the theatre, the Shah had expressed astonishment to some of his closest entourage at the mesmerising effect of my eyes. One of them told the Shah that he had read in a book that if someone had a female hyena's sexual organ in his possession, whenever he looked at a woman, he could subject her to his will. The Shah wanted to see whether this was true or not and that was why he had summoned me at sunrise.

When we were due to depart for Scotland, the Shah gave orders to the Amin-os-Soltan to write down the names of ten people to accompany him to Scotland and give the list to the court. Of course, as Abol-Qasem Khan Naser-ol-Molk had completed his studies at Oxford and had recently become the Shah's personal interpreter, he was chosen. On the morning of our departure, the court told the entourage to prepare their baggage, both those who were to accompany the Shah to Scotland and the others who were to remain in London, for court officials would come to escort the latter group to a hotel. Those who weren't going to Scotland had been told to wait on the ground floor of the palace before the departure of the Shah, so that they could be taken to the hotel, for the doors of the palace would be closed as soon as the Shah had left. Like the others, my baggage was duly taken to the hotel while we waited on the ground floor of the palace. We saw the Shah leave his apartment with his entourage. We drew back from the top of the stairs so that as the Shah came out we could bow to him and follow him down the stairs. By divine intervention, however, what had happened to Mirza Ma'sum and Mirza Taqi Khan[19] once again occurred here. Abol-Qasem Khan, who was behind the Shah, suddenly became giddy and fell from the top of the stairs to the bottom, where he lay unconscious. Everybody was stunned and the official host immediately ordered the court servants to take him to hospital.

When we emerged from the palace, the Shah looked around for his entourage as he was about to get into his carriage. His eye fell on me, so he told me to get into the carriage instead of Abol-Qasem Khan and sit down. I told the Amin-os-Soltan that all my luggage had been taken to the hotel and I had absolutely nothing with me, not even my shaving kit. How could I come? He said that fortune had smiled on me and that I shouldn't kick against it. I might be allowed to go and send for my belongings when we reached the first house where we were to stay. Our first stopping point was the prime minister, Lord

---

19 The interpreters for the Shah's second visit to Europe (1878), whose sudden illness gave the young author the opportunity to interpret for the Shah and thus to take his first steps on the path to fame and fortune (see Chapter 3).

Salisbury's summer residence,[20] where we arrived about sunset. The servants announced that we must be ready for dinner punctually at 7.30, but I hadn't had the opportunity to shave in the morning and so I wanted at least to shave my beard. Of the Shah's personal servants only Mehdi Khan was present and he was completely beardless. I asked him whether he had a razor. He said: 'Look at my face before you ask! But one of the eunuchs has bought some razors as presents for Tehran. Ask him for one!' I don't know whether the eunuch was joking or not but he said that he would charge me five shillings for one shave. I got out five shillings and gave it to him, took the razor and went to my room. I had prepared the soap and had shaved half my face when the Shah's butler entered the room in great haste. He took the razor and grabbed me by the hand, saying that it was the Shah's command that I come immediately, in whatever state I was. Although I pleaded with him, saying: 'Sir, be fair, have mercy! What would happen if Lord Salisbury, who saw me when we left, were to see me now in this state? Wait for me to shave the other half of my face!' He simply said that it was the Shah's command and dragged me off to the Shah's room.

The Shah was standing up and was very angry and distressed. He said: 'Reza, when we arrived from London, the steward told me that my jewel case was missing. I thought that it must have been left behind at Buckingham Palace. When Lord Salisbury telegraphed the palace and the police, however, the reply came back saying that it was not in the Palace and that the police had given orders for a search to be carried out. I cannot be satisfied with a routine police investigation, so I have told Lord Salisbury that the two policemen who accompanied me from London should go back there with you to investigate the whereabouts of this jewel case. By the time you get to London, it will be midnight, so the investigation will have to wait until tomorrow. Tomorrow, however, you must telegraph me at any hour to tell me what you have done and what steps the police are taking.' The Shah's butler then gave orders that I couldn't even return to my room: I would be taken to the door as I was and I must leave for London with the policemen.

As the railway station was close at hand, we took the train from there. When we arrived in London, the policemen suggested that I should go to the

20 Hatfield House in Hertfordshire.

Buckingham Hotel and they would go home. When I reached the hotel, it was after 11 o'clock and no one from the entourage was available. They had all either gone to bed or they had gone out for the evening. Nor was the manager there. The kitchen was shut and apart from the night porter, there was absolutely nobody on duty. I asked for a room, but he said that he had given all the good rooms either to the entourage or to other guests. The only thing he could do was to give me his room and he would sleep in the lobby. I thanked him but said that I had had no dinner. Could he give me something to eat? He said that he was sorry but the kitchen was shut and the cook had gone home. He said that if he could find anything in the larder, he would certainly give it to me. When he came back into the lobby from the kitchen, he placed a chair there and a small table, on which he laid a tablecloth. He brought a slice of dry bread with a piece of sausage and said that that was all there was. I asked him what the sausage was. He replied that it was pork. I told him to take it away: I wouldn't eat it. He then went and brought a cold chicken. I took a knife and fork and stabbed at the breast. Without exaggeration, ten or twenty huge worms emerged from its stomach and started to spill onto the table. I got up and shouted at him to remove it from my sight. It was now past midnight, so I went to the night porter's room to get some sleep. As soon as I got on to the bed, I saw that bedbugs had invaded it and were marching across my pillow in column formation, so I leapt out of bed. As I hadn't taken off my clothes and I was still wearing a frock-coat, I then went down to the lobby and sat on the chair with my head on the table, still itching from the bedbugs, but I couldn't sleep.

I kept on worrying how the police would ever be able to find the jewel case. As it was thought to contain jewels to a value of millions,[21] anybody who found it would never give it up. In that state, I decided that the next day I would go straight to Buckingham Palace, where I would search the royal treasurer's and the steward's rooms to see if they had left it there. If I didn't find them there, I would have to search the luggage carriage which had taken the Shah's trunks to the station. When these ideas came into my head, a ray of hope lit up my mind. Indeed it was almost as though I had already found the case. As I

---

21 In his travel diary, the Shah wrote that the case contained his travel diary, together with some secret papers and that he was very angry at its loss.

waited for sunrise, I forgot my hunger, my lack of sleep and the fact that I had no idea where my own luggage was. I kept on looking at my watch, counting the minutes until it was nine o'clock in the morning.

Instead of two ordinary constables, the chief of police had sent an officer and two intelligent constables. The officer asked me where I thought we should go. I replied that first we should go to Buckingham Palace. He said that it was no easy matter to get in there. First of all, permission would have to be obtained from the Lord Chamberlain, as otherwise no one would let us in. He asked me to wait a little, while he went to get permission. Less than half an hour later, he returned with written authorisation. They opened up the Shah's room, the box room and the Amin-os-Soltan's room, which we searched but found nothing. He then asked me where we should go now. I said that we should go to the coach stables. He said that permission to enter lay with the Master of the Horse and I should wait there while he obtained permission. This didn't take long: an official of the royal stables then accompanied us to the stables, where we found the carriage which had been used to take His Majesty's luggage from the palace to the station. I got into the carriage, which was all black and which had a long bench for the servants to sit on. I looked under it and there I saw the jewel case, which was also covered with black material so that nobody had been able to see it. I removed it and took it to the hotel, in order to telegraph to the Shah, although the case was by now officially in the hands of the police.

We came out of the hotel, where the Mokhber-od-Dowleh was sitting on a chair on the marble terrace at the top of the hotel steps looking out. He had seen me the previous day with the Shah and now he saw me with the police. When he saw the jewel case, you could have knocked him down with a feather. When I explained the what had happened to him, he said: 'Mirza Reza Khan, Abol-Qasem Khan's fall down the stairs yesterday and your finding the jewel case today are sure signs that you are favoured by heaven. You will certainly go very far in life. You must, however, first give me your promise not to forget my children when you are a great man.' He said that he thought that the telegram would arrive after me, so I should simply take the jewel case and go straight to Lord Salisbury's country house. I asked the departure time of the train and was told that it would leave at any time that I wanted. When I entered his Majesty's presence with the case, he jumped up joyfully and asked me to tell him everything that had occurred since I had left. I told him everything

Naser-od-Din Shah received by Lord Salisbury at Hatfield in July 1889 during the Shah's third visit to Europe. The Prince and Princess of Wales and the Shah's prime minister, the Amin-os-Soltan, can also be seen in the front. Reproduction by courtesy of the Marquess of Salisbury.

except the Mokhber-od-Dowleh's words. After showering me with praise, he told one of the eunuchs to tell the treasurer to give Mirza Reza Khan fifty napoleons as a reward.

I returned from London on a Sunday. Lord Salisbury, who was very religious, had gone to the chapel to pray, so the Shah said that we should go down to look at our host's library. By the time the Shah entered the library, Lord Salisbury had left the chapel, his wife had gone upstairs, and he was already in the library ahead of us. All the newspapers, including the illustrated London ones, had been placed on a very long, wide table. The Shah opened one and saw a photograph of a large cat, on which the Shah's crown had been placed. He turned over the newspaper and, very angry, turned round and started to climb the staircase in a rage. Lord Salisbury, who had observed this, was aghast. He opened the newspaper, saw the cat's head, understood what had

The Amin-os-Soltan, the Shah's prime minister, and Sir Henry Drummond-Wolff, British minister in Tehran, at Hatfield in July 1889. Reproduction by courtesy of the Marquess of Salisbury.

happened and asked me to go as fast as I could to persuade the Shah to talk to him for just a few minutes. Climbing the stairs as fast as I could, I somehow reached the Shah and gave him Lord Salisbury's request. The Shah thought that his host had urgent business with him, and was persuaded to come back down.

As the Shah entered the library, Lord Salisbury greeted him and took him over to a very large and spacious bookcase, which he opened. All the shelves were full of illustrated newspapers. He took out a newspaper from a shelf, showed it to the Shah and said: 'Look at these newspapers which all contain photographs of Lord Salisbury in various guises, even a pig's head, a monkey's and a cow's. Your Majesty, all the newspapers you see contain ridiculous and humorous pictures of me. I have never opposed them or protested at them for several reasons: first, our great men have said that this kind of newspaper is like the leaves from a tree which grows on the edge of a stream. They cease to be important when they fall off the tree and are trodden under the feet of passers-by. They become as insignificant as the leaves which have fallen into the stream. Second, in this country people say that if satirical pictures of our leaders don't appear in the newspapers, they are not considered figures of any weight. Frequent cartoons of a man in the press are signs of his importance. You should not be offended by the kind of thing which you have seen. The newspapers do the same thing to all kings and emperors. The reason for this stupid journalist's cartoon is that he knows French and the word "Shah" has two meanings in French. He had no intention of insulting you.' The Shah was apparently pacified by this explanation, for they came up the stairs together talking. Then the Shah retired to his room.

When we arrived in Edinburgh, the welcome given to the Shah by the government and the Lord Mayor was appropriately splendid. One very interesting event was the ball which, in accordance with local custom, was given in marquees for 2,000 people, all of whom, men and women, wore their national dress. The Shah did not like this ball, so he said that he wasn't feeling well and returned early to his residence. Actually, this was because Scottish national dress meant that men wore nothing below the knee, indeed they were completely naked, and as most of the male guests were old, the sight of their legs and knees covered with white hair was not a pleasant one.

A peer of ancient lineage who had no family and no heir to inherit his Scottish castle[22] sold it with all its furniture and fittings with the government's permission. Lord Rothschild, who lived in London and had British nationality, bought it for £10 million. As the Prince of Wales was reputed to favour Jews and protected them, the Shah had to go and stay there. Lord Rothschild had also invited the Prince, but Princess Alexandra didn't come. The Prince of Wales, however, was there together with their children. Rothschild's daughter, who was aged about sixteen, saw me in the garden and said that she had learnt

22 According to the Shah's travel diary, he was entertained to lunch at Halton Manor, Aylesbury, Buckinghamshire by Lionel Rothschild, where he was photographed, almost certainly by Aline Sassoon, a French Rothschild married to Sir Edward Sassoon, and then stayed the night of 7 July 1889 with the Baron Ferdinand de Rothschild at Waddesdon Manor, Buckinghamshire. It seems that the author's memory is misleading him, for the Shah was not a guest of the Rothschilds in Scotland.

photography in London, she had brought her camera with her and she wanted
to take photographs of the Shah, of the 'Aziz-os-Soltan and of any member of
the retinue the Shah indicated. She said that this should take place in a particular place in the garden, which she would show me. She told me that the 'Aziz-
os-Soltan should stand on the right and that I should stand immediately behind
the Shah so that my chest and head should be in the photograph. She asked me
to beg the Shah to accept, adding that if I would mention her idea to the Shah,
she would give her word of honour that on our return she would somehow or
other send me one of the photographs either in Iran or any other place that I
specified. I said that I would do my very best. I went and told the Shah what
had passed between Mademoiselle Rothschild and myself. He said that he had
no objection and accepted the young lady's request. Indeed if the photographs
turned out well, she was to send one to him. Mademoiselle Rothschild fixed
the time and place for the photography session, the Shah came and sat down,
with the 'Aziz-os-Soltan standing on his right and me standing behind him,
together with others whom the Shah ordered to join in. A year later, having
joined my new post at the consulate-general in Tiflis, I remembered to write a
letter to Mademoiselle at the address she had given me. A week later, a reply
came from her, enclosing a photograph and saying that she had also sent a
photograph to the Shah through the British Legation in Tehran.

One night we went to stay at the castle of Viscount Montrose, whose father
was a duke.[23] Our party were the only guests. The Viscount, with his mother,
the Duchess, and his wife, the Viscountess, and her sister were present. In the
evening, when they were about to go in to dinner, the Viscount asked me to
ask the Shah on his behalf to take his mother's arm and take her into dinner.
The Amin-os-Soltan should take his wife's arm and the private secretary
should take his sister-in-law into dinner. The Shah was sitting in a room with
the ladies, the Amin-os-Soltan and the secretary. Our host's wife was young
and pretty, the couple having married that year, and the Shah found her attractive. When I gave the Shah this message, he said: 'What kind of division of
spoils have you cooked up between you? I don't want to take this old woman's
arm and spoil my own dinner. Give her to the Amin-os-Soltan! I will take the

---

23 The Shah spent his first night in Scotland on 15 July at Buchanan Castle in Stirlingshire,
where his host was the fifth Duke of Montrose (1852–1925).

Viscountess into dinner.' I explained that this would be impossible. It would be a great insult to our host and would be talked of around the world. He said: 'If that is the case, then at least place the Viscountess next to me!' I said that naturally this was the way it would be: the Duchess would be on his right and the Viscountess on his left, so in due course he got up and took the old lady into the dining-room, where they sat down.

Detailed preparations had been made for a dance after dinner. As the village owned by our host was nearby, all the villagers had been invited to bring their musical instruments and torches and parade in front of the gateway where the Shah would be standing. In front of the house was a large lake, with boats moored on it. As soon as we got up from dinner, the Viscountess said to me that as the weather was a little cold that evening, she had told them to light a fire in one of the rooms near the dining-room, and if I liked, we could go and have a chat there. I said: 'With great pleasure. But you should go first and I will follow. If not, the Shah will see and I won't be able to come.' She left the room and then when the Shah and the Amin-os-Soltan were talking and couldn't see me, I saw an opportunity and went to the room she had mentioned. The lady was sitting close to the flames in front of the stove, so I sat down opposite her and started to tell the story of the Rothschild party. She asked me whether Princess Alexandra had been there. I said that she had not. She asked me to tell her the whole story. Who had been there? I replied that the Prince of Wales, his two sons and two daughters and the party who were now staying in her own house. She asked who was given the place of honour. I said that obviously it had been the Shah. She asked whether the party had all had breakfast together. I said that the Shah had had breakfast in his own room, as had the Prince of Wales, while I had eaten breakfast with our host and his wife in the dining-room. She asked what the party had done after breakfast. I said that the prince, the princesses, together with our host and his wife had gone to play tennis, while we went to watch. Then the Viscountess said that she was now warm, and withdrew her chair from the fire, leaving mine between her and the fire. Wanting to pay her a compliment, I said: 'You are a cruel woman, taking your chair away and placing me between two red-hot fires.' Suddenly I felt someone pull me by the ear. 'Get up! I have come to extinguish your fire,' said the Shah.

A short time later the party started. The villagers, carrying their torches and musical instruments, filed past the archway where the Shah was standing and took up their positions by the lake. The Viscountess had performed a wonder: she had decorated the shores of the lake with flowers, greenery and Chinese and Japanese lanterns. The Viscount gave the order and the villagers started to dance to the local tunes. First the women danced by themselves, then the men started to dance alone, and then the women and the men danced various dances together. After the dancing, the Shah said that he was tired and went to bed, with Saleh Khan, the eunuch, in attendance. Our host's mother then said that she was also tired and retired to her room. Then the Viscountess said that she and her sister knew how to row and as the boat would only take four people, they would invite the Amin-os-Soltan and myself on a boat trip round the lake, so that we could see the illuminations. We went down to the lake, and our host went to thank the villagers and tip them. The four of us then got into the rowing boat, each of the ladies took an oar, while we sat in the front of them, and off we went on round the lake. Meanwhile, when our host had said goodbye to the villagers and they had gone home, he also retired to his room.

Her sister said that the Viscountess had a good voice and suggested that we should ask her to give us pleasure by singing for us, so the Amin-os-Soltan and I begged her to do so, but she declined, saying that her voice wasn't good enough. We kept on begging her until finally she started to sing. Imagine what a feeling of happiness was created by the softness of the air, a full moon, the waters of the lake, in which the all the lanterns were reflected as in a mirror, and in front of us two fairy-like creature and a voice which would have made the nightingales fall in love! The Amin-os-Soltan and I lost consciousness, mesmerised by God's creation and the beauty of the earth and sky. The Amin-os-Soltan said to me: 'Reza, I don't know how long I shall live. It makes no difference whether it be twenty years, thirty years or a hundred years, but if after tonight I spend the rest of my life in prison and in fetters, I would not exchange this moment and all the subsequent misfortunes for a thousand royal thrones. For me nothing could compare with this pleasure.' I replied: 'Sir, Enjoy this happy moment which you say that you would not exchange for all the kingship in the world. At this very moment when the space between earth and sky is not wrapped in dust or clouds or rain and the gates of heaven are open, God is all powerful. Ask Him to grant you a better moment than tonight!' When this unfortunate man was murdered for no reason in front of the Consultative

Naser-od-Din Shah photographed at Ashridge, England in July 1889. By permission of the National Archives UK.

Assembly,[24] I couldn't help wondering whether when he spoke these sad words that evening, he knew what fate awaited him. A little after midnight, having rowed the whole way round the lake and returned to our departure point, we returned to our rooms with great regret that our moment of happiness had passed. The next day, as we were about to leave, the Viscountess gave me a photograph of herself on her wedding day and wrote on the back of it 'as a souvenir'. It is now in my photograph album at Daneshgah.

When we got back to London, we weren't taken to Buckingham Palace but directly to the coast, where the royal yacht *Victoria and Albert* was moored. All the entourage who had stayed at the hotel had gone on ahead there with

24 The Amin-os-Soltan was murdered by a member of a revolutionary society, the Social Democratic Party, in 1907 during the Constitutional Revolution.

all the baggage and were awaiting the Shah. There was also a guard of honour and a military band and several marquees had been erected. The Shah, his entourage and Sir Henry Drummond-Wolff, the British minister plenipotentiary in Tehran, who had accompanied the Shah for the whole of his visit to Scotland, went into the marquee to have coffee. The Prince of Wales and the ministers then entered, the guard of honour marched past the Shah, the Prince accompanied him to the foot of the gang-plank and to the sound of music the Shah bade a warm farewell to the Prince of Wales, who then shook our hands. We boarded the yacht, the band played a march and the guns thundered. His Majesty inspected the guard of honour and the yacht sailed for Amsterdam. I have nothing to say about the other courtiers because I was neither in competition with them nor was I jealous of them, but they had divided into two or three factions hostile to each other. I can't say that everyone enjoyed themselves but I certainly enjoyed my visit to England so much that for the rest of my life I have been unable to forget those happy moments and I have written and had published a short account in appreciation of them in *Montakhab-e-Danesh*.[25]

In Amsterdam, where following the death of her husband the reigning monarch was a queen, who was the mother of the present queen, the government received the Shah in an entirely seemly manner. One day, however, I was sitting in my room in the royal palace in Amsterdam when I was told that the Shah wished to see me urgently. The Shah was furious and he had a newspaper in his hand. I was certainly not expecting this. He told me to come in and as I entered, he threw the newspaper at me, saying that I was to take it and translate it quickly without showing it to anyone and then bring it back to him. Very disturbed, I took the newspaper and left the room. One of my three man group of allies said to me in a low voice that the Amin-od-Dowleh, who had gone on ahead, had sent this newspaper from Paris a few days before. The Shah had first sent it to the E'temad-os-Saltaneh, but my friend had no idea of what was in it. The E'temad-os-Saltaneh had said: 'I would rather be blind and that my hand lost its strength than do this. Give it to someone else to translate!' He had passed it on to Abol-Qasem Khan, who took it back to the Shah, saying

---

25 *Anthology of Knowledge* or, in a play on the author's name *Danesh's Anthology*, published in 1891 in Persian in Istanbul and in Tiflis in French in 1893.

that he didn't understand French. That was why the Shah had summoned me in this way and had given me the newspaper to translate.

From there I went to the Amin-os-Soltan's room and gave him an account of what had happened. He said: 'Quick! Read a little of it, while I keep an eye out in case one of the Shah's intimates comes and sees you with the newspaper in my company, having disobeyed the Shah's orders.' I saw written in capital letters: 'LE ROI PIQUE-ASSIETTE', meaning 'the king who makes holes in plates' or in other words 'the Scrounger King'. The Amin-os-Soltan trembled and told me to go away and translate the piece, as we shouldn't be seen together. I said that if those close to the Shah, such as the E'temad-os-Saltaneh and Abol-Qasem Khan, who had now left hospital and re-entered the Shah's service, wouldn't translate it, why should I? He said: 'You didn't write this, so you can't be blamed for it. Go and translate it quickly, as the Shah commands!'

The gist of the newspaper article was that the French government had asked the French parliament for a grant of 120,000 francs to spend on entertaining the most tyrannical king in the world, whereas the French parliament had unanimously and disgracefully rejected a request for 10,000 francs to buy surgical instruments for a French provincial hospital. Furthermore, when the Ministry of Education made a request for a 20,000 francs credit to open a primary school in a heavily-populated French province, parliament had unanimously rejected it, while granting a huge credit for the entertainment of a veritable Nero. The article continued that when the Shah had gone to Hazrat-e 'Abdol-'Azim[26] to seek a blessing for his journey, 200 of his hungry, naked soldiers who hadn't been paid for some time and were dying of hunger, wished to present a petition to the Shah. Aqa Vajih, who was behind the Shah's carriage, was pelted with stones by the soldiers and a stone hit the Shah's carriage. When the Shah asked Aqa Vajih what was going on, the latter, thoroughly frightened, had replied that the men were rebels, so the Shah gave orders for the soldiers who had thrown the stones to be seized and put to death. So, the article continued, the parliament shouldn't spend this 120,000 francs to the detriment of hospitals and schools and shouldn't admit this merciless individual to Paris.

---

26 Much revered tomb of a ninth-century descendant of 'Ali and of his son Hassan at Rey near Tehran, where Naser-od-Din Shah would himself be buried.

If his route took him through France at a time when Baha'is[27] were being shot in Iran, he should be allowed to do so but incognito and at his own expense. The Amin-os-Soltan told me to translate it to the end and then, as it was long and detailed, make a fair copy of it. He kept coming in and saying that the Shah said that when I had translated it, I was to bring it to him straight away.

Finally, I took the rough copy with the final version and the newspaper to the Shah's apartment. I was told that the Shah now wanted to go for a walk in the garden but was waiting for me. The Shah, who had seen me from afar, shouted out for me to approach. I was rooted to the spot and started to tremble. He took two steps forward and called out for me to come forward. I still remained motionless, trembling. His private servants and those courtiers who were there saw his mood and all fled to their rooms. The Shah didn't shout out a third time but came forward himself. At a distance of two yards from me he said: 'Have you translated the newspaper? Give it to me!' With my eyes I indicated the papers, which were under my arm. With a strange gesture he grabbed the papers and rushed down the stairs.

The private servants looked through the doorway and saw that the Shah had gone, so they went down the stairs very cautiously and followed him to see what he would do. I ran behind them. When they reached the foot of the staircase, they saw the Shah walking rapidly down the street to the end, where he sat down by the river on a bench. There he read the translation from beginning to end, then he started to tear up both the rough copy, the final version of the translation and the newspaper into tiny pieces, all of which he threw into the river. When he got up to come back, what a sight that was! How those private servants ran up the stairs! When the Shah arrived back, the corridor was entirely empty.

The Shah began to summon his entourage one by one and as each of them began to make excuses, he flew into a rage and told them to get out of his sight. This was the first time I had seen him behave like this and I asked my friends why the Shah was getting angry with people who had nothing to do with the newspaper. They said that any courtier who learnt the content of the

---

27 Baha'ism was a monotheistic faith founded in Iran by a religious leader known as 'the Bab' in the nineteenth century of the Christian era. Its followers were considered heretical and subversive by the clergy and were much persecuted.

newspaper must not think that the Shah's honour and power had been in any way adversely affected in the eyes of those around him, and everyone who knew his duty should incline his head and be obedient. In the immediate, however, this incident made no difference to his attitude towards France, for he summoned his private secretary and told him to send a telegram for the attention of the minister plenipotentiary there instructing him to call on the French minister of foreign affairs to say that he would arrive at the French frontier on such and such a date.

Since he had visited Holland on his previous journeys and had met the Queen of Holland, he didn't consider it necessary to stay in Holland and so he left almost immediately for France where he was obviously received with full honours. The President of the Republic and all the ministers met him at the railway-station, and the French minister plenipotentiary in Tehran had been appointed his official host. The Shah stayed at the Trocadero Palace. As there was very little room there, most of the entourage were put up at hotels. The French minister, whom I had known in Tehran before my posting to St Petersburg, said to me that if I wanted to be near the Shah and was willing to share a room with two or three others, he had a large room for me. I was very grateful and we four, the Fakhr-ol-Molk, Mehdi Khan, Ahmad Khan and I shared it.

On the night of the official party at the Opéra, at which everyone wore uniform or full evening dress, we were about to leave for the theatre when Haji Sadr-os-Saltaneh, who had been summoned from Washington, entered the palace reception room in uniform and said that he had heard that the Shah and entourage were going to the theatre and he was going with us. As he had arrived only that morning, I asked how it could be that the French government had been informed of his arrival soon enough to be able to issue him with an invitation to the theatre. He said that he hadn't been invited but didn't need an invitation. He had the right to go to where the Shah was: he was a minister plenipotentiary. At that moment the French minister in Tehran entered the room. Haji Sadr-os-Saltaneh went up to him, introduced himself to the Frenchman as an Iranian minister plenipotentiary and said that he intended to go to the theatre. The latter said that he was very sorry to tell him this but he could not go to the theatre without an invitation. He said that the gentlemen attending the theatre were all part of the Shah's entourage. On his arrival, the Shah had introduced them to the president of the republic, who had invited

The author photographed in Paris during the Shah's third visit to Europe in 1889. From the collection of Farhad and Firouzeh Diba.

them with special invitation cards. They all had numbered seats in the theatre and each one had to be sitting in his own numbered seat before the Shah arrived. Where in the theatre did he think that he could seat him? When Haji Sadr-os-Saltaneh heard this reply, he promptly left the room.

In due course, a servant entered saying that the carriage was ready and we should leave. We four had been allotted a large landau. Before we could all seat ourselves in the landau, Haji Sadr-os-Saltaneh came up and jumped into our carriage. I explained to him that we four had just managed to squeeze ourselves into it in our uniforms and anyway, after hearing our official host's reply, where did he think he was going? He said that the latter was talking non-sense. He was going and would sit in the Shah's box. He somehow managed to sit down on the carriage seat and as it was a long way from the Trocadéro Palace to the Opéra theatre, he began to talk. He said that even if the French didn't know how important he was, we Iranians should get this firmly into our heads. Mehdi Khan, who was a close intimate of the Shah and had made a study of this kind of person, with a view to telling the Shah and making him laugh, saw that he was in luck and said: 'Sir, how do you know that Iranians aren't good at assessing a man's value? Kindly tell us which Iranians here do not know how important you are! I certainly know how important you are.' Haji Sadr-os-Saltaneh replied that two months previously, a highly respected Washington hostess had written to tell him that several musical evenings were to be given at the opera house in aid of hospitals and the poor and that it would be much appreciated if he would agree to sing one of his nation's songs. If he was willing to do so, he should wear national dress. He said that in order to do honour to Iran he had accepted the invitation.

On the day specified, he had dressed in the long outer garment and cashmere shawl given him by the Shah, he had worn his jewelled sword and his medal with a portrait of the Shah, together with all his other medals. Unfortunately, he had been unable to find a shawl to go round his hat, so with only an Iranian hat on his head he had gone and recited a poem in Persian and then he had translated it into English. As soon as he went on stage, he said, there had been an extraordinary hullabaloo. Everyone, men and women, in the seats and boxes had got up and clapped and shouted 'Hurrah!' When he had finished, there was uproar. He had been obliged to repeat the performance not three but four times. Mehdi Khan said: 'Sir, could you enchant me by reciting the same poem in the same voice?' By this time we had reached the beginning of the Avenue de l'Opéra, where more than 100,000 Parisians had gathered in the fine weather to see the illuminations and the Shah. The more I kept on pressing Mehdi Khan's knee and saying that this was not right, the more determined he became. The minister began to sing the poem in English to his own tune. Just imagine four young people in very formal uniform sitting in an open landau, with an old man sitting between them singing in his own peculiar voice in English! The only two people not to be upset at being ridiculed by the French were Mehdi Khan and the Sadr-os-Saltaneh himself.

Every step of the way, a thousand rude noises rose to the heavens, as the French crowd made fun of us. However much I said: 'This really is enough, we are dying of embarrassment,' neither Mehdi Khan nor the Sadr-os-Saltaneh paid any attention. When we reached the Opéra, we saw the French minister standing in the corridor leading to the boxes and identifying the entourage.

He came up and stopped the Sadr-os-Saltaneh, saying: 'In what language do I have to tell you that you have no place here and that you have no right to enter?' The latter replied that he was entitled to a place there and he would now show him this. The huge door to the Shah's box was open. He suddenly pushed through into the box and stood behind the Shah's seat. He asked the Shah to tell the official host that he was his minister plenipotentiary and that he had the right to stand behind him: he didn't need a chair. The Shah, who wasn't aware of the background, told the Amin-os-Soltan to give him a chair and he would find out what he had to say for himself later. The Amin-os-Soltan passed on the Shah's command to the French minister, who had come to sit in the Shah's box. The minister left the box and ordered an ordinary dining chair to be brought which was placed behind everyone else's, and the Sadr-os-Saltaneh sat down. After the theatre, Mehdi Khan wanted to make the Shah laugh with his report of what this pompous man had done. The Shah was furious, however, at what had happened. As soon as he woke up the next day, he ordered the Amin-os-Sultan to send someone immediately to remove the Sadr-os-Saltaneh from Paris that very day and send him back to Iran. Haji Sadr-os-Saltaneh had some friends and family at court, however, who interceded for him pleading that as he was a minister, he should not be dismissed in such disgrace. As the Shah had also ordered the Mashkuh-od-Dowleh, his brother-in-law, to be sent away from Paris for some reason, the Amin-os-Soltan arranged that these two should go and stay in Istanbul, escorting the trunks which the Shah had ordered to be sent to Tehran by way of Istanbul. Their travel expenses were paid and they both left for Istanbul.

Naser-od-Din Shah was very respectful of women and was happy just to gaze at them: he loved beautiful women, but he was also extremely jealous in his dealings with them, to a point where if he saw a beautiful woman who pleased him at the theatre, he would look at her but if any of his courtiers also looked at her, he would be very displeased. Some of my friends in Moscow knew of this trait in the Shah's character and told the following story: On the same evening at the Opéra, he had been looking at two very beautiful actresses through his opera glasses from his seat immediately opposite the stage. Later that evening he said to Dr Tholozan, his private doctor: 'If possible, please tell those actresses to come to the Trocadero Palace tomorrow and take tea with me.' Obviously, the two actresses were proud to accept this

invitation. Indeed they were so pleased that they arrived at the Trocadero
Palace half an hour before they were due. Dr Tholozan put them in the tea-
room and told me to keep them occupied for a short time until the Shah came.
I thanked him but suggested that he entrust this task to someone else. I didn't
want to have anything to do with it. Mirza Reza Khan Mo'ayyed-os-Saltaneh
had come to Paris from Berlin, so Dr Tholozan referred this task to him. He
was happy to do this and kept the ladies busy talking. As soon as the appointed
hour arrived, Dr Tholozan went and told the Shah that the ladies had been
waiting for some time. The Shah asked who was in the room with them. Dr
Tholozan replied that he had sent the Mo'ayyed-os-Saltaneh to keep them
busy. When the Shah entered the room and saw the Mo'ayyed-os-Saltaneh
with them, he said nothing but made a sign that he should leave. After tea
and cakes, the actresses left and the Shah told Dr Tholozan, who was present
and translated some phrases which the Shah didn't understand, to give each
of them a tip. Then he summoned the Amin-os-Soltan and said: 'Mirza Reza
Khan Mo'ayyed-os-Saltaneh is minister plenipotentiary in Berlin. What is he
doing here? He must leave tomorrow.'

Before his departure from Tehran, the Shah had ordered Haji Mohsen Khan
Mo'in-ol-Molk, Iran's ambassador in Istanbul, to find an educated, beautiful Circassian girl, already trained, for him in Istanbul, buy her and bring
her to him. The Circassians who live round the Crimea are Sunni Muslims,
who know no trade or craft and thus are poor. Anyone who has a beautiful
daughter brings her to Istanbul and sells her. However, it is not described as a
'sale'. The father takes her to the house of a rich pasha and if she pleases the
wives of the pasha, he starts to bargain and then receives a sum of money as
a bride-price. He then hands his daughter over to the pasha's wife, who trains
her. These girls are taught to write, to sing, to play a musical instrument and
dance and when they reach the age of fifteen or sixteen, they are married off,
but the husband pays a considerable sum of money as a reward to the Pasha's
family for having educated and trained her.

On the day of our arrival in Amsterdam, the Shah told the Amin-os-Soltan
that he had sent the eunuchs to Istanbul to fetch a guest for him. The next day
I was to go to the railway-station at a certain time. The name of 'the guest' was
Hossein Khan. With the skill for which I was known I was to extract Hossein
Khan and the eunuchs from the throng of travellers arriving at the station

and bring them back in the government carriage which would be placed at our disposal. That evening Mehdi Khan told me that the eunuchs had in fact gone to Istanbul to fetch the girl whom the Moʻin-ol-Molk had bought for the Shah. If she arrived in Ottoman clothes, this would be a boon for French satirists, so they had dressed her in a man's clothing. It was even rumoured that there had been a marriage ceremony in Istanbul and she was to be the Shah's wife. As the Shah had confidence in me, he was sending me to bring her, but I should not speak to her or smile or even look at her in a meaningful way, for the eunuchs were spies. I should not forget what the Shah had done to the Moʼayyed-os-Saltaneh. I thanked my travelling companions very much for their loyalty to our agreement in keeping me fully informed.

At the appointed hour I went to the railway station and, as my friends had advised me to do, I went ahead, took the new arrivals aside and sat them in the carriage, while I travelled to the palace in another carriage. I certainly didn't look at her and still don't know whether she was beautiful or not or even whether she had dark hair or was a blonde. All that I know is that the Shah gave the Moʻin-ol-Molk £300, in addition to the cost of her clothes and travel expenses, and that the Shah wasn't particularly pleased either by her character or her face. He divorced her in Tehran, paid her travel expenses back to Istanbul and returned her to the woman who had sold her. As a result of this, he was displeased with the Moʻin-ol-Molk and dismissed him from the ambassadorship. After spending so much money on her, he had expected to find a better type of girl.

One day, the Amin-os-Soltan suggested that we should visit the Grande Exposition to see the tethered balloon for the first time. When we reached Paris, two people from the balloon company had invited the Shah to go up for a ride in the balloon. The Shah had been warned by everyone, however, that on one occasion a strong wind had torn the rope from its moorings, the balloon had then risen as far in the air as the amount of gas in it would allow and there it had stayed for several hours. Consequently the Shah refused the invitation and forbade his entourage from going up in the balloon.

As the Amin-os-Soltan and I approached the balloon, he suggested that we go and see what was going on. As we drew near, the spectators saw that we were wearing Iranian hats and recognised us as the Shah's courtiers. Some of the spectators had taken their places in the balloon, facing us from all four sides, and called out to us to encourage us to get into the basket too. Although we would both have liked to do so and look at the view, the Shah's command forbade us from doing so. The company share-holders, seeing us watching, wanted to provoke us. They started shouting out in a loud voice: 'Iranian gentlemen, you shouldn't be less brave than women. Look how confidently they get into the basket! We guarantee that the rope is very strong and will not tear.' Then the Amin-os-Soltan and I looked at each other. He said: 'What can we do? If we don't get in, Iranians will be humiliated, for people will say that we are less than women. Promise that you will not tell your companions that we went up in the balloon!' We looked all round us and saw that there were no Iranians present, so we finally got into the basket. When twelve passengers were seated, the balloon started to rise but it stopped as soon as it reached an altitude of five metres. Everyone was taken aback and thought that there was something wrong with it. We remained hanging in the air, but the engineer told us not to worry, for it would start to rise again very soon. After a pause of a few minutes, it started to rise again and at a height of 300 metres the balloon started to move off in a southerly direction, but as this did not cause the position of the basket to change, it continued to go up vertically. Meanwhile, the engineer was continually trying to boost our morale, so we weren't frightened. Fortunately the company had hired out about a dozen pairs of binoculars. From a height of 500 metres, they brought the balloon down gently and we got out safely, pleased to have at least seen such a great invention as the balloon.

We had two days rest after this event. On the third day at dawn, a servant came and told me that the Shah wished to see me. When I got up, Mehdi Khan also woke up and said: 'Your house is in ruins, I couldn't defend you yesterday. You disobeyed the Shah's express order. You got into the balloon with the Amin-os-Soltan, you were photographed and people were selling the photographs, which the eunuchs bought and took to the Shah. I was present when the Shah saw them, and he flew into a rage. He was angrier with the Amin-os-Soltan at having got into the balloon and taken you with him than he was with you but he ordered the eunuchs to summon you and the Amin-os-Soltan the moment he woke up. Take care to say nothing, so that he doesn't become even angrier!' From his explanation I understood that I was being advised to put all the blame for the incident on to the Amin-os-Soltan. I thanked him sincerely, but suggested that we should wait and see what happened.

I went to the Shah's apartment and saw that as in London, he was wearing a felt hat and sitting on a cushion with two eunuchs standing in front of him. Since it was a little early for the Amin-os-Soltan, I had arrived a few moments before him. I saw that the photograph was by the Shah's side. I understood that he thought that we would deny everything and he would then show us the photograph. He said: 'Tell me! Did you get into the balloon?' I replied very boldly that I had. He asked with whom I had done so. I replied that it had been with the Amin-os-Soltan. He asked whether any of his other servants had done so. I replied: 'No'. 'Did he not tell you that I had forbidden anyone to do so?' the Shah asked. I replied that the Amin-os-Soltan had communicated His Majesty's order to all his servants and members of the household. He said: 'In that case why did you disobey my order?' I replied that after a great deal of discussion between ourselves, we had felt obliged to get into the basket to preserve the honour of Iran and the reputation of His Imperial Majesty's servants.

At that moment the Amin-os-Soltan entered the room and stood listening to what I was saying. The Shah didn't interrupt me but said: 'Go on, tell me what this business of preserving honour was about!' I humbly told His Majesty exactly what had happened without exaggerating or changing anything. The Shah understood from the calm manner in which I was speaking that I was telling the truth, but he picked up the photograph and threw it in front of me, thus indicating that nothing in the whole world remained a secret from him. I picked it up and showed it to the Amin-os-Soltan. It was obvious that we had been photographed during our five minutes up in the air. As I saw that the Shah wished to speak to the Amin-os-Soltan, I bowed and left the room. Obviously, following the incident over the purchase of the rifles, the eunuchs had bought the photographs in order to damage me. As a result of the agreement between us four friends, however, we were able to escape from this difficult situation.

At that time the famous Sadi Carnot was the President of the French Republic. It was said that his father was a very cultivated man, whose surname was Carnot and who had given his son the first name Sadi in honour of our poet, Sa'adi. Since in French there is no letter 'ein', this gradually became Sadi. *Nazar Aqa*, Iran's minister in Paris, said that the president really loved Iran, and the garden-party which he gave at the Luxembourg Palace, his official residence, was clear evidence of this. He and his wife received us with smiling faces. In the garden itself and in the great hall which gave on to the garden, there were tables full of flowers and greenery on which sweet things, ice-creams, soft drinks and the best fruit available in Paris were offered to the guests. At Versailles we were also invited to a tea-party, when all the fountains were turned on.

A really strange thing happened to me at Versailles. A guide was showing the rooms and the furniture to us four friends. We duly arrived at Louis XIV's bedroom, in which there was a mattress, pillows and a bed which was so large that six people could sleep in it in perfect comfort without touching each other. Above the bed there was a niche with a mirror the width of the bed, so that when someone was in bed and looked at the mirror he saw himself as more than 300 people. In his presentation, the guide described how the king of France lacked for nothing in this world and was able to indulge in the most refined pleasures. This mirror had been specially made so that when he was in bed with one of his numerous mistresses, he could derive enough pleasure for 300 people, as he wanted to see 300 people making love. I said to my three companions that with their permission I would lie down on the bed for a minute so that I could see myself 300 times. They laughed and said that first the housekeeper wouldn't allow it, and if he did, what would be the point? I replied that they had heard the guide say that the owner of the bed had enjoyed the most refined pleasures and had left this world without any regrets. I also wanted to write in my travel diary that I had seen the world's wonders so that I could leave the world without regrets. They said that I really was an odd fellow: I didn't behave like a normal human being. When I had finally convinced them that my idea was a good one, I started to negotiate with the guide. I said that I would take off my boots as a sign of respect and look at myself as 300 people for just a few seconds. I would give him one napoleon as a souvenir. He said that he was afraid that his chief would hear us and dismiss him. I said that we four would promise not to tell anyone else and certainly not any of the other guides. I then took off my boots, lay down on the bed and saw even more than 300 people in the mirror. One could really say that nothing like this had ever been made in the whole world. When we reached the Troca-déro, Mehdi Khan made his report to the Shah, who summoned me and said: 'You are a sly fellow, why didn't you tell me? I would have wanted to see 300 versions of myself.' I said that first I had no idea that such a mirror existed in

Versailles and if I had known, I wouldn't have dared to tell him. For me to lie for a moment on Louis XIV's bed was an insignificant event and would not have excited any comment. However, His Imperial Majesty's actions, to which the whole world paid attention, wouldn't have been in the same class as those of his servants and would have received wide publicity. He said: 'Bravo! You spoke well.'

As had been the case with the reception at the Crystal Palace in London, the Paris reception was itself unique. It consisted of a soirée given in honour of the Shah on the banks of the Seine near the bridge now known as the Pont Alexandre III. Large vessels plied back and forth and both banks of the Seine were illuminated for several kilometres. All the boats, large and small, even launches, were illuminated by electric lights of various colours and there were military bands on the larger vessels. Even on the smaller boats and skiffs, there were musical instruments of every kind: pianos, guitars, cellos, percussion instruments, drums and flutes. Everyone had brought what they could and all these vessels and skiffs were decked out in French and Iranian flags. Foreign vessels had mixed their own national flags with those of France and Iran. On the French vessels there were all kinds of fireworks and on others people had fixed up makeshift fireworks such as rockets and multi-coloured ones fixed to frames.

When the festivities were over, the Shah left for Vienna, where the Emperor Franz Jozef also gave him a suitable welcome. His Majesty and the entourage were lodged at the royal palace. As the Emperor had been in mourning since the death at sea of the Empress, however, there were no more brilliant balls at the court in Vienna. Vienna, however, is famous for its theatre and its music. The best musicians train there. Infantry and cavalry uniforms are more elegant than in other European countries. Indeed the whole population of this town is generally better dressed and more elegant than the people of other European cities. On Naser-od-Din Shah's second visit to Europe, when he had visited many countries, twelve officers had been chosen by the Emperor of Austria to train Iranian soldiers. From then on, Austrian uniforms became quite a normal sight in Iran. Indeed, during the whole Qajar period the uniforms of generals, brigadiers, colonels and indeed all officers were all based on Austrian uniforms. As the Shah was by now very tired, he was allowed by the Austrian government to go to Budapest at his own expense and relax there for ten days. Nariman Khan, Iran's minister in Vienna, was sent to Budapest, where he rented two hotels, one for the Shah and ministers and the other for the entourage. Apart from the first day, when there was a guard of honour and the Austrian Emperor's brother greeted the Shah, he was free to do what he wanted. Hungarians are of Mongol descent, for they arrived with a horde from Mongolia and took over the country. Of course through racial intermingling with Europeans, there are many beautiful Hungarian women and the men are tall and well-made. The Austrian cavalry, the Hussars, who are renowned for their courage and manoeuvrability, are in fact Hungarians.

One day the Shah summoned me, together with one or two of his personal attendants, and said that he wanted to go for a walk in the city, as he hadn't been for a walk for some time. Our route led us past a hussar barracks. At the gate there was a patrol armed with rifles. The Shah expressed a wish to see the cavalry quarters for himself. I suggested to him that the guard wouldn't allow me to enter the barracks. He said that he would stay where he was but I should go up to the soldier. Perhaps an officer would come and I could tell him what the Shah wanted. Their commander would then come and escort us in. Several officers were talking on the parade ground, so I made a sign, one of them came over and I explained the Shah's wishes. He explained that the colonel com-mandant's lodgings were on the upper floor above the gate. He told me to wait a few minutes while he went and briefed him. The colonel immediately came out in a great hurry, bowed to the Shah and invited him to enter. The Shah said that he would like to see the horses. The colonel gave orders for the doors to be opened and we entered the stables. Hungarian horses are famous for their quality and most European cavalry regiments buy their horses there, for they are of good conformation and size. The Shah proceeded to inspect them. He then asked the colonel how many horses he had there and the latter replied that there were a little over a thousand. When the inspection of the horses was over, the colonel took us to the parade ground where the Shah asked him whether it would be possible to have a trumpet sound the reveille to summon the cavalry to come and saddle their horses. As all the cavalry lodgings were inside the barracks, the moment the reveille sounded, the men poured out from every door and in the twinkling of an eye every man was standing by his horse and saddling it. In a very short time they and their officers were stand-ing to attention in front of their colonel awaiting orders. The Shah then said that he wanted to see them charge, but beforehand he would like to see them drill. The colonel duly passed the Shah's orders to the commanders and asked the Shah to go to an appropriate place to review the parade. After some drill exercises, the cavalry went to the end of the parade ground and formed a line in front of us. Suddenly, when the colonel gave the order to attack: 'Charge!', they broke into a beautifully disciplined gallop. It was a truly wonderful sight. Exactly fifteen metres from the Shah the colonel gave the order to halt. It was as though these horsemen were immediately pinned to the ground. The Shah was full of praise for this exercise and asked the colonel to express his gratitude to the men, who gave three cheers for the Shah and were then dismissed. In perfect order they returned to tie up their horses to their mangers. The Shah later passed on his satisfaction to the Emperor through the latter's brother.

The Shah wanted to return to the palace. The colonel asked to be allowed to accompany him for a few yards, which the Shah graciously accepted, and the colonel said that he would like to ask one question: would it be possible for the Austrian instructors in Tehran to form and train this kind of brigade of hussars or not?[28] The Shah thought about this for a few moments and then told me to tell the colonel that since the arrival of the Austrian officers in Tehran we had not yet had time to form this kind of brigade. Two-thirds of our people were tribesmen and our horses were Arab horses. These tribes had many tribal chiefs who were passionate about horsemanship. From childhood their education was actually to catch deer at a gallop, not to shoot them with a rifle. In time of war, at the gallop they could sever an enemy's head from his body like a pumpkin with their swords. Although he had no hussars, any time he wanted he could summon 300,000 Iranian tribal horsemen and send them into battle anywhere he wanted.

From Budapest, we travelled directly to Tiflis where, on the first of Moharram of the lunar year of the Hijra 1307,[29] the Shah received an official welcome as he had done on our arrival from Iran and the 'Ala'-os-Saltaneh held a *row-zeh-khwani* at the consulate.

---

28 The Shah had been impressed by the Austrian cavalry on his second visit to Europe in 1878, but on this journey he was so struck by his Russian Cossack escorts that on his return to Tehran he asked for Russian military training and the Russian-officered Cossack Brigade was formed.

29 28 August 1889.

Prince Dondukov-Korsakov, the governor-general of the Caucasus, had gone to St Petersburg, so General Sherematiev, his deputy, was acting in his place. The general's wife was the honorary president of the Caucasus School for Noble Ladies, which was called the St Nina School. Four hundred girls boarded and studied there. One day this lady asked me to go and see her. She said that because of our friendship during my time as secretary in Tiflis, she wanted to do me a favour. It was as follows: I would remember the music teacher Monsieur Dekerschenk who on the occasion of Naser-od-Din's second visit to Europe had played 'Hail to the Shah!' to music by Strauss, the famous composer, in St Petersburg and how I had translated the words from Persian to French and then adapted the lines of poetry to Strauss's composition.[30] She had found one of Strauss's scores, which she had given to the girls at St Nina's School the previous month. They had rehearsed both the score and the words. She wanted to invite the Shah and his entourage to tea at the school, where she would stand in line with her 400 girl pupils, all dressed in white, and conduct them as they sang greetings to him. I cannot imagine that such a concert would have been given for the Shah anywhere else in Europe. Obviously, I complimented her on this idea and went and told the whole story to the ʿAlaʾ-os-Saltaneh, who asked for a copy of the composition and studied it. One day then, he invited the Amin-os-Soltan and the royal entourage to the consulate and asked for the music to be sung as a rehearsal, which the young ladies duly did.

On the appointed day, therefore, Madame Sherematiev invited everyone to the school, where Persian carpets and chairs had been placed in the courtyard. She had not said that it was I who had composed the lines of poetry, as she wanted it to be a surprise. Four hundred girls then started to sing in tune: 'Vive le Shah! May He Live For Ever!' When the Shah and the entourage sat down, 400 girls as beautiful as fairies, dressed in white, with curly hair, paraded before him, and when Madame Sherematiev gave the order, halted and formed lines. Then musicians from the Tiflis theatre orchestra started to play 'Hail to the Shah!' The Shah and the entourage stood up and then the

---

30 Johann Strauss the Younger composed military music to be played as the Iranian national anthem during the Shah's visit to Vienna on his first journey to Europe in 1873. The music seems to have been that used by the author on this occasion.

girls sang in unison in French the lines 'Vive le Shah!' It was so well received
by the Shah that at his royal command they played it again three times. The
Shah then called over Madame Sherematiev, thanked her, shook her hand and
asked who had composed the lines of poetry. At the time I was standing with
the entourage, so Madame Sherematiev came and took me by the hand into
the Shah's presence and said that I was the author of the poetry. The Shah was
very complimentary. When I had been a secretary at the consulate and Monsieur Dekerschenk had come and made me turn 'Hail to the Shah!' into French
poetry, I had never imagined that 400 schoolgirls would sing this to music in
the presence of the Shah himself.

Because of Moharram, it had been arranged that the Shah would leave
Tiflis on the 11th of the month in 1307.[31] I introduced to him in an appropriate
way the Sheikh-ol-Islam and the Qazi, who had been deputed by the government of the Caucasus to come and present official congratulations to the Shah
and I obtained a robe of honour for each of them from the Shah. In Iranian
Jolfa there was a huge gathering: leading personalities and ministers from
Tehran, Qazvin, Zanjan, Tabriz, indeed anybody who could come to greet His
Majesty did so. Mozaffar-od-Din Mirza, the Heir Apparent, was present with
all the members of his court. On the evening of our arrival, an official dinner
was given for our Russian hosts, at which the Amin-os-Soltan presided on
behalf of the Shah. As on the outward journey, I escorted the hosts and their
fine horses with their gold and silver harness to the tent. There were actually
two magnificent tents, one lined with shawls and the other with hand-printed
fabric. The reception was in the tent lined with shawls and the dinner in the
one lined with printed cotton. At the dinner Admiral Popov drank a toast to
the Shah and the Amin-os-Soltan proposed a toast to the Tsar. After dinner
the Shah received the official hosts in his personal tent and with his own hand
gave a bejewelled, diamond-encrusted portrait of himself to Admiral Popov,
while the Amin-os-Soltan gave medals and presents to our other hosts, who
thanked him and returned to the Kashmir shawl tent.

Admiral Popov said to me that as they were leaving for St Petersburg the
next day, he would like me to travel with them. As the Russians had brought

---

31 After 'Ashura, the tenth day of the month of Moharram, during which the Shi'a mourn
the death of the Imam Hossein and his family.

me from the capital, they were happy to take me back with them. He repeated his invitation officially to the Amin-os-Soltan but the latter said that I must first obtain the Shah's permission, so he went to the Shah's tent and told him what had happened. The Shah said that I should join the Russians for the night and he would give his decision in the morning. Word seeped out that he would not give his permission, so I accompanied our hosts to the riverbank in the same way as before and they departed.

Admiral Popov said: 'Since I have seen how hard you have worked on this journey and have told the Tsar all about this, I wanted to give you this good and no doubt unexpected news on our arrival in St Petersburg. However, since I do not think that you will be with us tomorrow, I will say goodbye to you with great regret and give you the good news now. The Tsar has awarded you the Order of Anna (Second Class) encrusted with diamonds. Not only is it the most beautiful Russian decoration but it is rarely given to foreign subjects.'

We slept that night very uncomfortably in the same room in the passport office. I didn't know what to do. Was I to return by those long, exhausting roads with post-house horses? It would be very difficult and I would have to pay my travel expenses myself. In the morning, I saw that the tents had been struck, the baggage loaded and everyone was leaving for Marand. I was the only person left there, without a tent, a horse or a servant. I was in utter despair. Of necessity I stood as near as I could to the Shah's carriage, so that he might see me and tell me what to do. On Iranian soil the Shah is a different person to the Shah abroad. Here in Iran there are so many doormen, attendants and mounted mace-bearers that it is literally impossible to approach him without his express command. Then the Shah emerged from his tent with the 'Aziz-os-Soltan and the Amin-os-Soltan. He told the *Hajeb-od-Dowleh* to summon me. When I approached him, I bowed and he told the Amin-os-Soltan that Mirza Reza Khan was not to go back to St Petersburg but should return to Tehran as part of his suite. I should sit in the 'Aziz-os-Soltan's carriage during the day and sleep in the Amin-os-Soltan's reception tent. When he reached Tehran, he would say what my duties would be. He then turned to the 'Aziz-os-Soltan and said: 'Dear one, Mirza Reza Khan will be your guest from here to Tehran. You must be very kind to him.' The Amin-os-Soltan made a sign to me that I was to kiss the Shah's foot. It was the custom of that time for the Shah to give permission for someone to kiss his foot, so I did so for the first time and then the Shah got into his carriage. The thing that most astonished people was that four horses with dyed tails pulled the 'Aziz-os-Soltan's royal carriage so that it would be clear that the person sitting in it was from the royal family. The Shah's order to the Hajeb-od-Dowleh was that the 'Aziz-os-Soltan's carriage should always be immediately behind his own carriage and should have precedence over all the other carriages, even the Heir Apparent's.

The Khans of Makou and the Avajaq, the Qarapapash and all the Shahsavan and Azabaijani Kurds had come to greet the Shah but as it was impossible to find provisions for them and their horses at the staging-posts which lay ahead, the Shah had decided to dismiss them when we set off from Jolfa. The Kurdish, Shahsavan and other tribal chiefs asked the Shah if he would halt for a while at the top of a hill and allow them to demonstrate their skills at shooting, galloping, firing backwards at a gallop, picking up handkerchiefs from the ground at a gallop, even wrestling an opponent out of his saddle at the gallop and carrying him off before he could fall to the ground. It is impossible to do justice with the pen to the skills shown by the tribal leaders and their sons on that huge plain during the hour-long demonstration. The most remarkable feat of all was when two young men faced each other and fought each other with spears. When one's spear shattered, the other combatant also threw away his spear, they then drew their swords and fought with a sword in one hand and a shield in the other, letting go of their reins so as to be free to use their shields while the horse continued to obey its master. The loser would then throw away his sword and flee like the wind. The winner would then gallop after him like lightening and grab him by the waist, lift him from the saddle and carry him off to wherever he wanted.

When the Shah ordered the demonstration to come to an end, he called for me and said: 'I know that you have never seen the courage and skill of the tribes. When I spoke to the colonel in Budapest, about our tribes, he accepted my word without question, but I know that you had your doubts. Now, however, I will ask you one question: Are the courage and skill of our tribesmen greater than those of the Hungarian cavalry?' I replied that truly there was no comparison. People abroad had no idea of the skill of these horsemen and indeed if anyone could actually describe it, no one would believe him. I suggested that it might be a good idea from time to time to invite foreign cavalry generals whose guest he had been to witness what we had just seen.

When we arrived in Tabriz, my father and mother didn't know that I was coming, for I hadn't had an opportunity to warn them. When I knocked on the door, they didn't recognise me. When I had left Tabriz, I had worn the clothes of a merchant's son, but now I was wearing the uniform of an adjutant general. Fortunately, my parents and my brothers and sisters were all at home. When my mother heard my voice, she cried: 'Oh! Reza!' and promptly fainted, whereupon my siblings brought rose-water and managed to revive her. Family and friends were informed and came to the house, with the men gathering in one room and the women in another. For the rest of the day, I was busy receiving guests. Everyone asked how I had managed to attain this position. Then I saw a *dervish* enter with a drinking bowl in one hand and a *dervish*'s axe in the other and started to recite a panegyric in praise of the Commander of the Faithful. It was my cousin Aqa Jaʿfar, who had said that he would become a *dervish* when we were children. As His Majesty wished to rest for a few days in the North Garden in Tabriz, he had given me a two day holiday so that I could spend time with my father and mother.

On the third morning, I was told that two royal footmen, dressed in their distinctive uniforms, had arrived from the court in a government carriage to take me to the North Garden. On my arrival there, Mozaffar-od-Din Mirza, the Heir Apparent, was standing with Mirza Fazlollah Khan, the chief secretary, and Mirza ʿAbd-or-Rahim Khan, the deputy-governor. A servant came and told me that the Shah was alone in the pool area of the house and wanted to see me. The pool area is only two steps up from the courtyard and a fountain of pure water flows from the floor. The water was very clear and the air there was wonderful. The Shah was sitting on a chair with a large table in front of him with different types of Tabriz grapes laid out on it for show. According to the gardener, there were fifty-two kinds. When the Shah saw me, I bowed and he ordered me to come forward. He said: 'You see how good Tabriz grapes are and how many varieties of them there are.' He asked whether the supply department had given me any. I replied that they had. Then with his own hand he took a bunch of seedless Tabriz raisin grapes and said: 'They certainly didn't give you any of these. Eat them!' I bowed and retired backwards. As the door to the pool area was open, the private servants, as was their wont, were following what happened to me. First the Heir Apparent, then the Amin-os-Soltan, then the deputy-governor all congratulated me warmly. I offered some of the grapes to each of them, but they said that this was really a mark of special royal favour, and suggested that I go away and eat them all. So the dream which I had dreamt at twelve years old about that very garden and which I had recounted to Haji Taqi, my cousin, all those years ago turned out to be true exactly as I had dreamt it.[32]

After a few days rest in Tabriz, the Shah left for Tehran. I rode in the ʿAziz-os-Soltan's carriage, as I had done up till then. Near Basmenj, he noticed that the Heir Apparent's carriage was in front of his, so he ordered the two mounted royal mace-bearers who preceded his carriage to go and halt the Heir Apparent's carriage so that his should travel in front. I pleaded with him not to do this, pointing out that when Mozaffar-od-Din Mirza became Shah, things would turn out badly for him, as the former would then remember this incident. I also thought that perhaps the Heir Apparent would think that I had persuaded the ʿAziz-os-Soltan to do this and I feared for myself. My words had no effect. 'It is now the period of Naser-od-Din Shah. After him, I don't want to remain alive. If I am still alive, let him do what he wants!' he said. The mace-bearers did not dare to go and stop the Heir Apparent's carriage horse, so they bowed from a distance and explained their mission. The Heir Apparent very calmly and coolly ordered his carriage to halt and let the ʿAziz-os-Soltan's go ahead. When the latter's carriage passed the Heir Apparent's, I was so ashamed that I hid myself in a corner of the carriage so that the latter couldn't see me.

The *Farman Farma*, who was then the commander of the Azerbaijan brigade and was the son-in-law of Mozaffar-od-Din Mirza, had contracted to repair the bridge at Mianeh which had been carried away by a flood, at a price of 12,000 *toman*s. He had not, however, received his money, so he didn't do the work. Unfortunately only three days before the Shah's cavalcade was to cross it, a flood had carried away two of the bridge spans, so the Shah and his entourage had to cross a bridge repaired with pieces of wood. The Amir-Nezam summoned the Farman Farma and got very angry with him. The prince said nothing. The Amir-Nezam said that he wouldn't receive one *toman* of the 12,000 *toman*s, which he would give to someone else to repair the bridge.

In Mianeh the Shah became very ill with dysentery. After thirty years of service at the court of Naser-od-Din Shah, Dr Tholozan, had insisted on

---

32 See Chapter 1.

leaving Iran and had retired to Paris. Dr Coupon,[33] another famous French doctor, had replaced him and was in attendance. Four well-known Tehran court doctors had come to greet the Shah and also attended him. Since the Shah didn't yet know Dr Coupon, he had no confidence in him and first asked the advice of his other doctors. His dysentery didn't get better and all those round him feared that he would die of the illness. Everyone thought of his own interests and the more the court advised his doctors to refer the matter to the French doctor, the more they spurned this advice and refused to do so. In accordance with Iranian custom, as the Shah lay on a mattress in his tent, the minister and nobles who were visiting the sick man remained standing. He said a few words to some of them. One day the Shah sent for me. I saw that his eyes were sunken and that he was deathly pale and very emaciated. This wasn't the Shah whom I knew. He looked at me weakly and said: 'You see, I am dying.' I was so affected that I began to sob loudly. The servants present came and removed me from the tent, saying that I shouldn't have wept, as it would make him lose hope and think that he was dying. I couldn't bear it, and went to see the Amin-os-Soltan in tears. I told him: 'Sir, in my view this king is very ill and will not survive this illness. You have hired Dr Coupon on the recommendation of Dr Tholozan. If these ignorant doctors who have studied nothing will not allow him to treat the Shah, what use is he?' He replied: 'What can I do? The Shah himself trusts them.' I replied that he was the prime minister of Iran. He should summon those doctors and order them to stop treating the Shah. He replied that he couldn't forbid what the Shah wanted. He would obey his orders. I said that I had thought of another solution. He should summon the doctors and point out to them the sick man's wretched state, suggesting very gently that they should consider that if the Shah were to pass away, chaos would result: there would be rivalry between the tribes, who would be at each other's throats, and the kingdom would catch fire. He should tell the doctors that they should sign a document stating that if they couldn't cure the Shah's dysentery within twenty-four hours, they would accept complete responsibility for this. If they weren't prepared to provide such a document, they should go and hand over to Dr Coupon.

33 Actually Dr Tholozan was replaced by Dr Feuvrier, who recounts the story of the Shah's illness in his book *Trois Ans à la Cour de Perse* (see Bibliography).

When the Amin-os-Soltan spoke to them, the doctors themselves admitted that the Shah was very ill and agreed not to stand in the way of Dr Coupon treating him, so the Tehran doctors, accompanied by Dr Coupon, were admitted into the presence of the Shah. Apparently they were persuaded that there should be a 'consultation'. As a result of this 'consultation', Dr Coupon said that only laudanum could cure him. The doctors agreed to this, and Dr Coupon prepared the dose, which he then administered to the Shah. After he had drunk it, the dysentery started to abate. Two days later the Shah's condition had improved so much that he gave orders to strike camp and continue his journey. Then, in order to curry favour with the Shah, ministers and other prominent people started to send presents to Dr Coupon for having cured the Shah. The latter was surprised and asked me why he was being sent presents. He had been sorry that he was on the government payroll and no use had been made of his services, so I explained to the doctor why these gentlemen were sending him presents.

When we reached Mianeh, all those who had accompanied the Shah from Tabriz were dismissed and everyone except the Farman Farma left. As I was sleeping in the Amin-os-Soltan's tent, the Farman Farma came to visit me and said how very happy he had been to meet me and become friends with me, as it was the first time that we had met. After a few minutes of ritual compliments and praising me, he said: 'My dear Reza, in the context of our friendship I have one request. If you can fulfil it, I shall be eternally grateful and you will not regret it. You know that in the evening the Amin-os-Soltan plays poker with several close friends among the Shah's private attendants. If you can ask the Amin-os-Soltan to allow me to be invited, I don't know how to show you enough gratitude for your kindness or how to repay your good deed.' Until then, I knew nothing about cards nor the close relationship between players or indeed their ultimate objectives, so I said that this would not be difficult. I couldn't imagine that the Amin-os-Soltan would object to inviting Prince Farman Farma, the heir apparent's son-in-law and the commander of the Azerbaijan Brigade, to play cards, so I replied: 'This is not as much trouble as you think, and of course I will do as you ask.' He said that as I shared a tent with the Amin-os-Soltan, when I made this request to him, I should take care that no one else was present, as he didn't want anyone to hear that the Amin-os-Soltan played poker, but he wanted to join the circle.

When the Amin-os-Soltan returned from an audience with the Shah and he was alone, I told him of the Farman Farma's request. He said: 'Drop this! Let it go! This man is a liar who doesn't know the meaning of truth. I never want him to play poker with me, for I know what he wants. He wants the 12,000 *toman*s which he wrongly claims from the government for a bridge which was swept away in a flood. Now he wants to be a real nuisance in order to make good his claim. When he approaches you, tell him that the players don't want to admit an outsider to their game!' The Farman Farma of course approached me again, so I passed on the message. He wouldn't give up and said that if they didn't want to play with him, he didn't want to play either. He simply wanted to come, sit and watch. He was, however, offended that although he was a member of the royal camp, he wasn't admitted to the Amin-os-Soltan's meetings. He continued: 'His tent is not a reserved area. In the summer heat, the skirt of his tent is open and I am an important man: I am the Shah's son-in-law and the commander of the Azerbaijan cavalry. Tell him that it would be a disgrace for me, an army officer, if the Amin-os-Soltan refused to admit me to his tent.' I reported his words exactly as he had said them. The Amin-os-Soltan replied: 'I am well aware of the Farman Farma's importunity, and he also talks too much. Tell him that he can come on one condition: he must not speak!' I was present that evening when he came but I didn't play, for I only slept there. He remained entirely silent. He first formed a partnership with another player, but he couldn't tell his partner what his object was, which was to lose to the Amin-os-Soltan. Every time one of the players refused the Amin-os-Soltan's bid, he bought in and lost. In this way he gave away cash. As he appeared credit-worthy, he gradually became part of the regular game. Every evening he lost large sums of money to the Amin- os-Soltan. He then left his account, took his promissory note with him, and left the game. After which he kissed me several times, thanked me, and promised to help me and to be my friend in every way in the future.

Chapter 7

Life at Court in Tehran until my
Departure for the Caucasus (1889–1890)

Mirza Reza Khan describes scenes from court life in Iran: on the one hand banquets, hedonistic musical evenings where dancers perform and alcohol is drunk, and on the other rowzeh-khwani ceremonies of lamentation on the anniversary of the martyrdom of the Shiʿa imams. Like other Qajar monarchs, Naser-od-Din Shah loved hunting and was himself an excellent shot. Court life was therefore to some degree peripatetic, as courtiers followed the Shah to his various hunting lodges. The author was summoned to Jajrud, north-east of Tehran in the Elburz mountains, in midwinter. There the Shah showed further signs of his exceptional personal regard for him by appointing him to the consulate-general in Tiflis. As the author is keen to point out, perhaps to avoid later accusations of corruption, the Shah also granted him all the income from the sale of Iranian passports to some 40,000 Iranians stranded in the Caucasus after the Russian conquest. It is clear that the Shah regarded the foreign-educated young man affectionately as someone unacquainted with Iranian customs and, when the Shah arranged a musical evening for him, he teased him as someone unused to flirting with male dancers.

This status had its dangers: if his enemies couldn't destroy him directly by shaking the Shah's trust in him, the Shah was known to be sensitive to clerical accusations of failure to protect Islam and a complaint to the senior clergy that Mirza Reza Khan was an infidel was likely to be equally effective. The author gives a graphic example of the power of a cleric, Haji Seyyed Karbalaʾi, part charlatan and part holy fool, who had no greater claim to sanctity than his lineage to the Prophet Mohammad and his ability to recite the Muslim prayers with his distinct Arabic pronunciation, but who could make even the Prime Minister the Amin-os-Soltan,[1] Mirza Reza Khan's protector, fear for his own position. The author pays a handsome tribute to the latter, describing his devotion to duty and his public generosity, but points out how even this was turned against him by his enemies. He claims to have given the Prime Minister disinterested advice to halt public criticism of him and to have skilfully mollified any incipient jealousy the latter might feel for him as the Shah's young favourite. Once again, however, one doubts whether he spoke to the Atabak quite as boldly as he claims: if he had done so, the Atabak's prestige would surely have been damaged, and with it, one suspects, his relationship with the author.

Given the perils of court life, it is interesting that Mirza Reza Khan refused a lucrative post at the newly-established Imperial Bank of Persia. It is, however, a mark of his high standing that not only was he able to do so without adverse consequences for himself but the Shah's gift of a new post in Tiflis set him on the path to wealth and some degree of financial security. His own distance from the snakepit of court politics for most of his career, combined with the presence of a powerful protector at court, were important factors in his subsequent success.

When we entered Tehran, the entire population had come out to welcome the Shah. On his orders, I was given lodgings in the guest quarters of the Amin-os-Soltan's residence. There were two rooms in a corridor: one for me and the other for one Haji Seyyed Karbala'i. This *seyyed* offended everyone: he showered abuse on everybody, and everyone, even the Amin-os-Soltan himself, put up with it. His entire body of knowledge consisted of being able to recite the five daily prayers at the appointed time in public. One of his skills was that he pronounced the Arabic hard consonants beautifully. This *seyyed* became the bane of my life. After the evening prayer, he would go to sleep and wake up at dawn, whereas I had been kept up until two or three o'clock at nocturnal gatherings attended by other leading figures. I had only just returned to my room and taken out my bedclothes, my eyes had not even closed in sleep when

---

1 The Amin-os-Soltan was also known as the 'Great Atabak'.

at the sound of the morning call to prayer he went to the pool in the courtyard to carry out his ablutions and called out to me in a loud voice: 'Mirza Reza Khan, get up and say your prayers!' I had no alternative but to do so. When we returned to our rooms, he would say: 'Leave your door open, as I do, so that I can hear the sound of your prayers! I am afraid that if you shut your door, you will go to sleep and fail to say your prayers.' I did as I was told and in return for my obedience, the *seyyed* became a great supporter of mine and sang my praises everywhere.

On one occasion, when twenty or thirty princes and distinguished people, including the *seyyed*, were gathered in the Amin-os-Soltan's house, and I was summoned by the Amin-os-Soltan, the *seyyed*, who got to his feet for no one, immediately rose when I entered the room and swore that he had never seen a better Muslim than me. These words of course were a particular blow to the Amin-os-Soltan's prestige because the *seyyed* had included him among those less favourably described. One day the Amin-os-Soltan asked me what I had done to turn the *seyyed* so mad that he attacked everyone. 'Just you wait until I show him what kind of a Muslim you really are, so that he will say that he has never seen a worse unbeliever than you!' At first I thought that the Amin-os-Soltan was joking. What had I done to make him want to prove my behaviour as irreligious? He said: 'The *seyyed* has been to the Shah and said the same thing. He has stirred up the people against me, so I will put him in his place.' On the next occasion when the *seyyed* got up as I entered the room and said that he had never seen a better Muslim than me, the Amin-os-Soltan said: 'I am surprised that you are such a simpleton that everywhere you go you introduce a man as the best Muslim you have ever seen when I have with my own eyes witnessed his debauchery.' The *seyyed*'s eyes almost came out on stalks. He made a movement towards the Amin-os-Soltan and said: 'Repent! Repent! Do not say that this Muslim is an unbeliever! You are slandering him.' The Amin-os-Soltan replied that this was not slander. He was saying this in my presence and I would confirm it for him. Then what would the *seyyed* have to say for himself? The *seyyed* then turned to me and it was as if his eyes had caught fire in his fury. He had a large stick and he said: 'In that case, I will immediately break his head with this stick.' All those present heard this exchange of words. The Amin-os-Soltan said to me: 'Before I question you, swear by the *seyyed*'s most righteous ancestor that you will tell the truth and will not deny what I say!' I replied that although there was no need for an oath, I would swear by this *seyyed*'s most righteous ancestor to reply truthfully to any question he asked me. Then the Amin-os-Soltan said: 'Gentlemen here present, pay attention!' He turned to me and said: 'Was it not you who in a Budapest hotel drank a glass of famous Hungarian red wine every night at dinner after the food?' I replied that I was indeed the Reza referred to by the *seyyed* and that I admitted that as the Aqa had said, in Budapest I used to drink a small glass of Hungarian red wine. Not only there but in every place where I was among friends, whenever I could lay my hands on a good wine, I drank it. I swore by God and his most noble prophet that I had drunk wine on the orders of 'a skilled physician', who gave me a certificate certifying that his prescription was based on the declaration of permissibility by the Prophet, who had declared that when a man was ill, it was permissible for him to drink wine when this was prescribed by a 'skilled physician'. After this admission I humbly suggested to the Amin-os-Soltan that he might read out the doctor's authorisation from the certificate and ask me what my illness had been.

On the subject of this illness of mine, when the 'Ala'-ol-Molk was consul-general in Tiflis and I was third translator, I had fallen seriously ill. The official Russian government doctor, Dr Schmidt, who was also the 'Ala'-ol-Molk's doctor and of German origin, came to examine me, then declared that I had typhoid and gave instructions for me to be taken to the Russian Mikhailovski hospital. The 'Ala'-ol-Molk said that since his son Javad had died in this gloomy hospital and its walls were stained with his blood, he couldn't bear to look at it and he couldn't allow Mirza Reza Khan to be taken there. I should stay in the consulate and the doctor should treat me there. My illness was very serious and when I was finally able to leave my bed, I had so little blood that the doctor ordered me to drink a glass of Kakhet red wine every day after food.

As I had not touched alcohol until then, I refused but the 'Ala'-ol-Molk insisted. I said that my father in Tabriz was renowned for his piety and if he heard that I had drunk alcohol, he would disinherit me. The 'Ala'-ol-Molk said that the Shari'a which forbids the consumption of alcohol allows, indeed even commands it when a doctor prescribes it for medical treatment. I had said that I would drink it on condition that if my father got to hear of it and asked questions, I could show him a medical certificate. Dr Schmidt had given me such a certificate, which fortunately I had always kept and which was available for inspection, so I said that if I was allowed to do so, I would go and fetch it. The *seyyed* was particularly insistent that I should do so, so I went and got it and showed it to those present. The Mohandes-ol-Mamalek was present, and he was given the document to read. He confirmed that its contents were as I had said. Haj Seyyed Karbala'i was very pleased and said to the Amin-os-Soltan: 'I hope that you are ashamed of yourself.'

One day, Count Montforto, who at the Shah's request had been sent by the Emperor Franz Jozef of Austria to re-organise the Iranian police, came to see me. Suddenly the *seyyed* entered the room. He asked who the visitor was, so I explained that he was a count and the chief of police. He said that he had heard that the Count was not a bad man. Indeed he was a good man. He then brought up a chair and sat down on it very close to the Count. Then in a very impudent manner, he said to him: 'Accursed Count, come and let me convert you to Islam!', which he then repeated three times. He pronounced the letter '*ein*'[2] in the Arabic word 'accursed' (*mal'oon*) so gutturally that his throat almost seized up. The Count replied: 'Who could refuse such a sweet and polite invitation to convert to Islam? First I suggest that you go and learn the art of polite manners, and then come and invite me to become a Muslim!' Thereupon the *seyyed* flew in a rage, rose to his feet and left the room.

From the moment he came to power, the Amin-os-Soltan arranged for *row-zeh-khwani* ceremonies of commemoration for the martyrs of Karbala to take place in his house throughout the whole ten days of 'Ashura. Each evening, dinner was provided for the people after the ceremonies. Three rooms were set aside for invited guests, while a table cloth was laid on the floor in the middle of the other rooms so that fifty people could sit down around it. Everybody who had remained at the commemoration ceremony until the end was free to take part in the dinner. As huge quantities of food were cooked and served, the rooms filled up and emptied three times in an evening, that is to say that each evening 600 people had dinner there. On this basis, just think of the huge expense which great men had to incur in Tehran with these ceremonies! As to the *molla*s reciting, one evening I counted more than forty of them mounting the pulpit. Of course there was not time for all of them to recite the ritual

---

2 Arabic guttural syllable which is normally pronounced more softly in Persian.

lamentations, so they simply went up, said prayers for the Shah and the Amin-os-Soltan and then came down again. But at the end of the ten days, each one was given money and a robe of honour. As the Shah had been in Tiflis during the ten days of ʿAshura that year,[3] the commemoration ceremonies were put back to the last ten days of the month of Safar.[4]

One evening at about sunset, a royal attendant came and whispered into the Amin-os-Soltan's ear: 'The Shah summons Reza.' The Amin-os-Soltan said that whenever the Shah wanted to see someone at that time of the evening, the person summoned should go and wait for his orders outside the door to the women's apartments. I was waiting for the Shah's orders there when a eunuch came out and said: 'The Shah has given orders that as Mirza Reza Khan has spent all his life abroad, where he attended the theatre most evenings, since there is no theatre here, he wants him to enjoy himself this evening. Therefore His Majesty has put the court musicians at his disposal this evening. They are ready in the ʿAziz-os-Soltan's house. He should go there and they will sing and play music to his command.' The eunuch gave me a purse, saying that it contained twenty gold coins, and told me to give it to the musicians as a gratuity at the end of the evening.

I duly took the purse to the ʿAziz-os-Soltan's house. He was in the women's quarters and there was absolutely no one else there but the servants and attendants, awaiting their orders. There was no audience apart from myself: the only people present were the singers, players of the tar,[5] of other string instruments and of tambourines. I was asked what I wanted them to play and sing. I told them what I had heard of two, three and four modes of Persian music, which they then played and sang for me. In accordance with the instructions which had come in advance from the women's quarters, the ʿAziz-os-Soltan's servants brought lamb kababs, dried nuts and fruits, and arak or wine for the musicians. I didn't want to detain them for long, so I distributed the twenty gold coins and returned to my lodgings. I saw that the *rowzeh-khwani* had finished but the dinner was not yet over. The Amin-os-Soltan was still at dinner, so

---

3 The author is referring to Tiflis as a land of infidels.

4 Safar is the second month in the Muslim year and follows Moharram, in which ʿAshura falls.

5 The tar is a stringed instrument.

I went and recounted the details of the evening to him. He said that this was the first time that the Shah had shown this kind of favour to any of his servants and this was particularly gratifying since, instead of my having to tip the musicians, he had given me twenty ashrafi gold coins with which to do this.

One day I was in the Amin-os-Soltan's house talking to his brother, the late Amin-ol-Molk. It was the day when *Ash-e-Qalamkar*[6] was being cooked. An attendant came and said that we had both been summoned by the Shah. The weather was conveniently fine, so carpets had been laid on the ground in the palace garden. The Shah was seated on a chair, while about twelve ministers and princes were sitting on the carpet. In front of each a particular species of herb had been placed, and different kinds of herb grown in spring on the banks of streams had also been provided. One minister was chopping spinach, another onions, another garlic and yet another chickpeas, with one peeling split peas. Isma'il the cloth-merchant had brought his own group of musicians in attendance, who played and sang. A fourteen-year-old boy, who had curled his hair and who was dressed as a girl, was dancing. At a sign from the Shah, the Amin-ol-Molk went and sat next to the ministers to take part in cleaning the herbs. The Shah ordered me to go and stand next to his chair. Then he made a sign to the musician to come and flirt with me. The more embarrassed I became, encouraged by the Shah, the more he persisted. The Shah commented: 'In Europe you used to pay court to female dancers. This is Iran and you must be content with male dancers.'

One day the Amin-os-Soltan told me that the Shah wanted to keep me in Tehran and appoint me a commissioner of the Imperial Bank,[7] his aim being to relieve me of any financial worry. The annual salary of this post was 3,000 *toman*s, there were no responsibilities associated with the job and no effort would be required. I humbly requested to be excused from this task and asked

---

6 The most elaborate and beautiful Persian dish, a kind of highly decorated goulash soup, introduced by Naser-od-Din Shah as a royal dish to be eaten at court and distributed to his subjects.

7 Shortly before the Shah's third visit to Europe in 1889, a concession was granted to the London-based Baron Julius de Reuter which resulted in the foundation of the Imperial Bank of Persia. It acquired a monopoly for the issuing of Iranian bank notes and acted as the state bank of Iran.

him to suggest that if the Shah wished to further bestow favour on me, he might give me another appointment abroad, for I couldn't remain in Tehran. The Atabak was very surprised and said that he didn't understand: from the day I had arrived in Tehran, I had become the object of envy of every Iranian. Not a day went by without much more senior people than myself sending intermediaries to plead with him to be given this appointment. I said: 'Sir, the only result of the Shah's boundless kindness to me is that each day it makes me another enemy. I want to leave, as the jealousy and intrigues of the courtiers pursue me even at home.' The Amin-os-Soltan was very keen that I should stay because he knew that I was his devoted servant, which indeed I was, for I had experienced nothing but kindness from him. As a result of my refusal, however, the post of Commissioner of the Imperial Bank was given to the Mohandes-ol-Mamalek.

One day, the Shah summoned me to the area where he was hunting deer, fox and partridge in the hills around Doshan-Tappeh. As he wanted to eat lunch where he was shooting, lunch of *polow* and stew had been put in covered dishes, and was being heated on brushwood. There were also cold dishes like vegetable omelette and mincemeat balls, with ample food both for masters and servants. Sometimes the game was driven by horsemen and sometimes by men on foot. By nature I didn't like killing animals, so when the master of the hunt offered me a gun, I refused but I was happy to be a spectator. Although I took no part in the hunt, I nevertheless followed it down through narrow defiles and up to mountain peaks. Provided that the objective is not to kill living things, I must say that following the hunt up hill and down dale, mounting and dismounting, is the best form of physical exercise. At lunch time, one can see with what a good appetite and with how much pleasure men eat their food.

The Amin-os Soltan's daily programme in those days was as follows: an hour before noon he would go to court, eat lunch there and he would only return to his residence after dinner at nine o'clock in the evening. From nine o'clock until two or three o'clock in the morning he would sit in his reception hall. That was the time he would receive friends, learned men and scholars or governors who had come to Tehran on leave or after removal from office. When the weather was very hot, a platform was erected over the pool, on which the gardener placed rugs, and on which he sat. When the weather was cold, he would receive in the great hall. He didn't make use of chairs or tables except in the room where he received foreign government representatives or other distinguished foreigners. In the summer season he was not in town but accompanied the Shah to his summer quarters. He went to the women's quarters to sleep at two or three o'clock in the morning, woke up at nine o'clock, dressed, and then looked into his personal affairs, his accounts and family matters. At ten o'clock he would leave the women's quarters.

As soon as he emerged from there, petitioners, *molla*s, *seyyed*s, merchants, tradesmen, peasants, in fact everyone who had a request, a complaint of injustice or a petition, were queuing up in a line thirty to forty yards long as far as the door of the reception area. The Amin-os-Soltan walked past all of them, taking their written petitions or listening to the oral ones, passing them on to an accompanying secretary and telling him to give him the details in the evening, when he would reply. As to those who had oral requests, he would hear them and instruct the secretary to write to such and such a department or governor. He would then emerge into the street, which would be full of beggars, men, women and girls of every description, the blind and the lame. More than 200 people would be waiting for the Amin-os-Soltan. He handled the matter in the following way: every day his steward would prepare ten *toman*s in half-*kran* coins, then he himself would give his donation, a token coin, to each supplicant with his own hand. Then he would give money to one of his servants whom he trusted. The beggars fell on the latter with such force, trying to grab as many coins as they could. It was such chaos that the man would have been overwhelmed. Then, however, the steward would turn to two other servants, who would rescue the man from the beggars. The man would then try to make his escape from the crowd by making his way towards Lalehzar, stopping every few metres to throw ten or twelve half-*kran* coins on the ground. The beggars fell on each other fighting to wrest the coins from the others.

This caused criticism of the Amin-os-Soltan all over town. People said that this kind of giving to the poor was not in order to please God but to boost his own reputation. It was in fact immoral, they said, because most of the people who gathered at the Amin-os-Soltan's house were not genuine beggars but merely idle people. By acting in this way, he was encouraging people to beg. Those close to him, his friends or those who wished to appear his friends, dared not alert him to this kind of comment. However, I thought it immoral to eat his bread and not to draw his attention to this great error on his part.

One day, when he was taking me with him to court, the street was so full of beggars that there was no room for his carriage to pass. They all got up and stretched out their hands towards the carriage, shouting: 'Give us our money with your own hand!' The more he shouted: 'I have given out the money. Go and get it from my man!' nobody paid the slightest attention. When he saw that he was going to be late for his audience with the Shah, he ordered the coachman to beat the beggars and open up a passage. They fell away on both sides of the carriage and finally we reached Lalehzar Street. The Amin-os-Soltan started to complain about the beggars, saying: 'Look at the disgrace they have brought on me! In this country one cannot do good to anyone. You see what happens. You know that every day I give ten *toman*s in ten *shahi* coins from my own purse for them and ten *toman*s to my man, as they well know. All they have to do is to take the money peaceably.' I took the opportunity to tell him to his face of people's criticisms exactly as I had heard them. He criticised the dishonourable behaviour of the beggars on the one hand and people's ingratitude on the other, saying that he had no motive but compassion for the poor. How could the gift of money to beggars be considered fame-seeking? If he didn't give money to beggars, God would hold him responsible for this, while if he did, he was censured by the people.

I asked his permission to tell him how the matter seemed to me. He could of course either accept what I said or reject it. He told me to say what I had to say. I said: 'I suggest that tomorrow morning before dawn you should station two attendants, one at the end of one street and the other at the end of the next one and that you shouldn't allow a single beggar to approach the door of your house. The attendants should say that in view of the scandal caused by the beggars the previous day, when several people's legs were injured under your carriage wheels, (as had indeed been the case), the Amin-os-Soltan would no longer give money in the street but had arranged to build a clinic with a monthly budget of 300 *toman*s where the blind, the lame and the disabled would be nursed.' He said that he thought that this was a good idea but doubted whether a budget of 300 *toman*s would suffice to open a clinic. I pointed out that the government had at its disposal several barracks at various places near the town gates. These were now empty and not a single soldier was stationed there. I proposed that on a trial basis he should take over one of these build-ings, which he could appoint people to clean, place reed mats on the floor, install water-pipes and provide water jugs. He should appoint a caretaker and order the local district headmen to make a public announcement that the blind, the lame and the crippled could go and stay in the clinic, where they would be given two meals a day. I said that as I understood matters, the real beggars wouldn't go there because they made a profession of begging. A monthly budget of 300 *toman*s would be entirely sufficient to give each impoverished person bread and yoghurt each day. If he saw that people stayed there and made their home there, so that this sum was no longer sufficient, he could ask the government for an additional sum. In this way he would enjoy a good reputation with God and with the people.

He thought this an excellent idea and said that he would entrust the matter to me. I thanked him but said that His Majesty had wanted to reward me with the post of Commissioner of the Imperial Bank and the sum of 3,000 *toman*s, so that I could live on 1,000 *toman*s and save 2,000 *toman*s for my old age. I hadn't accepted the post because I didn't wish to stay in Tehran. I was not up to the task which he wished to entrust to me, and I suggested that he would do better to entrust it to Tehran people who were at his service every day and would undertake to carry out any task he entrusted to them whole-heartedly. These should be men who knew the names of the local district headmen and of local people, at any rate until it became clear who was telling the truth and who was just talking nonsense, when he could get rid of those who were causing mischief.

Since the Amin-os-Soltan was to accompany His Majesty to one of his summer camps the next day, he didn't return to his house that night and the beggars who had gathered there scattered and left in despair. When he returned, he stopped stationing attendants in the streets and simply told two gatekeepers to tell the beggars that after the scandal there would be no more money.

The Amin-os-Soltan was by nature a very generous and kind-hearted man. Whenever he saw someone who had really been wronged or who had been impoverished by fire or flood, he would give him a helping hand. Sometimes I saw people following him as far as the door of his residence. He would then tell his servants to take a sum of money and give it to the poor petitioner in such a way that the latter should not know that it came from him. He didn't make enemies until someone did him wrong or denigrated him to senior clerics or to the Shah, and even then his enmity was not ferocious. As soon as they begged for forgiveness, he showed indulgence and I never heard him speak ill of anyone to the Shah. He might not praise someone, but he did not speak ill of them. Truly I viewed him as a noble, benevolent and generous man. I had often heard this and once saw him give a thousand *toman*s here and a thousand *toman*s there to poor deserving *seyyed*s, telling them to buy themselves a house.

After fourteen months residence in Tehran, the winter arrived. The Shah went to Jajrud with the Amin-os-Soltan and some courtiers. One day the Amin-os-Soltan summoned me there. When I arrived, there was a lot of snow and it was very cold. It was a long way from Tehran to Jajrud, and I arrived there in the evening. The Shah immediately sent for me. The ʿAziz-os-Soltan, together with his tutor, the Majd-od-Dowleh and Mehdi Khan were in the royal presence. I bowed. The Shah told me to approach. Before I could approach him, he said: 'Mirza Reza Khan, the services which you performed in defining the frontiers of Khorasan, and particularly in the matter of the agricultural and grazing land belonging to the people of Lotfabad, will always remain in my mind, and during my journey to Europe your honesty, truthfulness and trustworthiness have greatly pleased me. Since you do not wish to accept a post in Iran and have particularly asked for a post abroad, I thought that the most suitable post for you would be the Caucasus. As you studied there, you entered my service there, and you have formed friendly relations with the most important families there, all these factors will have a positive effect on the progress of your affairs.'

The Shah continued: 'I have told the *Qavam-od-Dowleh*, the minister of foreign affairs, that since Malkom Khan[8] was involved in the evil consequences of the lottery concession and he did not tell me the truth about it, he is to be dismissed. The Moʿin-ol-Vezareh, the consul-general in Tiflis, is to be sent to London with the title of ʿAlaʾ-os-Saltaneh and you are to replace him in Tiflis with the title of Moʿin-ol-Vezareh. You are now consul-general in Tiflis. I wanted to say a few words of my feelings for you in the presence

---

8 Iran's minister plenipotentiary in London.

of others. First you should know this: in Iran people think that a man's credibility, the respect due to him and his importance all depend on his wealth. Anybody who does not have money is of no importance to others and enjoys no credit with them. A man without money, even though he is the most learned of the learned and the most exceptional person in the world, is avoided like the plague, as people think that he might want to borrow money from them. I know full well that you have nothing and that your father has nothing, the flood having carried away everything he had. In the Caucasus we have at least 40,000 Iranian subjects. I have told the Qavam-od-Dowleh that he should entrust you with handling all the passports in the Caucasus. If you take one *manat* for every passport issued, in a year you will receive 40,000 *manat*, which is more than 20,000 *toman*s. Do not waste this money on silly things! Save it and become a man of substance! If you do well in this post, I will make you minister plenipotentiary in St Petersburg and will then send you on to become ambassador in Istanbul. Then I will bring you back to Tehran as prime minister.'

I was so affected by these words that tears of joy poured from my eyes, I couldn't say a word and I was completely tongue-tied. The Majd-od-Dowleh made a sign for me to kiss the Shah's feet, so I prostrated myself before him and did so. He saw in what a state I was and that I was speechless, so he told me that I was dismissed: I should go and rejoice in my good fortune. I withdrew backwards from the room. Those who were in the Shah's presence also withdrew and came and congratulated me. They wanted me to make promises to help them, but my throat was constricted and I was unable to reply.

I went straight from the Shah's palace to the Amin-os-Soltan's house, which was separated from the Palace by the Jajrud river. The weather was cold and I was out of breath by the time I arrived. The Amin-os-Soltan was sitting with his private secretary playing backgammon. The former laid aside the game and immediately asked me why the Shah had summoned me privately, without him or his private secretary being present. I replied that if he would give me a little time to catch my breath I would tell him in detail everything that had happened. When I had recounted the whole story in minute detail, he turned to his secretary and said: 'You see this man's gratitude: in return for all my efforts on this journey to Europe and all the cruelties which I have suffered from his courtiers, he still has not given me the title of Prime Minister.[9] I am his first minister and he knows that Mirza Reza Khan is my guest and yet within earshot he promises him the prime ministership. What do you have to say?' The secretary remained silent. I said to the Atabak: 'Sir, you know full well that if I become consul-general and demonstrate my competence to the Shah, and he then sends me as minister-plenipotentiary to St Petersburg, he can't make me ambassador in Istanbul on the same day. I will have to stay for six or seven years in Russia to prove my ability. Then for him to summon me from St Petersburg and send me to Istanbul as ambassador will take time. It took him twenty-five years to recall Haji Mohsen Khan Moʻin-ol-Molk from his embassy in Istanbul. He will have to leave me there for at least ten years. Please observe that if during this time the Shah doesn't change his mind, which would be unusual for him, as kings usually do so frequently, it will be many years before he summons me to Tehran. With the short lives we live, who knows who is going to be alive and who will die? Please do not upset your precious self over things which are simply speculation. I humbly suggest that you go back to your game.'

By way of diversion, please let me entertain you with a story which my uncle Haji Karim told me in my childhood. My uncle said that once upon a time a merchant made a loan to another merchant and the day of promised repayment duly arrived. At first, the creditor was too embarrassed to press too hard for repayment. One day a week, however, he would go to demand re-payment. As the debtor had no money, the creditor agreed to rely on the promise of repayment. Then he himself fell into financial difficulties, after which he went to reclaim his money every day. The debtor always said that the money would arrive the next day and promised to pay. This went on until enough money actually arrived to repay the debt. The debtor's son, who was present every day when the creditor called for repayment and was distressed and embarrassed in front of their neighbours, was delighted and thanked God that he would no longer be embarrassed. At that moment the creditor arrived. Instead of handing over the money, however, his father swore a solemn oath

---

9 'Sadr-e Aʻzam' or Prime Minister was a much-coveted title, which Naser-od-Din Shah, who liked to play one minister off against another, granted to few politicians, even though they carried out the functions of the post.

that he would repay the money the next day. In view of the oath sworn by the debtor, the creditor agreed to return on the morrow.

After the creditor had left, the son said to the father that he was well aware that his father had had no money and that he had had to postpone repayment. He had felt ashamed in front of the merchants from the next-door trading office and sometimes he had wept and prayed that God would provide the money. But now that his father had money, he asked, why had his father postponed repayment to the next day? The father replied: 'Son, you are still young and it is not right that you should criticise adults who are older than you. You have a long time to live before you reach my age and acquire my experience. I have put this matter off from today until tomorrow for the following reason: today and tomorrow are separated by a full night. Our learned men have said that the night is "pregnant" and we should wait to see what it brings forth at dawn. Three things could happen tonight, which could mean that the money stays here. Either there is an uprising, the Shah is killed and the country is in chaos, in which case I won't hand over the money; or the creditor dies and so I won't need to give him the money, which will stay here; or I die, you will be released from the debt and you won't have to hand over the money. If none of these three events happens, nothing is lost: he will come and get his money anyway.' I swore by God himself that I didn't tell this story so that (Heaven forfend!) anything should happen to the Shah or to the Amin-os-Soltan, but my purpose was to say that no one could know whether I would still be alive then and give him cause to worry.

The Amin-os-Soltan said that as a result of the affection which he had formed for me from the day when we first met, he hoped that all three of us, the Shah, I and he would still be alive then. If the Shah were to confer the prime ministership on me, it would be as though he was conferring it on him. He would be the first person to congratulate me. The next day I should go and see the Qavam-od-Dowleh, who was suffering from gout. He would write to the latter instructing him to provide everything I needed for my journey as soon as possible. He would also send him official instructions on behalf of the Shah that he should formally and in writing entrust the matter of the passports to me, so that I should have no financial worries in the future.

Chapter 8

The Consulate-General in Tiflis (1890–1895)

It is a little surprising that this period in Mirza Reza Khan's life occupies a relatively short chapter in his memoirs. The Tiflis Consulate-General was an important post, indeed almost a career staging-post for appointment as Minister Plenipotentiary in St Petersburg. It was also a double-edged sword: as many important visitors passed through Tiflis on their way to Europe or on the pilgrimage to Mecca, it was an ideal place to make influential friends. One mistake, however, could have endangered his whole career. It was also the time when the author married his first wife, Ludmila Jervis, half-Russian and half English, whom he doesn't mention.

Iranians have long memories for past injuries, but the author wasn't a cruel man. On his arrival in Tiflis in 1895 as the new consul-general, Mirza Reza Khan immediately took revenge for a long-nourished grudge against a colleague there and thus stamped his authority on the consulate. Cleverly, however, he allowed the sword of Damocles to hang over the man's head for some weeks, only to pardon and promote him at the very moment when the wretched man expected to be cast out penniless in a foreign land. The author had to deal with a cholera epidemic in Tiflis. Responsibility for spreading the disease was widely ascribed to resident Iranian workers. The author, however, acted deftly with the assistance of the large Iranian Armenian merchant community, whose organisational skills he admired, to defuse incipient anti-Iranian hysteria and prevent the expulsion of the entire Iranian community. Meanwhile, money from the sale of passports rained down on him from heaven.

He built three properties, one in Tiflis and two in the up and coming spa town
of Borjom, all of which he decorated in the Iranian style and two of which, the
Hôtel Firouzeh in Borjom and the Diamond Palace in Tiflis, survive to this day.
He gave a magnificent party to celebrate the Shah's birthday. Clearly, there
was no question of stinting on the quantity of Georgian Kakhet wine provided
for his guests, for the evening so impressed the governor of Tiflis, Prince Shir-
vashidze, that he said that he now understood the Muslim concept of paradise.

When we arrived in Tiflis, all the merchants and tradesmen came out to
welcome us, the merchants accompanied by a band, and the guilds each with
its own banner, together with Mirza Mohammad Beg, my deputy, and Taqi
Beg, the Russian language translator. The deputy head of the police and several
senior police officers were responsible for organising the official welcome ceremony for me on behalf of the governor of Tiflis.

The ʿAlaʾ-os-Saltaneh, whose leg was paining him, was awaiting my arrival
in the consul's residence. I was wearing uniform when I entered the town, as
flags were flying. Mohammad Aqa, the senior Iranian merchant, congratulated me on my arrival on behalf of the merchants, while ʿAli Beg, the chief
contractor, did so on behalf of all the guilds, and I made an appropriate reply.
I then reviewed the line of twelve people who had come to welcome me and
accompanied them to the consulate-general, where sherbet and cakes had been
prepared. There in the big reception room I again formally received the merchants and heads of guilds in front of a large oil painting of Naser-od-Din
Shah by an Iranian artist. The merchants had hired a military band, while the
guilds had arranged for two or three local Georgian and Armenian musicians
to play their instruments during the ceremony. Before going into the reception
room to receive the merchants, however, I went straight to call on the ʿAlaʾ-os-
Saltaneh. I saw that his leg really was hurting him. He said how happy he was
to see me and thankful that I had the post. He added that now that he had been
appointed minister plenipotentiary in London, it was as though the consulate
in Tiflis was also part of his responsibilities. Meanwhile, sherbet, cigarettes
and sweet things were being offered to the guilds and the welcoming party in
the street. After thanking the merchants, I went down into the street, where the
music struck up again with 'Hail to the Shah', after which I bade them farewell
and they departed.

On the day after my arrival in the consulate-general, I sent a message through Mirza Faraj Beg to Mirza Mohammad Beg,[1] my new deputy, who had treated me very badly on my first posting at the consulate, that he should fear the day when he first stood in front of me. The former told me that from the day when Mirza Mohammad Beg first heard of my posting to Tiflis he had enjoyed no peace of mind and had been unable to sleep peacefully. Mirza Mohammad Beg had served in the consulate for years and, having a wife, a son and two daughters, he had no savings and he was frightened that I would remember the past and dismiss him. Then without any money, where could he and his family go in this foreign land? I told Mirza Faraj Beg to tell him not to worry. If I had been a mean and vengeful person, heaven would not have granted me its favours. I was thankful that things had turned out as I had predicted all those years ago for, instead of dismissing him, I would promote him and increase his salary. The next day Mirza Mohammad Beg brought me the current list of passports and stood very humbly in front of me. He asked me to whom he should hand over responsibility for the passports. I told him that the passports would remain his responsibility and that for as long as I was in Tiflis he could be confident of keeping his position. I asked him how long he had served in the consulate. He said that this dated from the time of the mission of *Yousef Khan Mostashar-od-Dowleh.* I replied that in that case he had served for nearly forty years and that very week I would write to Tehran requesting that he should be given the title of Khan and be officially confirmed in his post as First Deputy Consul, and that is what I did. However, as soon as my successor arrived, he dismissed Mirza Mohammad Beg and put one of his own relatives in his place. What a difference there was between his expectations of me and what he actually experienced!

In the first year of my posting there, a serious epidemic of cholera broke out in Tehran and Tabriz and 300 people were dying every day in these towns. From Tabriz the disease spread to Tiflis, where it first broke out among the Iranian community. One day the merchants and the guild heads came in a group to the consulate-general. They informed me that, as most Iranians resident in Tiflis were workmen and lived three or four to a room, it was

---

1 See Chapter 3 for the author's previous comments on Mirza Mohammad Beg.

impossible to keep their lodgings under medical supervision or indeed to allot each one an individual, separate room. They would certainly spread the disease to the inhabitants of Tiflis. The governor-general of the Caucasus had therefore ordered that they should all be expelled and sent back under guard to Iran via Jolfa. The merchants reminded me that the road from Tiflis to Jolfa was at least a month's journey on foot and among the 10,000 Iranians there were women, children, old men and the sick. Half of these unfortunates would die on the way without medicines. Some way of keeping them in Tiflis must be found. After a great deal of consultation and much weighing up of all aspects of the problem, it was unanimously agreed that every morning the merchants themselves and the senior tradesmen would take bottles of antiseptic to the Iranians' lodgings, which they would inspect. They would then pour the antiseptic everywhere and ensure that the lodgings were kept clean. They would also draw up a list of tasks to be done and collect money, for which proper accounts would be kept. Outside the Muslim quarter and further on from the Mirzaiev factory, they would acquire an empty plot of land from the municipality and build a hospital out of wood, with wooden doors, walls, beds and chairs, large enough to accommodate eighty men and twenty-five women. There and then they drew up the list, nearly five thousand *manat* having been collected. It was decided that when I went to call on the governor-general, I would describe in detail what had been done, ask him to change his mind about expelling the Iranians, lend us some Russian doctors and provide us with some medicine.

As the Governor-General, General Sherematiev, was a kind and gentle man, he agreed to our requests. The next day, the merchants and guilds really put in a super-human effort. As most of the merchants there were Armenian Christians,[2] in the space of a few days the barracks were made ready. We then announced that the barracks were not only for Iranian citizens. Anyone who contracted this illness could be treated there. I observed that some of the inhabitants of Tiflis were so afraid of cholera, thinking that the Iranians were responsible for spreading the disease, that they refused to shake hands with them. So I wrote the following story in the semi-official Caucasus newspaper: 'One day a *molla* mounted his donkey and set off

---

2 The author clearly admires the industriousness of the Armenian community.

towards the city. On the way he saw a terrifying monster. He thought that it was a desert ghoul or indeed a *jinn*, so he started to recite: "I take refuge in the Lord" and blew a puff of breath in the direction of the monster. He saw that his prayer to ward off evil had no effect and the monster was getting closer to him. As soon as the monster came up to the *molla*, it greeted him and said: "Don't be frightened of me! I am the emissary of God and my mission is to kill those who neglect to mention the name of God. My name is Cholera." As soon as the *molla* heard the name of God and the emissary of God, his fear vanished. He replied: "Now that you are going to town, come and sit behind me on my donkey!" So he sat him behind him. When they reached the gate of the town, Cholera alighted and said that this was the parting of the ways. He was going in one direction and the *molla* in another. The *molla* asked how many people he would kill on God's orders. Cholera replied that he would kill exactly one thousand people. The *molla* said that he didn't entirely trust the cholera monster's word, so he asked him to promise not to kill any more than a thousand people. Cholera gave his promise and they went their separate ways. Now the governor of the town had given orders that the bodies of those who had died of the disease were only to be buried outside the town and that lime should be poured into their graves. After a week, the *molla* wished to return to his village, so he went and asked the gatekeeper how many people had died from cholera. The latter replied: "Ten thousand". The *molla* exclaimed: "Infidel, you have broken your promise. Faithless one, why have you killed so many of God's creatures?" Cholera replied: "*Molla*, calm down! Instead of cursing me, why have you not asked me for an explanation? I swear by the God who sent me to carry out his orders that I have killed no more than one thousand people. The other nine thousand died of fear, and I am not responsible for that".' This story made me famous. It was re-printed in other newspapers and even abroad. The phenomenon was confirmed by doctors, who gave examples of it and said that violent fear brought on diarrhoea.

During the days of the cholera epidemic, a letter reached me from the speaker of the local Consultative Assembly, who wrote that an Iranian suffering from cholera had urgently asked for someone from the consulate to come and witness his will. I told Mohammad Khan to go, but he said that he had a wife and children and if he caught the disease and died, there would be no one to provide for his family. Other members of staff gave the same reply. I became angry and told them to prepare the carriage: I would go to the Assembly. When I arrived, I saw the sick man, very thin and lying with a yellow liquid coming from his mouth. He was just skin and bone. He told me that he was called Aspetan, he was an Armenian from Salmas, and he had one sister, to whom his property would devolve. He had deposited so much money with such and such a Haji and so much with another Haji. After his death, the consulate should lend its assistance so that these men actually passed the money on to his sister.

I said to myself that he didn't seem to have cholera. Perhaps I should try to see whether I could treat him by hypnotism. So, in a loud commanding voice, I shouted: 'You rude man, you should be ashamed of yourself. The consul-general has come to your bedside and you are just lying there. Get up, son of a no-good father!' I saw that this appeared to have no effect, so I stamped my foot longer and louder and shouted: 'Get up, you rude man!' I saw that he moved, and opened his eyes. On the second occasion he actually sat up. The Speaker of the Assembly, who was present and witnessed my conversation with the sick man, was astonished. He nevertheless suggested that he should call the Assembly doctor to see if he could help cure the man. The doctor came and was also very surprised, saying: '"You have performed a real miracle. This man is cured. I will keep him here for a few days, give him some brandy and he will be fine.' I had saved the Armenian's life but I myself caught cholera and returned to the consulate-general, where I was treated. We both survived.

Two years after being posted to Tiflis, I had cause to remember the words of Naser-od-Din Shah. Money from issuing passports had started to pour down on me like rain. I had a sum of money in the government bank and I consulted several respected Iranian merchants as to where I could find a trustworthy home for all this money. They told me that the safest place to invest this money was in land. I should buy land in Tiflis and Borjom, which were places with a future. When I began to think about buying land, one of my close Iranian friends came to me and suggested that I should be prudent and act in accordance with the Arab proverb: 'Conceal your gold, your comings and goings and your allegiances!' He continued: 'As soon as they realise in Tehran how much income the consulate here enjoys, everyone will want to come here. If someone like Yahya Khan[3] takes over at the Ministry of Foreign Affairs, you will have nothing at all. Put your money in the bank and buy shares!' I replied that he didn't need to worry. I was buying this land openly on the orders of the Shah himself. I then bought land in Borjom close to the spa, where water is plentiful, at an exorbitant price and built the Hôtel Firouzeh there.[4] The architectural style there is similar to that prevailing in Iran. I brought a builder from Qazvin to carry out the stucco and mirror work, and also an Iranian painter whom I had located in Baku. Above each of the hotel's two doors, on a black stone slab I had lines of poetry engraved in gold. On one the lines went as follows:

One thousand and three hundred years had not yet passed[5]
When this humble cottage and patch of green field
Received the name of Firouzeh from friends and loved ones
To remain as a memorial to Mirza Reza Khan!

Above the other door was engraved:

Sa'adi said: A man's good name is a better memorial than a golden palace;
As for Mirza Reza Khan, let both a good name and a golden palace remain
    as his memorial in this world.

In the hills above Borjom I chose as my summer residence a large and very beautiful, level piece of ground, with wonderful views, facing the palace of the famous Georgian Queen Tamara. As that area was part of the inheritance of the Grand Duke Mikhail, the Tsar's uncle, who had no legal right to sell it or give it away, I leased a flat part of it on a 99-year lease. There I also built a house in the Iranian style, and had engraved the following historical text on the stone there:

---

3 Yahya Khan Moshir-od-Dowleh, the rapacious minister described in Chapter 5.
4 The building, having been a sanatorium in the Soviet period, has recently been inhabited by homeless families.
5 Since the beginning of the Islamic era.

The Hôtel Firouzeh, Borjom, in present-day Georgia, built by the author in 1892 while consul-general for the Caucasus.

When Arfaʿ-od-Dowleh chose his dwelling in the high hills of Borjom, as his name was superior,[6] he had to call it Daneshabad,[7] so that a trace of Mirza Reza Khan should remain for ever.

That year an article had appeared in the newspaper saying that a German engineer in the service of the Russian government had built two houses in

6 A play on the Arabic word 'Arfaʿ', which means 'higher'.
7 As previously mentioned, at the suggestion of Malkom Khan, minister in London, the author took the name of 'Danesh' or 'Knowledge'.

Gudovich street in Tiflis, one of which was a large two-storey house with a garden and the other next door to it a two-storey mansion.[8] Having finished his time in Tiflis, he was returning to Germany and he was selling them. I bought both of them and brought in the same painter and mirror-maker who had made the mirrors in Borjom. I had the ceiling of the big hall there completely lined with mirror work in hexagonal and octagonal shapes and I asked the painter to fill the spaces between the mirror-work with scenes from the *Thousand and One Nights* from a book recently published in Paris. Mirza ʿAli Khan Hakim Laʿli was there then and as the mirror work resembled diamond cutting, he called the building the 'Diamond Palace' and wrote two texts celebrating its construction, one of which was two lines of poetry engraved by Italian stone-masons on the marble plinth above the door to the mansion.

When the building was completed, it was agreed that in the year 1310 (1892 of the Christian era), as a kind of house-warming, I would celebrate the birthday of His Majesty with unparalleled pomp and circumstance, in order to express my thanks to him for his countless kindnesses to me. In the garden there were two pools: a hexagonal one in the middle of the garden and another small marble one in front of the Residence. Skilled Italian craftsmen had sculpted the latter pool in the shape of a round flat champagne glass. The top of the pool, with its long delicate base, reached the height of a man's chest. Now it had a fountain which functioned day and night. Water flowed from its sides into the circular marble basin and thence onto the flower-beds. Instead of water, I wanted fine Kakhet wine to pour from the fountain, fill the pool and provide drink for the guests. I planted four acacias as high as the glass stem at the four corners of the pool and attached them to scaffolding. A huge vat of red Kakhet wine was bought, the kind of vat which can contain 3,000–4,000 bottles and which Russian officers in Georgia used to fill with water and in which they would sit in the midsummer heat. These were brought into the garden and were raised and placed on the platform with the help of cranes used in the construction of government buildings. Then a rubber tube was connected from the vat to the pipe leading from the fountain in such a way that when the tap was turned on, wine shot upwards to the height of the platform

8 Arfaʿ made this building into the consulate-general. The building survives today in the re-named Chonkadze Street in Tbilisi.

and filled the pool. I asked the governor-general to send a military band to the garden that night and I ordered splendid fireworks from the government arsenal.

This display took place under the walls of the ancient citadel of Tiflis which overlooked the garden. I invited the aristocracy, the governor's staff and as many others as could fit into the great hall and the dining-room. I inserted a notice in the local newspaper that in honour of the celebration of His Majesty's birthday, the consulate gardens would be lit up and the gates opened to all comers. I had the gardens beautifully illuminated by Chinese and Japanese lanterns, and fortunately it was a moonlit night. 'Abdol-Baqi Qarabaghi, who had a fine voice, was then in Tiflis. He had played Iranian music for many years in Iran, and he had put together an orchestra of his own in Tiflis, consisting of a tar instrumentalist, a flautist, a violinist and two small drums. I stationed 'Abdol-Baqi on the balcony of the hall overlooking the garden and a military band in the garden itself. Four servants were standing round the pool with silver trays to serve drinks to the guests, since Georgians and Armenians really love Kakhet wine and they wouldn't be satisfied with just one or two small glasses. The area around the pool under the trees and the raised platform was decorated with colourful flowers and ornamental trees. Hundreds of Chinese and Japanese lanterns placed above and around the pool lit up the colour of the wine, which was rosé-coloured rather than dark red. How the wines sparkled in that brilliant light! The fireworks too greatly added to the brilliance of the evening.

Among the guests there were some very young and beautiful Georgian princesses. When the Governor of Tiflis, Prince Shirvashidze, who was a renowned, published poet in his own language, saw 'Abdol-Baqi and his orchestra on the balcony on the one side and the military band on the other, while the pool flowed with wine, with his compatriots, the princesses, and the fireworks forming a backdrop to this scene, he called me and said: 'Tonight you have converted me to Islam.' I asked him what he meant. He said that he had read the description of our prophet's paradise in several books of poetry but he would never have believed it. However, that evening he had become certain that paradise was indeed like such a place. He now believed that our Prophet's promised vision of paradise was well-founded.

During my five years in Tiflis, as the Diamond Palace had many bedrooms, I hosted all the important visitors who were on their way either to Mecca or to

Europe, who stayed as my guests during their time in Tiflis. On one occasion, a telegram arrived from the Ministry of Foreign Affairs saying that the Amin-e-Aqdas[9] was going to Vienna for eye treatment. Ahmad Khan, the step-son of the Sepahsalar, and the Sa'ad-os-Saltaneh, governor of Qazvin, were both escorting her to Vienna, accompanied by two eunuchs. I was instructed to go to Enzeli and accompany them to Vienna and back through Russia as far as Rasht, so very respectfully I accompanied the party to Vienna. On our return to Rasht, when I was about to take my leave, on behalf of the Shah they presented me with a fine Isfahan enamelled pen-box with a picture of Naser-od-Din Shah in uniform on it and inside it, together with a magnificent gold inkwell inlaid with jewels.

9 The Shah's influential wife referred to in Chapter 6. According Dr Feuvrier, the treatment for glaucoma was unsuccessful because undertaken too late and she became blind.

Chapter 9

The Embassy in St Petersburg (1895–1901)

This is in some ways the most important chapter in these memoirs as it covers the period when Arfa' was Iran's minister in St Petersburg and when in his own view he achieved more for his country than he had at any other time in his diplomatic career.

In the early 1890s, Russian-British rivalry was particularly acute: It was the time of the 'Great Game', when Iran became a battleground where the two countries' imperial interests played out. Russia sought territory for strategic and imperial reasons, while Britain, whose strategic interests were related to the defence of India from the Russian threat and which had greater access to investment capital, sought influence through commercial penetration. The result was constant competition between the two countries to obtain concessions, particularly for mining rights and the construction of roads and railways, or at least to prevent its rival obtaining them. The Shah and his ministers were keen to see the development of their country, no less keen to receive the personal financial benefits flowing from such concessions but, increasingly mindful of the opposition of the Shi'a clergy and merchant classes to the sell-off of their country to unbelievers, were concerned that a wide-ranging revolt against the Shah's rule would break out and worried that Russia and Britain would agree to partition the country between them. In 1890 a monopoly for the purchase and sale of all Iranian tobacco was granted to the British-owned Régie and, in the face of widespread protests, was cancelled by the Shah in 1892. Potential concession-holders and creditors were, however, faced with the problem of security for their investments. Iran's tax revenues were uncertain and sometimes insufficient to pay even its army. Foreign creditors were therefore unwilling to accept vague promises of payment and sought to attach the customs revenues as the only enforceable guarantee of their investment. In the context of the wider struggle for influence in Iran, however, Britain had in 1892 secured an undertaking from Naser-od-Din Shah that 'in no circumstances would the revenues of the Customs of Southern Persia be ceded to a Foreign Power', that is to say to any other power but Britain.[1]

Following the assassination of Naser-od-Din Shah in 1896, court intrigue around his successor, Mozaffar-od-Din Shah (1896–1907) soon caused the dismissal of Arfaʿs protector and prime minister, the Amin-os-Soltan, the Great Atabak, and his own consequent recall to Tehran.[2] *Faced with imminent ruin, the author bounced back with aplomb. The Shah found himself gravely embarrassed by what might seem to be a minor customs problem with an Italian merchant but which turned into a major commercial dispute, with all the main European powers arrayed against him. Arfaʿ was able to call for neutral arbitration of the dispute. The Shah was so pleased by the court's decision in favour of Iran that he confirmed the author in his post and awarded him the title of Prince, one of the first commoners to be given this title. Naser-od-Din Shah had long been gravely concerned that, following its victory over the Turkomans, Russia would invade Khorasan. In this context, the author's role in persuading the Tsar to cancel orders to send 10,000 troops through the holy city of Mashhad not only resolved a potentially explosive problem with the Iranian clergy and associated merchant community but helped to preserve Iran's territorial integrity. Finally, with Iran in desperate financial straits, unable to pay its Russian-trained Cossack Brigade or the gendarmerie, the author seems to have shown courage in querying his instructions to sign a loan agreement with Russia without further ado. As a result of his subsequent point-by-point renegotiation of its terms with Russian ministers, he claims to*

---

1 A guarantee given by Naser-od-Din Shah to the British Legation in 1892 in the context of an attempt to secure a foreign loan in Paris (Kazemzadeh, *Russia and Britain in Persia 1864–1914*, p. 307).

2 The intrigues were orchestrated by the Farman Farma, which goes some way to explain the author's unusually harsh words for the latter in Chapter 6.

have succeeded in removing the humiliating condition that Russian inspectors should supervise Iranian tax offices. Furthermore, by deleting the stipulation that the loan would be partly guaranteed by the revenues of Iran's southern Customs, he prevented what would almost certainly have been a serious Anglo-Persian and Anglo-Russian dispute. In 1901, however, when there was question of a second Russian loan to pay for the Shah's European travels, the Minister of Foreign Affairs, Mirza Nasrollah Khan Moshir-od-Dowleh, was able to secure the author's replacement as minister in St Petersburg by his own son.

After I had completed five years in Tiflis, just as Naser-od-Din Shah had promised, the ʿAlaʾ-ol-Molk was recalled from St Petersburg and appointed ambassador in Istanbul, while I was sent to St Petersburg with the title of Minister Plenipotentiary and Special Envoy. The most valuable services which I was able to perform for my government took place during my time there. From that year onwards, heavenly assistance laid the foundations for this. When I departed for St Petersburg, I took with me Mirza ʿAli-Akbar Khan, my brother, who later acquired the title of the Mofakhkham-os-Saltaneh, Mirza Karim Khan, later the Mobasser-ol-Molk, and Mirza ʿAli-Asghar Khan, my other brother, later the Baqaʾ-os-Saltaneh. In Vladikafkaz, we were received by Mohammad ʿAli Khan, the consul, and his wife Nisaʾ Khanum. In Rostov, Moscow and St Petersburg, the honorary consuls were wealthy Jews who owned fine mansions and had only accepted these honorary posts in order to secure invitations from the local governor. They had opened offices at their own expense and assisted Iranian citizens with the police and other bodies without financial reward. They really ran the consulates in a very honourable manner. All they wanted from the Iranian government in return for their services was the Order of the Lion and Sun for foreigners. In St Petersburg, in addition to the Consul-General, called Poliakov, there was a vice-consul called Rafaelovich, who was Poliakov's son-in-law.[3] Poliakov, the Consul in Moscow, who was the St Petersburg Poliakov's brother, entertained us for a

---

3 The immensely wealthy Poliakov family group were also heavily involved in attempts to obtain a Rasht-Tehran railway concession, as well as concessions to build roads and provide loans to the Shah.

day in Moscow and gave a splendid dinner for us. We entered St Petersburg on 10 May 1895. Samad Khan, who later acquired the title of Momtaz-os-Saltaneh and was made a prince, came to greet us with Poliakov and Rafaelovich. Samad Khan entered the railway carriage first and showed me a telegram from Tiflis saying that God had that day blessed me with a son. What should he be called? I replied that he should have my father's name, Hassan.[4] I took this event as a good omen.

A few days after my arrival in St Petersburg, a letter arrived from the Ministry of Foreign Affairs instructing me to go in full-dress uniform to Tsarskoe Seloe on a certain day, where the Tsar[5] and Tsarina were in residence, to present my credentials. I entered the magnificent royal palace and proceeded to the Great Hall. Baron Fredericks, the chief of protocol, with two young equerries to the Tsar and several officers of the Imperial Guard, were standing around and talking. The Tsar and the Tsarina received ambassadors separately. Their offices were next door to each other, with an intercommunicating door. Obviously the doors were closed. Baron Fredericks said to me: 'Your Excellency, first of all I will take you into the Tsar's presence. I will then introduce you and withdraw. The door will be shut and you will be alone in the imperial presence. You should make a short speech in one of four languages, Russian, French, English or German. When you have finished your speech, you will place the Shah's letter in His Majesty's hand. The Tsar will then reply to your speech in the language which you have used. You should remain silent. Then you will bow, retire backwards and then gently tap on the door. The imperial attendants will open the door, which they will leave open, and the arrangements for being received by the Tsarina[6] are the same. The Tsarina is very shy and she has only been married for about two months. Her mother died shortly after her birth and as she is the granddaughter of Queen Victoria of England, the latter took her in and brought her up, so she is quite unused to talking to men. When she talks, she blushes and her lips tremble. I always

4 Later Major-General Hassan Arfaʻ, Chief of Staff of the Iranian army and ambassador in Pakistan and Turkey under Mohammad Reza Shah Pahlavi.

5 Nicholas II.

6 Alexandra Feodorovna, formerly Princess Alix of Hesse, a granddaughter of Queen Victoria.

warn ambassadors and ministers of this before they are received in audience and I am now warning you in the same way. When I escort you into her presence, I will withdraw as I do with the Tsar, and the door will be shut. You will advance and stand before her alone. There is no need for a speech. If the Tsarina asks you a question, you should reply. If she does not, watch her lips! As soon as you see her lips tremble, you should bow and withdraw.'

Two Ethiopians were stationed in front of the door, chosen from among tribal leaders, who have to be very tall and are dressed in long robes of gold thread with small turbans made of silk and gold thread. Truly, these two doormen standing in front of the golden doors of the Great Hall add a particular magnificence to this reception. These two Ethiopians are not only tall but very well proportioned and handsome. Unlike Africans, they do not have thick, drooping lips. At great expense, the Russian government employs them and brings them over from Ethiopia. After the chief of protocol had briefed me, the doors were opened by the doormen. Fredericks escorted me into the presence of the Tsar, who was dressed in the uniform of a colonel and equerry to his father. (As Nicholas II had only reached the rank of colonel and equerry during his father's life-time and Alexander III's reign had not lasted long, out of respect for his father he would never wear a general's uniform as long as he lived.) I was wearing my uniform as an Adjutant General to the Shah. In accordance with Fredericks' instructions, I had prepared my speech in Russian and spoke from memory. Of course the speech was about international affairs: I recalled the friendship of Iran and Russia from ancient days; I expressed the hope that this friendship would increase as much as possible; I then transmitted the Shah's friendly feelings towards the Tsar and finished my speech. The Tsar said that he was very happy that I had been appointed. The governor-general of the Caucasus had reported that at the time of Alexander III's illness, when all the peoples of the Empire had gone to their places of worship with their religious leaders to pray for him, I had gone to the mosque known as the Shah 'Abbas mosque and had invited the Sheikh-ol-Islam and the Qazi to pray for his health. He had been impressed by these friendly feelings. Furthermore, when his brother George had been ill and had gone to 'Abbas-Toman near Borjom, I had gone to visit the sick man. Prince Shirvashidze had also described to him the reception I had given on the Shah's birthday and how Kakhet wine had flowed instead of water, so he knew me by reputation. He hoped that I would enjoy my time at his court in every way. I handed over my letters of appointment to him and bowed. Having taken the letters and made his speech, the Tsar fell silent. I bowed and withdrew backwards towards the door.

It was now my turn to be received by the Tsarina. As Baron Fredericks had said, I stood very humbly in front of her, watching her lips to see whether they were trembling, when I would withdraw. Suddenly her eyes fell on my chest and she saw my Victoria decoration, on which the Queen's face could be distinctly seen. She asked me where I had been awarded this decoration.[7] This one question gave me the opportunity to start to describe the Shah's visit to London and my journey to Scotland in the entourage of the Shah. I saw that she was so interested by my description of the reception at Buckingham Palace and of the parties given by the aristocracy that, instead of her lips trembling, she was smiling. Suddenly, I saw that the Tsar, no doubt thinking that it was some time since I had left his presence, open the door and enter the room singing a Russian song. As soon as he saw that I was still in the Tsarina's presence, he made a movement and shut the door. I realised that I had talked much too much, so I bowed and withdrew walking backwards out of the room. Baron Fredericks and the adjutants, who were standing on the other side of the door, were astonished. What spell had I worked to make the Tsarina speak so that I had remained in her presence for so long? I replied that I hadn't worked a spell. The representation of Queen Victoria had done the trick and had made me start to talk and recount the story of that journey. They all said that I should be aware of the value of this decoration: the medal would ensure the Tsarina's continuing favour.

At this point Baron Fredericks said that the Princess Galitsin, the Tsarina's principal lady-in-waiting, was waiting for me in the dining-room. He escorted me there and introduced me. Three ladies-in-waiting, two of whom I already

---

7 This decoration was sold with many of the author's possessions by Sotheby Park Bernet Monaco in 1983. The catalogue illustration shows that this was Queen Victoria's Star for non-Christians, which was probably created for distribution to members of the Shah's entourage during his 1889 visit and was later given by Queen Victoria to senior Indians as an acknowledgement of personal services to the Sovereign. It became obsolete on the creation of the Royal Victorian Order in 1896.

knew, were present. One was Mademoiselle Taube, whom I had got to know when I was the secretary in the Tiflis consulate-general. The other was the Princess Orbelliani, the leading Georgian aristocrat, whom I had also known in Tiflis. At lunch I was placed on the right of Princess Orbelliani and on the left of Baron Fredericks. The equerries and Monsieur Kanyar, the protocol officer, were also invited.

In my first year, preparations were being made for Tsar Nicholas II's coronation in Moscow. In the time of Alexander II, it was the custom for a parade to be held in the middle of May on the Champ de Mars just outside the summer park, where there is a flat area large enough for 50,000 troops to manoeuvre. In the presence of the entire imperial family, including the princesses, senior officers and the nobility, who were in temporary stands, Alexander II would review a parade of 30,000 troops of the St Petersburg garrison. However, after the death of Alexander II, who was killed by a revolutionary's bomb on his return from a reception, Alexander III was in mourning for a time and was in poor health, so this custom fell into disuse. Before leaving for Moscow and his coronation, Tsar Nicholas II wanted to revive this old custom.

A tribal chief's son, with whom I had become friends in Tiflis, had given me a Qarabagh Arab horse, which I had brought with me to St Petersburg. However, due to a heavy workload and too many official calls, I hadn't ridden it for some time. During my time on the Boundary Commission, I had ordered saddlery of silver and gold ornamented with rubies and turquoise to be made for me in Mashhad. In addition to its girth and bridle, it also had a neck-strap like those in Sassanian paintings and a neck pendant in the shape of a champagne glass, to which various objects were attached. When the horse was being saddled and the girth fastened, the groom said: 'Sir, this horse isn't used to the sound of bells. When it moves forward and the pendant touches its chest, it will get agitated and frightened. Please let me take the pendant off.' As the whole beauty of this harness lay in the pendant and its attachments, I rejected this idea. The horse was taken off and kept waiting in front of the Winter Palace, where I travelled in my carriage. I then mounted the horse but observed that it was indeed getting excited and frightened by the tinkling sound. As I waited for the Tsar to emerge from the palace, I walked my horse twice past the vast palace, so that it calmed down a little. The Tsar, the grand-dukes and the equerries started to move from the banks of the River Neva towards the parade ground, but it is a very long way from the riverbank to the parade ground, the Champ de Mars.

Up until that point, my horse was agitated and frightened but I somehow managed to control it. But when we reached the Summer Garden and the horse saw the life-size and sometimes larger than life stone or plaster statues of gods, Russian heroes and generals, terrifying monsters which the young Arab horse had never seen before in its life, it reared so badly that I lost control and it broke into a lightening gallop. First it galloped past the carriages belonging to the Tsarina and Grand-duchesses and then those carrying the Tsar and the Grand Dukes. I was so embarrassed by the horse's bad manners that I fainted and fell off. As I fell, however, my foot caught in the stirrup and the horse dragged me along the gravel road for a while, so that I lost the skin on my forehead. Then my foot fell out of the stirrup and I passed out. The noble animal thought that I was dead and stood over me sniffing my chest. At this point, the Tsar and the carriage containing the Tsarina and the princesses came up, and the Tsar ordered the cavalry guard to halt. A cavalryman was sent off, and a court carriage was brought from the parade ground, I was put into it unconscious and taken to the embassy in the coach with the Tsar's private doctor, who was in attendance. I saw the Tsar standing over me waiting for a carriage to be brought up. As there had been so much delay in proceedings, there was a rumour among the troops and those present that some harm had come to the Tsar. This lasted until he reached the lines of soldiers and stood in front of the Tsarina's box, when the march-past began. During the parade, the Tsar twice sent his equerries to the embassy to ask how I was. Meanwhile, I remained completely unconscious from the time I fainted and fell off my horse until about sunset on that day.

The Tsar's private doctor would come once a day until I recovered completely and could get up, and Baron Fredericks, the court chief of protocol, came to the embassy several times on behalf of the Tsar to enquire after my health. All the Russian newspapers were full of praise for the Tsar and gave a detailed description of how I had fallen from my horse and how the Tsar and Tsarina's coach had stopped where I lay on the ground until a coach had been brought up, and how the Tsar had sent his equerries to enquire after my health during the parade, emphasising the Tsar's compassion and humanity.

Two months later, we received an invitation to attend the coronation in Moscow. The expenses for these comings and goings are the responsibility of ministers plenipotentiary and ambassadors and are not paid for by the Russian government. The reason for this is that every foreign government sends a representative to congratulate the Tsar on his coronation and the Russian government cannot afford to pay both for these ambassadors extraordinary and those resident in Russia. The Iranian government had sent Prince Molk-Ara, Naser-od-Din Shah's brother, to Moscow with an appropriate number of senior figures to offer the monarch's congratulations. In fact, Mohammad Mirza, the Molk-Ara's son, who had the rank of secretary in the embassy extraordinary, took charge of it and the Molk-Ara did not interfere in any way in his son's decisions. The late *Mo'aven-od-Dowleh*, who had been consul-general in Tiflis and later became Minister of Foreign Affairs, was also part of this embassy extraordinary.

In order to thank the Tsar for his extraordinary kindness to me, I wanted to do something exceptional to celebrate the occasion, so I rented the third floor of a building to which I summoned an electrical engineer and told him that I wanted him to make a large electrically-illuminated lion, entirely lifelike, complete with eyes and eyebrows, and behind it a sun, all in proportion.[8] He was to put a shining sword in the lion's paw. However, he was to make this in such a way that spectators could not see that the whole thing was an assemblage of electric bulbs but rather the lion, the sun and the sword should be one single electrically-lit motif. The engineer understood the requirements and did his job admirably. When it was lit up, the whole of Moscow came, either on horseback or on foot, to see the spectacle. Several people even swore to me that they had seen the Tsar and Tsarina among the spectators in front of the lion and sun.

On the day before the coronation, one of the Tsarina's ladies-in-waiting saw me in the Nobles' Club. She said that she had some strange news: a few days before the departure of the imperial family from St Petersburg, the coronation programme had been brought to the Tsarina. When she read it, she noticed that the programme, planned according to Peter the Great's instructions and long-standing custom, would proceed as follows: on the day of the Tsar and the Tsarina's coronation, all the ministers, together with leading military and civilian figures, should arrive early at the Kremlin church and the entire imperial family of both sexes older than ten or twelve years, should also be in the

---

8 Iran's national emblem at the time.

church. When all the guests had arrived, a court herald would proclaim in a loud voice: 'All rise! Their Majesties are making their entry.' Obviously everyone present would get up. When the Tsar and Tsarina made their entry, they would make their way to the altar. Then the Grand Metropolitan would say a short prayer and give the imperial crown to the Tsar with both hands. The latter would place it on his own head. While he was doing this, the Tsarina would come and kneel before the Tsar, who would then take the Tsarina's crown from the priest and place it on her head. At this point the Tsarina had protested, saying how humiliating it would be for a woman to kneel in front of a man for her coronation in the presence of so many foreign dignitaries of different ranks and of heirs apparent and their wives. A crown was not worth this humiliation, and she refused to do this. The Tsarina Maria Feodorovna, the King of Denmark's daughter and Nicholas II's mother, very gently persuaded her to drop her protest, saying that as Peter the Great had written this programme for the coronation, it would be impossible to change it. Although the Tsarina was obliged to accept Maria Feodorovna's instructions, she was not at all happy about this.

Furthermore, as the Grand Metropolitan insisted that everyone should take off their hats in church and Naser-od-Din Shah was equally insistent that Iranians should not take off their hats in church, the result was that the Prince Molk-Ara delayed his arrival and arrived on the day after the coronation. I was also instructed not to enter the church at the time of the coronation but to stand outside the church by the door, if I could be allotted a place there, and to watch the ceremony inside church from there. I acted as instructed. The Iranian embassy extraordinary then arrived and was lodged in a hotel at the expense of the Russian government. The same day its members were received in audience by the Tsar so that it could present the Shah's letter of congratulation. In accordance with custom, I was also present.

Something happened on the day of the coronation which everyone took as a bad omen and made people say that this coronation would bring bad luck on Russia. According to ancient custom, on the day of the coronation the court would distribute a wooden basket containing a loaf of black bread, a large joint of cooked meat, a half-bottle of beer and two apples to every villager who came to Moscow from the surrounding countryside to watch the coronation. The thing that the villagers coveted the most in each basket was a china cup made in the imperial factories, on which the imperial eagle and the crown were painted. Underneath the crown the first letter of the Tsar's name and patronymic is written. On this occasion they had written N A, that is to say 'Nikolai Alexandrovich'.

At previous coronations, draconian security measures had been taken by the governor of Moscow to prevent disorder when these baskets were being distributed, so that people did not push each other and cause injury in order to get their basket first. On this occasion, however, more people than usual had gathered from Moscow and surrounding villages. Their numbers were estimated at 100,000. Either the government was unable to take the necessary measures to maintain calm or they were simply negligent. In any case, just as the Kremlin guns were firing a salvo announcing the coronation to the people and the distribution of the baskets was starting, the 100,000 spectators suddenly started to move from where they were standing towards those who were distributing the baskets. The ground was not level, for it had up and downs and hollows. People pushed and shoved each other, 10,000 people fell into the hollows and were crushed under the feet of those behind them. In order to remove the corpses as fast as possible, the police and security rushed to areas outside the town and requisitioned any wagons or carts they could find there, which they sent to the scene of the disaster, and piled the corpses on top of each other, barely covered with canvas or sackcloth.

As they brought the bodies past the thousands of spectators who had filled the surrounding area, the people became uneasy and began to feel anger and hatred at the sight, asking each other what had happened. From what place of execution had these bodies been brought? Obviously at this point the enemies of the government who have always existed in Russia, albeit in small numbers, were waiting for the opportunity to stir up every kind of suspicion among their sympathisers. They fell in behind the corpses and shouted 'May your coronation be blessed!' The police weren't present, as they were busy clearing up the area where the bodies were.

Unluckily for the Tsar, the French ambassador in Moscow, had organised a ball in honour of the coronation, for which all the decorations and Gobelin tapestries had been brought from the royal palace at Versailles. It was said that nearly 50,000 francs worth of flowers and greenery had been brought from Nice and the surrounding area, together with expensive table wines and more than a hundred cases of the best champagne to accompany the dessert. It was rumoured that the cost of the ball was many millions. After this ill-luck at the time of the coronation, which made the people of Moscow's feelings turn to hatred, the imperial family split into two groups: the one, of which the Tsar's mother was a member, said that going to a ball, playing music and dancing instead of there being a period of mourning would make the people angrier and was inhumane; in the other group was the Tsar's uncle, the Grand Duke Vladimir Alexandrovich, who said that a failure to attend the ball, when France had spent so much money on it and had brought all the decorations from the palace at Versailles, having just concluded a treaty of friendship with Russia, would cause offence. In the end the Grand Duke persuaded the Tsar to go to the ball but not to dance or play any part in the ball and let it be known that he had come to see what the French had spent so much money on for the ball and not for pleasure.

In the end, the Tsar came to the French embassy ball with the Tsarina, where I was also present. First, on the entry of the Tsar, the band played greetings to the Tsar and then to the President of the French Republic, followed by the French national anthem. Everyone in the area of the ball who heard the sound of the band objected, saying that the Tsar should not have attended. Nobody explained to them that the Tsar had gone to the ball to inspect the efforts made by the French and the royal furnishings and not for pleasure. The Grand Duke Vladimir's advice had caused greater offence to the Russian people.

In order to thank the Tsar for all his kindness when I fell off my horse, I gave a splendid reception for Muslim representatives of all the towns in the Caucasus, both Shi'a and Sunni. They came to offer their congratulations to the Tsar on the occasion of his coronation. Obviously, the Akhond Molla 'Abd-os-Salaam for the Shi'a and the Mufti 'Abdol-Hamid Effendi for the Sunnis were at the head of the line, and Muslim officers of the Imperial Guard like 'Ali Khan Nakhchivaneski and others were also invited. About sixty people sat down to eat. Of course the Tsar and Tsarina received a report about this party. During the period of the coronation, however, I had made a careless mistake and, had it not been for the Tsar's good nature, my mission to Russia would have ended differently and I would perhaps have been branded a failure for the rest of my life.

During my five-year mission in Tiflis, Prince Shirvashidze had been governor of the town and Monsieur Tchaikovski deputy governor. When the

Grand Duke George, then the heir to the Russian throne, fell ill, he was sent to ʿAbbas-Toman, which was part of the province of Tiflis, on the recommendation of the doctors. Prince Shirvashidze was in attendance on him in ʿAbbas-Toman, so in reality the deputy-governor was in charge in Tiflis. His house was near the Diamond Palace. Throughout my time in Tiflis, Monsieur Tchaikovski was very helpful to the work of the consulate-general, his wife being the daughter of a wealthy Moscow merchant. They used to give a dinner once a week for their friends and after dinner they would invite their guests to stay longer. They invited me to all these parties. Obviously the governor had come to Moscow for the coronation and Monsieur Tchaikovski remained in charge of the government in Tiflis, while his wife was staying with her father to see the coronation. Two days before the event, there was a gala performance at the imperial theatre, to which all crown princes with their wives, the prince of Qaradagh with his whole family, ministers plenipotentiary and ambassadors, the nobility and the diplomatic corps from every country were invited.

I received a note from Madame Tchaikovski asking me to come to her father's house to call on her, so I did so. She told me that there would be a ballet performance at the imperial theatre which would be about our prophet's paradise, with houris and handsome youths, the *Pool of Kawthar*,[9] jewelled castles and trees with leaves made of emeralds. Some 100,000 *manat* had been spent on this paradise, on the costumes for the houris, the handsome youths and the angels. There had never been a performance like this before and there would never be again. However, as her husband had remained in Tiflis and she had come to Moscow as a simple spectator, she hadn't received an invitation to the ballet. As a mark of our five-year friendship she was therefore making a plea for my help, which she didn't think that I would refuse. She asked me to take her with me to the theatre. I said that this was impossible: I had a place in a box and everyone in it had a numbered seat. Where could I find her a seat? She replied that she had thought of this. I could give her a seat allotted to one of my secretaries and she would give me her word of honour that she would

---

9 The *Pool of Kawthar* is described in the Qurʾan as a great pool which Allah grants his prophet on the Day of Judgment. Its water is clear, sweet and refreshing. Believers with good deeds will drink from it and quench their thirst caused by the horror of the Day of Judgment.

hide behind me throughout the performance, so that no one would see her. Her objective was to see the ballet.

As the way in which Madame Tchaikovski explained the matter to me seemed simple and easy, I agreed to do as she asked. It had been agreed that she would replace a secretary, and I entered the box first. The box belonging to the Tsar, the Tsarina and the imperial family was very large, and box no.6, which had been allotted to the Belgian minister and to me, was to the right of it. As his wife wasn't in St Petersburg, however, the second seat allotted to him was immediately in front of mine. As the Belgian minister had arrived before me, he had taken his seat, while the third seat behind him was occupied by his secretary. After I had sat down, Madame Tchaikovski entered. In breach of her promise that she would come simply dressed, she was literally drowning in jewels and she was both young and beautiful. As soon as the Belgian minister's eyes fell on her, he almost fainted and got up very quickly to give her his seat, while he sat in the secretary's place. Needless to say, every pair of opera glasses was trained on our box. I was confident, however, that when Madame had sat down, no one would pay any further attention to us.

Among the members of the imperial court, however, there was one person renowned for his irascible temperament. It was said that no one had ever seen him smile, let alone laugh. This man was Count Benckendorff, deputy chief of protocol, through whose hands all invitation cards passed. When from his box he saw Madame Tchaikovski, whom he knew personally, he was so angry that he left his box and came out to investigate who had invited her. The attendant in charge of the box replied that the Iranian minister had brought her with him. He then went to see the chief of protocol, Baron Fredericks, told him what had happened and asked for instructions. He made clear his view, however, that either Madame Tchaikovski had to be asked to leave the box and sent home or during the interval the attendant shouldn't allow her to go back into the box. Madame Tchaikovski had said that she wouldn't leave the box during the interval, in case she was asked to leave. The chief of protocol said that he couldn't give a view, as the matter had become rather complicated, but Benckendorff should go and consult the minister of foreign affairs, Lobanov Rostovski, and take his instructions from him. Benckendorff told the latter that on the basis of agreed official protocol, Madame Tchaikovski must be removed from the box by whatever means necessary. A Russian subject could not be allowed to flout contemporary protocol in the presence of the Tsar, and, as to the Iranian minister plenipotentiary's conduct, the Ministry of Foreign Affairs should ask the Iranian government to withdraw him and relieve him of his responsibilities. Prince Lobanov was a good-natured, level-headed old man, a good man, who said that he couldn't solve this difficult problem. Benckendorff should wait until the interval, when he would refer it to the Tsar and it would be up to him to give orders. The curtain fell and Lobanov told the Tsar what had happened. As the Tsar had an exceptional eye for beauty, he laughed and told him to drop the matter, commenting that he had noticed us both and that both Madame Tchaikovski and the minister plenipotentiary were an ornament to the box. As I too had put on several decorations ornamented with diamonds, these had caught the Tsar's eye and he had seen what was going on right from the beginning. Benckendorff became angrier than ever and went and sat in his box. Meanwhile, I knew nothing of what was going on. In the interval I went to the Minister of Foreign Affairs's box to pay my respects. The minister gave me a full account of what had happened and said that I should be very grateful to the Tsar: if the Minister of Foreign Affairs had acted on Benckendorff's proposal, I would have been finished. I swore not to be so reckless in future.

Before leaving St Petersburg for Moscow to attend the coronation, I had presented a French-language copy of my book *An Anthology of Knowledge* to the Tsarina by hand of the Princess Galitsin, who wrote in reply to express Her Majesty's gratitude to me. This kind letter made me think of celebrating this Moscow coronation in a poem in which I would recall the story of her kneeling and taking the crown from the Tsar, sympathising with her point of view. To this end I composed a *qasidah* in praise of her which I translated as literally as possible into French and gave to two members of the embassy staff to make a fair copy of it. When they had read it, however, both very politely said that they thought that it would be better not to send it to the Tsarina for two reasons: some of the lines had a scent of love-making in them and, with respect to the crowning of the Tsarina by the Tsar, there was an element of impertinence. Both of these factors would undoubtedly displease the Tsar and if that was the case, I would be unable to remain in my post. They said this with so much sincerity that I decided not to send the poem.

After the two men had left me, however, I thought of sending the translation of the poem to Princess Galitsin as a friendly and personal gesture before sending it to the Tsarina, writing that I had composed this poem and asking her for her personal view. Would it be possible to send it or not? Little by little this thought became uppermost in my mind and so I sent the translation to Princess Galitsin. When the members of the embassy learnt of this, they began to feel sorry for my position and were certain that the matter would end badly for me. Their supposition soon almost came true because when a week had passed without my receiving a reply from the Princess, I feared that she had passed on the poem and that it had so offended both of them that they thought a reply unnecessary. The Princess had been trained to reply to every letter.

On the eighth day after I had sent the letter, when I saw the expression of reproach on the faces of the staff at my having ignored their advice, I was sitting feeling very anxious at the Princess's silence, when a servant came in and said that a court servant with gold braid on his uniform had brought a letter, which he said he was only to give to the minister himself. As soon as my eye fell on the princess's seal, even though I hadn't yet opened the envelope, I could hardly restrain myself. I was so relieved that it no longer mattered to me whether the reply was positive or negative. All that mattered was that she had replied. I took out 100 *manat*, gave it to the servant and sent him on his way. I opened the letter and saw that the princess had written that she didn't know how to apologise enough for what had been necessarily a late reply. She had been so busy recently that she hadn't had a moment to study my translation of my superb *qasidah*. She didn't know whether I would forgive her. She was writing with great pleasure to say that I could without embarrassment send the *qasidah*, which contained pleasing and lofty sentiments, to Her Majesty the Tsarina. She was certain that Her exalted mind would be even more delighted by it than she was. The letter was signed: 'Your friend Princess Galitsin.' I was bursting with joy and immediately summoned the staff of the embassy. I thought that I would tease them, so I said: 'Gentlemen, I greatly regret that I didn't accept your advice and now it is clear that your experience is greater than mine.' I soon observed that these gentlemen weren't stupid enough to believe me and they had realised what was going on. They had seen from my expression that the matter was not at all as I was pretending, so I gave them the letter to read.

I sent off for a sheet of fine Khan Baleq paper, I gave the *qasidah* to Mirza Aqa Khan, whose *nasta'liq* script handwriting was better than anybody else's and I sent off the translation to the government printing press, where they wrote it out in ornamental script on the best card. It was a Tartar printing press, some of its workers having previously worked in Istanbul, where they had learnt the art of Turkish gilding. I gave them both the original *qasidah* and the translation. They gilded the original with gold and lapis lazuli. I then gave it to a German framer, who made two red-wood frames with glass in the Iranian style and I sent them with the particularly fine paper to the Princess Galitsin, saying that in my humble way I wished to record in poetry the happy hours of the sacred coronation of Their Majesties and in doing so to provide an example of Iranian culture and outstanding oriental skills. I added that if this insignificant gift from this humble servant met with the favour of Her Majesty Alexandra Feodorovna, Empress of all the Russias, then the supreme honour conferred on me would raise my head to the heavens. The princess wrote in her reply that she had been honoured to present the royal offering to Her Majesty, the study of which had been a cause of great joy to the royal mind and the composition of which was greatly admired by her. She now wished to free herself from the great burden which had been placed on her and convey to me Her Majesty's gratitude and heart-felt pleasure. After this, every time there was an official reception at court for the diplomatic corps and the Tsarina processed along the line of ambassadors and ministers plenipotentiary, she only said two words in conversation and they were always addressed to me, so that my colleagues became very jealous of me.

Now it was the custom in Russia in those days that after a coronation, the Tsarina would commission a charitable foundation, such as a school for orphans, free hospitals for the treatment of the poor, free maternity hospitals, mental asylums or other such things. Committees were formed to raise money and these committees gave instructions as to how such funds should be raised, whether at the theatre or by lottery, concerts and such like. On this occasion, the decision was taken that the Tsarina would give a charity bazaar in the halls of the Winter Palace, where ambassadors and ministers would bring samples of their country's products to sell, with any profits over the cost price being given to the charity committee. It was also decided that there should be a 25 per cent mark-up on the basic price of the goods. A few months before the event, plans were announced and ambassadors invited to participate, with stall places allotted in alphabetical order in the hall. I had no means of buying goods from Iran and transporting them to St Petersburg and no merchant would pay to send for his own goods from there, as they would lose money if they did not sell, so I thought of a plan: two Armenians, one from Iran and the other from the Caucasus, had a shop in St Petersburg which sold Iranian goods such as carpets, printed cloth, flower embroidery, silk embroidery and paintings, pen-cases, mirror frames, inlay work and wood-carving. I asked them to come to the embassy, where I told them about the committee's objective and the rules. We agreed that there would be a profit margin for them of 10 per cent on the basic purchase price in Iran and that they would write out a complete list of all the goods which they wished to sell, together with the prices, including the 10 per cent profit, which I would then give to the committee. The committee would allow them an additional 25 per cent profit on sales, and the final price was then fixed and the final inventory of goods and prices was then handed to the merchant owning them. It was agreed that the goods would be on sale for three weeks.

When the charity bazaar started, the Iranian stall was particularly good. The Armenian merchants had made great efforts, they stationed their own sales assistants in the hall for the period of the sale and they were extremely courteous to buyers. On the day of the official opening, His Majesty the Tsar, together with the Tsarina, the princes and princesses attended and started from stall 'A' until they reached stall 'P' for Persia. At other stalls they simply passed by and thanked the stallholders. At our stall they stopped for a while and asked for explanations of where the goods had been produced, which the salesmen explained through me. They stayed there for a full half-hour and when they left, I accompanied them until they left the building. When the charity bazaar was over, all the invoices went to the profit committee. The Iranian stall had sold goods worth 80,000 *manat*s and was more successful than those of other minister plenipotentiaries. Of that sum 20,000 *manat*s were handed over to the committee. The things that really sold like hot cakes were Persian rugs and carpets. In return for this help, the Tsarina herself made small stamp boxes out of wood from the Tsarskoe Seloe park, which she stuck together with her own hands, and on which she incised a flower in the form of a metal stamp. She sent me one of these boxes through Princess Galitsin and this is now in my museum at Danesh-gah in Monaco. Although it is made of simple wood, it is the most precious thing shown to visitors there because it is the work of the Tsarina's own hand.

At this time a telegram arrived from Tehran instructing me to give a suitable reception at the embassy to celebrate the fiftieth year of Naser-od-Din Shah's reign. There was of course no need for this telegram, as out of gratitude for the many particular favours shown me by this great monarch, I was already ready to serve him and sacrifice myself for him in every possible way. This telegram merely provided an added incentive. I gave instructions for the electrically-illuminated lion and sun, which I had had made in Moscow, to be placed on the top of the embassy building. As the windows on one side of the embassy building gave onto the street and the view from them stretched into the distance, I gave orders not only for the area around the windows to be lit up but for the centre of the windows to be decorated with various geometrical shapes in the form of electric lightbulbs. I invited the minister of foreign affairs, the minister of court, the Tsar's chief of protocol, ambassadors, ministers plenipotentiary and their wives to the official dinner. Unfortunately, on the very day, a telegram arrived from Tehran announcing that on a visit to the Shrine of Hazrat-e ʿAbdol-ʿAzim in Rey to give thanks for his fifty-year reign, the Shah had been shot and killed by an opponent of the regime. The embassy was to go into official mourning. Obviously, because of the great favours which I had received from the Shah, I was in a terrible state. The world seemed to darken. I went to my bedroom, fell on the bed and wept so much that I lost consciousness. When I came to my senses, I gave orders for the embassy to be draped in black and wrote letters to the guests informing them of what had happened and asking for their indulgence.

After the death of Naser-od-Din Shah, who had recently conferred on me the title of Arfaʿ-od-Dowleh, Mozaffar-od-Din Shah confirmed me in my post at the Russian imperial court. Although this diary of mine is not an account of the services which I have rendered to my government, two major events involving the Iranian government took place during my five-year stay at the Russian court. They are also relevant to the story of my life.

Some ten years previously, an Italian merchant called Consonno had brought sixty cases of precious artefacts with him to Tehran: valuable paintings and marble sculptures, mosaic tables, articles of toilette, expensive perfumes, inlaid wooden boxes etc. When he arrived at Enzeli, he paid 5 per cent customs duty for these goods and was given a receipt. As at that time there was no proper road between Enzeli and Tehran, the transport of these cases to

Tehran turned out to be very expensive since the villagers actually had to carry them over some mountain passes. These objects remained in Tehran for some years, for at that time this kind of object wasn't fashionable, nobody would buy them and the merchant was forced to take them back to Italy. The Enzeli customs house prevented their re-export, saying that as they were leaving Iran, he should first pay 5 per cent customs tax. As there was then no Italian consul in Enzeli or Rasht and responsibility for Italian subjects was in the hands of the Russian consul, Consonno appealed to him on this matter. The consul replied that since he had paid 5 per cent duty on these goods when they entered Iran and had obtained a receipt for this payment, in accordance with the Treaty of Turkomanchai, the Iranian government had no right to take another 5 per cent customs dues.[10] According to the terms of the agreement between the Iranian government and Italy, Italian subjects in Iran were to benefit from all the rights that Russian citizens enjoyed under the Treaty of Turkomanchai.

Consonno wrote to the consul asking him to show this agreement to the customs. The customs house still wouldn't accept this. Consonno then produced several Russian subjects as witnesses. Now, at that time there was no customs warehouse in Enzeli, so the cases were left in the open air in front of the customs house, while, taking the Russian consul's affidavit with him, Consonno went off to Rome. After several months under the Gilan rain, the contents of the cases were completely ruined. Then the Italian Ministry of Foreign Affairs obtained affidavits from the foreign ministries in London, Paris, Austria and Germany, countries which traded with Iran, stating that in accordance with the affidavit sworn by the Russian consul, the Iranian government had no right to impose customs dues and that it must pay damages.

At this point Consonno prepared an invoice, which he gave to the Italian Ministry of Foreign Affairs claiming four million francs in damages from the Iranian government on the basis of the inventory he had drawn up. The Italian foreign ministry then instructed the Italian minister in Tehran to seek to obtain this sum in compensation from the Iranian government. The Iranian government, however, did nothing and failed to reply in a frank, correct manner to the embassy letters. Finally, the Italian government lost patience

---

10 A commercial agreement was part of the treaty, whereby the maximum rate of duty on Russian goods entering Iran was fixed at 5 per cent.

and instructed its minister to lower the Italian flag, break off relations and hand over his responsibilities to the German embassy. After the departure of the Italian minister, things became difficult. At that time, the tripartite agreement between Germany, Austria and Italy was concluded and the German embassy advised our Foreign Ministry that this problem must be solved quickly or an Italian warship would go to Bushehr and sequestrate all goods in the customs, which would cause the Iranian government much greater losses. The Iranian government panicked and instructed the Foreign Ministry to ask Iran's ambassadors serving abroad to advise on how to solve the problem.

At that point my advice was sought. As I was fully briefed on the matter, I wrote that the commercial interests of the great powers would lead them to support Italy, in case such a thing befell one of their own subjects: that is to say where a foreign national who had imported commercial goods into Iran had then been unable to sell them and was then forced to pay customs exit charges when he applied to re-export them to his own country. Obviously, therefore, they would support Italy. Sweden, however, had no trade with Iran and it was very unlikely that it would start to trade with Iran in the near future. As the King of Sweden had a reputation for correct behaviour and neutrality, I suggested that we should if possible persuade our opponent, Italy, to entrust the matter to the King of Sweden for arbitration.[11] My reasoning was that if we were adjudged to be right in this matter, the Swedish government would not hesitate to say so in its judgment. My proposal was accepted and Italy was persuaded to accept arbitration. At that time the government had made me minister plenipotentiary in Norway and Sweden in addition to my mission in St Petersburg, so I went to Sweden to persuade the King to accept the role of arbitrator. By a fortunate combination of circumstances, I arrived at the time

11 In fact this was the second case brought against the Persian government by Italy on this matter. In 1891, Sir William White, the British Ambassador at Constantinople, who had been asked by the parties to resolve the dispute, ruled that Consonno had acted illegally in refusing examination of his goods by the Persian Customs. However, the Customs, having failed since 1882 to impound the goods, were responsible for their deterioration and should pay 78,000 francs as compensation for their loss. In 1894, despite the decision being irrevocable, Count Donato addressed a further demand for indirect damages to the Persian government. It seems that it was the second claim which Prince Arfaʿ was able to have referred to the King of Sweden (FO/4682).

of the celebrations of the twenty-fifth anniversary of King Oscar's succession to the throne. The King accepted arbitration and appointed Monsieur Elliot, the public prosecutor of the kingdom, as his representative. Monsieur Elliot assembled all the leading lawyers in Sweden and their verdict was that in international law, the rule on all merchandise entering a country from abroad was as follows: as soon as the owner of goods entering a country had paid the usual customs taxes, these goods were legally in that country. Consequently, all the taxes which are levied on local goods in that country can be demanded of him. So duties could be levied on Consenno's merchandise and in accordance with usage and the terms of the Treaty of Turkomanchai, the Iranian government had the right to levy customs dues on all goods leaving Iran. Therefore Consonno had no right to leave his cases at Enzeli and everything that had happened had been his own fault. The judgment also stated that not only should Iran not have to pay anything but the Italian government must pay the costs of the arbitration.

When I sent the arbitration judgment through *Mirza Hassan Khan Pirnia* (later the Moshir-od-Dowleh), then second secretary at the embassy in St Petersburg, to the ministry in Tehran, a telegram arrived from Mirza Nasrollah Khan Moshir-od-Dowleh, who was the latter's father and minister of foreign affairs, that as a reward for this service His Majesty Mozaffar-od-Din Shah had been gracious enough to confer on me the title of Prince. In the relevant *farman*, it was stated that I would enjoy all the rights and privileges of the royal family.

However, a short time later, the Shah dismissed the Amin-os-Soltan, the Great Atabak, from his position as prime minister,[12] exiled him to Qom and imprisoned all his people. The Farman Farma became prime minister.[13] The Shah was told that Arfaʿ-od-Dowleh was a particular supporter of the Amin-os-Soltan and that so long as I remained in St Petersburg, I would deliberately impede any progress in Iran's affairs. They obtained the Shah's permission

12 The Amin-os-Soltan was dismissed in November 1896.

13 The Farman Farma in fact became Minister of War in the cabinet of the Amin-od-Dowleh but was held to have played a major role in the dismissal of the Amin-os-Soltan. This no doubt goes some way to explain the author's hostility to the Farman Farma in Chapter 6.

to dismiss me and send the Ehtesham-os-Saltaneh in my place. A telegram arrived from the new foreign minister, Haji Sheikh Mohsen Khan Moshir-od-Dowleh, saying that His Majesty had recalled me and that I should travel to Tehran with all speed. I didn't know that the Ehtesham-os-Saltaneh had been appointed in my place and only learnt this from the director of Iranian affairs at the Russian foreign ministry, who also told me that the minister had sent a letter to the Tsar requesting agreement for this appointment, but the latter had not yet replied. At this point a letter from a friend arrived warning me that if I were to return to Tehran, the moment I arrived the Farman Farma intended to send me to Qom with the Atabak. Despite this, I preferred prison in Tehran to remaining in despair in St Petersburg, so I started to make my preparations for my journey. My friends there came to the embassy and said how sorry they were that I was leaving. Then a letter came from the Princess Galitsin saying that Her Majesty the Tsarina was sorry to hear of the misfortune which had befallen me and expressed her heartfelt sympathy.

Two days before my departure from St Petersburg, a 300-word coded telegram arrived from the Ministry. The minister had written that at the beginning of Mozaffar-od-Din Shah's reign, Monsieur Butsev, the Russian minister in Tehran, had called on the Shah to say that for the previous few years the Russian government had installed a quarantine station near the Afghan frontier in Sistan, sending doctors there and arranging that all travellers from India should be medically examined there, so that if the cholera bacteria was detected in them, they should not be allowed to enter Russian territory. The Russians were concerned that they would bring the germ with them to Ashkabad.

A month previously, the Russian minister had declared that since Iran had no troops in Sistan, the Russian government wished to send a permanent garrison of 300 Cossack cavalry to Sistan via Mashhad to protect the members of the quarantine station from frontier rebels. He had asked His Majesty the Shah's permission for the troops to cross the frontier, and His Majesty had given it. As soon as the 300 Cossacks reached Quchan, however, a great cry arose from all the religious scholars of Mashhad, Najaf and Karbala, indeed from all religious scholars throughout Iran's domains. Those from Mashhad sent a clearly-worded telegram saying that they would not allow Russian Cossack feet to trample on the sacred soil of Khorasan. If the Iranian government was incapable of preventing this, they would declare a jihad.

Meanwhile, of course, the English were fanning the flames from the sidelines. The Foreign Ministry, however, had explained the situation to the Russian minister, asking him to send a telegram to the Ministry of Foreign Affairs, requesting the withdrawal of the Cossacks. The ministry did not know at what time the minister's telegram had reached the Tsar, but in any case the Tsar had given orders to General Komarov, the military governor of Ashkabad, for 10,000 troops to be sent in support of the 300 Cossacks, who would then be able to pass through Mashhad. They were to arrest and punish any *molla* who opposed the Shah. In his telegram, the minister of foreign affairs added that the Shah had ordained that if I could think of a way-out and prevent this invasion, not only would I remain in post but the Shah would confer on me extraordinary favours. My view was that as matters had gone as far as this and formal orders had been given to the military governor of Ashkabad, diplomatic action was unlikely to be successful. However, it would be better for me to put the true facts on paper anyway. So I wrote a softly-worded letter to the Russian Ministry of Foreign Affairs doing just that.

In the meantime, a second telegram reached me from the Iranian government explaining that, as we considered Mashhad to be holy ground, with no one except Muslims being allowed to tread on that most sacred soil, when Russian Cossacks had arrived in Quchan, religious scholars from Mashhad and indeed from the whole Shiʿa world had risen up and were threatening to declare a jihad. Of course the Russian Ministry of Foreign Affairs was well-informed about the Iranian people and were aware of the potential influence of religious scholars on them and on the tribes, who made up three-quarters of the population. It was also crystal-clear that a foreign hand[14] would also be involved in this agitation. I was therefore instructed to explain the importance of the matter to the Russian government with the utmost clarity and request that they cancel the departure of the Cossacks for Sistan. The government of Iran was itself prepared to send troops to protect the quarantine mission. At the end of his telegram, our minister of foreign affairs had added that if I was successful in persuading the Russian government through the Ministry of Foreign Affairs to accept our request, then in addition to my remaining in post, His Majesty the Shah would confer on me particular favours.

---

14 Clearly the British were suspected.

I took the minister's letter to Count Lamsdorf, the Russian Minister of Foreign Affairs. He read it carefully from beginning to end. He said that since the dispatch of troops to Sistan had become such an important matter, when the Tsar had been offended by the Shah's and his government's hesitation and inconsistency, he didn't think that I would succeed in this matter, as 10,000 troops were about to set off from Ashkabad and they couldn't wait for the return of His Majesty the Tsar from Finnish waters, where he was taking a holiday with the Tsarina. To help me, he would send my communication to the Tsar on the ship which was carrying the government report on the matter to him, so that His Majesty could decide what should be done. When reports reached him while he was with the Tsarina, the Tsar would read them out to her, and sometimes she even helped him by reading them herself. Luckily, my report and the letter reached the imperial yacht when the Tsarina was busy reading reports. When she reached the end of the letter, she asked the Tsar to give orders for the Cossacks to return to Russian territory and for the troop movement order to be cancelled. She also suggested that the Iranian minister plenipotentiary should remain in his post, since she had heard that he was very popular with everyone. Anyway, however this actually happened, the Tsarina managed to persuade the Tsar to take this decision.

I was sitting in the embassy when Monsieur Palanson, the head of the Iran section of the Foreign Ministry, came in crying out cheerfully to me from the doorway: 'Good news! Good news!' He said that on the Tsar's orders, the Minister of War had sent a telegram to General Komarov, military governor of Ashkabad, cancelling the marching orders for the troops to enter Iran and recalling the Cossacks from Quchan. I immediately telegraphed the good news to the Foreign Ministry. They communicated to me the grant of more boundless royal bounty, saying that not only was I not to be recalled but the Diamond Epaulettes (Second Class) had been awarded to me.

The scale of hospitality in St Petersburg was such that foreigners, particularly diplomats and members of the embassy staff who were not accustomed to this kind of life, couldn't live there for more than two or three years. The great families there were very hospitable. When they invited guests to dinner, before they actually sat down to dinner, there would be another table called the 'zakuski' table. I repeatedly counted twenty to twenty-five dishes on that table. The first of these would be fresh caviar and two kinds of pressed, salted caviar, five or six kinds of fish, sardines, salmon, tuna fish and other good things. Then there were several kinds of roast meat, partridge, pheasant and quail, several kinds of liver, of goose hearts and of various pickles. With all these dishes alcoholic drinks, such as arak, cognac, whisky, cinzano and madeira were offered. The host or, if he was married, his wife would offer arak and vodka to the guest and would drink to his health and the guest would then have to drink one or two toasts to the health of his host. (When the glass was drained, the etiquette was that the host would fill the guest's glass and the latter would then drink a toast to him.) After the host's health had been drunk, the host would offer other drinks. If the truth is known, when the guests went into dinner, they had already filled their stomachs and whatever they ate at the dinner table actually became a burden on the stomach and further eating was difficult. They also drank a great deal at dinner, which lasted from eight o'clock until ten o'clock or even later. Obviously at dinner new wine, old wine and champagne were served, glasses were continually re-filled and at 11.30 or midnight the ball would begin.

In the fourth year of my posting to St Petersburg,[15] a long coded telegram arrived from the prime minister, the Amin-os-Soltan. He wrote that the government in Tehran had started negotiations there with Monsieur Butsev, the Russian minister, for a loan of 20 million *manat* from Russia. The minister suggested that I should take part in the negotiations with Monsieur Witte, the Russian finance minister, who had been given considerable freedom of action in his work. I was instructed to call on him to see what the conditions for this loan would be and then urgently telegraph the result to Tehran. In reply, I telegraphed that I did not think it a good idea that the government should take a foreign loan and that if this was really necessary, I didn't think that it was in the national interest that we should borrow from Russia or England. Instead I proposed firstly that the salaries and allowances of senior government servants and ambassadors should be reduced by half and that this process should start with me. Second, a small tax should be placed on landed property and houses, as people would certainly not grudge paying a small sum.

In its reply telegram, the Ministry of Foreign Affairs thanked me for my patriotic proposals. I was however no doubt unaware of the fact that for several

---

15 Probably in late 1899. The loan agreement was finally signed in St Petersburg in January 1900.

months the Cossacks and the gendarmerie had not been paid, and if they were not given several months' pay quickly, they would certainly mutiny. Other ministries were also well behind in paying salaries, for due to drought no taxes had been received from the provinces. The government was therefore obliged to raise this money from another source. Consequently, it was in negotiation with the Russian government and would shortly decide what my instructions would be.

Ten days later a letter of instructions arrived from the Ministry of Foreign Affairs. In it were two copies of the loan agreement and a short letter of instructions: the moment this treaty arrived, I was to call on the Minister of Finance, hand it to him and we were both to sign both copies. I was then to send one copy to the ministry, whereupon the Russian government would transfer twenty million *manat* to Iran. The treaty was written in French and Persian, so I summoned Samad Khan and we read it together from beginning to end. We saw that the most important condition of this loan was that the Iranian government would pledge Iran's customs duties from both northern and southern points of entry as a loan guarantee. A Russian official would also have to supervise this process. If even these revenues were not sufficient to amortise both the capital and the 5 per cent interest on the twenty million *manat*, then the taxes of the country would have to be used to ensure payment. When I read this, I was so upset that my first reaction was to say: 'Let God's will be done! So be it!' Nevertheless, on further reflection, I replied to the ministry that these conditions were not loan conditions: they amounted to the sale of the whole kingdom of Iran. If the government wished to sell off the country, the price should not be twenty million or even 200 million. The right sale price was many hundreds of millions of *manat*. I couldn't put myself and my family in a position where we would be eternally cursed by Iranians, who would say that we had sold off Iran for a derisory sum. I entreated the ministry to spare me this task and accept my resignation. The reply came immediately: this loan was absolutely necessary, Iran would make its interest payments on time and wouldn't allow things to go so far. I was to go and call on Witte, however, to see whether the conditions could be made less onerous. In any case the government was anxiously awaiting my telegram. A mutiny by the infantry and cavalry was imminent and the situation was terrible.

Truly in this kind of difficult situation, God Almighty lends his assistance, for on the evening before my appointment with Witte, the Tsar was giving an official ball in the Winter Palace, to which I and the staff of the embassy were invited. The etiquette for a ball was that ambassadors with their wives were placed in order of precedence on the right-hand side of the entrance to the Great Hall, while members of their staff were placed one or two paces behind them. In the same way, ministers plenipotentiary and their staff were placed on the left hand side of the entrance. When the Tsar and the Tsarina entered in court dress and the band struck up the national anthem, the two would start from the right: first the Tsarina would ask after the health of the ambassadors' wives and then the Tsar would do the same with the ambassadors. Then they would move to the entrance and in the same way start to greet those on the left.

After the arrival of the above-mentioned telegram, I had decided that if my offer of resignation wasn't accepted, I would leave the embassy without it having been accepted. I was therefore in a distressed state and I didn't want to talk to anyone. The Tsarina came up to me and asked me very kindly whether I had composed any new poetry and whether I had published memoirs of my journey to Europe as part of Naser-od-Din Shah's entourage in a volume similar to *An Anthology of Knowledge*. I replied that I had recently been very busy and the only poetry I had written had been at the request of the King of Sweden, when I had recited an elegiac poem commemorating the twenty-fifth anniversary of his coronation. She asked me to send her a copy of the poem with a translation. Then the Tsar approached and asked me what news I had from Tehran. I said that the news was grim. The Tsar was very surprised by my words and asked me to tell him the news. Monsieur Kanyar made a sign to the other ministers and their staff who were standing near to move away from me a little. I said: 'Your Majesty, as a result of the drought this year, the government of Iran has been forced to take a small foreign loan. Your Majesty's ministers haven't allowed us to take this loan from France and Holland on easy conditions. The conditions they have proposed show that they want to buy up Iran for twenty million *manat*.' The Tsar said: 'Don't think that I will put this right! Don't you see what beautiful women there are here? You should go and pay court to them!' The Tsar then passed on. The Tsar had spoken in such a way that those near and the members of the embassy should hear what he said.

When the imperial couple had finished greeting the ministers, Monsieur

Kanyar came up and said that the Grand Duchess Xenia, the Tsar's sister, wished me to be her partner for the quadrille and opposite me would be the Tsarina's sister, the Grand Duchess Helen, the wife of the Grand Duke Sergei, the governor of Moscow. I gave my sword to a member of the embassy and started to dance. I have included the photograph of this party in *Perles d'Orient*,[16] where you can clearly see my partner facing me. At one o'clock in the morning, Their Majesties left and the ball came to an end.

His telegram remained in my mind all night and I even had nightmares about it. At nine o'clock in the morning, I heard a servant knocking on my bedroom door and asked him what the matter was. He said that a messenger from the minister of foreign affairs had come and asked me to call on the minister immediately, so I dressed and went to the ministry. Lamsdorf,[17] the minister was seated, while Monsieur Witte was standing and pacing up and down. The Minister of Foreign Affairs got up and sat me down in front of him. Monsieur Witte came up to me and, without shaking my hand, he very angrily asked: 'Why have you been complaining about us to the Court? We haven't forced Iran to take a loan from us. Iran has urgently asked us for money and we have simply stated our conditions. This is no reason for you to have complained to His Majesty.' The prospect of Tehran's anger, a sleepless night and the minister's failure to shake my hand, which showed a lack of respect, made me act uncharacteristically. I got up angrily and replied: 'Yes, Monsieur Witte, I was right to complain and I will complain again. Nazar Aqa, our minister plenipotentiary in Paris had arranged that France would make us a loan of 100 million francs on easy conditions, but you intrigued and wouldn't allow it. The Sa'ad-od-Dowleh, our minister in Belgium, had also arranged for banks in Belgium and Holland to make us a loan, but you threw a stone in the works and would not allow it. England is busy in the Transvaal and hasn't time to get involved in this kind of thing, so you want to buy up Iran for twenty million *manat*.'

Monsieur Lamsdorf was a man of few words. He took Witte by the hand and sat him down opposite, placing me next to himself. He said that at the ball

---

16 A volume of French poetry which the author had published in Istanbul in 1904. Unfortunately, the editor's copy of this book doesn't contain this photograph.

17 Count Vladimir Lamsdorf was in fact Deputy Foreign Minister until June 1900, when he replaced Count Mikhail Muraviev as Foreign Minister.

the previous evening the Tsar had asked him to sit down with us and final-
ise the loan on easy terms. Monsieur Witte immediately calmed down and I
expressed my gratitude to the Tsar. Then he opened the copy of the agreement
which had been sent from Tehran and said that I should specify every point
to which I objected. When he reached the clause which specified that Iran
would give the customs revenues of both the southern and the northern points
of entry as a guarantee for the loan, I said that this was my first objection. We
had no right to offer our customs revenues as a guarantee: England had Naser-
od-Din Shah's signature on this point.[18] Witte said that they were well aware
that the English had obtained the Shah's signature on this point. The Shah
had made a mistake. As the English were being defeated again and again in
the Transvaal and they were in a very bad state, the Russians wanted to take
advantage of this opportunity to free the Iranian government from the obligation of Naser-od-Din's promise. I said that this was an extraordinary thing to
say. The British government wouldn't be destroyed or crushed under foot by
Boer weapons. When the Transvaal war was over and England sent warships
to occupy the only customs house in the south, which was at Bushehr, what
would be his reply to that? Witte said: 'Praise be to God! You Iranians really
are afraid of the English. All the English forces are tied up in the Transvaal
and yet you are now frightened of their shadow.' I saw that arguing with Witte
was pointless, as he was renowned for his obstinacy, so I turned to Count
Lamsdorf and said: 'You are an expert on international affairs. If, in breach of
the signature which the English extracted from Naser-od-Din Shah, we offer
you the customs revenues of the south as a guarantee and the English send
warships, will you undertake officially and in writing that you will bring to
bear the full range of your naval and land forces to expel the British and that
you will not ask Iran to pay the costs of the war?'

The two ministers looked at each other. Then the minister of foreign affairs
said that they were willing to remove the southern customs guarantee from
the document. Since the Tsar had given orders for them to be lenient, what
other comments did I have to make? I asked him to read out the agreement so
that I could make my comments. He read out the terms until he reached the

---

18 The Shah had given this undertaking in October 1897 during negotiations for an earlier
foreign loan, confirming Naser-od-Din Shah's guarantee of 1892 to the British government.

passage where a Russian official would come and sit in the customs house to supervise matters. I said that I couldn't accept this either. Supervision could take place if one side hadn't fulfilled its obligations, but it was unthinkable that a Russian could come and give orders to customs officials when there had been no breach of the agreement. I proposed that we should write that if the government of Iran regularly paid its instalments, the Russian government would have no right of supervision, but that if it couldn't or wouldn't pay instalments due, then the Russian government could appoint an official to inspect and supervise matters. Witte said that I wanted to negate all the conditions of the agreement: why didn't I simply take out my pen and strike them out?

Count Lamsdorf took my side against Witte, saying that my objection was logical. If Iran regularly paid the loan in instalments, then there was no need for supervision. I of course agreed with this. The minister of foreign affairs then politely said that they accepted my two proposals. Did I have any further points to make? I asked him to kindly continue reading and if I had any points to make, I would do so. He reached the point where it was stated that if the customs dues for both the south and the north were insufficient to pay the instalments on the loan, then government taxes would be used to guarantee payment of these. I asked them to be fair. I pointed out that all Iran's trade with Turkey, Europe and the Caucasus passed through the northern customs. How could the northern customs revenues, which amounted to six times the instalments due, conceivably not suffice to cover these payments? There was no need for this condition. The imposition of this condition was either a result of ignorance or of sheer obstinacy. Count Lamsdorf said that I was no doubt aware that there were thousands of agreements in the world where it was impossible to foretell what would happen in the future. Was it not possible that Turkey would declare war on Iran and that the northern customs would be entirely shut, leaving Russia with no guarantee for the payment of instalments? I said that I was not an unreasonable person and that I agreed that this was possible: there could be war, the customs could be shut and there could be no revenue. We should simply write that in those circumstances the government would guarantee to pay the instalments at the agreed time without specifically committing government tax revenues. The Russian finance ministry could then send two people to the provinces to go and supervise this process there. Then if the Iranian government guarantee turned out to be worthless and the instalments were not paid, the Russians had a minister plenipotentiary in Tehran and would be perfectly capable of securing payment of the instalments by diplomatic pressure. Lamsdorf also accepted this.

I said that I had no further comments to make. He said that they would make a fair copy of the agreement that day and send it to the Ministry of Finance. I should come to sign it. I said that I couldn't do this the same day, as I had to report the facts to the Ministry of Foreign Affairs and the prime minister and receive fresh instructions. He said that the Russians were in no hurry. It was Iran which needed money urgently. I should send my telegram and then reply formally, so that he could inform the Tsar of the details. I sent a telegram to the Ministry of Foreign Affairs and the prime minister. A reply came back praising me for the service which I had rendered and instructing me to complete the matter, sign the agreement and receive the transfer of funds.

As the Russians were aware that the government of Iran had previously taken a loan of some five million from England, with the customs revenues of the south pledged as a guarantee, and a condition of the Russian loan was that from the twenty million Russian loan five million would go to repay the English loan and free up the southern customs revenues, the threat to southern customs revenues from Britain would be removed. The Russians didn't attach much importance to this condition. I thought, however, that it was in the interest of the Iranian government and people that this condition should remain in the agreement, so that the first interest payment made on Russian monies received should be earmarked to repay the English loan, so that the customs revenues of the south should be freed from foreign interference.

In 1899, a peace conference of the representatives of twenty-five countries, of which Iran was one, was held in Holland at the invitation of Tsar Nicholas II. I was appointed the Iranian government's principal representative to it. From the beginning of the conference, the German representatives were implacably opposed to Russian government proposals. The first Russian proposal was that the signatory governments would undertake not to increase their land or naval forces for a period of five years and during this time they wouldn't manufacture any new weapons such as artillery, rifles, mortars etc. They would be content with the armaments which they possessed on the day the agreement was signed. It was claimed that there would be several great benefits from such an agreement: first, state budgets, together with the exorbitant and onerous

Mozaffar-od-Din Shah and the then Russian Heir Apparent, The Grand-Duke Mikhail Aleksandrovich seated on the Shah's first visit to Russia in 1900. The author and the Amin-os-Soltan are standing in the middle of the back row.

taxes which afflicted people, would be reduced: people would then breathe easily, and workers who worked in artillery and small arms factories would go and till the land, thus increasing the prosperity of the country. The money spent on murderous weapons could be used to finance schools and hospitals. As governments would be relieved of anxiety on these matters for five years, they would take no further steps toward war and bloodshed.

The German representatives replied that war had countless advantages: most of the progress made in the world came from war; indeed war prevented the German people from becoming lazy. Preventing the manufacture of new artillery and weapons, which was itself a branch of industry, would be a hindrance to industrial development. Indeed it would be inconceivable to create obstacles for industry, for the world should make progress in all branches of industry. One of the blessings resulting from the manufacture of artillery and small arms had been that wars between countries had become less frequent: every time there had been a war, it had been followed by ten to fifteen years of peace. Before these new weapons of war existed, however, when armies fought with arrows and swords, wars between nations had been a permanent feature of history. Indeed, war was the natural task of humankind and it was impossible to prevent it.

In those days it was rumoured, and I do not know whether the rumour was true, that the reason for the German Emperor's opposition was that he had been the first monarch to think of inviting others to a peace conference, which he intended to do standing in front of Jesus's tomb on his visit to Jerusalem.[19] When he reached Istanbul, however, clever spies heard of the Kaiser's idea and informed the Russian government, so that it acted first before the Kaiser reached Jerusalem and himself invited the Russian government. As a result, it was said, the Kaiser gave orders that the Tsar's ideas should not be allowed to become a practical reality.

The conference dragged on and no progress was made. The German newspapers started to publish derogatory comments. In Berlin a postcard was printed with a picture of the Tsar dressed as a Russian *muzhik* or peasant with a red shirt, peasant boots, a huge stomach and the imperial crown on his head. In front of him was a round table with several plates on it. On his right were ten or twenty bottles of arak. He had one in his hand and was drinking from it. He was so drunk that his eyes were glazed over and in that state he was making a speech: 'Just give me a moment to eat this food and then come and fight me!' The name of each dish was written on it: 'Finland, Estonia, Lithuania, Poland, Crimea, Ukraine, Bessarabia, Georgia, Armenia, Bokhara, Samarqand, Merv, Ashkabad, Siberia, Caucasus, Baku, Erivan, Kars, Ardahan etc.'

When this postcard was brought to the Tsar's attention, he was displeased by the lack of progress, by the existence of the postcard and indeed by this sort of German propaganda. He therefore wrote to Monsieur Staal, the principal Russian representative, instructing him to bring proceedings to an end but to make the following speech on behalf of the Tsar for the history of the world: 'Out of respect for the peace of the world, in my desire to free people from all this killing and for the sake of human kind, I invited governments to try to find a solution. Even if it is not possible to rid humanity of this scourge for

---

19 Kaiser Wilhelm II visited Istanbul and Jerusalem in 1898.

ever, at least it should be possible, through arbitration,[20] to bring peace to the world and end international disputes for a period of five years. Unfortunately my peaceful, constructive ideas have been misinterpreted. Clearly I am not responsible for the actions of my predecessors but during the five years of my reign, I have striven to the best of my ability for the benefit of mankind. Since I can see no positive result from this conference, however, I call on history to be my witness to this and hereby bring its proceedings to an end.'

Monsieur Rafaelovich, the cousin of our honorary consul in St Petersburg, who was the secretary-general of the conference and whom I knew, told me all the background. In all truth, I was unable to regard the Tsar, who had shown me so much kindness and humanity when I fell from my horse, as a drunken tyrant, as portrayed to the citizens of the world on the postcard. At the closing official session, therefore, when the other delegations had assembled but before Monsieur Staal, the Russian ambassador in London and the Tsar's representative at the conference, read the Tsar's speech, I decided to ask permission to speak, go up to the rostrum and describe without embellishment how, when I fell from my horse, the Tsar had stood over me until the carriage arrived. However, at the end of my speech I did add with some warmth that the Tsar was young and was only at the beginning of his reign and I quoted the line of Sa'adi that when 30,000 troops paraded in front of him in perfect order,

He looks to his friends as a king looks proudly to his army.

I spoke as follows: 'On that proud and glorious day, he didn't forget an unfortunate foreigner but twice sent his aide-de-camp to enquire after his health. This kind of man cannot possibly be described as vain-glorious: the Tsar's sense of duty came from a sincere heart. At the official dinner in the royal palace, you heard how movingly Her Majesty the young Queen Wilhelmina entreated you gentlemen to achieve something in the first year of her reign, so that this peace conference shouldn't end fruitlessly and you leave empty-handed. It is not right that two kings with good intentions who love the world should make humanity despair of them. However we may be able to achieve this, we must

---

20 An agreement on arbitration of international disputes was one of the few positive results of the 1899 Peace Conference.

Mozaffar-od-Din Shah, photographed on his first visit to Russia in 1900. From left to right standing, his Russian official host, the author and the Amin-os-Soltan.

not leave here empty-handed.' The delegates, especially those who supported Russia, all applauded so much and shouted 'Bravo!' that the majority decided that the conference shouldn't end until a result had been achieved.

After my return to St Petersburg I became very ill. It was a very strange illness, I had a very high temperature and I sweated so much that my pillows were so soaked in sweat that they had to be changed every half hour and I suffered from diarrhoea with stomach convulsions. Several doctors were called in but they were unable to diagnose my illness. In the end one of them said that my intestines had been displaced. I would have to be operated on and my intestines put back in their proper place. The doctor who made this recommendation himself admitted that this was the most difficult of operations and one

Prince Arfa', photographed
in St Petersburg in 1901.
From the collection of
Farhad and Firouzeh Diba.

from which few people recovered. The news of my serious illness and prob-
able death spread through St Petersburg society. The news reached the court,
which sent the same doctor who had attended me following my fall from my
horse. At the very moment when the doctors were deliberating as to whether to
open up my stomach and return my intestines to their proper place, this doctor
arrived and strongly opposed an operation, recommending a completely different remedy. Then they all agreed that the air of St Petersburg didn't suit
me and I couldn't live there. I absolutely must change my place of residence.
Despite all the kindnesses of the imperial court, this whole matter was very
difficult for me. At times I even preferred death to leaving St Petersburg for
ever. At this juncture, however, a telegram came from the Atabak saying that
His Majesty had made the 'Ala'-ol-Molk governor of the province of Kerman

and had appointed me ambassador in Istanbul.[21] I gave a copy of the telegram to the imperial doctor and asked him to inform the Tsar at an appropriate moment that he had recommended that I should leave St Petersburg and that I had just received a telegram, in which I had not been asked for my opinion but ordered to return to Tehran before going on to Istanbul.

On my arrival in Tehran, an official was sent to Shahabad by Mirza Nasrollah Khan Moshir-od-Dowleh, who was then minister of foreign affairs, to greet me. I was taken to his house at Rostamabad in Shemiran. There was only one building there, which contained the women's quarters. However, a tent had been pitched in the garden as the Moshir-od-Dowleh's reception area, with a small tent next door to it for me to sleep in. *Mirza Hassan Khan Pirnia*, his son, who had been appointed by his father to be my official host, greeted me. Suddenly my rheumatism, a souvenir of St Petersburg, flared up again. The Tehran doctors said that I should go to the hot baths every day and have a massage. The Moshir-od-Dowleh had a bathhouse in the women's quarters but I really couldn't go there every day and cause inconvenience to everyone. Then, the Atabak, the prime minister, suggested that I should go into Tehran to his park, where there was a good bathhouse in a corner of the house, together with several rooms, where I could stay. So I moved there. It really was a good bathhouse with hot and cold water, with the hot water being changed every day.

When the Russian loan was received, Mozaffar-od-Din Shah gave a gratuity of 100,000 *toman*s to each of his courtiers, at which point all the courtiers used this as an excuse to give a party in honour of Arfaʿ-od-Dowleh. All these splendid parties were accompanied by groups of musicians and singers. The party given by the Hajeb-od-Dowleh was very like the house parties given by British aristocrats. In Nazabad he had built a two-story European-style house with numerous reception rooms and bedrooms. The guests organised their own parties there in turn, and all the guests ate and slept there for three days.

---

21 Bamdad suggests a different version of events: following the first Russian loan negotiated by Arfaʿ, when a second loan became necessary, the Foreign Minister Mirza Nasrollah Khan Moshir-od-Dowleh didn't wish further commission money to go into Arfaʿ's pocket, so he secured the latter's dismissal and his replacement by his own son, Mirza Hassan Khan Pirnia, as minister in St Petersburg. The Amin-os-Soltan then arranged for his protégé's appointment to Istanbul.

Several groups of musicians were invited, of whom eighty were women. Their job was to dance and sing, playing a wind instrument and the tambourine. Most of these women had a husband or brother to protect their reputation: they were not immoral women. The head of the group was Monavvar-e-Shirazi. At fifteen, the famous Malek-ot-Tojjar, the Bushehr millionaire, had made her his temporary wife and taken her with him to India. He had shown her Bombay, Calcutta and Delhi and had taken her to all the theatres, and particularly the ballet. As she was naturally very intelligent and clever, she learnt most European ballets off by heart, together with Iranian dances and songs. She was truly one of the outstanding Iranian artists of her time. She was dark-skinned and charming, not really beautiful but outstandingly attractive. Every evening guests would give her sixty or seventy *toman*s. Indeed they were happy to do so. Her best role was the Afghan dance. She had a variety of costumes from every country, both male and female. When she wore Afghan male costume, she looked exactly like an Afghan chieftain and when she put on Kurdish clothes, she became a real Kurdish Bey's son. When she was given money, she filled a small glass with wine, placed it on her forehead and performed different dances with it on her forehead without the glass ever moving. Then she would move in front of one of the guests and would bend down until her head was in front of him, when he would take the glass and drink to her health. The guests would then open their purses and hand out tips, which were never less than ten ashrafis. This Monavvar always attended parties with her sister and mother and had thus managed to preserve her chaste reputation. During this three day and night party, the Hajeb-od-Dowleh gave these dancers lodging in another courtyard and provided them with bedding, lunch and dinner. Obviously, he spent enormous sums of money on this party.

On the first evening, the Hajeb-od-Dowleh came and said to me that he wished to put on a show in my honour, the like of which I had never seen before and never would again, on condition that I took no part in drawing up the programme and did exactly what he said. I agreed. The Great Atabak, the prime minister, hadn't yet arrived, but a large chair with arm-rests had been brought and put in the place of honour for him. I was told to sit on it in a dignified manner and not to laugh. Then two guests were nominated as members of my staff and our host then went to the musicians, who were in the small pavilion, and told them that an Indian maharajah was on a visit as a guest of Mozaffar-od-Din Shah and that a party was being organised there in his honour that evening on behalf of the Shah. All the women should come up to be introduced to him, and parade before him, bowing as they did so. Most of the time I somehow managed to restrain myself but there were moments when I just couldn't help bursting out laughing.

Postscript (1902–1937)

After St Petersburg, Prince Arfaʿ served as ambassador in Istanbul from 1902 until 1910. This promotion should have been the summit of his diplomatic career, but there is a sense of anti-climax. For someone who believed in the power of personal influence in diplomacy, it seemed that the world that Arfaʿ knew was collapsing and he was caught up in the turbulence of international events which gave him little scope for achievement. While there are interesting passages which could be the subject of further research, to this Western reader, at least, his later memoirs are much less interesting than the earlier pages, which chronicle his meteoric rise from provincial obscurity to grandee of the Qajar regime and which are an interesting documentary source both on life in mid-Qajar Iran and on relations with Tsarist Russia.

After the death of Mozaffar-od-Din Shah in 1907 and the accession of Mohammad ʿAli Shah, one senses that Arfaʿ began to lose influence in Tehran. Furthermore, in the last years of Sultan ʿAbdol-Hamid the Sunni-Shiʿa divide continued to be a cause of friction between Ottoman Turkey and Qajar Iran, and the author seems to have spent much of his time in Istanbul fire-fighting. Ottoman suspicion that a senior Iranian cleric had insulted the first three 'righteous' Caliphs of Islam, who were regarded as usurpers by the Shiʿa, almost caused a breach in relations between the two empires and the author's recall to Tehran, while the Sultan, conscious of Iran's military weakness, was not averse to supporting Kurdish Sunni tribesmen against the Iranian government and to sending troops to occupy areas of Iranian territory near their common frontier, which made Arfaʿ's position difficult.

During his time in Istanbul, the 1905 revolution in Russia, the 1905–9 Constitutional Revolution in Iran and the overthrow of Sultan ʿAbdol-Hamid by the Young Turks in 1908, at which he had a ringside seat, caused him great anguish: he supported the modernisation of the Islamic world but he was emotionally attached to the traditional ways and to the personalities whom he had served over the years: the 1907 assassination of his protector, the long-standing prime minister, the Amin-os-Soltan, was not only a bitter personal blow but deprived him of his most powerful supporter at court. Meanwhile, in Istanbul, where the Anjoman-e-Saʿadat and other Iranian revolutionary societies were active, he was sometimes regarded by the local Iranian community as an agent of tyranny and was even the object of an assassination attempt. In Tehran, however, it was whispered that he supported the revolutionaries, a suspicion which no doubt further undermined his position there. He claimed in later life that Mohammad ʿAli Shah, who allied himself with Russia and bombarded the new parliament, the Majles, in an attempt to put down the Constitutional Revolution by force, was not a man he could serve. In reality, however, he seems to have temporised as best he could.

Matters came to a head in 1910, when the Iranian government ceased payment of embassy salaries and after protesting to Tehran, Arfaʿ resigned, so he says, on grounds of ill health, and left for France. In fact he was dismissed. As he writes early in his memoirs, he had never liked living in Iran and from then on he was to spend most of the rest of his life in Europe. While in Istanbul he had given instructions for a house to be built for him in Monaco. 'Daneshgah', once again in a mixed oriental and European style, survives to this day as the 'Villa Ispahan'. There he summoned his second wife, Elsa, the daughter of a Finnish-born violin professor at the Stockholm Conservatoire de Musique, and their two children, who had, it seems, moved to Dresden from Istanbul. Meanwhile, he paid an extended visit to Pierre Loti, the French orientalist whom he had come to know in Istanbul, witnessed the funeral of King Edward VII in London, and spent the summer in the eastern United States, where as an exotic oriental prince, he seems to have created something of a sensation with the press. After a year and half in Monaco, he returned to Tehran in 1913, where he became Minister of Justice in the cabinet of Prince ʿAlaʾ-os-Saltaneh, his predecessor as consul-general in Tiflis, but except for his decision to re-design the façade of the ministry building in the Achaemenid style, he makes no mention of his work in the ministry. Writing in the 1930s under the new Pahlavi regime, silence on his past political activity was perhaps the prudent option. On the outbreak of the First World

War and the collapse of the government, he made his way back to Monaco by way of Istanbul where, while staying at his old embassy, he was approached by Enver Pasha, the Ottoman Minister of War, who invited Iran to join the German/Ottoman war effort and send troops to the Caucasus front against Russia, ignoring any British threat to southern Iran. Arfaʿ found the financial subsidy offered Iran by Enver entirely inadequate; nor was he persuaded by Enver's promise to return Tiflis and five Caucasus khanates, part of Iran's empire before the Russian conquest, after the war had been won. Enver was displeased by this response and the author, together with his successor as ambassador, reported the conversation to the foreign ministry. Iran declared her neutrality.

Arfaʿ spent the whole period of hostilities in Monaco, completing the construction of Daneshgah with two statues of Cyrus and one of Darius, to which he added a Peace Gallery filled with mementos of the 1899 Hague Peace Conference, cultivating his reputation as an apostle of peace with the local press and later lobbying, ultimately unsuccessfully, to be awarded the Nobel Peace Prize. He had been awarded a prize by the Académie Française in 1909, and in 1919 he was elected a member of the Société des Gens de Lettres.

After the Great War, he appears to have played only a minor unofficial part in assisting the Iranian delegation to the Versailles Peace Conference in Paris in their efforts to obtain compensation from the belligerent powers for the war damage caused by their breaches of Iran's neutrality. These collapsed, he says, when the Anglo-Persian Agreement of 1919 was signed, making Iran a virtual British protectorate, and under the terms of which Iran agreed not to press claims for compensation from Britain. In the end, however, the Agreement was rejected by the Majles. He then returned to an impoverished, unstable Iran, where he refused the poisoned chalice of the prime ministership but was pressed to become Iran's first representative at the newly-formed League of Nations in Geneva. His own considerable property and investments in Russia had by now been confiscated by the Bolsheviks, and he had to negotiate hard to receive a salary and expenses. He couldn't travel to Europe through revolutionary Russia, Iraq was convulsed by a revolt against British rule and he was obliged to travel south via Isfahan, where he commented on the appalling state of disrepair into which Iran's most beautiful monuments had fallen, and Shiraz. On the road between the two cities, he was attacked by Qashqaʾi tribesmen, his travelling companion, the son of Arbab Kaikhosrow,[1] was murdered and he himself was left for dead in the desert.

After his miraculous escape and the recovery of his property, including his beloved decorations, he travelled on to Geneva, where he served as Iran's representative at the League of Nations from 1920 to 1928, and where, he says, he gathered around him the representatives of the smaller League member states and struggled to defend the rights of small countries against the bullying of the Great Powers. He goes on to describe his most important battles at the League as follows:

1. By hard bargaining, he won a considerable reduction in Iran's annual membership fee to the League.

2. In 1925 he was instructed to inform the Secretariat of the League of Soviet Russia's many flagrant breaches of Iran's northern border. At the suggestion of the Secretary-General of the League, he was able to publicise these hostile acts in the local and international press. He accompanied this by a statement of Iran's firm intention to invoke Articles 10 and 16 of the League's Covenant, which provided for all member states to assist a League member which was the object of external aggression against its 'territorial integrity and existing political independence'. This threat was duly reported to Moscow and the situation on Iran's border improved.

3. He defended Iran's opium exports from commercial rivals, who, he says, sought to use the League to ban the export of the Iranian medicinal product.[2] Arfaʿ pointed out that the reason for the success of Iranian exports was that Iranian opium contained 18 per cent morphine, whereas exports from China, Japan, British India and Russian Turkestan were markedly inferior in quality. The complaint against Iran was, he asserted, no more than an attempt to destroy a commercial rival. He was able to form a committee of the League, which

---

1 Arbab Kaikhosrow (1874–1950) succeeded Arbab Jamshid (1850–1932) as head of the Zoroastrian community in Iran and was the Zoroastrian member of the Majles.

2 The revised International Opium Convention, to which Persia was a party, was signed in 1925 and entered into force as a registered League of Nations treaty in 1928.

Daneshgah, now known as the Villa Ispahan, built by Prince Arfaʿ in Monaco from 1910. By courtesy of Wak Kani.

examined the matter and declined to make any recommendations against Iran's opium exports.

4. Since the days of Naser-od-Din Shah, Iranian shipping in the Persian Gulf had been subject to British supervision and Iran was forbidden

from launching new vessels of any size there without British permission. In 1925, he was able to secure a Council vote, he says, exempting Iranian shipping from such formalities.

5. Above all he strove to prevent the British government, which was fearful of being drawn into a military confrontation with the newly-formed Soviet Union, from amending or qualifying Articles 10 and 16 of the Covenant of the League. In his defence of these articles, he pointed out that the protection given by these articles was the only reason why Iran and other small countries had joined the League. In September 1921, a vote of the Assembly of the League rejected a resolution calling for the revocation of these articles.

However, he writes that in 1926 the British government was cleverly able to insert into the text of the Treaty of Locarno, to which Iran was not a party, a clause restricting the ambit of Article 10. Where, following aggression against a member state, the Council of the League had to decide whether to send an armed force to defend it, the restriction stated that in so doing it should take account of the geographical position of that country and of the state of its armed forces. With that limitation, the author says, Britain attained its objective of emasculating Article 10 of the League's Covenant. The Assembly of the League approved the Treaty with exaggerated haste, Arfaʿ says, and he was prevented from speaking in the debate. Without seeking further instructions from his government, it seems, he then wrote to the President of the League to protest that the Treaty of Locarno had reduced the effectiveness of Articles 10 and 16, and that this was not in the best interests of the League.

Britain, France and Germany then instructed their ambassadors in Tehran to ask the foreign ministry whether in so doing Prince Arfaʿ had acted on his government's instructions or on his own initiative. The government of the Mostowfi-ol-Mamalek in Tehran closed ranks and supported him, but the powers intrigued against him and brought this government down. The more compliant Mehdi Hedayat Mokhber-os-Saltaneh replaced him as prime minister, the Iranian government duly ratified the Treaty of Locarno, and Arfaʿ was dismissed from his post.

In the course of his career, he had sometimes exceeded his official instructions but, no doubt due to high-level patronage in Tehran, he had always survived, but in Geneva his luck ran out: British displeasure, allied to intrigue by enemies at home, seems to have ended his glittering career. Compelled by Reza Shah, founder of the new Pahlavi dynasty, to abandon the constellation of Qajar and foreign decorations he so prized in favour of a solitary new Homayoun Order, he declined the Shah's invitation to become chairman of the Council of Ministers, requesting permission to return to Europe. He was finally able to leave Iran in 1931 for Monaco, where he lived out his last years but he returned to Tehran to complete his memoirs, where he died in March 1937.

Glossary of Qajar Names and Titles

Chapter 2

(Mirza) Fath ʿAli Akhondzadeh or Akhondov (1812–78). Son of a landowning family from Iranian Azerbaijan, he moved to Tiflis where, instead of a career as a Shiʿa cleric as planned, he became a standard-bearer for Western secular thought and an atheist. From 1850 advised the reform of the Arabic-Persian alphabet. Writing in both Persian and Azeri, he combined love of Russia, writing a famous poem commemorating the death of Pushkin, love of liberty, many of his friends being exiled Decembrists, and Iranian nationalism. Known as 'the Molière of the Orient', he wrote the first comedies in Azeri literature and is celebrated as the greatest Azeri poet and intellectual of the nineteenth century. (Bamdad Vol. 3 p. 55).

Chapter 3

(Haji Mirza) Hossein Khan Moshir-od-Dowleh/Sepahsalar (1828–81). Studied briefly in Paris. Consul in Bombay (1851). Consul in Tiflis (1855–8). Minister/Ambassador in Istanbul 1858–70). Minister of Justice and of Pensions (1870). Minister of War and commander of the army/Sephsalar (1871). Prime Minister (1871). Accompanied Shah on first visit to Europe (1873). Dismissed but appointed Foreign Minister (1873) and re-appointed Minister of War (1874). Dismissed from all posts (1880). Governor of Khorasan (1881), where he died. (Bamdad Vol. 1 p. 406).

(Mirza) Javad Khan Saʿad-od-Dowleh. Studied telegraph technology in Tiflis. Originally from Tabriz, where he was Head of the Azerbaijan Telegraph

Department with the rank of Colonel (1871) and then of Tehran Telegraph Department as Brigadier under the Mokhber-od-Dowleh, who gave him his daughter in marriage. Iranian representative at the Vienna Exhibition (1873) and the Paris Exhibition (1878). On his divorce, the Mokhber-od-Dowleh dismissed him and he joined the Ministry of Foreign Affairs. Ambassador to Belgium (1892–1902). Minister of Commerce (1905). Deputy in the First Majles (1906). According to Bamdad, one of the most influential figures in period of the Constitutional Revolution. In 1907, he became briefly Minister of Foreign Affairs under Mohammad ʿAli Shah and pro-Shah and anti-constitution. After fall of the Shah, took refuge in the Russian Embassy and then left for Europe. Ahmad Shah appointed him Prime Minister in 1914–15 but following a public outcry, changed his mind (Bamdad Vol. 1 p. 288, Churchill folio 494/611).

(Mirza) Mahmoud Khan ʿAlaʾ-ol-Molk (1845–1925). Brother of Nezam-ol-ʿOlamaʾ of Tabriz. Large estates in Azerbaijan. Arfaʿ's protector and first chief in Tiflis, where he was consul-general for the Caucasus until 1882, then minister plenipotentiary in St Petersburg until 1895 and ambassador in Constantinople until 1901, when appointed Governor-general of Kerman province, where he co-operated with the British. Minister of Education in 1904. Accompanied Mozaffar-od-Din Shah to Europe in 1905. (Bamdad Vol. 4 p. 39, Churchill folio 82/611).

(Mirza) Malkom Khan (1833–1908). Armenian convert to Islam. Studied in Paris (1843–52). Official government translator (1852–6). Counsellor Cairo (1863) and Istanbul (1864). Founded secret nationalist society, 'Faramoush-khane', devoted to Westernising reform (1856). Adviser to prime minister Mirza Hossein Khan Moshir-od-Dowleh Sepahsalar (1872). Ambassador to Britain (1873–89). Removed by Naser-od-Din Shah because of his involvement with the Lottery Concession scandal. Titles, rank and salary revoked (1891). Founder of London opposition newspaper *Qanun*, clandestinely circulated in Iran. (1890.) Appointed ambassador to Italy by Mozaffar-od-Din Shah in 1898 with title of Nezam-od-Dowleh. Died 1908. (Bamdad Vol. 4 p. 139).

(Mirza) Mohammad 'Ali Khan Mo'in-ol-Vezareh/ 'Ala'-os-Saltaneh, Prince (1835–1918). Consul-General in Bombay and Baghdad. From an Azerbaijan family. Married to sister of the Amin-od-Dowleh. Governor of Gilan (1880). Arfa''s predecessor as Consul-General in Tiflis (1882–90). Minister Plenipotentiary in London (1890–1906). Created Amir-Toman by Naser-od-Din Shah. Awarded the British decoration, the GCVO. Created Prince in 1905. Minister of Foreign Affairs (1906–08), where he started to carry out wide-reaching reforms in the ministry. Headed Iranian delegation to coronation of King George V (1911). Prime Minister (1913–14). Served as Minister of Foreign Affairs and twice as Prime Minister during the First World War. (Father of Hossein 'Ala', Prime Minister under Mohammad Reza Shah Pahlavi). (Bamdad Vol. 3 p. 447, Churchill folio 84/611).

(Mirza) Mohammad Hassan Khan Sani'-od-Dowleh/ E'temad-os-Saltaneh (circa 1840–96). Family originally from Maragheh in Azerbaijan. Son of the Hajeb-od-Dowleh, master of the household to Naser-od-Din Shah early in his reign. Educated at the Dar-ol-Fonoun, where he studied military sciences. In 1860 he became governor of Shushtar under his father. In 1861 he became assistant to his father, then Minister of Justice. Military attaché in Paris (1864–8), where he also completed his studies. Returned to Iran, where he became the Shah's French translator (1868), reading foreign newspapers and books to the Shah. Head of official publications office (1872), which published the newspaper *Ettela'*. Courtier, scholar and, like his master, Naser-od-Din Shah, a prolific diarist and historian of the reign. In charge of the Shah's correspondence and from 1883 minister for publications, censorship and propaganda. As such, one of the Shah's most influential advisers, and a rival to the Amin-os-Soltan. (Bamdad Vol. 3 p. 330, Curzon pp. 430 and 469, Churchill folio 181/611).

(Mirza) Mohammad Hossein Khan Foroughi/Zoka'-ol-Molk (d.1907). Family originally from Isfahan. As editor of *Iran*, the official gazette, in Naser-od-Din Shah's time, he came under the control of the E'temad-os-Saltaneh. Director of the translation bureau and of government publications. Official translator from Arabic and French. Under Mozaffar-od-Din Shah, he directed his own newspaper, Tarbiyat, and was known as a man of

progressive ideas. Among other translations of European works, he translated Morier's *Haji Baba* into Persian. Father of Mohammad ʿAli Foroughi,
tutor to Arfaʿ's son Hassan and Iran's prime minister in the 1940s. (Bamdad
Vol. 3 p. 384, Churchill folio 594/611).

(Sultan) Morad Mirza Hesam-os-Saltaneh (1818–83). Son of ʿAbbas Mirza and
uncle of Naser-od-Din Shah. Governor of Khorasan (1850–4). Conqueror
of Herat (1856). Only military leader considered able to repel Turkoman
attacks. Again governor of Khorasan but dismissed for insubordination in
1872 by Prime Minister Mirza Hossein Khan Moshir-od-Dowleh Sepahsalar, of whom he became a bitter enemy. Also governor of Fars, Kurdistan
and Kermanshah (Bamdad Vol. 2 p. 104).

Chapter 4

(Mirza) ʿAli Asghar Khan Amin-os-Soltan/Atabak-e-Aʿzam (1857–1907). Of
Georgian extraction, son of Aqa Ibrahim Amin-os-Soltan, the Shah's
butler and head of the Shah's household. Inherited his father's title and
functions on the latter's death in 1883. Became inter alia Minister of Court
and head of Customs before becoming Prime Minister in 1888. Accompanied Naser-od-Din Shah on his third visit to Europe in 1889. Working
closely with the British minister, secured the Shah's agreement to the
Imperial Bank concession and the opening of the Karoun River (1888–9).
Described in 1891 by Curzon as intelligent, energetic, apparently a forceful character and skilful in foiling the intrigues and jealousies of his many
rivals. Discredited over cancellation of Tobacco Régie concession in 1892
but regained his position by turning from the British to the Russians.
Briefly exiled to Qom following assassination of Naser-od-Din Shah and
accession of Mozaffar-od-Din Shah in 1896, but in 1898 he was confirmed
as prime minister. Following his much-criticised role in securing Russian
loans in 1900 and 1902, he went into exile abroad in 1903, but was recalled
as prime minister by Mohammad ʿAli Shah in 1907. Assassinated by an
extremist in the same year. (Bamdad Vol. 2 p. 387, Curzon Vol. 1 p. 426,
Churchill folio 115/611).

(Haji Mirza) 'Ali Khan Amin-od-Dowleh (1844–1904). Very wealthy land-owner, courtier and minister. Naser-od-Din Shah's private secretary (1870). Minister for the Shah's private correspondence (1873). Head of Mint (1875–1876). Chairman of Consultative Council (1875–90s). Minister of Posts (1876–95). Given title of Amin-od-Dowleh (1883). Court Minister (1889). Led appeal against the Tobacco Régie (1891). One of few Westernised Iranians, who later became known as an early progressive, liberal leader. Principal rival of the Amin-os-Soltan and, after the accession of Mozaffar-od-Din Shah, in 1896 replaced him as prime Minister, but he was replaced in 1898. Thought by foreign legations to have lacked energy. Described by Curzon as 'the most honourable and capable among the Shah's ministers, of courtly manners, liberal sympathies and great cultivation'. (Ancestor of Dr Ali Amini, reforming prime minister under Mohammad Reza Shah Pahlavi.) (Bamdad Vol. 2 p. 354, Curzon Vol. 1 p. 428, Churchill folio 93/611).

Mohammad Taqi Mirza Rokn-od-Dowleh (1846–1900). Son of Mohammad Shah and half-brother of Naser-od-Din Shah. Governor of Tehran (1857) and of Zanjan (1872). Governor of Khorasan (1876–81; 1883–4; 1887–91). Member of Consultative Council (1886). Governor of Fars (1892). Reputedly timid and with a tendency to temporise in politics. (Bamdad Vol. 4 p. 412, Curzon Vol. 1 p. 168).

(Mirza) Nasrollah Khan Moshir-od-Dowleh (1840–1907). Originally from Na'in. Worked his way up the foreign ministry before becoming Minister in 1899. A leader of the Constitutional Movement (1902–08). Foreign Minister again from 1902–05, before becoming the first Prime Minister following the introduction of the Constitution (1906–07). Died in suspicious circumstances during the Constitutional Revolution. (Churchill Folio 391/611).

Soleiman Khan Afshar-Ghassemlou Saheb-e-Ekhtiyar (d.1892). Chief of the Afshar tribe. Entered government service in 1829. Married daughter of Fath 'Ali Shah (1833). Accompanied Mohammad Shah to Herat, where he took part in the campaign to recover the city for Iran (1837). Commanded troops in Astarabad (1864). Governor of Gorgan (1868–75), where he campaigned against the Turkomans. Appointed army commander in Khorasan (1879).

Head of the Iranian delegation to the Akhal-Khorasan Boundary Commission (1883–6) (Bamdad Vol. 2 p. 116).

Chapter 5

(Mirza) Ibrahim Mostowfi Moʿtamad-os-Saltaneh. Father of future prime ministers, Mirza Hassan Khan Vossouq-od-Dowleh and Ahmad Qavam, Qavam-os-Saltaneh. Chief accountant for Azerbaijan (1880–92). Joined the court in 1892. In 1900 became chief aide to Malek Mansour Mirza, Mozaffar-od-Din Shah's second son, governor-general of Fars. (Bamdad Vol. 1 p. 28).

(Haji) Mohammad Hassan Amin-oz-Zarb. Enterprising late nineteenth-century Iranian merchant and financier with agents in all Iranian cities and substantial trading interests abroad. In partnership with the Amin-os-Soltan, he held the concession of the royal mint. In 1879, he proposed the foundation of a bank funded entirely by Iranian capital. The proposal was not approved by the Shah. In 1884, he obtained the monopoly for the construction, subsequently partly completed, of a railway from Mazanderan to Tehran (Bamdad Vol. 3 p. 348)

(Mirza) Nezam-od-Din Ghaffari Mohandes-ol-Mamalek (circa 1845–1915). Bureaucrat, diplomat and courtier. First cousin of Farrokh Khan Kashi Ghaffari Amin-od-Dowleh, and thus a cousin of the latter's son, the Moʿaven-od-Dowleh. In 1859, he was sent to study at the Ecole Polytechnique in Paris and later graduated from the Dar-ol-Fonoun and School of Mines. Reputed to be one of the most educated Iranians of his time, particularly in mathematics. Interpreter to the Amin-os-Soltan, to whom he remained faithful throughout, and, according to Bamdad, because of his role in the translation of the Imperial Bank concession, he was protected by the British, who rewarded him with a KCMG in 1903. From 1889–1903 he was a commissioner of the Imperial Bank of Persia, in 1892 became Ministry of Foreign Affairs representative in Khorasan and in 1897 Minister of Mines. From 1908, he was Minister of Public Works and Culture in successive cabinets, and in 1914 Minister of Commerce and Culture in

the cabinet of the Mostowfi-ol-Mamalek. (Bamdad Vol. 4 p. 383, Churchill folio 374/611).

(Mirza) Sa'id Khan Ansari Mo'tamen-ol-Molk (1816–84). Private secretary to Mirza Taqi Khan Amir Kabir (1848–51). Foreign Minister (1853–73). Governor of Gilan (1869). Member of Consultative Council (1871). Keeper of Shrine of Imam Reza in Mashhad (1873). Re-appointed Foreign Minister (1880). (Bamdad Vol. 2 p. 66).

(Mirza) Yahya Khan Moshir-od-Dowleh (1822–92). Younger brother of Mirza Hossein Khan Moshir-od-Dowleh Sepahsalar (see No. 2 above). A protégé of Mirza Taqi Khan Amir Kabir. Like his brother, he studied in France. Married to Princess 'Ezzat-od-Dowleh, a sister of Naser-od-Din Shah. Aide-de-camp and interpreter to the Shah (1858). Keeper of privy purse and chairman of the Consultative Council, head of the Shah's bodyguard. He accompanied the Shah on his first visit to Europe (1873). Briefly governor of Fars, then Mazandaran (1875). Given brother's title on latter's death and made minister of Commerce and of Justice (1881). Minister of Foreign Affairs but dismissed in 1887 over British objections to his allegedly pro-Russian actions. Re-appointed Minister of Commerce and of Justice (1889). Curzon describes him as the least oriental and most European of the ministers he met, reputedly pro-Russian, living in grand style but burdened by huge debts. (Bamdad Vol. 4 p. 438, Curzon Vol. 1 p. 429, Churchill Folio 391/611).

Chapter 6

'Abdol-Hossein Mirza Farman Farma (1859–1939). Son of Prince Firouz Nosrat-Dowleh. Educated at the Austrian Military Academy in Tehran. With a keen interest in Western sciences, he acquired a reputation as an enthusiastic builder of bridges and roads. Commanded troops in Kerman province (1882) as a Colonel. Commander of Qarasuran gendarmerie forces in Azerbaijan (1884). Promoted Major-General (1887). Married Princess 'Ezzat-od-Dowleh, Mozaffar-od-Din Shah's daughter (1888), while his sister was married to the Shah. Successively commander of Azerbaijan

troops, governor of Kerman twice, of Kurdistan, Fars, Kermanshah and Azerbaijan. Under Mozaffar-od-Din Shah, influential in securing the dismissal of the Amin-os-Soltan in 1896 and became minister of war in the government of the Amin-od-Dowleh, who succeeded him. Exiled to Baghdad (1899–1903). On his return, he sided with the constitutionalists in the Constitutional Revolution (1905). Later he was sent to quell inter-tribal fighting in Azerbaijan. Created Pasteur Institute of Iran. War Minister and then briefly prime minister (1915). Governor of Fars (1916–21), where with Sir Percy Sykes he was instrumental in forming the South Persia Rifles. Following Reza Shah's coup (1921), he was briefly imprisoned, many of his estates were confiscated and he died under continuing house arrest. Father of many remarkable sons and daughters, whom he sent to be educated abroad. (Bamdad Vol. 2 p. 247, Churchill folio 216/611).

Abol-Qasem Khan Qaragozlou Hamadani Naser-ol-Molk/Na'ib-os-Saltaneh (1865–1927). Grandson of Mahmoud Khan Qaragozlou Naser-ol-Molk, prominent tribal chief, courtier and minister. Abol-Qasem was the first Iranian to have studied at Oxford University. Courtier and translator to Naser-od-Din Shah. Accompanied Shah on his third visit to Europe in 1889. Following accession of Mozaffar-od-Din Shah and the dismissal of the Amin-os-Soltan, he became Foreign Minister in Amin-od-Dowleh's government (1896) and remained in this post in succeeding cabinets. In the Constitutional period, briefly Prime Minister under Mohammad 'Ali Shah but imprisoned for resigning without royal permission. Released on British intervention and left for Europe. Appointed by the Majles as Regent for the young Ahmad Shah (1910–14). (Bamdad Vol. 1 p. 66, Churchill folio 435/611).

'Ali Qoli Khan Mokhber-od-Dowleh (1829–1903). Born in Shiraz, the eldest son of Reza Qoli Khan Hedayat, writer, poet and tutor to the future Mozaffar-od-Din Shah. Accompanied his father on an embassy to Khiva. He became one of the first students at the Dar-ol-Fonoun. In 1859 joined the Telegraph Department and was responsible for supervising the construction of the telegraph from Tehran-Karaj-Zanjan-Tabriz. In 1860, he was appointed honorary Colonel, director of the Telegraph Department, second Deputy Minister and was given the title of Mokhber-od-Dowleh. Also

awarded the British decoration of Commander of the Indian Empire (CIE) for his telegraph work and later KCIE (1902). In 1871, he was appointed Minister of Telegraphs, in 1878 concurrently Minister of Education, and in 1882 Minister of Mines, to whom the Shah rented the mines for a period of fifteen years. In 1897, after dismissal of the Amin-os-Soltan, he was also appointed the head of the Mint, head of the Treasury and Minister of the Interior. Accompanied Naser-od-Din Shah on his second (1878) and third (1889) visits to Europe. (Bamdad Volume 2 p. 455, Churchill folio 411/611). Curzon describes him as a person of ability and enlightenment, although lacking in ambition (Vol 1, pp. 266 and 430).

Mostafa Khan Hajeb-od-Dowleh/Amir-e-Moʿazzam. Son of Mohammad Reza Khan Beiglarbeigli. In 1892, he replaced his uncle as head of the Heir Apparent's household. In 1896, when the Heir Apparent became Mozaffar-od-Din Shah, he remained as head of the royal household with the title of Hajeb-od-Dowleh and later of Sardar, where, according to Bamdad, he became very rich. He was replaced on the accession of Mohammad ʿAli Shah but given the further title of Amir-e-Moʿazzam under his successor, Ahmad Shah. Not liked by the British Legation. (Bamdad Vol. 5 p. 293, Churchill folio 244/611).

Nazar Aqa Yamin-os-Saltaneh. An Assyrian Christian from Orumiyyeh, Born 1827. Studied at the Lazarist school in Istanbul, followed by studies at the Dar-ol-Fonoun, where he specialised in history and geography. Translator at the Iranian consulate-general in Tiflis (1854–5) and then second translator at the legation in St Petersburg. In 1858–9, he was appointed first translator at the Iranian Embassy in Paris under Hassan ʿAli Khan Garrousi Amir Nezam. Returned to Tehran with his chief in 1866–7, where he worked at the Foreign Ministry. In 1869–70 replaced the Mostashar-od-Dowleh as Chargé d'Affaires in Paris. Minister plenipotentiary in Paris from 1873–4 until 1904–05. With Nariman Khan, his Assyrian colleague and Minister in Vienna, he was granted a concession to build a paved road from Jolfa to Tehran in 1891–2. (Bamdad Vol. 4 p. 387).

Zobeideh Khanom Amin-e-Aqdas (d.1893). Like her brother, Malijak 1, the child of an impoverished Kurdish shepherd. Introduced to court by the Shah's favourite wife, Anis-od-Dowleh. Although only a 'sigheh' or temporary wife, she attained high status, great wealth and great influence over the Shah. Supervised the Shah's private apartment, where the crown jewels were kept, and the Shah's most important seal. Like her ally, the Amin-os-Soltan, she reinforced her influence by playing on the Shah's weaknesses, not least his intense attachment to her nephew, Gholam-'Ali Khan 'Aziz-os-Soltan, Malijak 2. (Bamdad Vol. 2 p. 251, Curzon Vol. 1 p. 410).

Chapter 7

(Mirza) 'Abbas Khan Qavam-od-Dowleh (d.1897). Twice Minister of the Interior (1885–8). Replaced Mirza Yahya Khan Moshir-od-Dowleh as Foreign Minister in 1888. In 1889, signed renewal of Russian Caspian fishing concession. Remained in this position until his death in 1896. According to Curzon, he was a cypher, renowned only for his wealth, and control of foreign affairs rested with the Amin-os-Soltan. (Bamdad Vol. 2 p. 211, Curzon Vol. 1 p. 428).

Gholam-'Ali Khan 'Aziz-os-Soltan, known as Malijak 2 or 'Little Sparrow' (1879–1940). Successor to his father, known as Malijak 1, son of a Kurdish shepherd and page of the private quarters, as Naser-od-Din Shah's boy favourite. Nephew of Zobeideh Khanom Amin-e-Aqdas, the Shah's influential wife, who used him to maintain her influence over the Shah. Sickly and impudent child who, to the fury of courtiers and those in government, was showered with wealth and attentions by the emotionally deprived Shah. The Shah became subservient to his whims and so, reluctantly did the court. Entitled "Aziz-os-Soltan' in 1886, an apparent insult to the Amin-os-Soltan. Made Amir-Toman (1887) and married to the Shah's daughter. Keeper of Royal Seal (1889). Lived on comfortably until 1940. (Bamdad Vol. 3 p. 20, Churchill folio 126/611).

Chapter 8

(Mirza) Yousef Khan Mostashar-od-Dowleh (d.1896). Son of a Tabriz merchant.

Following entry to the Ministry of Foreign Affairs, he was consul in Astrakhan from 1854 to 1863. Then briefly Chargé d'Affaires in St Petersburg, followed by Consul-General in Tiflis from 1852 to 1858 and then Chargé in Paris (1868–71). In 1872, he became adviser to the Minister of Justice before returning to the Ministry of Foreign Affairs in 1873 as deputy minister and then as its representative in Azerbaijan. In 1882, he was appointed deputy Minister of Justice with the title of Mostashar-od-Dowleh. An early partisan of liberal thought, who in 1886 wrote a treatise on replacing the Islamic alphabet, in 1882 he admitted writing material critical of Iran under a pseudonym and was imprisoned. On his release, he became Consul-General in Bombay from 1884–1886 before returning to his old post as the ministry's representative in Azerbaijan. He was again imprisoned because of his relationship with Mirza Malkom Khan. (Bamdad Vol. 4 p. 490).

Chapter 9

(Mirza) Hassan Khan Pirnia Moshir-od-Dowleh (1871–1935). Eldest son of Mirza Nasrollah Khan Moshir-od-Dowleh (see no. 13 above). Educated in Russia. Attaché in Embassy in St Petersburg under Prince Arfaʿ. Accompanied Mozaffar-od-Din Shah on his first visit to Europe (1900) as interpreter. Following the 1900 Russian loan negotiated by Arfaʿ, Bamdad says, the Moshir-od-Dowleh didn't wish further commission money to go into Arfaʿ's pocket, so secured his dismissal and his replacement by his own son as minister in St Petersburg (1903). When his father became prime minister in the Constitutional period (1906), the Mirza Hassan Khan became a leading proponent of an electoral law. On his father's death in 1907, he was granted his father's title of Moshir-od-Dowleh. Between 1907 and 1923, he was four times Prime Minister, four times Foreign Minister, founded the Military Academy while Minister of War and held an almost uninterrupted series of cabinet posts until his retirement in 1923, following which he devoted his life to writing a history of ancient Iran. According to Bamdad, unlike his father and most of his contemporaries, he was an honest and patriotic man. (Bamdad Vol. 1 p. 323, Churchill folio 392/611).

(Mirza) Ibrahim Ghaffari Moʿaven-od-Dowleh (1861–1918). Son of Farrokh
Khan Kashi Ghaffari Amin-od-Dowleh and thus a cousin of the Mohandes-
ol-Mamalek (see no. 17 above). In Naser-od-Din Shah's time, like many
members of his family, he was a member of the royal household. In 1892, he
became head of the commercial court and in 1894 the Ministry of Foreign
Affairs representative in Azerbaijan. He was Consul-General in Tiflis from
1895 to 1896 and Minister of Commerce under Mozaffar-od-Din Shah in
1897–8. In 1904, he was appointed Minister Plenipotentiary for the Balkans
resident in Bucharest. In 1910, he became Minister of Foreign Affairs in
the cabinet of Mahmoud Vali Khan Sepahdar-e-Aʿzam, then Minister of
Commerce in 1911 and Minister of Finance in 1912. In 1914, he was again
appointed Minister of Foreign Affairs in the cabinet of the Mostowfi-ol-
Mamalek. (Bamdad Vol. 1 p. 19, Churchill folio 358/611).

Table of Measures used in Qajar Iran

Weight

Tabriz *mann* = 3 kilograms.

Mesqal. Generally used for expensive items such as saffron, jewellery and gold = 4.7 grams.

Sir. Used for domestic items, such as vegetables, garlic etc. = 75 grams.

Kharvar = 100 *mann*s of Tabriz= 300 kilograms, original a donkey load.

Coinage

Ashrafi. Gold coin of varying value, often given as wedding presents, part of dowry.

Kran. Basic unit of coinage in Qajar times, which became the rial in Reza Shah's time. In 1873, it was worth about £3 or $4.50 in today's currency.

Shahi. 20 *shahi*s = 1 *kran*.

Toman. 1 *toman* = 10 *kran*s.

Dinar. 10 *dinar*s = approximately 1 *toman*, so 1 *dinar* = 1 *kran*.

Bibliography

Arfaʿ, General H., *Under Five Shahs* (John Murray, 1964).

Bakhash, S., *Iran: Monarchy, Bureaucracy and Reform under the Qajars 1858–1896* (Ithaca Press, 1978).

Bamdad, F., *Sharh-Hal-e-Rejal-e-Iran dar qarn-e-davazdah, sizdah va chahardah-e-hejri* (Ketabforoushi Zovvar Tehran Shahabad, 1972 and later).

Browne, E. G., *The Persian Revolution 1905–1909* (new edition Mage Publishers, 1995).

Churchill, G. P*., Biographical Notices of Persian Statesmen and Notables* (Biographical Notes, British Library: India Office Records and Private Papers, IOR/R/15/1/746, in *Qatar Digital Library*: <http://www.qdl.qa/en/archive/81055/vdc_100000000193.0x0002d2>).

Curzon, E. G., *Persia and the Persian Question* (Frank Cass & Co, 1966).

Diba, F., 'Arfaʿ: Gained in Translation', *Journal of Qajar Studies* Vol. VII (2007).

Feuvrier, Jean-Baptiste, *Trois Ans à la Cour de Perse* (reprint by Facsimile Publisher of New Delhi, India, 2015).

Issawi, C. (ed.), *The Economic History of Iran (1800–1914)* (University of Chicago Press, 1971).

Kazemzadeh, F., *Russia and Britain in Persia 1864–1914* (Yale University Press, 1968).

Khomeini, Hedayati A., *Zendeginameh-eh-siyasi va ejtemaʿi-ye-Mohammad ʿAli ʿAlaʾ-os-Saltaneh (Prince Mohammad ʿAli Khan)* (Entesharat-e-Touri, Tehran 1390).

Moʻizzi, F., *Mirza Reza Khan Arfaʻ-od-Dowleh* (*Tarikh-e-Moʻaser-e-Iran* published by the Institute of Iranian Contemporary Historical Studies, Vol. 6 no. 23 Autumn 2002).

Neshat, G., *The Origins of Modern Reform in Iran 1870–1880* (University of Illinois Press, 1982).

Rezvani, M., and Qaziha, F., *Ruznameh-eh-Khaterat-e-Naser-od-Din Shah dar safar-e sevvom-e-farangistan* (Tehran, 1374/1995).

Werner, C., *An Iranian Town in Transition: A social and economic history of the elites of Tabriz (1747–1848)* (Harrassowitz Verlag, 2000).

Yarshater, E. (ed.), *Encyclopaedia Iranica* (online).

Index

Page numbers in *italics* refer to illustrations